THE COSMOPOLITAN FIRST AMENDMENT

We live in an interconnected world in which expressive and religious cultures increasingly commingle and collide. In a globalized and digitized era, we need to better understand the relationship between the First Amendment to the United States Constitution and international borders. This book focuses on the exercise and protection of cross-border and beyond-border expressive and religious liberties, and on the First Amendment's relationship to the world beyond U.S. shores. The examination reveals a cosmopolitan First Amendment that protects robust cross-border conversation and commingling, facilitates the global spread of democratic principles, recognizes expressive and religious liberties regardless of location, is influential across the world despite its exceptionalist character, and encourages respectful engagement with the liberty regimes of other nations. The cosmopolitan First Amendment is the product of a variety of historical, social, political, technological, and legal developments. Its principles and justifications are presented through an examination of the First Amendment's relationship to foreign travel, immigration, cross-border communication and association, religious activities that traverse international borders, conflicts among foreign and U.S. speech and religious liberty models, and the conduct of international affairs and diplomacy.

Timothy Zick is Professor of Law at William & Mary Law School. Professor Zick has twice been selected for a College of William & Mary Plumeri Award for Faculty Excellence and has been appointed the Cabell Research Professor and the Robert and Elizabeth Scott Research Professor. Professor Zick has published numerous articles on free speech issues. He has testified before Congress regarding First Amendment rights of public expression and petition and has been a frequent commentator on the First Amendment in print and other media. Professor Zick is the author of *Speech Out of Doors: Preserving First Amendment Liberties in Public Places* (Cambridge University Press, 2008).

The Cosmopolitan First Amendment

PROTECTING TRANSBORDER EXPRESSIVE AND RELIGIOUS LIBERTIES

Timothy Zick

William & Mary Law School

CAMBRIDGE UNIVERSITY PRESS

CAMBRIDGE
UNIVERSITY PRESS

32 Avenue of the Americas, New York NY 10013-2473, USA

Cambridge University Press is part of the University of Cambridge.

It furthers the University's mission by disseminating knowledge in the pursuit of education, learning and research at the highest international levels of excellence.

www.cambridge.org
Information on this title: www.cambridge.org/9781107547216

© Timothy Zick 2014

First published 2014
First paperback edition 2015

A catalogue record for this publication is available from the British Library

Library of Congress Cataloguing in Publication data
Zick, Timothy.
The cosmopolitan First Amendment : protecting transborder expressive and religious liberties / Timothy Zick, William & Mary Law School.
  pages   cm
Includes bibliographical references and index.
ISBN 978-1-107-01232-5 (hardback)
1. United States. Constitution. 1st Amendment   2. Freedom of expression – United States.   3. Law – American influences.   4. International and municipal law.   I. Title.
KF4558 1ST.Z53   2013
342.7308′53–dc23   2013027358

ISBN 978-1-107-01232-5 Hardback
ISBN 978-1-107-54721-6 Paperback

To my parents, Suzanne and C.J.

CONTENTS

Acknowledgments   *page* ix

Introduction 1

PART I   SCOPE AND THEORY

1 The First Amendment's Transborder Dimension. 25

2 Transborder Perspectives: Provincialism and
   Cosmopolitanism 61

PART II   CONVERSATION AND COMMINGLING

3 Mobility and Expressive Liberties. 103

4 Cross-Border Communication and Association 132

5 Falsely Shouting Fire in a Global Theater. 164

6 Expressive Liberties Beyond U.S. Borders 199

7 Transborder Religious Liberties 228

PART III   THE COMMUNITY OF NATIONS

8 The First Amendment in International Forums 265

9 Cosmopolitan Engagement 303

10 Exporting the First Amendment. 346

Notes   375
Index   439

ACKNOWLEDGMENTS

I would like to thank the following individuals for generously reading and commenting on the proposal, early drafts of the book, or specific chapters: Derek Bambauer, Joseph Blocher, Danielle Citron, James Dwyer, Peter Margulies, Jason Solomon, Anna Su, Marketa Trimble, and Alexander Tsesis. Special thanks to Anna Su for encouraging me to include a discussion of the First Amendment's religion clauses, and for her help on issues relating to religious liberties. Special thanks, as well, to William W. Van Alstyne, for the many informative and provocative conversations we have had about the First Amendment. I would also like to thank several research assistants, whose work contributed substantially to the completion of this project. Many thanks to Mary Button, Chris Healy, Cari LaSala, Lily MacCartney, Rob Poggenklass, and Tom Ports.

Although I have been thinking and writing about transborder First Amendment issues for some time, in this book I did not reproduce previously published material. However, the framework for the general argument of the book was presented in two previously published articles: "Territoriality and the First Amendment: Free Speech At – and Beyond – Our Borders, 85 *Notre Dame L. Rev.* 1544 (2010), and "The First Amendment in Trans-Border Perspective: Toward a More Cosmopolitan Orientation," 52 *B.C. L. Rev.* 941 (2011). Much of the material in Chapter 5 is drawn from a third article, "Falsely Shouting Fire in a Global Theater: Emerging Complexities of Transborder Expression," 65 *Vand. L. Rev.* 125 (2012).

INTRODUCTION

When most Americans think about First Amendment liberties, they likely envision domestic activities and concerns. They think, for example, in terms of speakers, religious institutions, and government officials that are acting within the United States. In traditional terms, the First Amendment contains a critical set of limitations on domestic governance. Its provisions facilitate local self-governance and define domestic or local political communities.

Scholars, courts, and government officials have considered the First Amendment's domestic domain in exhaustive detail. However, far less attention has been paid to the manner in which First Amendment liberties intersect with and relate to international borders.[1]

To be sure, some scholars have recognized the impact of globalization, digitization, and international human rights protections on freedoms of speech, press, and religion.[2] They have examined global and comparative issues relating to expressive and religious freedoms.[3] Legal scholars have also examined the special influence of the Internet on freedom of expression.[4] But, leading casebooks, treatises, and other scholarly treatments of the First Amendment still focus almost exclusively on domestic or intraterritorial issues and concerns.[5] Nowhere in the popular constitutional "stories" books will one find an entry for *Lamont v. Postmaster General*, which invalidated federal postal restrictions on the receipt of information sent by foreign speakers.[6] Even with the important comparative and other work that has been done, particularly in recent years, the First Amendment's relationship to territorial borders remains conceptually, doctrinally, and jurisprudentially underdeveloped.

In our globalized and digitized era, it is important that we have a clearer understanding of the First Amendment's relationship to territorial borders.[7] Speech conflicts and controversies increasingly have a transborder element. For example, offensive videos and other communications now reach global audiences in seconds, riling foreign audiences with different expressive and religious laws or norms. Transborder First Amendment issues, including surveillance of U.S. citizens' international communications, criminalization of various contacts between Americans and designated foreign terrorists, and conditional subsidies restricting foreign speech, have been adjudicated in U.S. courts. Transnational litigation has brought foreign speech and religious laws to the doorsteps of U.S. courts. Meanwhile, a weakened U.S. press corps struggles to provide access and reporting from foreign locations. Finally, U.S. officials and policymakers are faced daily with decisions regarding how to conceptualize and regulate a global communications infrastructure.

Today the domain, relevance, and authority of the First Amendment are being questioned as never before. This book adopts a different orientation or perspective with regard to the First Amendment.[8] It focuses attention outward rather than inward – toward and beyond American shores rather than within them. I present and defend a cosmopolitan approach or perspective regarding the First Amendment's nondomestic or transborder dimension.

In basic terms, a cosmopolitan approach encourages lawmakers, courts, and citizens to focus on the dynamic intersection between the First Amendment's doctrines, principles, and norms and international borders. It recognizes the crucial role our First Amendment plays in terms of facilitating transborder communication, commingling, and connectivity. A cosmopolitan focus also requires that we think more carefully and systematically about how the First Amendment limits governmental power beyond U.S. shores, intersects with foreign speech and religious liberty regimes, and affects global marketplaces of information and ideas.

The perspective I advance requires that officials, courts, and citizens address or, in some instances, reconsider a wide range of issues relating to the nondomestic First Amendment. For instance, we do not have a clear conception of the First Amendment's relationship to foreign travel and immigration. Nor, surprisingly, is there any consensus regarding the extent to which the First Amendment protects cross-border speech, association, press, petition, and religious liberties, or the justifications for granting such protection. Scholars have only begun to explore the extent to which First Amendment doctrines relating to harmful speech, including the prohibition on incitement to unlawful action, treason, and disclosure of secret information, apply to communications that cross international borders. The geographic scope or domain of the First Amendment, including whether its limits extend to U.S. government actions abroad and whether its protections apply to citizens and/or aliens when they are located beyond U.S. borders, are subjects that have not been systematically addressed. Further, in our increasingly inter-connected world, we ought to have a better understanding of the manner in which foreign speech and other laws intersect with exceptional First Amendment protections; this includes development of systematic approaches to resolution of ensuing conflicts and U.S. recognition of foreign libel and other judgment. Finally, we ought to think more carefully and systematically about the extent to which the United States can or ought to export First Amendment doctrines, principles, or norms to other nations and the manner in which any such exportation ought to be accomplished.

Adopting a more cosmopolitan perspective would not entail replacement or derogation of the more traditional conception of the First Amendment as a set of constraints on domestic governance. Indeed, I will argue that some domestic protections are critical to ensuring broader First Amendment rights in the transborder context. However, a cosmopolitan perspective reveals a less provincial, more mature, and more globally embedded First Amendment than the tra-ditional conception allows. This change in orientation will allow us to think more clearly and holistically about the nondomestic aspects of our First Amendment. And it will, as I explain in the chapters that fol-low, have tangible effects on laws, policies, and debates regarding the First Amendment in the twenty-first century.

THE PHILOSOPHER, PASTOR, PHARMACIST, AND PUBLISHER

First Amendment history is replete with colorful and controversial characters, and more than a few scoundrels. These include the Ku

Klux Klan members who threatened to march in Skokie, Illinois; Larry Flynt of *Hustler* magazine; and, most recently, members of the Westboro Baptist Church, who communicate deeply offensive messages near military funerals. First Amendment eras have distinct representatives. These include antiwar dissidents, communists, members of Jehovah's Witnesses, and civil rights protesters.

To render more concrete the dimension I will focus on in the book, I want to introduce a new generation of First Amendment protagonists – the Swiss philosopher, the Florida pastor, the Massachusetts pharmacist, and the Australian publisher. Their actions and the responses to them highlight some of the characteristics and complexities of the First Amendment's transborder dimension.

Tariq Ramadan is a prominent Swiss philosopher, poet, and writer who sought to enter the United States in 2004 to accept an academic post at Notre Dame University. Ramadan is an expert in the interpretation of Islamic texts and preaches, among other things, the virtues for Muslims of inclusivity and integration. After he obtained a nonimmigrant visa, the State Department informed Ramadan that the visa had been revoked, allegedly on the ground that he "espoused or endorsed" terrorism – advocacy that was prohibited under the USA PATRIOT Act.

Ramadan eventually resigned from his appointment with Notre Dame. When he next applied for and was denied a visa to enter the United States for the purpose of participating in various conferences and academic events, the American Civil Liberties Union filed a lawsuit challenging Ramadan's exclusion. This time the State Department alleged that Ramadan's visa application had been denied on the ground that he had provided material support, in the form of charitable contributions, to designated foreign terrorist groups. The government defended its denial of the visa application, in part on the ground that it was authorized to deny entry to aliens even if the exclusion was based solely on ideological or associational grounds. After many years of litigation that claim was never resolved. Secretary of State Hillary Clinton eventually lifted the ban on Ramadan's entry.

Despite the outcome in Ramadan's case, free speech activists continue to assert that the executive has barred entry to foreign nationals based on the content of their speech or the nature of their associations.

Although President Obama has been urged to denounce any such constitutional authority, he has steadfastly refused to do so. The executive branch continues to take the position that it does not need congressional approval to exclude aliens for any reason, including on the basis of their prior statements or affiliations.

Pastor Terry Jones of Gainesville, Florida, courted international controversy by first threatening to burn and later actually setting fire to a copy of the Koran. Although his actions were protected speech under the First Amendment, Jones had been warned by high-level government officials, including President Obama, not to go through with his controversial plans. The President warned that the burning of the Koran would be an international "recruitment bonanza" for Al Qaeda. Jones nevertheless held his Koran "trial" and carried out the punishment. His actions were broadcast around the world. After Jones's threat to burn the Koran and again after the deed had actually been done, deadly riots broke out in Afghanistan. Several people were killed during those clashes.

Jones's actions are part of a new category of incendiary domestic communications that, once globally distributed, sometimes lead or contribute to deadly events beyond U.S. borders. Like the Koran burning, the distribution of a movie trailer for *Innocence of Muslims*, a film that portrayed Mohammed as a greedy philanderer, was also linked to deadly riots in several Muslim nations. In addition, the Obama Administration initially linked the distribution of the trailer to the attack on the American Embassy in Benghazi, Libya. Although it later backed away from that claim, the distribution of the trailer on the Internet was linked to global protests and violence. Global distribution of offensive materials, such as the *Innocence of Muslims* trailer and images of the Koran burning have sparked a robust debate concerning American free speech exceptionalism and the need, according to some, for global speech standards in an interconnected world.

Tarek Mehanna is a Sudbury, Massachusetts pharmacist who traveled to Yemen in 2004 in an unsuccessful search for a jihadist training camp. Mehanna later translated several jihadist tracts and videos into English for distribution on the Internet. Mehanna was convicted of violating U.S. law by conspiring to provide material support to a foreign terrorist organization in violation of U.S. law. He was sentenced to seventeen and a half years in prison. The government's case against Mehanna focused substantially on his writings and statements. The jury did not specify whether the conviction was based on Mehanna's trip to Yemen, the translation of Arabic documents, or some combination.

Many such material support prosecutions have been initiated in recent years. Prosecutors can point to a Supreme Court precedent, *Holder v. Humanitarian Law Project* (2010), which broadly rejected First Amendment free speech and free association challenges to material support laws. In that case, the Court held that prosecution of American citizens who sought to teach groups designated by the United States as foreign terrorist organizations how to file petitions with the United Nations and to peacefully resolve disputes in international forums, would not violate the First Amendment. Indeed, the government argued that the material support laws were broad enough to forbid the filing of an amicus brief on behalf of such groups in a U.S. court. According to the Court, all of this otherwise protected speech activity may be criminalized by the government even though there is no evidence that the speaker intended to further the organization's criminal or violent activities. Material support prosecutions raise important questions regarding the balance between national security, foreign affairs, and Americans' ability to communicate and associate with foreign nationals located beyond U.S. shores.

Julian Assange is an Australian-born journalist, publisher, and Internet activist. Assange became a controversial worldwide figure when his website, WikiLeaks, published a trove of documents relating to America's execution of the wars in Iraq and Afghanistan. Assange received the documents from a private in the U.S. Army, who has since pleaded guilty to disclosing the documents. Assange and WikiLeaks, along with major international media outlets including the *New York Times, Le Monde,* and *Der Spiegel,* later published a cache of U.S. diplomatic cables, some of which had been designated "confidential" or "secret" by the United States. The U.S. Department of Justice has opened a criminal investigation, and has indicated that Assange who is currently living inside the Ecuadorian embassy in London, might be prosecuted under the Espionage Act of 1917 or other U.S. criminal laws.

The WikiLeaks case raises a number of intriguing First Amendment questions and concerns. One question is whether Assange, a foreign national, would be entitled to raise a First Amendment free speech or free press defense to prosecution. Further, the Espionage Act has never been used to prosecute a newspaper, website, blog, or other publisher of truthful information. Its application in the WikiLeaks case could jeopardize domestic press rights and weaken U.S. moral and diplomatic claims in international forums where it frequently presses for expansion of expressive liberties. The WikiLeaks case exposes a new model of global information distribution. The rise of a global fourth estate complicates state efforts to control access to information. It also highlights a shift of power, from state actors to private information intermediaries, in terms of regulating global communications.

The experiences of Ramadan, Jones, Mehanna, and Assange demonstrate some of the complexities associated with the exercise of First Amendment liberties in an emerging global theater. Like countless other aliens before him, Ramadan sought to cross American borders in order to engage in scholarly, cultural, and religious exchanges with American audiences. Jones was speaking not only to a domestic audience consisting of residents of Gainesville, citizens of Florida, or citizens of the United States, but to a worldwide audience consisting of a variety of cultures and religious faiths. Owing to potential national security and diplomatic concerns, his expressive conduct garnered the attention of government officials in the United States, including President Obama. It also contributed to violent reactions thousands of miles away, in nations that criminalize religious offense and ridicule. Mehanna's Internet postings regarding Islam and jihad led to his conviction for conspiring to provide material support to foreign terrorists he had never actually met. Finally, Assange's dissemination of secret information precipitated a debate regarding the extraterritorial application of U.S. laws and constitutional protections, the character and implications of a new global press, the scope of press freedoms, and the power of government to control cross-border information flow.[9]

Transborder Expressive and Religious Liberties

As these and other examples in the book demonstrate, the First Amendment has a critically important transborder dimension. Expressive and religious activities routinely traverse and, in the digital era, may even transcend territorial borders. Communications that originate inside the United States can produce effects far beyond its shores. People converse and commingle across international borders. Films, political commentary, propaganda, scientific information, and other materials routinely cross these borders, both in traditional and digitized forms. Americans travel abroad for purposes of engaging in artistic expression, information-gathering, cultural exchange, protest, humanitarian aid, and religious communion. They communicate, associate, and worship, sometimes in person and with increasing frequency in virtual forums, with aliens located abroad. All of this traffic runs in two directions. Information flows from foreign locations across American borders, seeking access to U.S. audiences, marketplaces, and forums. Like Tariq Ramadan, individual aliens seek entry to the United States for purposes of academic, artistic, religious, and other forms of exchange.

Today, information flows across territorial borders with extraordinary speed and ease. Owing to globalization and digitization, the world is now connected as never before. Long-anticipated global marketplaces of ideas may now at last be emerging. The benefits of these emerging marketplaces are clear. They include the free cross-border flow of information, diverse forms of cultural commingling, and new forms of cross-border and beyond-border collaboration. But there are obvious costs as well. Some of this contact and commingling is potentially or actually harmful. As some of the preceding examples indicate, the global flow of information poses new regulatory challenges. Thus, in the context of the distribution of the *Innocence of Muslims* trailer, President Obama asserted before a United Nations assembly that governmental control of global information flow is now obsolete. This claim, if accurate, has serious implications, not only for the exercise of expressive and religious liberties, but also for state sovereignty, national security, foreign affairs, and international trade.

As they long have, First Amendment activities also continue to occur beyond U.S. shores. Americans travel abroad for purposes of gathering information, protesting, and engaging in other expressive and religious activities. The U.S. press operates foreign bureaus and publishes information abroad. Many American universities have opened foreign campuses. Many religious institutions and faiths operate on a global scale. The U.S. government funds foreign speech and press activities, and often conditions that funding on certain requirements or limits. The government also engages more directly in expressive activities, including press and propaganda programs, abroad.

Owing to the prevalence and central importance of expressive activities in transborder contexts, First Amendment rights of speech, press, and association will be the principal focus of the book. However, religious liberties also have a transborder dimension. Limits on foreign travel, restrictions on various forms of cross-border communication and association, application of U.S. terrorism and other federal laws, and other restrictions affect the cross-border and beyond-border exercise of First Amendment religious liberties.

Moreover, as religious persons and practices traverse territorial borders, issues of tolerance, discrimination, and assimilation arise within the United States. Global connectivity and territorial fluidity have contributed to domestic conflicts regarding religious liberties. For example, debates regarding the location and building of mosques in the United States, and application of Shari'a law by U.S. courts, have been precipitated and influenced by events beyond American shores. Finally, U.S. citizens, employers, and government officials work, operate, and regulate in foreign nations. It is thus important that we examine the geographic scope or domain of the First Amendment's religion clauses, and how these provisions might apply abroad.

As I have indicated, at this point our conception of the First Amendment's nondomestic dimension is underdeveloped, particularly when considered relative to the domestic sphere. Earlier I noted some broad areas of inquiry. Among the more specific questions that have not yet been clearly answered, many relate to *cross-border* expressive and religious activities:

- Does the First Amendment prohibit exclusion or deportation of aliens on the basis of ideology, association, or religious beliefs?
- Does the free speech guarantee apply to citizens' speech that is directed *solely* to foreign audiences?
- Do citizens located in the United States have a First Amendment right to associate with aliens located abroad?
- Do aliens who are legally resident in the United States have full First Amendment rights?

- Does the federal ban on aliens' campaign contributions in American elections violate the First Amendment?
- Does the federal "deemed export" rule, which bars certain American institutions from sharing sensitive information with foreign nationals in their employ without a license, violate the First Amendment?
- Can domestic First Amendment rights be derogated by importation of international standards through treaty enactment?
- Does the First Amendment bar recognition and enforcement by U.S. courts of foreign speech laws or judgments based on foreign speech laws?
- Does the First Amendment permit U.S. localities to bar courts from citing or enforcing foreign religious laws and judgments?

Other questions relate to *beyond-border* or extraterritorial activities of U.S. citizens, aliens, and government officials:

- Does the First Amendment fully protect American citizens' speech, association, and press activities abroad?
- Can a U.S. citizen located abroad be subjected to targeted killing by the American government based solely on Internet communications and other speech activity?
- Are aliens detained by American forces outside the United States entitled to free speech protections?
- Does the doctrine of unconstitutional conditions, which limits the extent to which officials can condition receipt of U.S. funds, apply to subsidies provided to foreign speakers?
- Does the principle that the U.S. government must speak with a single voice in the foreign affairs realm mean that individuals, corporations, and subnational government have no free speech rights in such contexts?
- Does the First Amendment place any limits on the federal government's propaganda and other communications activities abroad?
- Does the Free Exercise Clause apply to citizens' or aliens' religious activities abroad?
- Does the Establishment Clause limit collaboration between U.S. officials and foreign religious leaders, institutions, or communities?

We ought to have clear answers to many or most of these questions. However, we have leapt headlong into a globalized and digitized era without resolving these and other fundamental issues. Answering these nondomestic First Amendment queries remains vitally important.

President Obama's claim that cross-border information flow cannot be controlled by governments in the twenty-first century seems overstated. Moreover, even today, limits on foreign travel, ideological exclusion of aliens, restrictions on religious practices and associations involving aliens marked as dangerous by the U.S. government, and restrictions on U.S. press activities abroad restrict cross-border First Amendment liberties.

Although the Internet has justifiably been celebrated as a great advance in terms of facilitating global communication and information flow, technological capability does not confer formal legal immunity. Nations, including established Western democracies, are actively censoring Internet speech.[10] Even the United States, which extols the virtues of global information flow, frequently requests that social media and other websites remove certain content even though no court has deemed it unlawful. American intelligence agencies have engaged in broad surveillance of U.S. citizens' cross-border communications. And Congress has recently considered enactment of intellectual property laws that would restrict both domestic and foreign information-sharing.

The First Amendment in Global Perspective

This book examines a variety of issues that relate to the exercise of individual First Amendment liberties. However, I will pursue a broader agenda. The proposed cosmopolitan turn involves situating or, more accurately, re-situating the First Amendment in proper global perspective. In brief, I want to take a closer look at how the First Amendment relates to and operates within the community of nations in the twenty-first century.

Although many members of the community of nations support robust speech and religious liberties, nations interpret the substance of these rights quite differently. Many countries do not share America's understanding of the scope and substance of expressive and religious liberties. Indeed, among the world's expressive and religious liberty models, the American First Amendment is a distinct outlier. While many Americans and U.S. officials strongly defend the First

Amendment's exceptional protections, foreign audiences and leaders of foreign nations have pressed for universal standards prohibiting the dissemination of hate speech and other harmful content. Indeed, this was a common theme among many world leaders following the distribution of the *Innocence of Muslims* trailer.

This international disagreement highlights a broader lesson or point. The American First Amendment does not exist or operate in isolation from the rest of the world. Indeed, it has a distinct relationship with the community of nations. Thus, for example, First Amendment principles and values are implicated in various international forums. In many international venues, federal and subnational governments, along with various organizations, corporations, and individuals, engage in speech activities. The United States propagandizes and distributes information abroad, operates media outlets in foreign lands, and works with religious leaders and institutions all over the world. U.S. officials negotiate and enter treaties that address both international and domestic expressive and religious liberties. U.S. courts are increasingly being asked to recognize and enforce foreign libel, hate speech, and other laws or judgments. In the digital era, nations are asserting extraterritorial power to restrict speech that affects or harms domestic interests. French courts have sought to apply French law to the communications of U.S. speakers. British libel plaintiffs have sought enforcement of their judgments in U.S. courts. German plaintiffs have pressed for enforcement of foreign privacy norms against U.S. publishers. At the same time, as it has for most of its history, the United States continues to seek to export First Amendment standards and principles to foreign nations.

As my four protagonists show, the First Amendment has a complex and dynamic relationship with the world beyond America's borders. Throughout history, it has been a beacon drawing aliens to our shores; a portal for facilitating international and global dialogue, collaboration, and exchange; and a vehicle by which democratic cultures, practices, and norms can expand across the globe. The First Amendment has also been a longstanding curiosity in nations where libelous, hateful, and other potentially harmful forms of expression are restricted or prohibited; a haven, according to some critics, for hateful and other potentially harmful speech; and a culturally embedded and contingent liberty model that is not deemed fit by many for international export.

We ought also to remember that the First Amendment does more than protect expressive and religious liberties. Indeed, as a fundamental matter its provisions impose obligations and responsibilities on U.S. officials. Officials in all three branches of the federal government ought to think carefully about the fundamental goals and purposes that the First Amendment will serve in the twenty-first century. If it is to continue to be a beacon, a facilitator of transborder information flow, and a catalyst for global democracy, then the United States will need to adopt and articulate perspectives and policies that support these goals. Courts will need to consider how to balance the government's interests in foreign affairs, immigration, and national security with individuals' liberty to engage in transborder speech and other activities. Government officials will need to examine U.S. policies and practices regarding the conduct of foreign affairs, international trade, global intellectual property rights, and foreign propaganda to ensure that First Amendment commitments are honored and that the U.S. leads by positive example. Finally, American citizens must think carefully about when, whether, and how to defend the First Amendment's unique and exceptional protections to increasingly skeptical, and sometimes hostile, global audiences.

A Cosmopolitan First Amendment

My goal is not simply to draw increased attention to the nondomestic aspects of the First Amendment. As we think about the foregoing issues, it is useful to examine them through different lenses or perspectives. In Chapter 2, I present two different conceptions of the First Amendment insofar as it relates to transborder activities and some of the broader concerns I have mentioned. I label these conceptions or orientations *provincial* and *cosmopolitan*. My central claim is that we ought to adopt a more cosmopolitan orientation with regard to the First Amendment's transborder dimension. This orientation has important implications for transborder expressive and religious liberties, and for the manner in which our First Amendment operates within the global community of nations.

Before I summarize what I mean by a cosmopolitan perspective, let me first explain the competing vision or orientation that led me to it and convinced me of its merits. At various times, U.S. laws, policies, court decisions, and scholarly commentaries have adopted a territorially bounded and provincial perspective regarding the First Amendment. According to this account, transborder activities are located at or very near the First Amendment's periphery. Under the strongest version of provincialism, the First Amendment's domain ends, conceptually and perhaps literally as well, at the water's edge. The underlying supposition is that the First Amendment relates solely to and governs only domestic communities and concerns.

Provincialism is a distinct view of the world and, more specifically, of the First Amendment's scope or domain. Like cosmopolitanism, First Amendment provincialism exists on a scale or spectrum rather than as an absolute. Not surprisingly, few would admit to being provincialists; indeed, most would fight the label, which is generally considered pejorative. Although I criticize the perspective I do not wish to cast aspersions. Rather, I argue that in a basic definitional sense, provincialism focuses too much attention on the local or domestic. One of my central criticisms is that courts, officials, and commentators have not devoted sufficient attention to the First Amendment's intersection with international borders.[11]

First Amendment provincialism is deeply rooted in our national and constitutional histories. It is anchored in structural constitutional principles. Provincialism is based on narrow conceptions of citizenship and self-government and broad conceptions of federal power both at and beyond U.S. borders. Thus, under some traditional accounts, the First Amendment does not fully apply, or perhaps apply at all, to cross-border communications or associations. Moreover, it imposes little or no constraints on government officials when they act abroad. Even with regard to U.S. citizens, courts and elected officials have often assumed, without expressly deciding, that the First Amendment applies extraterritorially.

Many U.S. citizens and officials are ardent defenders of American and First Amendment exceptionalism. Although provincialists would welcome other nations' adoption of First Amendment doctrines and principles, they strongly resist consideration or application of foreign or international speech or religious laws within the United States. The traditional view is that Americans are exporters, not importers, of standards and principles relating to expressive and religious liberties. Indeed, the First Amendment is viewed by some as an impenetrable protective barrier against importation of foreign expressive and religious liberty standards and norms.

This is merely a snapshot of the provincial conception of the First Amendment. I should add that this orientation is not provincial from a comparative perspective; most nations have far more provincial laws than does the United States. Rather, it is provincial by the lights of *our own* First Amendment, which I take to be the proper measure. By this measure, provincialism is a dated perspective based largely upon twentieth-century attitudes, principles, and conditions. Among other things, it fails to account for developments in transborder communication and information flow, the geographic expansion of American power, the decline of territorial sovereignty, and human rights and other developments within the community of nations.

I offer an alternative, and more cosmopolitan, orientation with regard to the First Amendment and its transborder or nondomestic dimension. Like scholars in other disciplines, I come to the term "cosmopolitan" with some ambivalence – perhaps even a bit of trepidation.[12] I use it not to "suggest an unpleasant posture of superiority,"[13] but rather to offer a distinct perspective regarding an underdeveloped dimension of the First Amendment. Like provincialism, cosmopolitanism is a perspective, an orientation, a set of general principles that can be usefully applied when considering nondomestic First Amendment concerns. Like provincialism, cosmopolitanism is best conceived as spectral rather than absolute.

I do not minimize or discount the importance of the First Amendment as a guarantor of domestic expressive and religious liberties. I come not to bury the First Amendment but, in many respects, to praise and preserve it insofar as this is possible. First Amendment cosmopolitanism is not a dogma or ideology. Nor is it, to be clear from the outset, the basis for arguing in favor of world citizenship, a world order, or the application of global standards regarding expressive and religious freedoms. The cosmopolitan perspective I will advance is "rooted," rather than universal.[14] Thus, it does not require that

Americans disregard local attachments in favor of nondomestic, trans-border, or global ones.

Cosmopolitanism conceives of the exercise of transborder expressive and religious liberties as core rather than marginal or peripheral First Amendment concerns. Indeed, it adopts the view that a central purpose of the First Amendment is to facilitate "cosmopolitan conversation," commingling, and (ideally) international understanding.[15] Since the founding of the nation, Americans have looked beyond U.S. shores for opportunities to engage in cosmopolitan intercourse and exchange. Core First Amendment justifications and values support these endeavors. Insofar as individuals desire to be or act as cosmopolitan Americans, the First Amendment supports that choice.

Cosmopolitan outlooks and concerns are not to be imposed on U.S. citizens. The government cannot force citizens to take interest in matters beyond their local communities. However, as I will discuss, government can facilitate international engagement and education with regard to diverse cultures and ideas beyond our borders. In an interconnected world, government has some responsibility to ensure that citizens have access to information that originates or relates to matters beyond territorial borders. Thus, I argue that U.S. policies ought to encourage domestic dissemination of factual information regarding foreign nations and cultures, support a robust American press that can facilitate global information flow, and ensure that Americans have full access to information that is disseminated by their own government in foreign nations.[16]

Cosmopolitanism rejects the idea that expressive and religious liberties are strictly or narrowly determined by territorial borders. Rather, in an interconnected world, expressive and religious liberties ought to be viewed as presumptively portable. Various international treaties to which the United States is a signatory require that these freedoms be protected "regardless of frontiers." Among other things, this means that barriers to citizens' – and in some cases aliens' – transborder expression, association, and religious practices ought to be rare, narrowly circumscribed, and carefully scrutinized by courts. To invoke a common phrase, cosmopolitanism holds that the First Amendment generally "follows the flag" – or, perhaps more accurately, follows the government as it acts abroad.

Beyond fully recognizing and protecting individual transborder rights, a cosmopolitan First Amendment would extend its basic protections and principles to international forums and, in some instances, to the conduct of foreign affairs. In light of the First Amendment's commitment to truth-seeking and self-government, cosmopolitanism suggests that we ought to have a robust foreign affairs marketplace in which private, subnational, and national participants debate policy and U.S. officials are sensitive to free speech, press, and religious establishment principles.

Moreover, from a cosmopolitan perspective, we ought to resolve conflicts between the First Amendment and other liberty models through dialogic and pluralistic approaches, rather than through protectionism or attempts to impose U.S. standards in foreign countries. Consideration of, and even some degree of receptivity to, outside norms, judgments, or legal interpretations ought not to be rejected merely *because* these things are deemed "foreign." A focus on persuasion and pluralism, rather than the reflexive defense of First Amendment exceptionalism, ought to lead to respectful engagement with transnational actors and legal sources.[17]

At the same time, cosmopolitanism does not reject the notion that U.S. officials will seek to export First Amendment standards and norms. The First Amendment competes, as it long has, with other liberty models. What type and degree of convergence will occur, and in what direction, will be determined at least in part by the substance of this exchange. This, incidentally, is the pluralistic approach that undergirds the First Amendment's own free speech and other guarantees.

The conception of the First Amendment that emerges from the cosmopolitan perspective is quite different from the traditional provincial model. The changes would not be merely attitudinal or theoretical, although these would be important alterations in their own right. Tangible effects would follow a cosmopolitan turn. For example, under this approach:

- Americans would have fundamental, First Amendment–based rights to travel abroad.
- U.S. citizens would enjoy full First Amendment rights to associate with aliens at home and abroad, and foreign visitors could not be excluded on the basis of speech or association activities.

- Existing laws that restrict cross-border communications would be subject to the same First Amendment standards as domestic restrictions, and in some cases invalidated as a result.
- Citizens' First Amendment rights would extend and be enforceable beyond international borders.
- In some limited circumstances, aliens located abroad would be entitled to First Amendment protections.
- The First Amendment's religion clauses would be applicable in both cross-border and beyond-border contexts.
- Nongovernmental organizations, citizens, and subnational governments would be permitted or invited to participate in foreign affairs conversations.
- Some foreign laws and judgments implicating expressive and religious liberties would be enforceable in U.S. courts.
- U.S.international trade, telecommunications and other policies would balance the desire to export First Amendment principles and norms with respect for the preservation of foreign speech and religious cultures.

General Objections and Preliminary Responses

I recognize that some, perhaps even most, of the principles, justifications, and effects of First Amendment cosmopolitanism will be contested. The most committed exceptionalists, internationalism skeptics, constitutional originalists, and perhaps even a significant segment of the American public may react negatively to some of my claims. Moreover, detractors will claim not to be provincialists, but rather defenders of the First Amendment and its core liberty provisions.

Many will object specifically to the domestication of laws and regulations that implicate foreign affairs and national security concerns; to the claim that aliens are entitled to First Amendment protections; to the notion that foreign laws and judgments may apply or be entitled to recognition in the United States; and to the idea that transnational sources are relevant to First Amendment interpretation or application. We live in an era of increasing social and political tension with respect to foreign ideologies, faiths, and cultures. Foreign incursions, particularly insofar as constitutional liberties are concerned, remain cause for great concern and even alarm in some circles.

I recognize that I bear the burden of demonstrating that transborder liberties are part of the First Amendment's core. I hope to carry that burden by showing that embracing nondomestic speech and other rights is fully consistent with our venerable First Amendment tradition. There are reasons to be sensitive to national security, foreign affairs, and other concerns at and beyond U.S. borders. However, this does not mean that the federal government ought to have plenary power to restrict cross-border information flow. Not every communication or person that approaches or intends to cross international borders raises compelling foreign affairs concerns. Nor is it plainly the case that domestic associations are more deserving of robust First Amendment protection than those involving cross-border communication and commingling. Finally, concerning the fear of foreign incursion, I do not propose to replace domestic liberties with international, supranational, or global standards (although I do not rule out some changes).

Students of American history, and in particular of First Amendment history, will recognize that some of the foregoing objections and concerns are not new, but cyclical. Today's controversies regarding incendiary cross-border speech, association with U.S. enemies, and importation of foreign constitutional norms mirror those from our past – from the founding era's Alien and Sedition Act controversies, up through twentieth-century campaigns against communism and other perceived foreign threats. Particularly during times of economic distress, foreign persons and ideas have been the focus of significant public angst and concern.

Many Americans have looked back on such periods with a mixture of surprise and regret – surprise that our forebears treated foreign speakers or ideologies as per se threats, and regret that draconian measures such as imprisonment and deportation were imposed on visitors solely on the basis of speech, belief, creed, and association. The reaction may well be similar when the specter of terrorism and the perceived threat from "foreign" persons, ideas, and beliefs give way to the next perceived threat emanating from beyond our borders.

The notion that *our* First Amendment has nothing to do with "foreign" persons, ideologies, and faiths, or with the community of nations, ignores our past. What is worse, this perspective may actually imperil our future. Our First Amendment is intricately connected to emerging global marketplaces of ideas, increasingly relevant to matters of global as opposed to purely domestic concern, and frequently in dialog and active competition with other liberty regimes across the globe.

Whether we like it or not, we occupy a world where cultures and legal systems are intertwined. Foreign officials and citizens in nations across the globe are critically examining the First Amendment's doctrines, principles, and norms and questioning their suitability in this interconnected world. At home, contemporary discussions regarding the First Amendment must take into account twenty-first century realities, including the global dimension of social and political activities, the rapidly changing nature and globalization of the press, the rise of transborder conflicts centering on religious ideologies and laws, the decline of strict territorial models of governance, and the increase in international engagement by citizens and public officials at all levels of government.

My primary goal is to advance a conception of the First Amendment that is responsive to the challenges of an increasingly globalized world and liberating to an increasingly digitized and mobile citizenry. The First Amendment ought also to constrain a government whose powers increasingly affect the speech, association, press, and religious liberties of citizens and aliens across the globe. This, too, is fully consistent with the liberty-enhancing conception of our First Amendment.

Although I focus on the nondomestic aspects of the First Amendment, my project is not wholly detached from local concerns. By working through unresolved transborder problems and systematically examining transborder First Amendment concerns, we may come to understand and appreciate better the substance and strength of America's commitment to expressive and religious liberties. I hope this, at least, will be cause for critics to engage First Amendment cosmopolitanism on its merits.

The Basic Outline of the Book

The book has three parts. Part I places the First Amendment in transborder perspective. Chapter 1 introduces and explains the concept and scope of the First Amendment's transborder or nondomestic dimension. Chapter 2 describes, compares, and contrasts the provincial and cosmopolitan First Amendment perspectives.

Part II focuses on individual liberties, in particular transborder conversation and commingling. Chapter 3 addresses the relationship between personal mobility and the First Amendment. It focuses on issues relating to international travel and immigration. Chapter 4 examines the First Amendment's connection to cross-border speech, press, and association. Chapter 5 examines the complexities of cross-border communication in an emerging global theater, with a particular focus on offensive, incendiary, and other potentially harmful content. Chapter 6 considers the protection of expressive liberties beyond U.S. shores. Chapter 7 examines transborder issues relating to First Amendment religious liberties, including the free exercise of religion and protection against religious establishment.

Part III adopts a broader perspective. It examines the relationship between the First Amendment and the community of nations. Part III focuses on three distinct aspects of that relationship. Chapter 8 examines the manner in which First Amendment standards and principles apply in a variety of international forums. It discusses the rights of persons and institutions to speak in such forums, the limits that apply to individual and governmental speech there, and the extent to which the First Amendment intersects with and influences foreign affairs and foreign relations concerns. Chapter 9 addresses U.S. engagement with transnational laws, judgments, and standards relating to expressive and religious liberties. Finally, Chapter 10 discusses U.S. efforts to export First Amendment standards, principles, and norms to other nations.

PART I   SCOPE AND THEORY

1   THE FIRST AMENDMENT'S TRANSBORDER DIMENSION

OUR THREE FIRST AMENDMENTS

This is a book about the First Amendment's transborder dimension. I examine a wide variety of cross-border and beyond-border activities, subjects, and issues, with a focus on the First Amendment's relationship to territorial borders. Given the scope of the project, I cover a great deal of literal and conceptual ground. It is important, then, to offer a general framework and to define some general parameters for the discussion that follows.

As noted in the Introduction, the basic plan of the book is to introduce terms and concepts in this and the next chapter, then to focus on individual liberties in Part II, and finally to discuss the First Amendment's relationship to the community of nations in Part III. Although there are overlapping themes and concerns, these will serve as rough subject matter divisions. For framing and illustrative purposes, however, let me begin by proposing that there is actually not one, but three, distinct First Amendments.[1] Each version or conception is defined by its relationship to U.S. territorial borders.

The *intraterritorial* First Amendment governs the exercise of expressive and religious liberties within the territorial boundaries of the United States (including its territories).[2] Unlike most works on the First Amendment, this book does not focus on intraterritorial concerns, except insofar as they may relate to or could be affected by transborder activities, processes, or regulations.

The *cross-territorial* First Amendment operates at borders the United States shares with other countries. Its general domain is cross-border exchange of various sorts – of persons, information, materials, and ideas. The cross-territorial First Amendment also includes the importation of foreign constitutional norms and standards. Questions arising in this domain include the extent to which the First Amendment protects cross-border communication and association, and whether the First Amendment permits recognition and enforcement in the United States of foreign laws and judgments relating to expressive and religious liberties.

The *extraterritorial* First Amendment governs the exercise of expressive and religious liberties, and defines the corresponding limits on governmental power, in foreign territories. Here the principal questions relate to the First Amendment's geographic scope or domain. I examine whether and to what extent the First Amendment limits U.S. actions in foreign nations. More broadly, I discuss how the First Amendment operates in global forums, including in the context of U.S. foreign policy and international diplomacy. Finally, I discuss the extent to which the United States can export and ultimately transplant First Amendment standards and norms abroad. Insofar as the First Amendment is interpreted to apply or exert legal or political influence beyond U.S. borders, it has an extraterritorial dimension.

In general, when thinking about the First Amendment, we can envision concentric circles. As depicted in Figure 1.1, purely local

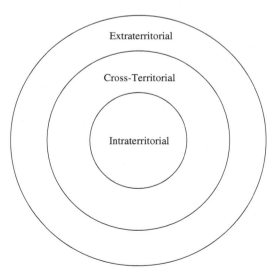

Figure 1.1 The Three First Amendments.

or domestic expressive and religious activities occur at the center; cross-border activities are represented by the next ring or level; and beyond-border activities extend to the outer ring, which represents activity and effects occurring primarily in foreign territories. This book focuses on the two "outer" rings or levels, which together represent the First Amendment's transborder dimension. An important goal of my project is to bring matters within these outer rings, which have typically been considered peripheral concerns, closer to the core of our First Amendment. As we will see, the First Amendment operates differently, if at all, at these outer rings.

In more specific terms, it is helpful to divide the relevant concerns along two axes, one relating to citizenship (who is affected) and the other to territorial location (at or beyond the border). Table 1.1 identifies some of the expressive and religious activities that occur in the First Amendment's transborder dimension. As Table 1.1 indicates, I discuss the rights of both citizens and aliens (resident and non-resident), and the effects of American regulatory power both at and beyond U.S. borders. In general, my principal focus is not on where legal effects

Table 1.1 Activities in the First Amendment's Transborder Dimension

	Cross-Territorial	*Extraterritorial*
Citizen	(1) Travel abroad (2) Communication and association with aliens abroad (3) Charitable donations to foreign religious organizations (4) Enforcement of foreign laws or judgments against U.S. defendants	(1) Political protest (2) Press activities (3) U.S. funding of religious programs and projects (4) Participation in foreign affairs debates
Alien	(1) Immigration exclusions (2) Recognition and enforcement of foreign judgments in the United States (3) Obtaining information "deemed" to be exported abroad (4) Receipt of information abroad that originates in the United States	(1) Detention or prosecution based on expression or religious practice (2) Speech conditions on U.S. subsidies (3) U.S. propaganda and provision of technology in repressive nations (4) Export and transplant of U.S. laws and First Amendment standards, principles, norms

actually occur, but rather on the territorial dimension in which specific expressive and religious activities take place. Thus, for example, although a citizen might be prosecuted in the United States for communicating with or on behalf of foreign terrorists, the expressive activity is considered cross-territorial insofar as it traverses international borders. As the concentric circles in Figure 1.1 indicate, the divisions are not rigid or formalistic. Activities can and often do implicate more than one First Amendment dimension.

I have three primary goals in this initial chapter, which is largely descriptive. First, I outline the First Amendment's transborder or non-domestic dimension. This will convey the scope of the book. Second, I provide a basic overview of some of the comparative and transnational aspects of global expressive and religious freedoms. This will help to clarify the scope of the project as it relates to transborder liberties, and will place the First Amendment in a more cosmopolitan or global perspective. Third, I introduce some of the historical, political, legal, social, and other events that have influenced or shaped the contours of the First Amendment's transborder dimension. Although the transborder First Amendment has been a work in progress throughout American history, my primary focus is on twentieth and twenty-first century developments.

THE CROSS-TERRITORIAL FIRST AMENDMENT

There are two principal areas of concern regarding the cross-territorial First Amendment. The primary issue is the extent to which the First Amendment applies to and protects the cross-border flow of persons, information, and ideas. The activities in question include foreign travel, immigration, and various forms of cross-border communication and association. The cross-territorial exercise of expressive and religious liberties is the central concern of Part II of the book. A second concern involves the cross-border transmission of constitutional standards and norms. First Amendment liberties are of course implicated in this exchange, as, for example, where a U.S. court is asked to enforce a foreign libel or hate speech judgment against an American speaker. However, there is also an international relations aspect to enforcement of foreign judgments and laws. Questions relating to the cross-border flow or exchange of constitutional standards and norms, and specifically conflicts between First Amendment and foreign standards, are addressed in Part III of the book, which examines the First Amendment within the community of nations.

Cross-Border Movement, Communication, and Association

In the domestic realm, information-gathering, the transmission and receipt of ideas and materials, and various associational activities (intimate, large-scale, secular, sectarian) are all core First Amendment activities. These activities are also prevalent in cross-territorial contexts. People, information, ideas, cultural practices, and religious activities all traverse U.S. borders.

Egress and Ingress – International Travel and Immigration

Ever since U.S. passports were first required for international travel, federal laws and policies have restricted citizens' cross-border movement. At times, permission to travel abroad was denied solely on ideological or religious grounds. Further, during both war and peacetime, presidents have imposed area travel restrictions on U.S. citizens and resident aliens. Economic embargoes also limit travel by U.S. citizens to certain foreign nations, and thus restrict exchange with aliens in those targeted nations.

Millions of Americans travel abroad each year, and millions hold dual citizenship status.[3] Foreign travel is closely connected to a number of First Amendment liberties.[4] When they leave the country, U.S. citizens can gather first-hand information about foreign nations, cultures, and people.[5] They can speak directly to and associate with aliens, fellow citizens, co-workers, and family members located abroad. As a result of their ability to exit, citizens can engage in a variety of educational, artistic, and religious activities across the globe.

For millions of Americans each year, foreign travel provides an important opportunity to converse with global audiences and commingle with the world at large. It allows citizens to assess the effects of U.S. foreign policy abroad without any governmental filter. These activities remain important in the digital era, in which technology has facilitated effective forms of virtual exchange.[6] Even in this era, many people wish to communicate and associate in person.[7] Depending on the specific nature and character of particular transborder relationships and endeavors, many individuals must travel abroad and meet with others in person.

U.S. restrictions on the cross-border movement of citizens have long affected cross-border political, intellectual, academic, social, artistic, and religious exchanges. Although Congress loosened or eliminated some restrictions on cross-border exchange in the post–Cold War period, current U.S. laws continue to limit citizens' foreign travel. An economic embargo affecting citizens' travel to, and activities within, Cuba remains in place today. Under current federal law, foreign travel can be restricted if officials determine that it might adversely affect the national interest. Recently developed travel "watchlists" and "no-fly" programs have imposed additional burdens on foreign travel.

Despite the seemingly close connections between egress and First Amendment values, the Supreme Court has never expressly recognized the ability to venture beyond the nation's borders as a fundamental constitutional right.[8] Nor has international travel achieved such recognition indirectly, through the First Amendment or some other constitutional guarantee. As discussed in Chapter 3, based on national security and foreign affairs concerns, courts have generally deferred to legislative and executive policies regarding limits on foreign travel. Many Americans would likely be surprised to learn that they have no judicially recognized First Amendment or other fundamental constitutional right to exit the United States.

The cross-border flow of persons also runs in the opposite direction. First Amendment interests are often implicated when aliens seek to enter U.S. territory. Aliens seek entry to the United States for cultural, artistic, religious, educational, and other purposes.

Visa and immigration laws can significantly restrict these forms of cross-border exchange. Like all other sovereign nations, the United States asserts and exercises the power to exclude foreign persons from its territory. It does so for various reasons, including that the alien has violated U.S. laws or is otherwise deemed inadmissible. U.S. laws have also provided for the exclusion of aliens based solely on ideological, religious, and associational grounds.

Alien exclusions affect not only the aliens' ability to communicate and associate with U.S. audiences, but the rights of U.S. citizens to speak to, worship with, and generally associate with the excluded persons. The Supreme Court held in *Kleindienst v. Mandel* (1972) that aliens do not have constitutional standing to challenge their exclusion from the United States on First Amendment or other constitutional grounds.[9] Thus, even when U.S. laws are being applied directly to restrict their movement, aliens cannot claim any First Amendment expressive or religious protection.[10] The Court acknowledged that visa denials may implicate the First Amendment rights of citizens to speak to and associate with certain applicants in person. However, it held that government officials need only provide a minimal, reasonable basis to support visa denials or other alien exclusions. The Supreme Court has never squarely addressed whether the exclusion of aliens by the U.S. government based *solely* on ideological or associational grounds violates the First Amendment.

Although ideological exclusions have decreased since the 1990s, in part owing to amendments to federal immigration and other laws, visa restrictions continue to hamper cultural, artistic, and other forms of exchange with alien visitors. Although current federal immigration laws bar ideological exclusions, national security laws may allow them. Civil liberties groups claim that executive officials continue to deny visas to aliens for purely ideological reasons. Past and present presidents, including George W. Bush and Barack Obama, have maintained that they have the statutory and constitutional authority to exclude terrorists and other potentially dangerous aliens based on these individuals' announced support for terrorism or their affiliation with terrorist groups. The exclusion of Tariq Ramadan, which I discussed in the Introduction, is a prominent recent example.

The cross-border movement of persons implicates fundamental First Amendment concerns relating to access to information, self-government, autonomy, and various forms of association. Chapter 3 addresses this critical aspect of the First Amendment's transborder dimension.

Cross-Border Communication and Information Flow

Within the United States, communications and materials flow freely across *state* territorial borders. The intraterritorial First Amendment protects this robust exchange. A wide variety of information and material also flows across U.S. territorial borders. These include traditional materials such as pamphlets, letters, magazines, books, films, religious tracts, and works of art. In addition, technology has facilitated the cross-border sharing of and trade in CD-ROMs, computer software, and bytes across territorial borders. Today, of course, an increasing amount of material flows across borders through the digital channels created by the Internet.

Like the ability to leave and enter U.S. territory, the cross-border flow of information and informational materials is an important aspect of the First Amendment's transborder dimension. However, as discussed in Chapter 4, the constitutional status of cross-border communication and information flow has never been clearly and definitively resolved.

Congress and executive agencies have long exercised broad customs, foreign commerce, and foreign affairs powers to regulate cross-border communication. Historically, many U.S. laws and policies have restricted cross-border information flow. These laws and regulations have sometimes been based explicitly on ideology, religion, or other content-based grounds. Some of the most egregious viewpoint-based restrictions on cross-border communication and information flow were repealed or amended as the Cold War came to an end. Further, certain categories of "informational materials" have now been exempted from federal customs, defense, and other regulations. Congressional liberalization was a specific reaction to perceived abuses by executive regulators. However, U.S. international commitments and agreements also played a role in eliminating some barriers to cross-border information flow.

This does not mean that the United States now has an open borders policy when it comes to cross-border information flow. Current federal laws prohibit the export and import of a wide variety of materials, only some of which can be classified as unprotected expression. Further, U.S. laws expressly ban or restrict certain cross-border communications that fall well short of espionage, treason, or other federal crimes. For example, the Logan Act, passed in 1799, makes it a crime for a U.S. citizen to engage in any "correspondence or intercourse" with a foreign regime or its principals "with intent to influence the measures or conduct of any foreign government" with respect to a matter of dispute with the United States "or to defeat the measures of the United States."[11] By its terms, the Logan Act would subject to a fine and/or a term of imprisonment a citizen who sent an e-mail or letter to the leader of a foreign government urging him to reject U.S. policies with respect to Israel, nuclear disarmament, or global warming. Less seriously, it might even bar events such as the recent trip by Dennis Rodman, the former N.B.A. star, to North Korea to meet with Kim Jong-un.

Other laws, some dating from the World War II era, restrict cross-border information flow by limiting the distribution of foreign propaganda and the sharing of scientific and technical information with alien recipients living in the United States.[12] Until very recently, federal law also limited citizens' access to, and domestic distribution of, United States propaganda messages delivered in foreign countries.[13] Further, U.S. surveillance practices have apparently swept up vast numbers of communications between U.S. citizens and aliens located abroad.[14] Even the laptops and other devices that we carry with us on overseas trips, which are often filled with our diaries, photographs, and other information, have thus far received no First Amendment immunity or other protection from border searches and seizures.[15]

The First Amendment speaks with a different voice at international borders. Courts have not generally recognized robust First Amendment rights to engage in cross-border communication and exchange. With regard to incoming foreign communications, the Supreme Court held in *Lamont v. Postmaster General* (1965) that citizens have a First Amendment right to receive foreign propaganda that has entered the postal stream.[16] However, subsequent commentary and judicial decisions have not interpreted *Lamont* expansively. Indeed, the decision has been cited most often for the proposition that the Free Speech Clause protects an implicit right to receive information in domestic contexts, rather than for its relationship to cross-border communication and information flow.

In general, the extent to which the First Amendment protects cross-border communications is not well settled. Indeed, some courts and scholars have questioned whether the Free Speech Clause applies to citizen speech that is directed – presumably by whatever medium – *solely* to alien audiences abroad. Further, scholars have questioned whether traditional free speech justifications apply to cross-border communications with aliens. Thus, surprisingly, today it remains unclear whether or to what extent the First Amendment protects an e-mail sent by an American citizen to an alien living in France.

Although it may seem to transcend territorial borders, digitized expression is not immune from regulation. Congress has amended various trade and customs laws to expressly include digital forms of information-sharing, including Web-based communications and materials. U.S. laws and regulations that restrict the communication of inciting messages, criminalize the provision of support for foreign terrorist organizations, and punish espionage-related activities apply to both domestic and cross-border communications.

As we shall see, the Internet has challenged but not prevented regulation of cross-border communication and information flow. Indeed, as scholars have observed, Internet filtering and censorship are quite common. As one study notes:

> The reality today is that Internet censorship is a growing practice both east and west of Vienna, with the filtering of Internet content carried out by both established Western democracies and transitional ones. Indeed, the countries where Internet matters the most as the sole carrier of real news media are the same countries whose governments, posing as 'defenders' of the public, filter and block the most online content.[17]

The United States continues to restrict cross-border exchange by focusing on content distributors located within its territory.[18] Moreover, in the United States and other nations, censorship is not always direct or coercive. Rather, officials communicate requests for blocking or other measures to Internet service providers, social network websites, and other distribution sources. The U.S. government frequently requests that American Internet service providers remove content from their websites. The combination of territorial regulation and soft censorship may be at least as successful as traditional interception of content at the border.

As I discuss in Chapter 5, the Internet has created a global theater in which harmful and offensive cross-border communications can be cheaply and rapidly distributed across the globe. In that theater, incendiary, offensive, and hateful expression has raised national security and foreign affairs concerns and has generated conflicts among nations that provide different levels of protection for such speech. When Pastor Terry Jones set fire to a copy of the Koran in Gainesville, Florida, the effects were felt almost immediately thousands of miles away. Using the Internet, speakers can now incite violence from within or beyond U.S. borders. As the recent disclosures by WikiLeaks and Edward Snowden showed, they can also disseminate government secrets and other information from locations beyond the legal jurisdiction of harmed states. U.S. courts and officials have not systematically considered or addressed this emerging aspect of the cross-territorial First Amendment.

As I discuss throughout the book, in the twenty-first century the judicial branch will not be the only, nor perhaps the most important, architect of the cross-territorial First Amendment. Legislators, executive officials, and regulators will have to decide what sorts of communications, technology, trade, and intellectual property laws and policies to adopt with regard to communications that increasingly flow across international borders.

Cross-Border Association

Citizens and aliens frequently engage in cross-border exchanges and collaborations. These associations take place both in real places, as a result of international travel, and in electronic or virtual forums. As I discuss in Chapters 4 and 5, the status of cross-border association is another underdeveloped aspect of the cross-territorial First Amendment.

Cross-border associative rights may be restricted in a number of ways. Limits on territorial egress and ingress, as well as regulation of cross-border communication, can restrict the ability to associate with others for familial, religious, cultural, and other expressive purposes. Federal laws restricting the operation of foreign missions in the United States, and laws prohibiting the provision of "material support" to designated foreign terrorist organizations, interfere with or ban certain associational activities. The longstanding federal ban on contributions by aliens to U.S. political campaigns also affects cross-border associational activity.[19]

Charitable and other forms of cross-border religious fellowship are an important part of the First Amendment's transborder dimension. As I explain in Chapter 7, religious affiliation and association may be uniquely and disparately affected by material support and other federal restrictions on cross-border association. In particular, these laws restrict cross-border charitable activities. Indeed, some argue that the Muslim practice of *zakat*, which involves the provision of charitable aid, has been particularly susceptible to prosecution and chill under these laws. Since September 2001, several American-based Muslim charities that provide aid in the United States and abroad have been aggressively prosecuted under U.S. material support laws. As the American Civil Liberties Union wrote in a recent report, "Tragically, U.S. counterterrorism laws make it more difficult for U.S. charities to operate in parts of the world where their good works could be most effective in countering extremism and enhancing security."[20]

Courts, government officials, and constitutional scholars have not devoted significant attention to this aspect of the cross-territorial First Amendment. The Supreme Court's recent decision in *Holder v. Humanitarian Law Project* (2010),[21] which upheld restrictions on U.S. citizens' peaceful association with members of designated foreign terrorist organizations, has focused some attention on this aspect of the First Amendment's transborder dimension. As we shall see, however, in that case the Court did not recognize a substantively meaningful First Amendment right to associate with aliens located abroad.

Import of Foreign Laws, Judgments, and Constitutional Standards

The United States is a member of the global community of nations. The First Amendment does not exist or operate in isolation from the expressive and religious regimes of other nations. Its standards, principles, and norms are frequently debated and discussed in global forums. Further, the potential importation of foreign expressive and religious standards and principles is part of the cross-border trade in information and ideas. Although this trade affects individual liberties, it is also related to larger concerns regarding comity among nations and, more generally, the First Amendment's relationship with the community of nations. Issues relating to import of foreign laws, judgments, and constitutional standards are discussed in Chapter 9. As this discussion shows, there is a robust ongoing debate in the United States regarding recognition of foreign judgments relating to both expressive and religious liberties.

Global and Comparative Perspectives on
Expressive and Religious Freedoms

This is an appropriate place to describe, in general terms, some of the comparative differences between the First Amendment and other liberty models. When examining the First Amendment's transborder dimension, we must keep in mind that nations' receptivity to foreign laws, as well as substantive standards relating to expressive and religious freedoms, vary considerably across the globe. This is not a book about comparative constitutional law. A comprehensive overview of expressive and religious freedoms across the globe is thus beyond its scope. The literature on comparative constitutionalism, which of course includes many works relating to freedom of speech and religion, is far too extensive to engage in this book.[22] However, as part of my effort to place the First Amendment in transborder perspective, I briefly highlight some of the important procedural and substantive issues relating to global expressive and religious freedoms. Here and throughout the book, my comparative focus will primarily be on other Western democracies rather than more authoritarian or autocratic regimes.

Although the United States was the first to protect freedom of speech in a written constitution, today most nations provide some form of constitutional or statutory protection for freedom of expression. In addition, international as well as supranational laws and conventions provide broad protection for such rights. For example, the Universal Declaration of Human Rights (UDHR) provides in Article 19: "Everyone has the right to freedom of opinion and expression; this right includes freedom to hold opinions without interference and to seek, receive and impart information and ideas through any media and regardless of frontiers."[23] The International Covenant on Civil and Political Rights (ICCPR), a global treaty, contains a similar free speech guarantee.[24]

The free speech provisions of the UDHR and ICCPR have been models for numerous regional conventions and treaties. In addition, a number of signatory nations have altered their domestic laws in a manner that tracks these guarantees. As Gerald Neuman has observed, "[s]ome national constitutions elevate human rights treaty norms to the level of constitutional rights; others expressly make international human rights norms a source of guidance in constitutional interpretations."[25] To varying degrees, constitutional courts across the world also take international interpretations of human rights into consideration.[26]

In most democratic nations, courts also engage in some degree of comparative constitutional interpretation. Thus, they look to interpretations by other nations when deciding the meaning of their own constitutional guarantees. This does not mean that the foreign interpretations are considered binding or even persuasive. In some instances courts explicitly adopt foreign interpretations, whereas in others they refer to foreign constitutional interpretations in explaining why they interpret a particular freedom or liberty differently.

In addition, all members of the European Convention on Human Rights (ECHR) must comply with supranational laws. This includes interpretations of the ECHR's free speech guarantee, which are issued by the European Court on Human Rights (ECtHR) in Strasbourg. Article 10 provides: "Everyone has the right to freedom of expression. This right shall include freedom to hold opinions and to receive and impart information and ideas without interference by public authority and regardless of frontiers."[27] Article 10 limits the scope of these rights by making them subject to:

> ...such formalities, conditions, restrictions or penalties as are prescribed by law and are necessary in a democratic society, in the interests of national security, territorial integrity or public safety, for the prevention of disorder or crime, for the protection of health or morals, for the protection of the reputation or rights of others, for preventing the disclosure of information received in confidence, or for maintaining the authority and impartiality of the judiciary.[28]

Although member nations are given a "margin of appreciation," or some measure of deference, with regard to whether a domestic speech restriction is necessary owing to the foregoing limitations, ultimately they must implement any adverse ruling by the ECtHR. In some cases, this entails formally amending or altering domestic constitutional laws so that they are consistent with the Court's decisions.

In the United States, the influence of treaty obligations on domestic free speech law is limited in a number of respects. Under the U.S. Constitution, international treaties are part of the "supreme law of the land" and Congress has all "necessary and proper" powers to carry these agreements into execution.[29] The Supreme Court has interpreted the Constitution as providing that Congress has the power to enact legislation implementing treaty obligations and that treaty provisions prevail over conflicting prior legislation only if they are "self-executing" – which means that they are judicially enforceable on ratification, without any implementing legislation.[30]

Whether or not they are self-executing, the U.S. Supreme Court has held that treaty provisions cannot contradict or modify U.S. constitutional individual rights guarantees.[31] The U.S. Senate generally makes clear when it ratifies international treaties that they do not create individual rights enforceable in U.S. courts, and in any event are enforceable only insofar as they do not conflict with the First Amendment. Moreover, the United States has inserted reservations, declarations, and understandings into a number of international treaties relating to expressive freedoms.[32] Although some critics question whether these reservations are legitimate under international law, they are now standard practice in American diplomacy.[33]

As noted, constitutional courts around the world generally look to decisions from other nations when interpreting domestic laws and constitutional guarantees relating to expressive and religious freedoms. In contrast, the U.S. Supreme Court has stoked domestic controversy by merely *citing*, in a handful of decisions, foreign decisions and legal sources.[34] In general, the U.S. Supreme Court and lower courts resist citation to and reliance on foreign constitutional law. In First Amendment cases, judicial citation or reference to transnational legal sources is extremely rare.

The United States is not subject to the jurisdiction of any supranational constitutional authority. It is a member of the Organization of American States (OAS), which has adopted a Convention on Human Rights that includes a free speech guarantee. The Inter-American Commission on Human Rights issues annual reports on alleged rights violations, and the Inter-American Court adjudicates any disputes regarding alleged violations that are referred to it by the Commission. To date, the United States has refused to submit to the jurisdiction of the Inter-American Court.

U.S. resistance to transnational law and processes is based partly on concerns regarding fundamental principles of national sovereignty. However, U.S. resistance to foreign and international laws and standards also rests on a desire to preserve the exceptional nature of First Amendment protections.[35]

The First Amendment's Free Speech Clause grants exceptionally broad protection for expressive freedoms relative to the constitutions and laws of other nations. This is true in areas ranging from antigovernment speech, to restrictions on campaign donations, to commercial speech, to privacy, to sexually explicit expression. The First Amendment also grants exceptional protection to the freedom to assemble in public places and freedom of the press. In many parts of the world, press freedoms are tenuously recognized or not protected at all.

Again, my purpose is not to catalogue the many specific ways that American First Amendment guarantees differ from speech and other protections provided in legal systems across the globe. Rather, I want to highlight a few prominent examples that we will revisit in subsequent chapters. I focus on the illustrative examples of incitement to unlawful action, defamation, and hate speech.[36]

In the United States, modern First Amendment free speech doctrine originated in cases involving speech that allegedly incited others to unlawful acts, such as interference with the draft or overthrow of the government. The standard the Supreme Court ultimately adopted requires an intent to incite unlawful action, actual words of incitement, and a likelihood that unlawful action will occur imminently.[37] This standard is one of the most speech-protective ever developed. Under it, officials are not permitted to punish or suppress the teaching or advocacy of unlawful action or speech that is merely critical of governmental policies, actions, or officials.

As we will see, this certainly does not mean that the First Amendment protects all forms of violent advocacy. However, the traditional or baseline incitement standard does protect a much wider range of speech than do international and supranational laws. Simply put, other nations tend to balance the government's interests in order and security and the speaker's interest in communicating or advocating his position in a manner that is less speech-protective than the American incitement standard. In many nations, including Western democracies, where there is a pressing social need speech that merely advocates unlawful action can be prohibited or criminalized. Moreover, in some nations, speakers can be jailed for merely criticizing governments and government officials.

In recent years, in response to the terrorist attacks in the United States and elsewhere, many nations have explicitly altered or amended their laws to prohibit the mere advocacy of terrorism. Israeli penal law prohibits any incitement to violence or terror. In the United Kingdom, speakers may be arrested and prosecuted for statements that "glorify" terrorism or seek to indoctrinate others with inflammatory rhetoric.[38] Similar prohibitions have been enacted in other European nations including Denmark, Spain, and France. The thirty-four countries of the Council of Europe signed its Convention on the Prevention of Terrorism, which directs each state party to criminalize "public provocation to commit a terrorist offence."[39] These and other laws differ markedly from the First Amendment's incitement standard.

The First Amendment's exceptional speech protections with regard to defamatory speech have received significant global attention and notoriety. In *New York Times v. Sullivan*[40] and subsequent cases, the United States Supreme Court interpreted the First Amendment as placing strict limits on certain kinds of state common law defamation claims. In the United States, public officials and public figures must prove not only that statements published about them are false and have harmed their reputations, but that the statements have been made with "actual malice" – either knowledge of their falsity or reckless disregard for their truth. The Supreme Court has interpreted the First Amendment to require that speakers have the widest possible latitude or "breathing space" when criticizing or speaking about public officials and public figures, or debating matters of public concern. The Court has afforded this breathing space not only to false statements, but even to vulgar parodies of public officials and public figures.[41]

As Frederick Schauer has noted, although U.S. defamation doctrine has perhaps moved some nations away from the strictest forms of common law liability for defamatory statements, "the overwhelming reaction of the rest of the world to the American approach has been negative."[42] As Schauer has explained:

> Believing that the American model places far too much weight on the freedom of the press side of the balance, and far too little on the reputational side, the rest of even the developed democratic world

has been satisfied to leave largely in place defamation remedies and standards that the United States continues to find unacceptable under the First Amendment.[43]

In sum, after careful consideration of *Sullivan* and the U.S. approach to defamation, other nations have struck a different balance between individual dignity (which includes personal reputation) and speaker autonomy.[44] This balance reflects nations' historical, legal, and social values.[45]

Finally, the United States is also an outlier in the area of what is often referred to as "hate speech." Generally speaking, hate speech consists of communications that are deliberately insulting, abusive, threatening, or demeaning to certain persons or groups and designed to stir up hatred against them.

In general, the First Amendment has been interpreted to bar regulation of speech based on its content in all but the most narrowly drawn circumstances. The Supreme Court has held that government cannot punish speakers solely for expressing hatred toward individuals or groups. Thus, although officials may treat the burning of a cross as a true threat to individual safety, they may not restrict cross-burning on the grounds that it expresses hatred or contempt for a particular person or group.[46] Nor can they prevent someone from burning a copy of the Koran, even if the intent behind this symbolic act is to insult Muslims or their religion. The First Amendment has been interpreted to protect a wide range of hateful and insulting speech. This construction remains the subject of fervent debate, both within the United States and across the globe.[47]

In contrast, Article 20(2) of the ICCPR requires that "[a]ny advocacy of national, racial or religious hatred that constitutes incitement to discrimination, hostility or violence shall be prohibited by law." Either pursuant to the ICCPR or on their own initiative, many European and English-speaking countries have adopted legislation that forbids various types of insulting, degrading, or hateful expression. As Jeremy Waldron recently explained, "Many advanced democracies willingly embrace the idea of restrictions on hate speech."[48] For example, Norway's law forbids "publicly stirring one part of the population against another" and any utterance that "threatens, insults, or subjects to hatred, persecution, or contempt any person or group of persons because of their creed, color, race, or national origins." German law forbids attacks on "the human dignity of others by insulting, maliciously maligning or defaming segments of the population." In Canada, it is a criminal offense to advocate genocide, publicly incite hatred, or "willfully promote hatred."

As with incitement and defamation, First Amendment protection for hate speech is a product of American experience and history. In general, European and other nations have decided that society's interests in protecting and preserving individual dignity outweigh speakers' interest in conveying hateful messages. This difference in perspective has created new conflicts in the digital era. With the rise of the Internet, many hate groups have located within the United States to avoid criminal prosecution and civil liability in other nations. Consequently, many nations now view the United States as a haven for hate speech.[49]

As this brief, and admittedly incomplete, summary of comparative free speech substance shows, although the community of nations generally recognizes freedom of speech as a protected right most nations diverge from First Amendment doctrines in significant respects. In an increasingly interconnected community of nations, this is bound to create some transnational tensions and conflicts regarding free speech protection. As Rodney Smolla has observed:

> We need to think carefully about these differences, because the new technologies that increasingly knit the globe into one giant electronic village will tend to create an international marketplace for free speech, *which will in turn create enormous pressures toward uniformity in free speech policies*. There will be pressure from one direction on the rest of the world to adopt notions of free speech more like America's. There will be a corresponding pressure from the opposite direction for America to water down its free speech principles to conform more closely to the rest of the world's.[50]

The First Amendment also provides somewhat exceptional protections for religious freedoms. For many reasons, there is less crossterritorial pressure or tension with regard to importation of foreign religious laws or standards. For one thing, the vehicles for transmission and transplantation of foreign religious laws and principles are not as numerous or readily apparent. However, as with free speech, international treaties may touch on certain religious freedoms. As we shall see, certain tensions and conflicts arise extraterritorially, in particular when we consider how First Amendment anti-establishment or free exercise principles might apply beyond U.S. borders. As well, global and comparative perspectives will be useful in terms of assessing U.S. efforts to export religious freedom principles based on the First Amendment, a subject discussed in Chapter 10. Here I briefly mention some of the principal distinctions between the First Amendment's religion clauses and the global environment with regard to religious freedoms.

Owing to the tremendous differences in cultural and historical experience in nations across the globe, it is even more difficult to generalize about religious freedoms than it is with respect to expressive ones. Even within European democracies there is a wide variation in terms of church–state relationships. When one considers nations in other parts of the world the diversity of approaches multiplies. Some nations are relatively homogeneous when it comes to matters of religion, others are decidedly pluralistic. Some nations have officially adopted state religions, while others informally recognize particular faiths.

However, we can make some general observations regarding religious freedoms as part of the system of global human rights. International and supranational law expressly provide for protection of religious freedoms. Article 18 of the UDHR provides: "Everyone has the right to freedom of thought, conscience and religion; this right includes freedom to change his religion or belief, and freedom, either alone or in community with others and in public or private, to manifest his religion or belief in teaching, practice, worship and observance." Article 18 of the ICCPR and Article 9 of the ECHR protect the same substantive rights. Again, the ECHR protects these rights subject to limitations that are considered by states to be "necessary in a democratic society in the interests of public safety, for the protection of public order, health or morals, or for the protection of the rights and freedoms of others."[51]

The structural and procedural observations made earlier with respect to freedom of speech apply as well to freedom of religion. The United States is not directly subject to human rights treaties or instruments that address religious freedoms. As in the case of free speech, when it has agreed in principle to an international covenant, the United States has routinely insisted on and obtained reservations, declarations, and understandings that preserve the First Amendment's approach with regard to religious freedoms inside the United States. The United States is not subject to any supranational laws or the jurisdiction of supranational institutions with regard to religious liberties.

With regard to substance, the First Amendment's Establishment Clause and Free Exercise Clause have been interpreted to require that officials maintain a degree of separation from, and neutrality regarding, religious faiths and religion in general that is unique within the community of nations. This interpretation has developed as a result of many events and circumstances that are peculiar to American history, law, and politics. The basic approach can be traced to the religious pluralism of early American society, and to the colonists' experience with religious wars and persecution in Europe.

Although the religion clauses have given rise to a complex jurisprudence, we can at least mark the general boundaries that relate to the book's discussion of religious liberties. The Free Exercise Clause, while allowing for the enforcement of generally applicable civil and criminal laws, essentially prohibits government from targeting religious beliefs or practices or interfering with the inner workings of churches and religious institutions.[52] The Establishment Clause prohibits certain forms of direct governmental support for religion and the public endorsement of religious symbols, and prohibits government from discriminating among religions or discriminating against religion itself.[53]

Most nations do not have a formal Establishment Clause. However, similar concerns are addressed in constitutional provisions guaranteeing religious liberty and equality.[54] Constitutional courts throughout the world routinely address religious discrimination and endorsement issues. Although generalizing with regard to global religious freedom is, as noted, a perilous endeavor it is clear that the First Amendment's religion clauses have been interpreted in a manner that is somewhat exceptional within the community of nations. As a few examples will illustrate, this is particularly true with regard to anti-establishment principles.

The conception of a "wall of separation" between state and religion is uniquely American. Unlike the central command of the Establishment Clause, the laws and jurisprudence of many nations do not expressly prohibit an official established religion. Indeed, in several nations constitutional provisions and laws expressly recognize official

state churches. Some nations in the Middle East officially recognize
Islam. Further, in nations such as Germany, Belgium, Switzerland,
and Austria, laws and precedents allow governments to differentiate
among religious groups so long as they have a substantial reason for
doing so.[55] International and supranational laws do not generally dis-
turb these deeply rooted historical relations between church and state.[56]
Courts apply a considerable margin of appreciation with regard to religious endorsement.

Moreover, in contrast to the United States, in many nations there
is no strict separation between public school education and religion.
In some nations, public schools are essentially religious schools. In
many, direct state financial support for sectarian educational institutions is permitted.[57] Indeed, in many European countries, constitutional provisions either permit or require the teaching of religion in
public schools.[58] Further, unlike in the United States, in some nations
government officials may participate in public religious ceremonies
or displays, crucifixes may be placed in classrooms, and school prayer
is either expressly or impliedly permitted.[59] This stems from very
distinct national and international understandings of state neutrality toward religion.[60] In sum, the extent to which state and religions
intersect and the manner in which they relate to one another varies
widely across the globe. However, it is fair to say that the U.S. concept
of separation of church and state has not generally been adopted in
foreign nations.

Conceptions of free exercise of religion also vary across the globe.
National, international, and supranational laws generally treat protections for religious belief and rights of conscience as fundamental human
rights. However, in many nations the balance between individual and
community rights differs in significant respects from that struck in
the United States. For example, rather than adopt a tiered-scrutiny
approach in which laws targeting religious practices receive heightened
review and generally applicable laws receive minimal review, constitutional courts interpret the concept of "reasonable accommodation"
more flexibly under a proportionality approach.[61] Some scholars have
claimed that the protection afforded under Article 18 of the ICCPR
to religious free exercise is more substantial than protection granted
under the current First Amendment approach.[62] However, under the

principle of margin of appreciation, the ECtHR has deferred significantly to member states' determination of whether limits on free exercise are necessary in a democratic society.[63]

In any event, in a variety of specific contexts, foreign courts have interpreted free exercise principles in a manner that diverges sharply from certain First Amendment precedents. For example, some constitutional courts have upheld the authority of public educational institutions to regulate the wearing of specific forms of religious garb and symbols.[64] In some nations bans on veiling, which would clearly offend First Amendment free exercise principles, are considered a means of protecting the secularism of the public sphere.[65] International, regional, and national laws also place some limits on proselytizing and attempts to convert others to a different religious faith.[66] These laws and constitutional interpretations diverge from conclusions reached in various Supreme Court precedents interpreting the First Amendment's Free Exercise Clause.[67]

Again, my goal here is not to provide an exhaustive description of comparative, international, and supranational law with respect to religious freedom. However, it is important as we engage in an examination of the First Amendment's transborder dimension that we recognize the diversity of global approaches to establishment and free exercise concerns. As Americans work, travel, and communicate across borders, citizens bring claims against foreign defendants, U.S. officials engage with religious leaders and communities abroad, and the United States seeks to export religious freedom to the rest of the world, religious laws and norms will intersect and sometimes come into conflict.[68] These points of intersection and conflict are an important aspect of the First Amendment's transborder dimension.

Mechanisms of Importation

Foreign expressive and religious standards might be imported into the United States in a number of different ways. For example, aliens who have obtained foreign libel judgments have sought to enforce those judgments in U.S. courts. Moreover, in an increasingly interconnected world where communications can be rapidly disseminated across vast territories instantaneously, nations have increasingly called on one another to recognize and enforce foreign speech laws extraterritorially.

Foreign plaintiffs, courts, and officials have sought to enforce foreign hate speech, privacy, and other laws inside the United States.[69]

Concerns regarding importation of foreign religious laws, judgments, and principles have also been on the rise in the United States. Some Americans consider efforts to enforce laws and principles of religious faiths whose adherents live primarily outside the United States as a form of cross-border importation.[70] As recent controversies involving enforcement of Shari'a laws show, in many instances resistance to this form of importation and First Amendment protection for religious pluralism come into direct conflict.

Foreign laws and standards might also enter the United States through execution of international treaties or other forms of transnational legal processes.[71] As the preceding summary shows, the United States generally views itself as an exporter, not an importer, of laws and standards relating to expressive and religious freedoms. Insofar as the First Amendment is concerned, the United States has consistently adopted an attitude or perspective of resistance to foreign influences and sources of law.[72] In addition to using treaty reservations to resist importation of foreign laws and standards, the United States has enacted legislation that bars U.S. courts from recognizing and enforcing foreign judgments that are based on libel standards that do not meet strict First Amendment standards.[73] In addition, a number of American states have recently enacted laws or constitutional provisions that purport to bar judges from considering foreign and international law, and in some cases from specifically enforcing Shari'a law.[74]

Whether the United States can maintain this posture of resistance, in particular with regard to freedom of speech and, if so, whether this is a normatively desirable approach in the twenty-first century are pressing questions.[75] In the current century, some form of engagement with the transnational is inevitable. U.S. officials may not be able to keep all aspects of foreign laws and cultures from crossing U.S. borders.

As Rodney Smolla observed more than two decades ago, as the world becomes more tightly interconnected the United States must think carefully about how receptive to foreign and international laws it can or ought to be. As discussed in Chapter 9, legal scholars have proposed several approaches to resolving international conflicts regarding expressive freedoms. These include application of uniform foreign judgment recognition standards, development of global free speech standards, creation of a "safe haven" for online expression, and cosmopolitan or pluralist approaches to resolving conflicts of law.

There is, of course, a certain inherent tension between receptivity to foreign laws and standards and preservation of First Amendment liberties at home. I address this issue in later chapters. At this point, I suggest only that the choice need not be one between wholesale importation of foreign standards and the strongest form of First Amendment exceptionalism. Perhaps it is possible for the United States to demonstrate, as the Declaration of Independence states, "a decent respect for the opinions of mankind" regarding expressive and religious freedoms without sacrificing its longstanding commitment to these freedoms.[76]

THE EXTRATERRITORIAL FIRST AMENDMENT

The First Amendment also has an important and diverse extraterritorial dimension. Citizens, aliens, multinational corporations, members of the American press, and various American governmental units participate in expressive and religious activities beyond U.S. shores. American power, activities, and influence extend well beyond the nation's territorial borders. The First Amendment has long influenced global debates and conceptions of expressive and religious liberties. Finally, the United States continues to attempt to export and transplant First Amendment standards, principles, and norms across the globe.

Does the First Amendment Follow the Flag?

A variety of expressive and religious activities occur beyond U.S. territorial borders. As discussed earlier, foreign travel is an important aspect of the First Amendment's transborder dimension. U.S. citizens travel abroad to gather information, understand foreign cultures, attend American universities, report from foreign locations, and protest U.S. policies. Some are employed by American companies operating abroad, and seek protection in that context under U.S. laws and First Amendment provisions.[77]

Further, Americans have long engaged in religious fellowship and other sectarian activities abroad. Missionaries, proselytizers, and sectarian charitable organizations have operated extensively in foreign nations. Indeed, in certain historical periods, religious groups have worked hand-in-hand with federal officials to carry out American foreign policy abroad.[78]

The United States has also funded projects in foreign nations that involve, and sometimes directly benefit, foreign religious institutions. Faith-based initiatives under Presidents George W. Bush and Barack Obama have raised concerns regarding direct and indirect forms of U.S. support for sectarian projects overseas. Similarly, post–September 11, 2001 civic education programs that support the development of moderate forms of Islam abroad have raised Establishment Clause concerns.[79]

The foregoing activities and programs raise the question whether the First Amendment, either in whole or in part, follows the flag or follows the government as it operates abroad.[80] If so, to what extent do First Amendment guarantees protect citizens or aliens while they are located abroad and to what extent do or should these provisions restrict U.S. governmental activities in foreign nations?

The First Amendment's extraterritorial scope or domain has not received significant judicial or scholarly attention. The Supreme Court has assumed, but never expressly held, that U.S. citizens enjoy free speech, association, press, or petition rights when they are subject to U.S. regulations abroad.[81] However, courts have consistently declined to grant relief to American speakers or press members acting beyond U.S. shores.[82] Whether the First Amendment Establishment Clause or Free Exercise Clause applies to U.S. projects, diplomatic ventures, or citizens overseas has also not been definitively settled.[83]

Answering these and related questions is important to a full understanding of the extraterritorial First Amendment. Chapter 6 addresses issues relating to the extraterritorial application of the First Amendment's free speech, press, assembly, and petition clauses. Chapter 7 addresses extraterritorial application of the First Amendment's religion clauses.

The First Amendment in International Forums

In a variety of international forums, U.S. officials speak on behalf of the nation and conduct its foreign affairs. The United States funds and operates media outlets, engages in informational and propaganda campaigns, and distributes billions of dollars in funds to governments, institutions, and communities across the globe. In conducting the nation's international diplomacy, government officials meet and engage in dialog with foreign leaders. Thus, in forums across the world the United States acts as a sovereign, a speaker, and a subsidizer of a variety of expressive and religious activities.

Chapter 8 examines the role and application of the First Amendment in these international forums. The extent to which the First Amendment applies or is implicated in international forums and foreign affairs has not been systematically addressed. In general, courts have been reluctant to entertain constitutional claims that involve foreign affairs and core diplomatic functions. However, governmental participation in global forums raises a number of important First Amendment questions. These include whether states, localities, and other speakers have speech rights in international forums, the application and limits of the government speech doctrine in the foreign affairs realm, the extent to which the unconstitutional conditions doctrine can limit the speech of U.S. citizens and foreign speakers, and whether the Establishment Clause imposes any limits on the conduct of foreign affairs.

As we shall see, these questions raise both individual liberties concerns and broader issues regarding the First Amendment's influence on the international stage. I will argue that whether or not citizens, states, or individuals have judicially enforceable expressive or religious rights in international forums, the First Amendment ought to guide or inform U.S. activity in international forums. I will urge that basic First Amendment principles be used as a framework for analyzing participation in international debates; American propagandizing abroad; U.S. intervention in foreign speech cultures; and U.S. engagement with foreign religious leaders, organizations, and communities.

In sum, examination of the extraterritorial First Amendment will raise issues of constitutional domain as well as political issues regarding the projection of U.S. power. Resolving both types of issues is critical to understanding the First Amendment's transborder dimension.

Exporting the First Amendment

For much of its history, the First Amendment has competed for acceptance with other constitutional models around the world. The cross-border flow mentioned earlier moves in two directions. Foreign laws, judgments, and constitutional norms could be imported into the United States. The United States also seeks to export First Amendment standards, norms, and principles beyond its borders. Like import of foreign standards and principles, this is part of a cross-territorial exchange of ideas. However, because the goal of this exportation is to broadly affect rights, policies, and behaviors in foreign nations, it is also appropriate to think of exportation as an important aspect of the extraterritorial First Amendment.

As I have mentioned, when it comes to expressive and religious freedoms the United States considers itself to be solely in the export business. As I discuss in Chapter 10, the United States has long made concerted efforts to export First Amendment standards, principles, and norms across the globe.[84] In the wake of the Second World War and during the postwar period the United States engaged in a vigorous campaign at the United Nations to codify First Amendment–like speech, press, and religious freedoms.[85] Other export mechanisms, aimed less at codifying standards than altering policies and behaviors, include U.S. propaganda and informational campaigns, cultural exchange and free trade policies, extraterritorial application of trade and intellectual property laws, judicial decisions, and laws respecting foreign judgments.

Some of these American efforts have borne significant fruit.[86] Owing to American diplomatic and other actions, expressive and religious freedoms are now considered fundamental human rights across vast geopolitical domains. Basic First Amendment principles have been well received in many parts of the world, and have led to liberalization of some foreign restrictions on expressive and religious freedoms.

At the same time, as I have noted, in most specific respects the rest of the world has largely rejected First Amendment doctrines and standards.[87] In a variety of global marketplaces of ideas relating to constitutional liberties, the United States has steadily lost ground to other models and regimes. This is the case not just with respect to the American model of First Amendment freedoms, but also regarding the American constitutional model more generally.[88]

As other scholars have argued, in the twenty-first century, constitutional pluralism will likely be the dominant perspective in comparative constitutional law.[89] No single expressive or religious liberty regime is likely to be adopted as a global standard. It has long been clear that the United States has neither the raw power nor the global influence to enshrine First Amendment standards into international or supranational law. If the First Amendment is to retain purchase in the community of nations, the United States will need to focus on alternative export strategies and mechanisms. Chapter 10 examines some of these alternatives.

THE CONTOURS OF THE TRANSBORDER DIMENSION

So far, I have outlined the basic parameters of the First Amendment's transborder dimension, and previewed some of the issues that will be addressed in subsequent chapters. Over the years, a variety of historical, sociological, political, legal, institutional, technological, and international factors have shaped and altered the contours of the First Amendment's transborder or nondomestic dimension. In the text that follows I offer some general and preliminary comments regarding these factors. Subsequent chapters consider these influences in more specific and concrete contexts.

Historical Events and National Orientation

Nations might be said to possess collective orientations or perspectives regarding foreign persons, norms, ideas, and cultures. In America, the basic ideal of openness to foreign persons, cultures, faiths, and ideas has been, and indeed remains, an important aspect of national culture and mythology. Americans generally like to think of their nation as a welcoming place for immigrants and a haven from foreign ideological and religious persecution. Indeed, this is a critical part of the American historical narrative.

However, as is true of citizens of other nations, Americans' openness to foreign persons and influences has ebbed and flowed over time in response to domestic and international events. At various points in our nation's history, foreign persons, ideas, and influences have been treated with suspicion, fear, and outright hostility. Indeed, fear of foreign influences and attachments is deeply rooted in American history. The Constitution's framers were not isolationists. However, they were deeply concerned about the dangers of foreign influence and corruption. Thus, for instance, they allowed only "natural born citizens" to hold the office of president and prohibited the granting of foreign titles of nobility.[90]

Fear of foreign persons and ideas has also been codified in U.S. laws. Not surprisingly, negative and suspicious orientations toward the outside world have been most prevalent during times of domestic strife, war, and international conflict.[91] In the eighteenth and nineteenth centuries, aliens were imprisoned, deported, or denied permission to travel abroad based solely on the content of their speech, the nature of their associations, or their religious beliefs. The Alien and Sedition Acts of 1798 provided for the deportation and prosecution of aliens and others considered "dangerous to the peace and safety of the United States."[92] As James Madison wrote to Thomas Jefferson just before passage of the Alien and Sedition Acts, "Perhaps it is a universal truth that the loss of liberty at home is to be charged to provisions against danger, real or pretended, from abroad."

Notwithstanding the ratification of the First Amendment, throughout American history journalists and others have been prosecuted under federal laws based on their speech, press, and associational activities. As Anthony Lewis has observed, "Again and again in American history the public has been told that civil liberties must be sacrificed to protect the country from foreign threats."[93]

With regard to development of the First Amendment's transborder dimension, the first half of the twentieth century was perhaps the most important formative period. Through two world wars, general concerns regarding the importation of foreign ideologies including anarchy, communism, pacifism, Trotskyism, and socialism gave rise to broad-scale government efforts to punish speech and association, deport and exclude aliens, prohibit citizens' foreign travel, and otherwise suppress foreign faiths and ideologies. During this period, foreign visitors, organizations, and ideologies were often treated as "clear and present dangers" to the domestic body politic. Americans who adopted radical foreign ideas were considered unpatriotic, accused of treason, and imprisoned for merely espousing such ideas or joining with others to do so. During wartime periods, but also in more peaceful times, the American mood has sometimes been jingoistic.

Of course, not all Americans held such attitudes. Nor were all national policies, even during these tense periods, explicitly hostile to foreigners or foreign influences. Immigrants, including many prominent intellectuals, were welcomed into the United States. However, in general, from the early twentieth century through the end of the Cold War, national attitudes and policies certainly hardened against cross-border exchange. Aliens were treated as political outsiders situated, even when they were in the United States, beyond the First Amendment's protective domain. Foreign creeds, ideologies, and influences were considered, in the words of the Supreme Court, "clear and present dangers."[94]

As noted earlier, the end of the Cold War brought a degree of thawing and liberalization of laws and regulations restricting cross-border movement and information flow. However, American borders have remained closed to a variety of informational sources and activities. Legal restrictions on cross-border exchange have never been fully domesticated, in the sense that the First Amendment applies fully to them. In certain political quarters today, fear of socialist ideas, Nazi-inspired ideologies, and European cultural fads remains quite sharp – if not, to be sure, as acute as this mood was during the Cold War period.

In more contemporary periods, the global war that the United States and other nations are waging against foreign terrorists has influenced national attitudes regarding foreign speakers, associations, and faiths. It has produced national laws and policies like the USA PATRIOT Act, the prohibition on "material support" to foreign terrorist organizations, surveillance of cross-border communications and domestic associations, and proposed additional limits on foreign contributions to U.S. political campaigns. In states and localities, these attitudes are manifested in immigration laws, proposals to limit or exclude Shari'a law, and local restrictions on the building of mosques.

With regard to the community of nations, two world wars convinced Americans that exporting the First Amendment would provide a form of insurance against the rise of authoritarian governments. Thus, in international forums after World War II, U.S. officials sought to export the First Amendment as a universal model for expressive and religious liberties. On the international stage, U.S. officials sought to embed First Amendment–like standards and principles in international legal instruments and agreements.

Today, Americans continue to view the First Amendment as a shining example of constitutional liberty in a pluralistic nation, one that separates us from both repressive regimes and other democracies around the world. The First Amendment undeniably provides some exceptional protections to U.S. citizens. However, with regard to perceived foreign dangers, the U.S. approach is not as exceptional as many Americans might believe. In certain contexts, including restrictions on cross-border communication and association and exclusion of alien visitors, U.S. policies and practices do not look so different from those of many foreign nations.

In sum, national attitudes toward the world beyond U.S. borders have significantly influenced the contours of the First Amendment's transborder dimension. As a general matter, what Richard Hofstadter has called "the paranoid style in American politics" has limited the extent to which the First Amendment's free speech and religious liberty guarantees have been considered applicable to foreign persons, ideas, and creeds. At the same time, Americans have long contended that the freedoms enshrined in the First Amendment are fit for export to nations across the world.

Institutional and Legal Influences

National orientations are often inscribed in positive law. The policies and decisions of U.S. legislative, executive, and judicial institutions have significantly influenced the contours of the First Amendment's transborder dimension. These decisions and policies have generally tracked, and in some cases have contributed to, some of the parochial and exceptionalist orientations discussed earlier.

In general, although for somewhat different reasons, all three branches of the national government have adopted and applied a territorial framework with regard to expressive and religious liberties.[95] Under this framework, robust First Amendment protection appears to stop at the water's edge. Moreover, all three branches have generally treated territorial borders as barriers to recognition of foreign laws relating to freedom of speech.

Congress has broad constitutional powers to regulate foreign commerce, immigration, and other matters relating to the U.S. international borders. It has passed laws restricting a broad range of cross-border and beyond-border expressive, associational, and other activities. Congress has also authorized foreign spending and other policies that have affected the contours of the extraterritorial First Amendment.

The President also possesses broad powers relating to territorial sovereignty, particularly in the areas of national security and foreign affairs. The executive has restricted foreign travel, regulated press activities abroad, and prosecuted cross-border crimes relating to national security. Executive agencies, both familiar and less well known, including the United States Agency for International Development, the Bureau of Educational and Cultural Affairs, the Department of Homeland Security, United States Customs and Border Protection, the United States Bureau of Industry and Security, and the U.S. State Department all extensively regulate and participate in the construction of the transborder First Amendment.

Primarily as a result of judicially developed doctrines and principles, the federal courts operate under greater institutional constraints than the other branches of government. In areas such as immigration, foreign affairs, and national security courts generally grant broad deference to political actors and policies. They may also decline to adjudicate some transborder claims, either under the so-called political questions doctrine or by construing statutes narrowly to avoid First Amendment questions. As a result of these and other limits, the judicial branch has not fully recognized and enforced transborder First Amendment liberties.

In sum, through exercise of their constitutional powers, all three branches of the federal government have significantly influenced the First Amendment's transborder dimension. Through their policies and decisions, each branch continues to actively participate in shaping this dimension in the twenty-first century.

Digitization and Globalization

Factors and forces beyond the corridors of government are presently having an extraordinary impact on transborder expressive and religious activities. In particular, the digitization of communications and the rise of globalization are altering expressive and religious practices. These forces are posing unique challenges to governmental authority and, in particular, the territorial framework that has long governed cross-border information flow.[96] As we shall see, that framework has not yet been vanquished. However, social forces are placing considerable pressure on traditional regulatory models and mechanisms.

To some degree, early technologies such as print, radio, and television bridged territorial distance. These technologies linked the peoples of distant nations, expanded opportunities for transborder exchange and information flow, and altered geopolitical relations. In the twentieth and twenty-first centuries, the rise of the Internet and digitized communication has done more than any previous technological advance to alter the basic relationship among sovereigns, citizens, and territorial borders.[97]

Digitization has facilitated global communication and information flow on a massive scale. It has linked geographically distant cultures and expanded opportunities for cross-border association and fellowship. As scholars have argued, digitization has made possible the creation of an "international marketplace of ideas."[98] Digitization and information flow have in turn played a central role in the process of globalization. Here I am using globalization in a broad sense, to refer to the phenomena of deterritorialization and global interconnectedness.[99] Insofar as First Amendment liberties are concerned, the most important aspects of globalization include the ease and frequency of foreign travel and international collaboration, the facilitation of cross-border information flow and trade, and the transformation of traditional press models.[100]

Global interconnectivity has reopened what seemed to be well-settled issues relating to the First Amendment's transborder dimension. For example, scholars have begun to develop new theories or justifications for freedom of speech and association that focus on how people communicate and collaborate in the digital era.[101] Scholars and courts have also questioned basic presuppositions regarding territoriality and rights. Among other things, they have noted that determining which nation's law applies to a particular activity no longer seems to depend exclusively on the location of the actor or regulator.

As digitized speech and collaboration have begun to transcend borders, new dangers and concerns have arisen. As I discuss in Chapter 5, digitization has facilitated the global transmission of hate speech, international terrorist activities, and cross-border criminal conspiracies. It has also facilitated global piracy with regard to intellectual property. The Internet's emerging global theater will give rise to many difficult regulatory and national security challenges. How officials respond to these challenges will significantly affect the future contours of the First Amendment's transborder dimension.

In the twenty-first century, people, informational materials, ideas, ideologies, cultural norms, and religious faiths all traverse international borders with extraordinary frequency and speed.[102] As a result of this global interconnectedness, people can converse and commingle to an unprecedented degree. Instead of being strictly separated by territorial borders, the world's economic, cultural, and religious systems are increasingly in contact with one another. This will create opportunities for both transborder cooperation and conflict. How citizens and officials respond to these opportunities will also have a significant impact on the future contours of the First Amendment's transborder dimension.

Territorial Sovereignty and International Engagement

Although territorial sovereignty remains the fundamental organizational principle within the community of nations, territorial borders are becoming less certain markers of sovereign authority. A number of

forces, including digitization and globalization, have decreased the significance of the links between law, culture, and geography. Changes to
territory and territorial sovereignty will challenge not only traditional
governmental powers to regulate and control cross-border information flow, but also to preserve intraterritorial legal and constitutional
domains.[103]

Transnational processes such as treaties, multinational agreements,
and contacts (formal and informal) between U.S. officials and foreign
actors and institutions have pushed comparative and transnational
constitutional issues to the fore. With regard to the First Amendment,
these processes have highlighted some sharp differences among international human rights regimes, foreign laws, and America's exceptionalist approach to expressive and religious freedoms.[104]

Transnationalism and international governance will not completely
eliminate territorial sovereignty. However, like other forces, they will
cause domestic and transnational laws and actors to come into more
frequent contact with one another. As mentioned earlier, a number
of international treaties and agreements address freedom of speech,
press, assembly, belief, religious conversion, and proselytization. In
addition, transnational legal sources address specific subjects ranging
from limits on travel or movement, to global distribution of art, music,
and films, to global rights in intellectual property. Future treaties, covenants, and protocols may address the regulation of hate speech on the
Internet, global press freedoms, and international protection of religious freedom.

This does not mean that U.S. legislative, executive, and judicial
officials will necessarily be influenced by these processes and contacts. However, as it continues to participate in transnational processes
the United States will face pressure to alter or abandon some of its
exceptional First Amendment standards. The extent to which the First
Amendment will remain an outlier in comparison to the rest of the
world's rights regimes is uncertain. In part, the contours of the First
Amendment's transborder dimension will be determined by the manner in which officials resolve the tension between American exceptionalism at home and transnational engagement abroad.

2   TRANSBORDER PERSPECTIVES

Provincialism and Cosmopolitanism

As Chapter 1 demonstrated, the First Amendment has an important transborder or nondomestic dimension. This chapter describes two general orientations or perspectives with regard to that dimension. The first perspective, which in essence views the First Amendment as an exclusive and exceptional set of intraterritorial limits on government, I will call *provincial.* The second approach, which I will call *cosmopolitan,* adopts a more outward-oriented perspective with regard to expressive and religious liberties. In addition, the cosmopolitan approach is more deeply engaged than the provincial account with the First Amendment's operation and standing within the community of nations.

As will become clear, these terms have both descriptive and normative aspects. Further, we ought to view provincialism and cosmopolitanism as perspectives or orientations that are embraced by degrees rather than in absolute terms. Thus, for example, weaker forms of provincialism would support granting protection to certain cross-border speech and religious activities. Similarly, First Amendment cosmopolitanism acknowledges that transborder activities can be subject to significant legal restrictions.

I want to avoid the tyranny of labels. However, I also want to describe and critically examine what I believe are two distinct perspectives regarding the First Amendment. In the text that follows, I describe the basic tenets of the provincial and cosmopolitan perspectives. I adopt and defend a cosmopolitan approach. As will become clear, my goal in presenting and defending a cosmopolitan perspective is not to urge significant displacement of, or departure from, First Amendment standards or principles relating to domestic liberties.[1]

Thus, I do not argue that international human rights laws and universal norms relating to expressive and religious liberties are or ought to be binding in the United States. Nor, for that matter, do I contend that First Amendment standards ought to be universally adopted by other nations. I advance a more limited form of cosmopolitanism with more modest goals.[2] Among other things, I hope to convince readers that transborder liberties are core rather than peripheral guarantees. More generally, I want us to think more critically and systematically about the First Amendment's global footprint in the twenty-first century.

FIRST AMENDMENT PROVINCIALISM

I use the term "provincial" to describe one orientation or perspective regarding the First Amendment and its transborder dimension. I use this term not in the judgmental sense, in which it is typically associated with narrow-mindedness or lack of sophistication. I do not denigrate those who believe that the First Amendment is principally, if not exclusively, intended to protect citizens located within U.S. borders from certain forms of governmental regulation and from foreign influences. There is, as I discuss, some support for this position. Rather, I use the term provincial to denote a general orientation regarding the First Amendment that is limited in terms of geographic range or scope, somewhat insular in terms of outlook and biases, and strongly exceptionalist. Some have suggested "democratic" may be a better term for this approach. However, as will become clear, part of my objection to provincialism relates specifically to its rather narrow definition of democratic community.

There is no single authoritative or systematic account of First Amendment provincialism. However, the provincial perspective is represented in many judicial decisions, federal laws, and scholarly commentaries. It has been articulated over time, by all three branches of government, in explicit and implicit holdings, policies, statements, and claims. In its strongest form, provincialism envisions not three First Amendments, as I proposed in Chapter 1, but merely a single intraterritorial dimension. In general terms, provincialism views the First

Amendment as a set of protections for U.S. citizens against certain kinds of domestic regulation and a shield against importation of foreign laws, standards, and judgments. More specifically, as I discuss later, First Amendment provincialism is based on (1) parochial accounts of constitutional origins and community; (2) an expansive interpretation of territorial sovereignty and federal power in transborder contexts; (3) an inward-looking, territorial orientation regarding First Amendment justifications; (4) a narrow conception of transborder liberties; and (5) a strong , often reflexive, defense of First Amendment exceptionalism.

Constitutional Origins and Orientation

According to the traditional account of the Constitution's origins, "the framers created the Constitution for internal purposes, and its intended audience was the American people."[3] From this perspective, the Constitution itself was inwardly oriented and directed – its provisions related exclusively to domestic concerns, and the founding took place outside or beyond the then-existing community of nations.

As I discuss later, there are several reasons to question this narrative. However, First Amendment provincialism appears to accept and is based on this parochial account of constitutional origins. According to this narrative, the First Amendment was ratified for the exclusive benefit of political communities located within the United States and was not intended to signify or convey anything to the world beyond American shores. The supposition appears to have been that a domestic institution was prohibited from infringing the rights of members of the domestic political community within domestic territorial borders. As the U.S. Constitution's Preamble and other provisions confirm, the new government was barred from abridging or denying the expressive and religious liberties of "the People of the United States."

As developed, the provincial conception of constitutional community is based primarily on location and status. From its provincial inception, the First Amendment was intended to benefit the citizens of the contiguous United States while they were located within U.S. borders. Membership in the political community was determined primarily by the status of citizenship. Thus citizens, who are entitled to all benefits bestowed under the social contract, enjoy robust protection with regard to expressive, religious, and other constitutional liberties when exercised within the geographic boundaries of their domestic political communities.[4]

By contrast, under the provincial account aliens are considered community outsiders. In its strongest form provincialism denies that aliens have any First Amendment rights – even when they are located within the United States.[5] The Alien and Sedition Acts of 1798 were enacted on this assumption. This view has never been formally repudiated. Thus, in a Cold War–era case that has not been overruled, the Supreme Court held that aliens can be removed from the United States even for purely ideological or associational reasons.[6] More generally, nonpermanent resident and perhaps even permanent resident aliens have no First Amendment rights to participate in self-governance activities. This includes voting or spending money in U.S. elections, activities that lie at the heart of the First Amendment free speech guarantee.[7]

The provincial orientation is based on certain instrumental suppositions and justifications. With regard to the First Amendment, the framers believed that the exercise of expressive and religious liberties would help citizens build and strengthen domestic constitutional communities. On this view, those who ratified the First Amendment were not at all concerned with protecting citizens' communications or relationships with audiences beyond American borders or the rights of citizens who traveled and commingled with aliens abroad. Moreover, they had no reason to be concerned about the effects of U.S. power abroad, as American influence did not generally extend beyond its territorial borders. Even if it did cross borders, the Constitution was not then understood to follow the flag. From the perspective of the founding generation, transborder activities and concerns had little or nothing to do with local self-government or the building of domestic political institutions.[8]

From the provincial perspective, the framers' orientation with regard to aliens and audiences abroad was sometimes one of skepticism, wariness, and even fear. George Washington frequently inveighed against the dangers foreign influence posed to the American political system.

As James Madison observed, "[s]ecurity against foreign danger is …
an avowed and essential object of the American Union."[9] This attitude
is deeply rooted in American constitutional history. As discussed in
Chapter 1, some framers feared foreign entanglements and influences.
Their concerns are explicitly inscribed in constitutional text – for
example, in the ban on foreign gifts, the prohibition on titles of nobility, restrictions on foreign emoluments, and provisions addressing eli-
gibility for election to Congress and the presidency.[10] Fear of foreign
influence was, of course, not entirely irrational. As it sought to break
foreign bonds, the new American republic was indeed vulnerable to
foreign plots, intrigue, and attacks.

Over time, however, the definition or concept of "foreign danger"
broadened considerably. It sometimes came to include a general wariness or skepticism with regard to foreign persons, ideas, and influences. Indeed, the defining conflicts that shaped early interpretations
of the First Amendment in the twentieth century involved efforts
to suppress ideologies – Jacobinism, radicalism, anarchism, socialism, and communism – that were viewed as emanating from foreign sources and lands.[11] The Alien and Sedition Acts of 1798 were
enacted specifically to protect Americans from revolutionary French
political thought and terrorism. As Anthony Lewis has observed,
"The French Revolution of 1789 had led to Jacobin Terror and the
guillotine. Some Americans, especially those of conservative outlook, feared that France would export its ideology."[12] During certain
periods of American history, protecting the American people against
foreign danger meant protecting them from foreign fads, influences,
and political creeds.

This wariness has also extended to foreign religious faiths and
institutions. The American colonists had escaped religious persecution abroad. The Constitution expressly prohibits imposition of any
religious test for public office and otherwise evinces concern for separation of church and state.[13] Meaningful protection for religious pluralism did not arise primarily from these textual provisions or from
the fact that a Bill of Rights was ratified. Insofar as such protection has
been achieved, it is owing to domestic political struggles during which
certain religious faiths have been treated as "foreign."

For example, during the American struggle for religious pluralism, Mormon citizens were denied the right to travel abroad and some
aliens were denied the right to enter the country owing specifically
to their religious beliefs. Today, many Americans strongly believe that
the United States was founded as, and remains, a "Judeo-Christian
nation." Non-mainstream religious beliefs, including Islam, continue
to be viewed with a certain measure of suspicion – as if they too constitute a kind of "foreign danger."

In sum, the provincial perspective regarding constitutional origins and community is inward-oriented. First Amendment liberties
were granted to domestic insiders based on location and status, in an
effort to provide support for domestic community-building and self-
governance. In contrast, foreign persons, ideologies, and faiths have
often been viewed as dangerous to domestic community and order.

Territorial Sovereignty and U.S. Power

The framers of the Constitution were, of course, not unaware of the
world beyond their borders. When they constituted the new federal
government, the framers granted it broad powers to protect domestic
interests against "foreign dangers" and to engage with other members
of the community of nations.

Thus, the framers granted Congress the power to regulate commerce with foreign nations, to define crimes on the high seas and
against the law of nations, and to establish rules relating to naturalization.[14] Congress was also granted broad powers relating to national
defense.[15] In addition to being the nation's Commander-in-Chief and
having the power to enforce congressional laws, the executive was
granted powers to conduct foreign affairs and relations. Sometimes
this was to be done by the president alone, but in many cases foreign
affairs were to be conducted in consultation with the U.S. Senate.[16]
Over time, the bulk of the nation's power in the area of foreign relations has accrued to the president. Further, the legislative and executive branches have been granted "plenary" power over immigration.[17]
The Supreme Court was granted the power of judicial review in some
cases touching on foreign relations, including cases arising under

treaties and affecting foreign ambassadors.[18] The states, by contrast, were expressly precluded from entering into treaties or otherwise conducting foreign affairs.[19]

Together, this basic framework or structure authorizes the federal government to engage in commercial, political, and diplomatic intercourse with the international community. The granted and implied powers represent the core of American territorial sovereignty.[20]

From a provincial perspective, these powers are broadly construed and subject to few limits. As the Supreme Court has stated, "It is axiomatic that the United States, as sovereign, has the inherent authority to protect, and a paramount interest in protecting, its territorial integrity."[21] Owing to this orientation, relative to domestic liberties constitutional liberties at the border have always enjoyed a somewhat diminished status. In certain contexts, the Supreme Court has made clear that the Constitution does not always operate with the same force at the international border as it does domestically. Thus, for example, the Court has established a border search exception to the Fourth Amendment that permits customs and other officials to conduct searches without warrants or reasonable suspicion.[22] This was necessary, according to the Court, primarily to ensure that federal officials could protect the United States and its people from dangerous packages, materials, and items originating abroad.

During most of our nation's history, a similar supposition has affected the First Amendment's operation at international borders. Officials have prevented persons and materials from crossing international borders on grounds that would clearly violate the First Amendment in domestic or local contexts.[23] As we shall see, although some restrictive federal laws and regulations have been repealed, the provincial idea that the First Amendment is silent or speaks differently at the international border is still embraced to some extent by all three branches of the U.S. government.[24]

From a provincial standpoint, territorial integrity and sovereignty concerns generally trump or substantially weaken First Amendment liberties. Federal officials must have the authority to police and maintain the boundaries of the American constitutional community and to defend the United States against foreign threats and dangers. Whenever a contested activity intersects in some fashion with international borders, provincialists argue that courts must defer to governmental assertions of national security and foreign affairs concerns.

Provincialism's strong, indeed plenary, conception of federal power with regard to foreign affairs and national security affects more than the exercise of individual liberties. It also influences the provincial conception of the First Amendment's scope or domain – that is, the areas where its limits and principles are considered relevant and applicable.

Under a provincial approach, territorial borders remain critical markers of governmental authority. Domestic and foreign affairs are sharply distinguished. The federal government acts in a variety of international forums. It regulates, subsidizes, and speaks across the globe. From a provincial perspective, the First Amendment does not generally limit or even guide these extraterritorial activities. Thus, for example, U.S. propaganda and informational programs, as well as collaborations with foreign religious leaders, essentially occur outside the purview of the Free Speech Clause and the Establishment Clause.

Further, in the realm of foreign affairs, provincialism views the national government's voice as supreme and preemptive. As the sole representative of the American constitutional community in its dealings with foreign powers, the federal government can generally preempt or silence the voices of citizens, subnational governments, nongovernmental organizations, and multinational corporations that may also wish to speak on matters of international or global concern. These actors' interests are considered to be primarily or exclusively domestic in character and scope.

First Amendment Justifications

Provincialism also holds distinctive views concerning the justifications for freedom of speech and other First Amendment liberties. These justifications tend to look exclusively inward, toward the domestic political and social concerns of citizens.

Traditional justifications or theories relating to freedom of speech, press, and religion tend to have an inherent parochial bias or orientation.

This bias is in some sense quite natural. First Amendment justifications are rooted in the provincial conceptions of constitutional origins and community which, as noted, focus on supporting domestic expressive and religious communities.

The principal justifications for free speech and press rights stress the need for individual self-government in domestic political communities, vibrant local and national marketplaces of ideas, and a vigorous press capable of checking domestic governmental abuses.[25] Alexander Meiklejohn's celebrated town hall meeting, which was conceptualized as a focal point for self-government, is quintessentially local in both character and orientation.[26] Meiklejohn's self-governance justification for freedom of speech focuses on the rights of domestic audiences to receive information from their fellow citizens that relates to matters of public concern in their respective local communities. This focus on domestic political communication and debate is a defining feature in the work of many prominent free speech theorists.[27]

Other traditional free speech justifications, including truth-seeking and self-actualization, have also been primarily oriented toward the exercise of speech rights within the contiguous United States. Both the search for truth and concerns regarding speaker autonomy seem to dissipate or halt at the water's edge. Robert Kamenshine succinctly summarized this orientation when he wrote that "generally cited First Amendment values have little or no application" in nondomestic contexts.[28] As Kamenshine argued, "We are not constitutionally committed to facilitating [First Amendment] objectives abroad."[29] According to some scholars, this is especially true with regard to aliens living in foreign nations.[30]

First Amendment press rights have also been conceptualized in a provincial fashion. Courts and scholars have generally conceived of the press as operating within a national forum.[31] According to traditional accounts, the press facilitates citizen self-government by informing domestic communities, ensuring governmental transparency, and checking governmental institutions and officials as they act in the United States.[32] Under a provincial account, to operate effectively as a fourth estate the domestic press primarily needs access to domestic leaders and institutions. Its principal function is to inform and educate the American public with regard to matters of public concern within U.S. borders.

Finally, justifications for First Amendment religious liberties focus primarily on concerns regarding official support for or discrimination against domestic religious institutions. Scholars acknowledge the influence of international persecution of American colonists on modern conceptions of religious liberty. However, with very few exceptions, analyses of First Amendment religious liberties have not specifically addressed transborder or nondomestic concerns.[33] The Supreme Court has not had occasion to address such concerns either. The Court has developed concepts such as the "reasonable observer," which is at present central to application of the Establishment Clause's endorsement standard, in the context of local political communities.[34] Some scholars have implied or suggested that the antidiscrimination, equality, and anti-establishment values underlying the religion clauses may not be applicable beyond U.S. borders.[35]

In sum, although they are not necessarily limited to provincial concerns, traditional First Amendment theories or justifications exhibit an inward-facing or intraterritorial orientation. The most systematic consideration has been given to free speech justifications, with several scholars arguing or assuming that the traditional justifications apply only in domestic contexts. The more implicit assumption with regard to free press and religious liberties appears to be that the justifications for protecting them are also closely related to the functioning of domestic political communities.

Quasi-Recognition of Transborder Liberties

Relative to the other branches of the federal government, courts have played a somewhat minor, but still important, role in terms of defining the scope of the First Amendment's transborder dimension. Courts have explicitly or implicitly recognized that citizens possess some nondomestic First Amendment rights. Rights receiving at least some judicial recognition include the right to receive information originating abroad; to listen in person to foreign speakers; to engage in expressive activities in foreign nations; and to contest the expenditure of American tax dollars on foreign sectarian projects.[36]

However, these First Amendment liberties are not recognized to the same extent as their domestic counterparts. When confronted with First Amendment claims in nondomestic contexts, courts have generally used an interpretive modality under which liberties have attained only a "quasi-recognized" status. Although judicial deference is one characteristic of this approach, quasi-recognition is not simply a function of the deference typically granted to the federal government in transborder contexts. Rather, quasi-recognition places transborder liberties in a unique and separate category of rights that are thinly recognized and not deemed fundamental.

As a judicial modality, quasi-recognition consists of five basic elements: (1) reluctance to fully recognize and justify transborder First Amendment liberties; (2) articulation of unique limitations on those liberties; (3) demotion or devaluation of certain transborder activities, such as the right to travel abroad; (4) substantial reliance on federal immigration powers and judicial precedents involving immigration and travel; and (5) reflexive deference to foreign affairs and national security concerns.

Courts have been reluctant to fully recognize and justify transborder First Amendment liberties. On some occasions, they have simply avoided the question by declining to decide whether such rights exist or ruling against plaintiffs on other grounds.[37]

In other cases courts have simply assumed, without formally or expressly deciding, that citizens do enjoy certain nondomestic First Amendment liberties. These courts have not articulated any justification for granting such protection.[38] Similarly, courts that have recognized extraterritorial speech and press rights have generally offered no First Amendment theory or justification for doing so.[39] The Supreme Court has itself merely assumed, without expressly deciding, that citizens have a right to free speech beyond U.S. borders.[40] Courts have also described issues regarding recognition of transborder liberties, such as whether U.S. citizens' communications with foreign audiences are protected under the Free Speech Clause, as "open questions."[41]

In some cases, courts have subjected transborder First Amendment liberties to limitations that are not applicable in domestic contexts. Indeed, some of these limitations are flatly inconsistent with long-settled doctrine. For example, one court concluded that U.S. publishers who intentionally disseminate communications abroad may thereby waive First Amendment protection for such communications.[42] No similar waiver theory applies with regard to free speech or press rights exercised in domestic forums. Another court claimed that cross-border associations involving more than one entity may not be protected by the First Amendment's freedom of association – another limitation that has no parallel in domestic contexts.[43]

Further, in transborder contexts, courts have altered fundamental doctrines in a manner that cuts against judicial recognition of First Amendment rights. For example, in domestic First Amendment cases involving symbolic conduct, courts and scholars have long expressed concern that any symbolic act, including violent criminal activities, might be characterized as expressive and thus protected to some extent. In transborder cases, by contrast, this all-conduct-may-be-characterized-as-speech concern has been turned on its head. As a result, the following have all been characterized as regulations of *conduct* rather than *speech*: restricting a citizen's foreign travel where the express purpose of the travel was to gather information about a foreign culture[44]; revoking a citizen's passport in response to disclosure of sensitive information about American clandestine operations;[45] closing down a foreign mission operating in the United States[46]; and punishing a citizen for traveling abroad to engage in a "human shield" protest.[47] Of course, no court would ever think of characterizing censorship of a book as a regulation of the conduct of writing, or a parade permit requirement as a mere regulation of public movement. However, in transborder contexts, courts often treat what are arguably expressive activities, or at least activities with an expressive element, as forms of pure conduct.[48]

As noted, provincialism does not entail the outright rejection of all transborder First Amendment liberties. However, even some transborder liberties that courts have recognized have thereafter been demoted or narrowed in scope. For example, with regard to the right to foreign travel, Supreme Court decisions from the 1950s and 1960s suggested a close connection among foreign travel, freedom of speech, and freedom of association.[49] However, as I discuss in Chapter 3, the Supreme

Court later explained that the right of citizens to travel abroad is protected not by the First Amendment but through application of the Fifth Amendment's Due Process Clause. The Court explained that cross-border travel is not a strong "right," such as the one that protects interstate travel within the United States, but a much weaker "freedom."[50] The terms are important. They determine the amount or degree of constitutional protection afforded to foreign travel, particularly when engaged in for expressive purposes.[51]

Quasi-recognition also results in part from courts' application of immigration and foreign travel precedents to disparate and sometimes inapposite contexts. Thus, decisions recognizing U.S. power to determine who may enter or leave the country have been treated as relevant, if not dispositive, in lawsuits challenging U.S. funding conditions affecting foreign expression and cross-border expressive association claims.[52] Application of these precedents has raised questions concerning justiciability and resulted in application of minimal standards of judicial review with respect to other transborder First Amendment liberties.[53]

As discussed earlier, the provincial orientation is based in part on broad deference to federal power in areas such as immigration, foreign affairs, and national security. Courts have long exercised judicial restraint in these areas. In some cases, judges must defer to the expertise and judgments of military and other government officials, who are charged with protecting the nation's borders and carrying out its policies overseas. No one would suggest, for example, that U.S. enemies captured on foreign battlefields are entitled to assert free speech or assembly rights in such places.

Quasi-recognition is not based on any ordinary form of deference to the political branches. Rather, in nondomestic contexts, quasi-recognition rests on extraordinarily broad conceptions of both the federal sphere of authority and the character of federal power. Courts seem to treat any utterance or association that happens to intersect with territorial borders as activity that touches on foreign affairs and implicates national security. Indeed, as we shall see, federal courts have come close to recognizing broad foreign affairs, national security, and immigration *exceptions* to the First Amendment.[54] Even when they purport to recognize transborder liberties, courts reflexively defer to federal interests.

All three branches of the federal government have at times treated transborder liberties as peripheral, rather than core, First Amendment concerns. Indeed, this has been part of a longstanding interbranch dynamic relating to transborder liberties. As an interpretive modality, quasi-recognition has at times licensed the political branches to enact laws, regulations, and policies that restrict transborder information flow, association, and other activities. It has prevented nondomestic First Amendment liberties from achieving full jurisprudential status and recognition.

First Amendment Exceptionalism

As I noted in Chapter 1, the United States has adopted an exceptional approach to expressive and religious liberties. Those who adopt a strong provincial orientation with respect to the First Amendment's transborder dimension insist that the United States preserve free speech and other exceptionalist First Amendment doctrines. Among other things, this counsels officials to be skeptical of participation in transnational legal processes and wary of other possible avenues by which foreign or international standards might be imported to the United States.

Defense of First Amendment exceptionalism has long been a central plank of United States foreign policy. In the context of negotiating and entering treaties and multinational agreements, American officials rely on reservations, declarations, and understandings that limit the scope and application of international instruments that might affect expressive and religious liberties within the United States. In U.S. courts and legislatures, this approach has been evident in near-blanket refusals to enforce or recognize foreign libel and hate speech judgments, resistance to application of or even citation to foreign laws, and discrimination against religious laws and practices deemed foreign to the U.S. political community.

From a provincial perspective, foreign sources and authorities carry no persuasive or other weight within "our" constitutional community or with respect to "our" First Amendment. Thus, whenever foreign expressive and religious standards conflict with U.S. standards, the conflict must be resolved in favor of the American approach. Thus, in cross-border contexts in which the sovereign interests of French, German, and other foreign nations are implicated, the First Amendment essentially acts as a trump card or a barrier to foreign entry.

In American cultural and political debate, many take pride in rejecting European and other international constitutional standards regarding expressive and religious freedoms. Within the American polity, there has long been strong sentiment that the United States knows best and has arrived at the correct interpretation of expressive and religious freedoms. Thus, according to some provincialists, there is little or nothing to be gained from comparative analysis or transnational engagement. As a matter of national policy, the United States resists importation or application of foreign speech and religious laws, standards, and judgments.

At the same time, the United States has long taken the position that other nations ought to adopt *its* exceptional protections for expressive and religious liberties. As discussed in Chapter 10, like resistance to foreign laws the exportation of First Amendment standards has been an important part of U.S. foreign policy. Further, resistance to importation and exportation are, in a sense, flip sides of the same coin. Thus, the refusal to recognize foreign speech standards may result in imposition of First Amendment standards abroad.[55]

The United States also encourages nations to respect expressive and religious liberties as universal human rights. For example, the International Religious Freedom Act, signed by President Bill Clinton in 1998, authorizes the president to impose sanctions against foreign nations that, in the opinion of U.S. officials, have violated international standards regarding religious freedom. Some have criticized this approach for basing sanctions and judgments on *American* conceptions of expressive and religious freedom. Again, rather than assess liberties from a pluralistic perspective, the provincial account assumes the primacy of the American model.

To summarize, from the beginning First Amendment liberties have been viewed by many as a set of exceptional guarantees against domestic federal (and later state) encroachment. Under this view, First Amendment liberties exist solely for the benefit of citizens of domestic political communities, and in particular so that they may engage in self-governing and self-fulfilling activities. Moreover, under a provincial approach, outside the nation's territorial boundaries and beyond these domestic functions, First Amendment liberties are subject to plenary or broad exercises of federal power and entitled only to a form of judicial quasi-recognition. Finally, the provincialist views the First Amendment as a shield or barrier against importation of foreign laws and judgments, while at the same time arguing in favor of exportation of U.S. standards and principles.

First Amendment provincialism is an attitude or perspective that is deeply ingrained in American culture, politics, and law. Although I argue for a different orientation, let me first concede that some of provincialism's fundamental precepts are not without merit and historical support. Constitutional protections do of course exist *primarily* for the benefit of members of the domestic constitutional community. Moreover, exceptional First Amendment protections for expressive and religious liberties are indeed a hallmark of the American constitutional and political system. Robust protection for expressive and religious freedoms has produced undeniable benefits for Americans and for U.S. domestic political communities. Last, the federal government undoubtedly must have the authority to police cross-border exchange, to seek to preserve and protect domestic communities, and to conduct the nation's foreign affairs. These are irreducible aspects of national sovereignty.

However, despite its attributes, provincialism has led to a conception of the First Amendment that is too narrow, territorial, and parochial in orientation and effect. I will propose a more cosmopolitan orientation or perspective, one that both more accurately reflects the actual domain of transborder or nondomestic liberties and situates the First Amendment within the community of nations. In short, I hope to show how a more cosmopolitan conception of the First Amendment can benefit citizens, aliens, and the global community.

FIRST AMENDMENT COSMOPOLITANISM

First Amendment cosmopolitanism differs sharply from First Amendment provincialism. The differences relate primarily to perspectives on constitutional origins and orientation, degrees of recognition and support for transborder First Amendment liberties, and postures toward broader transnational and international concerns. In more specific terms, a cosmopolitan conception of the First Amendment (1) adopts a less parochial perspective with regard to the world beyond our shores, including foreign persons, ideas, attachments, and authorities; (2) views transborder conversation and commingling as central First Amendment activities and concerns with global implications; (3) relies on and is consistent with, although it supplements and broadens, traditional First Amendment justifications; and (4) features broad but not unlimited territorial and conceptual domains. Further, although cosmopolitanism challenges and globally situates First Amendment exceptionalism, it does not call for its ultimate demise.

In making the case for this more outward-oriented First Amendment, I borrow from both philosophical and basic definitional conceptions of cosmopolitanism.[56] I do not, however, argue in favor of world citizenship, convergence on universal standards regarding expressive and religious liberties, or establishment of global governance. Rather, I emphasize such things as global connectivity, the need for cross-cultural conversation, and respect for global constitutional pluralism.[57] Although the version of cosmopolitanism I defend challenges traditional conceptions of territoriality and territorial sovereignty, it does not dismiss or discount the nation-state or the importance of domestic connections. Rather, it contemplates a "rooted" form of cosmopolitanism in which Americans remain attached to their localities but are also interested in and connected to distant places and cultures.[58]

The Constitution's Cosmopolitan Heritage

According to the traditional account of the Constitution's origins, the framers were focused exclusively on internal concerns and communities. They drafted a charter with a territorially bounded, discrete domestic constitutional community in mind. According to the provincial narrative, as the framers met in Philadelphia and in the state ratifying conventions, events and circumstances beyond U.S. borders were far from their minds.

An implication of this narrative is that the First Amendment's guarantees, adopted just a few years later, were also part of this provincial project. Thus, according to the conventional account, the Constitution's structural and liberty provisions were adopted for the benefit of a territorially bounded people. The protections of the First Amendment, in particular, were adopted to encourage conversation and collaboration at home, with fellow citizens. This is consistent with the provincial claim that freedoms of speech, press, assembly, petition, and religion were intended to operate as restrictions on domestic laws or actions that interfered with domestic self-governance and community-building.

Although the provincial origins account has long been part of our constitutional narrative, scholars have begun to show that it is substantially incomplete and indeed may be misleading. A competing, more cosmopolitan, narrative exists with regard to the founding of our nation, our Constitution, and, I will argue, our First Amendment. The account I provide is not intended as an originalist analysis of either the Constitution itself or the First Amendment's text. As David Strauss has observed with regard to the latter, "the text and the original understandings of the First Amendment are essentially irrelevant to the American system of freedom of expression as it exists today."[59] I focus more generally on the extent to which "[l]ooking beyond our borders came naturally to the Framers."[60]

The cosmopolitan narrative traces back to the Revolutionary era. During that period, many Americans adopted a worldly perspective with regard to foreign laws, nations, and cultures. Many of the leading colonists had cosmopolitan social and political ties or habits.[61] As Gordon Wood has observed, during this period "[b]eing a gentleman signified being cosmopolitan, standing on elevated ground in order to have a large view of human affairs, and being free of the prejudices, parochialism, and religious enthusiasm of the vulgar and barbaric."[62]

To acquire this larger view, prominent American colonists frequently traveled abroad. There they regularly associated with foreign officials, as well as friends and acquaintances. In addition, many early Americans were participants in "the republic of letters," which has been described as a "transnational public sphere" in which thinkers "communicate[d] across space, including national boundaries and, Americans believed, oceans."[63] In this sphere, American public officials and other influential figures exhibited substantial interest in and respect for foreign thinkers, ideas, and cultures. This outward orientation would later be manifested in foundational documents such as the Declaration of Independence, in which Americans expressed their intention to pay "a decent respect to the opinions of mankind."[64]

Thus, from the beginning, Americans sought to engage with persons and cultures beyond their borders. They conceived of rights to travel abroad and to participate in global intercourse as fundamental human rights.[65] As a means of preserving peace among all civilized nations, the American colonists exhibited a certain benevolence and respect for foreign persons and nations – including those considered to be enemies of the United States. In sum, the early American colonists exhibited a "sensibility to the opinion of the world" and to the judgments of other nations.[66]

This cosmopolitan orientation carried over to the founding period. As legal scholars and historians have observed, the Constitution's founding was not a provincial event.[67] As David Golove and Daniel Hulsebosch have argued, "[t]he fundamental purpose of the Federal Constitution was to create a nation-state that the European powers would recognize, in the practical and legal sense, as a 'civilized state' worthy of equal respect in the international community."[68] According to these authors' cosmopolitan account, the Constitution was intended primarily for an international, rather than a domestic, audience. That is, as they constructed a system for local democratic self-governance, the framers had one eye sharply fixed on the world beyond U.S. international borders.

The framers adopted this orientation because they were seeking to integrate the United States and its citizens into an already-existing community of nations. Full integration required international recognition of the United States as a legitimate sovereign. However, during the founding period more than official diplomatic and international recognition was at stake. As Golove and Hulsebosch observe:

> Membership in this larger civilization – linked across space by cultural ties of sympathy, benevolence, and commerce – was desirable in its own right, and served the psychological needs of the many

founders who viewed themselves not just as members of a family, voluntary association, profession, town or city, state, and nation, but also as 'citizens of the world.'[69]

The framers were indeed concerned with erecting specifically *American* governance institutions, and with protecting the domestic liberties of the new nation's citizens. However, traditional accounts of constitutional origins and history ignore or minimize the close connections between this domestic project and persons, events, and influences beyond U.S. borders.[70] Transborder relations, the law of nations, and an abiding concern regarding international recognition were all aspects of the "international dimensions of the Federal Constitution."[71]

As noted earlier, the framers were certainly aware of foreign dangers. However, they also appreciated the need to protect cross-border conversation and diverse forms of nondomestic commingling. The drafters and ratifiers of the original Constitution understood that they were creating a framework for facilitating cross-border trade, social intercourse, and foreign diplomacy.[72]

The framers could not have anticipated that the United States would become a superpower. Although the text is not dispositive, it is significant that the framers drafted a document that contains strikingly few explicit geographic limitations.[73] The First Amendment, in particular, does not bar Congress from making any law abridging *domestic* freedom of speech, or establishing religion *on U.S. soil*. Its text is written in universal terms.[74]

The men who proposed, debated, and ratified the First Amendment had witnessed first-hand the importance of overseas fact-gathering and correspondence by American diplomats to the project of world citizenship.[75] The Constitution's framers were also acutely aware of religious persecution and official endorsement of religion by foreign governments, and of the need to restrain the newly created federal government in matters of faith and conscience.

Like the original Constitution, the Bill of Rights was a demonstration of America's status and its civilized nature. Indeed, it was presented to the world as one of the first human rights charters. To be sure, the First Amendment departed from European models in some significant respects. At the time of ratification, American officials understood that what they were doing was indeed exceptional relative to other nations. With regard to matters such as freedom of the press and church-state relations, the framers broke ranks with the community of nations. However, they did so in a manner that was self-consciously cosmopolitan.

Thus, the First Amendment's guarantees were a product of international engagement and comparison. Many framers, early jurists, and legal commentators studied and learned from foreign thinkers and political systems.[76] They borrowed First Amendment concepts, ideas, and principles, including the vitally important prohibition on prior restraints, from these systems.[77] Moreover, colonists' experiences in foreign nations led directly to the adoption of other First Amendment protections. In some instances, constitutional protections were adopted only *after* considering, and rejecting, approaches that had been adopted by other nations. Thus, as mentioned, explicit protection for certain religious freedoms was deemed necessary in part owing to a history of religious persecution at the hands of foreign governments. Universal freedoms of conscience and religious free exercise were imported to the colonies and, later, to U.S. territories.[78] In these respects, the First Amendment was itself a product of transborder borrowing, exchange, engagement, and global experience.

To be sure, the United States has not always acted in a manner consistent with the Constitution's cosmopolitan roots and ideals. From the Alien and Sedition Acts of 1798, to the mid-twentieth century ideological conflict focusing on communism and socialism, through the current era of antiterrorism laws and policies, the United States has sometimes suppressed cross-border exchange and treated aliens and foreign creeds as unwelcome foreign dangers. However, in an important sense even these illiberal episodes are part of a cosmopolitan constitutional narrative. The First Amendment came of age in the United States not in isolation from the rest of the world, but in large measure as a result of global connectivity.[79] Clashes and conflicts involving foreign persons and ideas helped to frame and articulate the First Amendment's free speech and other guarantees.

In sum, the U.S. Constitution, including its Bill of Rights, was not forged in isolation from the community of nations. Indeed, according to an ascendant cosmopolitan narrative it was adopted to achieve recognition within that community. The framers knew that the Constitution they drafted would be situated in an international community, and would be compared to existing international laws. They also knew that providing protection for citizens' rights and ensuring international recognition would both be instrumental in terms of facilitating the global circulation of people, ideas, and commerce. Although they were certainly aware of foreign dangers, they also carried forward a Revolutionary era commitment to cosmopolitan conversation and collaboration in a "transborder sphere" that traversed borders and oceans. The First Amendment ultimately would come of age in that sphere.

Protecting and Facilitating Transborder Liberties

From the beginning, curious Americans have sought information regarding the world beyond their territorial borders. They have participated in transborder economic, social, and political intercourse. As a result of globalization and the digitization of communication these activities have become increasingly frequent and even routine. The exercise of some First Amendment liberties seems to transcend territorial borders.[80] For most Americans, local attachments and concerns will, of course, continue to be of central importance to daily life.[81] However, for an increasing number of citizens, global connections will become increasingly important. From a cosmopolitan perspective, one of the First Amendment's core functions is to ensure that the channels of global exchange and intercourse remain as open as possible. Repealing, amending and avoiding enactment of laws that obstruct or interfere with this activity is one way to advance this purpose. However, I argue that the United States also ought to adopt policies regarding education, trade, technology, and the press that facilitate global information flow, transnational understanding, and international cooperation with respect to global problems.[82]

Cosmopolitan Conversation and Commingling

First Amendment cosmopolitanism locates transborder expressive and religious liberties closer to the core of the First Amendment's domain than its periphery. Part II of the book focuses on the various forms of cosmopolitan conversation and commingling that the cosmopolitan First Amendment would protect and facilitate.

Transborder conversation is facilitated by global information flow, which takes many forms. These include sending informational materials – letters, emails, films, pamphlets, works of art, computer code – across international borders. Transborder commingling is a similarly broad concept. It encompasses a wide variety of interactions and associations across and beyond borders. Commingling can be intimate (i.e., familial), expressive, physical, virtual, commercial, spiritual, artistic, journalistic, or some combination of these forms.

Cosmopolitan conversation and commingling are traditional First Amendment activities. As I have observed, many early Americans believed that transborder exchange was actually *virtuous*. They traveled abroad, maintained foreign ties and relationships, and participated in a "republic of letters" in which individuals "communicate[d] across space, including national boundaries and, Americans believed, oceans."[83]

Despite some isolationist eras and tendencies, Americans generally remain curious about the world beyond their shores.[84] They maintain strong ties to world communities and engage in conversations with citizens and aliens regarding collective issues of global importance. Americans share common causes, from global climate change to global hunger, with persons and organizations across the world. Millions of U.S. citizens actually reside in foreign nations. Many of these individuals hold dual or plural citizenship, an act that Peter Spiro has described as a form of international association.[85]

Moreover, as a result of immigration patterns, U.S. citizens have come into frequent contact with aliens within American borders.[86] Although it is true that these resident aliens are not part of the formal constitutional community, they are part of what Martha Nussbaum has referred to as "our community of dialogue and concern."[87] Thus, their concerns and claims are indeed relevant to internal political debate and deliberation.

Meaningful transborder conversation requires that Americans have some level of understanding with respect to foreign laws, cultures, and norms. The robust flow of individuals and information across territorial borders facilitates cross-cultural dialogue and understanding. Fueled by economic necessity, technological advances, and a rising global appetite for social connection, our world is now characterized by extraordinary levels of cross-border communication and collaboration. The Internet, in particular, has fused territorial borders and ushered in a new era in which global connectivity is the norm. In addition to these and other organic forms of cross-border exchange, federally funded education initiatives and financial support for foreign press activities would also facilitate effective conversation and commingling.

As global interconnection increases, transborder conversation and commingling may become as critical to expressive and religious freedoms as their domestic counterparts. Accordingly, First Amendment cosmopolitanism encourages judges, officials, and policymakers to focus more explicitly on the connection between the First Amendment and activities such as foreign travel, immigration, online and face-to-face communication, transborder research and reporting, religious proselytizing abroad, cross-border cultural exchange, and global education. These activities ought to be considered important components of a mature, contemporary, and robust First Amendment.

Of course, some nondomestic conversation and commingling may pose serious threats to national safety and security. As Kwame Appiah has noted, "Conversations across boundaries can be fraught, all the more so as the world grows smaller and the stakes grow larger."[88] Cosmopolitan conversation and commingling can facilitate the spread of hateful ideas and incite violence on the basis of race, or religion, or sexual orientation. These activities may further entrench rather than break down stereotypes.

Like liberty itself, First Amendment cosmopolitanism is an ideal. The question, as always, is whether the benefits and values associated with expressive and religious liberties are worth the attendant risks. Nearly two decades ago, First Amendment scholar Rodney Smolla provided the cosmopolitan response: "But in the end, the towering hopes of the world for a new century of pluralistic tolerance and peace must be wagered on the faith that the free flow of information across

international borders avoids more wars than it causes, averts more terrorism than it feeds, uncovers more violations of human rights than it
incites...."[89]

First Amendment Justifications

Adopting a cosmopolitan perspective would not entail a radical shift
in the way we think about core First Amendment values, principles,
and justifications.[90] Indeed, we need not start entirely from scratch to
justify a more cosmopolitan conception of First Amendment liberties.
Although traditional justifications and theories may not be completely
up to the task, most are generally amenable to cosmopolitan interpretations. I use traditional justifications to provide a basic theoretical
foundation for extending First Amendment protection to various nondomestic activities. However, I also supplement this foundation with
distinctly cosmopolitan considerations including contemporary justifications for First Amendment liberties, U.S. treaty obligations, and
respect for human rights.

As discussed earlier, with regard to freedom of speech, traditional
justifications focus on self-governance, the search for truth, and individual autonomy.[91] The self-governance values associated with freedom of speech are often implicated in transborder contexts.[92] We
need merely to conceive of a twenty-first century analog to Alexander
Meiklejohn's famous town hall meeting, in which citizens received
information concerning critical governance matters. That analog is an
emerging global theater, an agora that includes both traditional and
digitized forms of transborder exchange and information flow.[93]

The domain of American self-governance has never been limited to
local town halls, statehouses, or the halls of Congress. In our interconnected world, a self-governing individual must not only have access
to information regarding local or national communities, but in many
instances must also have some sense of how domestic politics and policies will affect foreign peoples, cultures, and communities. She must
be aware of matters that occur, and conditions that exist, beyond U.S.
borders. In a globalized and digitized world, these things increasingly
affect domestic debates and politics. Speech abroad, including communications by U.S. officials, informs our politics both at home and
abroad.

Much of this information now crosses territorial borders in digital form. But even with the Internet, not all of the information required for self-governance will be at one's fingertips. Some of it will be available only more directly, at its foreign source. Thus, for example, American citizens often wish to travel abroad to seek information and experience foreign cultures first-hand. Further, we need a strong American press corps to inform domestic audiences and check governmental abuses that occur beyond U.S. shores.[94] Traditional conceptions of self-governance thus provide a strong justification for protecting the right to gather and receive information that originates beyond U.S. borders.

Information and knowledge are global commodities that are not always directly linked to domestic self-governance. In our interconnected world, it makes little sense to think of the metaphorical "marketplace of ideas" as a physical place or places strictly bounded by U.S. territorial borders.[95] Simply put, the search for truth does not stop at the water's edge. The First Amendment's domain ought to be broad enough to facilitate robust participation in cross-border and beyond-border political, artistic, scientific, educational, and religious exchanges. Transborder speech marketplaces actually predate the Internet era. Now, owing to the fact that speech frequently crosses or transcends borders in digital form, global speech marketplaces are even less strictly separated by territorial borders. Even speech that takes place abroad, and relates solely to events beyond our borders, may be of considerable interest to sizeable domestic constituencies within the United States.

When we think of marketplace theories or justifications for free speech and press, we ought to do so with the explicit understanding that the marketplace is not fixed or purely domestic in nature, but is constantly expanding. U.S. courts, officials, and policymakers ought to anticipate and orient themselves toward this new reality. As Rodney Smolla has observed, "If an international marketplace of ideas is to emerge, all the nations of the world must come to respect the free flow of information across all international borders. The United States, with its magnificent First Amendment tradition, would do well to set the example."[96]

Individual autonomy justifications relating to both expressive and religious liberties are also relevant in transborder contexts.[97] The community of nations has long recognized the importance of these liberties to individual self-fulfillment. Although they are of course not universally respected, in most parts of the world freedoms of thought, belief, and speech are considered fundamental human rights. The process of self-actualization and the development of core personal beliefs often involve transborder pursuits and exchanges. Fully autonomous persons must be free to pursue ideas, interests, and information without regard to territorial boundaries or frontiers.

Structural arguments also support a more expansive First Amendment domain. As Akhil Amar has argued, Bill of Rights provisions act as structural safeguards.[98] These safeguards generally bind the government without regard to frontiers or territory. Under this view, prior restraints on speech and establishments of religion are offensive to the First Amendment regardless of where they occur. Structural theory is most relevant to questions relating to extraterritorial application of First Amendment limitations. However, the structural approach also informs our understanding of the First Amendment's scope or domain in other ways, some of which relate back to the origins account discussed earlier. Structural theory suggests that expressive and religious liberties were never considered to be merely domestic limitations. The framers sought to ensure that these liberties would be respected whether people exercised them in the United States, at its borders, or in foreign lands.

In examining transborder or nondomestic expressive and religious liberties, we are of course not confined to traditional First Amendment justifications. Although these justifications are generally flexible enough to apply in the First Amendment's transborder dimension, there are more specific cosmopolitan justifications for extending protection beyond the purely domestic.

For example, as Jack Balkin argues, the traditional self-governance justification for freedom of speech is simply "too narrow in the age of the Internet."[99] Balkin observes that "what people do on the Internet transcends the nation state; they participate in discussions, debate, and collective activity that does not respect national borders."[100] He claims that these activities "should not be protected only because and to the degree that they might contribute to debate about American politics, or even American foreign policy."[101]

Balkin claims that free speech ought to be protected insofar as it contributes to what he refers to as "democratic culture."[102] This is "a culture in which individuals have a fair opportunity to participate in the forms of meaning making that constitute them as individuals."[103] Balkin argues that freedom of speech in the digital era is characterized by mass participation and interactivity. He further claims that in this era the focus of free speech has shifted toward nonpolitical expression and popular culture. To protect individuals' ability to participate in contemporary culture-making, Balkin argues that officials must adopt policies that facilitate certain forms of digital conversation and commingling. Owing to the nature of the Internet and digital communication, much of this activity will occur at or beyond U.S. borders.

Balkin's theory has attractive cosmopolitan characteristics. The democratic culture he envisions would seem to transcend territorial borders. Balkin's theory is responsive to changing social conditions relating to information flow. It is sensitive to the need to protect digital speech and cross-cultural collaboration. Further, the theory of democratic culture acknowledges that the digitization of speech can lead to the spread of democratic practices and ideals – perhaps across and among the cultures of the world. As Balkin notes, whether these cosmopolitan effects will be realized depends on how officials, administrators, and technologists manage and regulate modern channels of communication and new technologies. He thus rightly encourages officials to think beyond narrow conceptions of domestic democratic self-governance.

Balkin's conception of democratic culture is compatible with the more outward-oriented, cosmopolitan perspective I am advancing. A cosmopolitan First Amendment supports freedom of movement – of persons, papers, and ideas as well as bytes – and the free exchange of information across borders. It does so because cosmopolitan conversation and commingling will create opportunities for transborder learning, understanding, innovation, and transmission of democratic ideals. As Rodney Smolla observed: "There is no better way to advance the progress of science, social justice, and culture, no better way to conquer hunger and disease, no better check on tyranny and exploitation, no better nourishment for the art, music, and poetry that stir the human spirit, than a world committed to open cultures and freedom of speech."[104]

Cosmopolitan First Amendment justifications such as Balkin's and Smolla's look well beyond domestic communities to broader global values and principles. Although there are obviously local differences, values such as democratic culture, liberty, autonomy, and freedom of belief are embraced across the globe. As noted earlier, some scholars have argued or suggested that the United States is not generally committed to pursuing traditional First Amendment objectives beyond its own borders. Insofar as this claim suggests a territorially bounded commitment to First Amendment freedoms, it ignores both the Constitution's cosmopolitan origins and national commitments to global expressive and religious freedoms.

In foreign policy, the United States has long supported robust protection for expressive and religious liberties throughout the world. During World War II, President Franklin Roosevelt identified freedom of expression and freedom to worship as two of the "four freedoms" for which the Allies were fighting abroad. By virtue of various international agreements and covenants the United States has formally committed to protecting global expressive and religious liberties.[105] These commitments transcend borders. Expressive and religious liberties are entitled to protection "regardless of frontiers."[106] By endorsing this basic orientation, the United States has expressed a commitment to the ideal of universal human rights.[107] This universal commitment provides further justification for protecting nondomestic expressive and religious liberties.

The acknowledgment that we are all in some sense members of a global community and that we share certain universal values does not eliminate or diminish local concerns or attachments. Support for transborder conversation and commingling, in particular, is not designed or expected to lead to sameness, homogeneity, or any single truth.[108] Rather, these activities will allow individuals who are separated by geography to learn from one another; to share and critically examine political, legal, religious, and cultural differences; and to acquire new perspectives regarding these and other matters.[109] Ideally, by bringing the foreign "other" into view, breaking down stereotypes and misperceptions, and creating new spaces for cooperation and exchange, transborder conversation and commingling can facilitate the process of learning from difference and cross-cultural understanding. We can acknowledge and celebrate local differences while still recognizing certain universal commitments.

Sovereignty and Territoriality

To conceive of the First Amendment in more cosmopolitan terms, it is not sufficient to examine or re-examine justifications for extending protection to nondomestic liberties. Fundamentally, we must also reconsider the relationship between territorial borders and sovereign power. As Kal Raustiala has observed, "the nature of the relationship between law and land raises profoundly significant political, economic, and social questions."[110] This law–land relationship significantly affects the scope and substance of the First Amendment's transborder dimension.

As discussed earlier, provincialism is based on traditional principles of territorial sovereignty. These principles include a conception of broad, even plenary national powers in nondomestic contexts. First Amendment cosmopolitanism adopts a different position regarding the relationship between territory and sovereign authority. Although it does not deny the existence or importance of territorial sovereignty, a cosmopolitan approach rejects the existence of a stark foreign–domestic divide with regard to constitutional rights and sovereign power; adopts a less deferential posture toward federal laws and regulations that affect transborder expressive and religious activities; and contends that the First Amendment ought generally to be deemed a structural limit on the extraterritorial exercise of governmental authority.

Territorial Sovereignty and Constitutional Domain

In its most basic sense, sovereignty consists of exclusive control over a defined territory. Within each territory, the sovereign's laws apply to the exclusion of other laws. Further, under traditional conceptions of sovereign power a nation's authority to enforce its laws generally does not extend beyond its own territory and constitutional guarantees do not extend beyond national borders.

In the twenty-first century national boundaries, nation-states, and territorial sovereignty continue to exist. Individual nations continue to largely exercise control over the cross-border movement of persons, a defining attribute of sovereignty.[111] Further, to at least some degree, even in the digital era nations continue to control the flow of information across their borders.[112] However, as political scientists, sociologists, and international law scholars have observed, modern events and forces, including globalization, digitization, and the increased prevalence and influence of international human rights laws, have eroded or altered traditional ideas of territorial sovereignty.[113]

Indeed, conceptions of constitutional and legal domain have changed significantly. Contemporary social, political, and legal conditions have combined to reduce governmental control with regard to the cross-border movement of materials and information. Thus, absent a radical step such as installation of a national filter, the United States could not exclude from its borders all obscene materials on the Internet that originate in foreign nations. Global exchange and connectivity, rather than rigid territorial separation, are becoming the norm.

Today, many nations assert legal authority over events beyond their borders, and extraterritorial application of constitutional guarantees is becoming more common. As Kal Raustiala has observed, "The human rights revolution of the postwar era has rested on the principle that all individuals possess rights, rights that transcend whatever domestic law or national sovereignty might dictate."[114] Today, international and foreign laws bid through various mechanisms for acceptance or application in domestic forums, and sovereigns frequently seek to expand the territorial domain of their own laws. Speech, in particular, crosses territorial borders in a manner that significantly complicates issues of jurisdiction and international comity. Which nation's laws ought to apply to digital speech that transcends national borders is a complex and pressing question.

A more cosmopolitan conception of the First Amendment acknowledges and indeed generally embraces the decline of territorial sovereignty. This embrace is tempered, to some extent, by the concern that importation of foreign laws could degrade domestic First Amendment liberties. In the future, the United States will be drawn into some difficult conversations with other nations regarding the scope of expressive and religious liberties. As I discuss in Chapter 9, the United States ought to enter those conversations with respect and appreciation both for its own conception of such liberties and for the diverse approaches adopted by other nations. The aspiration is that on balance, the decline of territorial sovereignty will lead to more frequent and more robust transborder conversation and commingling. However, the permissible degree and substance of this conversation and commingling will not always be determined by American lights or standards. Sometimes, the judgments of foreign nations and institutions will be entitled to respect and comity – even if they are not the judgments Americans would reach.

At the same time, a cosmopolitan First Amendment would have a relatively expansive territorial scope or domain. The conception of territorial sovereignty under which location is determinative of a person's constitutional rights has come under increasing pressure and criticism.[115] Under a cosmopolitan approach, citizens' First Amendment expressive and religious liberties would presumptively be deemed portable – that is, they would apply regardless of geographic location.[116] If U.S. citizens are going to participate fully and confidently in global debates and international exchanges, they will need access to persons, information, and ideas located beyond U.S. borders. Further, citizens ought to have firm assurances that when they, or their speech or other activities, cross international borders this will not result in waiver or abandonment of First Amendment protections. Although application of the First Amendment beyond U.S. borders ought to respect domestic laws and cultures, the core of citizens' expressive and religious liberties must be preserved. In short, wherever the U.S. government acts to suppress the expressive or other liberties of its citizens the First Amendment follows and constrains it.

More controversially, a cosmopolitan orientation with regard to the First Amendment leaves open the possibility that aliens abroad might also be entitled to some protection against certain forms of U.S. intervention and regulation.[117] As the United States projects and exercises its power across the world, it ought to abide by domestic and international commitments relating to free speech and freedom of religion. As Louis Henkin has succinctly made the point, "Our federal government must not invade the individual rights of any human being."[118] First

Amendment limitations will obviously not apply in all circumstances abroad, or to all aliens in foreign nations. Nor will these limits apply in precisely the same manner abroad as they do at home. However, under a cosmopolitan approach aliens would not be deemed beyond the First Amendment's domain simply because our government regulates or otherwise acts on them beyond U.S. borders.

This expanded conception of constitutional domain has some support in the courts and the academy. In a decision that ultimately rejected extraterritorial application of the Fourth Amendment, Justice Kennedy nevertheless stated that "the Government may act only as the Constitution authorizes, whether the actions in question are foreign or domestic."[119] In a more recent decision invalidating U.S. detention policies with regard to enemy combatants, the Court expressly rejected the government's argument that the Constitution applies to aliens only when they are within the territorial United States.[120] Thus, the Supreme Court has expressly rejected a formalistic territorial conception of constitutional domain.

As Kal Raustiala has observed, "Over the last half-century many Americans have come to see the Constitution as a far-reaching document whose roving powers can rein in almost any malfeasance."[121] In a far more limited sense, First Amendment cosmopolitanism insists that when the United States acts as a visiting power in a foreign nation, and when it exercises jurisdiction and control over citizens or aliens there, it must respect individual expressive and religious liberties. In this context the First Amendment is cosmopolitan insofar as it constrains the U.S. government across the globe.

Domestic/Foreign and Internal/External
The decline of territoriality has implications beyond sovereign authority and constitutional domain. Provincialism rests in part on the supposition that there are clear physical and conceptual divisions between domestic and foreign, or internal and external, spheres of individual activity and nation-state authority. A cosmopolitan conception of territoriality does not wholly reject distinctions between domestic and foreign constitutional communities. However, it questions the conceptual strength and relevance of such formal distinctions insofar as transborder First Amendment liberties are concerned.

As the Supreme Court has instructed, we ought to approach territoriality realistically and pragmatically rather than formalistically. For example, as noted earlier, some commentators have suggested that free speech protections apply only when a speaker directs communications to an audience comprised of fellow citizens. However, today we cannot assume that an audience is composed of *either* citizens *or* nonresident aliens. Audiences across the globe increasingly comprise a mixture of citizens and aliens. In many cases, Internet speech reaches broad, geographically dispersed, and mixed audiences.

Moreover, in today's communications environment information conveyed or published abroad will almost always find its way back into the United States through digital and other channels. This includes books, press reports, and even U.S. propaganda that is published or distributed abroad. In many instances, citizens' speech that is published, or republished, in a foreign country will affect domestic self-governance and the search for truth. Aliens' speech may also contribute to domestic debates regarding American foreign policy, immigration, and other matters of public concern.

Traditional conceptions of governmental power also assume that exercises of U.S. authority are *either* domestic *or* foreign in character and effect. In reality, however, the foreign and domestic spheres are often blurred or intricately connected. This is in part owing to the fact that expressive and religious activities often cross or transcend national boundaries. For example, financial aid provided to religious groups abroad may benefit domestic sectarian institutions. Similarly, regulatory and funding decisions made by U.S. agency officials inside the United States may profoundly affect expressive and religious liberties on both sides of the international border.[122] Domestic regulations relating to Internet access, global piracy, and international trade will also have both domestic and international effects.

In sum, global interconnectivity complicates the traditional supposition that the world can be divided into discrete domestic and foreign spheres. Doctrines, justifications, and principles that rest on formal separation of the domestic and foreign, the internal and external, fail to acknowledge twenty-first century realities relating to information flow and sovereign power.

Governmental Power in the Transborder Dimension

The erosion of territorial sovereignty and the observations above regarding internal and external spheres also affect the way we conceptualize exercises of governmental power at the border. Courts have been reluctant to interfere with the decisions of the political branches, particularly the executive, with regard to immigration, foreign affairs, and national security.[123]

Many scholars have criticized the basis for and extent of strong or plenary deference in such areas.[124] I share their concerns. Of course, officials must have substantial power to address transborder concerns relating to territorial ingress and egress, intercourse with foreign nations, national security, and international diplomacy. However, the deference afforded to national officials in these transborder spheres ought not to translate into broad exceptions to First Amendment protection.

A cosmopolitan approach rejects the methods and principles that have led to the quasi-recognition of transborder First Amendment liberties. Insofar as possible, this approach contends that review of U.S. laws and regulations affecting transborder expressive and religious activities ought to be *domesticated*. In other words, they ought to be treated the same as domestic restrictions of similar character.

This is a controversial perspective with regard to federal power in many of the cross-border and beyond-border contexts discussed in the book. However, we have grown too accustomed to the idea that activity at the border lies within the exclusive province of federal authorities and that the First Amendment speaks, if at all, in a muted voice in the transborder dimension. The United States ought to honor its domestic and international commitments to protect expressive and religious liberties "without regard to frontiers."

Cosmopolitanism and the Community of Nations

With regard to individual liberties, cosmopolitanism highlights the First Amendment's transborder heritage; recognizes and enforces transborder liberties; and reassesses the relationship among territory, sovereignty, and rights. However, as an orientation or perspective, First Amendment cosmopolitanism addresses concerns beyond individual liberties. Provincialism is territorially bounded, rigidly insists on First Amendment domestic exclusivity and exceptionalism, and adopts an export-only perspective. Cosmopolitanism, by contrast, takes a more universal, engaged, and pluralistic approach to the First Amendment's place within the community of nations. Part III of the book examines the First Amendment's application, influence, and status within the community of nations. Although individual rights are an important part of this discussion, broader concerns regarding the First Amendment's status and applicability in global forums, its relationship to transnational legal sources, and the appropriate extent of its exportation beyond U.S. shores, will be the principal focus of this discussion.

Global Forums

The United States participates in a variety of global debates and conversations. It takes official positions on issues of global significance, conducts foreign affairs and international diplomacy, and participates in transnational processes. In these contexts, the First Amendment is not generally considered to be enforceable in the courts. However, this does not mean that First Amendment principles are irrelevant or provide no guidance at all for U.S. officials. In these global forums, First Amendment principles ought to be given due consideration and, in some instances, to influence the nature and character of official actions.

I do not propose that First Amendment limitations be applied to such activities as core diplomatic and military functions. Rather, as discussed in Chapter 8, cosmopolitan principles encourage U.S. officials to be mindful of the First Amendment's core commitments when participating in global forums. Thus, for example, cosmopolitanism rejects the notion that the federal government must always speak as the sole, impliedly preemptive, voice of the United States in every global forum.[125] In an interconnected world, the United States ought to encourage a diverse and robust conversation in which subnational governments, citizens, nongovernmental organizations, and corporations actively participate. This approach is consistent with core First Amendment values.

Further, cosmopolitanism contends that when the U.S. government speaks in global forums, it ought to do so in a manner that takes into account the limitations of the Free Speech Clause and the Establishment Clause. This might affect both the extent and character of U.S. propaganda, spending conditions imposed on foreign recipients, or collaboration with foreign religious leaders and communities.

Again, the idea is not to impose formal constitutional limits on U.S. diplomacy or the conduct of foreign relations. Rather, U.S. officials ought to apply general First Amendment marketplace, self-government, and anti-establishment principles in the global forums in which they participate. This will protect and enhance the First Amendment liberties of U.S. citizens and institutions and produce benefits associated with the free exchange of ideas. Respecting First Amendment commitments in global forums will also allow the United States to lead by positive example when speaking and acting beyond its borders.

Global Engagement

As mentioned earlier, in an interconnected community of nations expressive and religious activities will increasingly come under the jurisdiction of many nations at once. Speech will cross over international borders instantly, religious norms and practices will migrate with relative ease, and international agreements affecting expressive and religious liberties will continue to be enacted and enforced.

The United States has adopted a strong defensive posture with regard to importation of foreign judgments, laws, and norms. It has sought to preserve First Amendment exclusivity and exceptionalism by treating territorial borders as a protective shield – even if this means imposing American free speech standards on foreign libel plaintiffs, or discriminating against religious norms that are deemed to be "foreign" to mainstream or traditional faith communities. More generally, the United States has rejected any sort of engagement with transnational legal sources that might affect exceptional First Amendment standards and principles.

Under a cosmopolitan approach, the United States would adopt a more respectful and dialogic perspective with regard to foreign laws, influences, and norms. This does not entail sacrificing First Amendment exceptionalism altogether. As I will show, fears that this will occur through treaty ratification or other transnational means are overstated. However, it is possible to allow for the recognition and enforcement of some foreign laws and judgments without threatening the First Amendment's core protections or principles. Moreover, legal scholars have developed pluralistic and cosmopolitan conflicts principles that can be applied to resolve transnational judgment recognition and similar disputes.[126]

As a member in good standing of the community of nations, the United States cannot continue to maintain a discriminatory posture regarding foreign expressive and religious laws. More generally, the United States ought to be open to learning, through legal processes and conversations, from foreign approaches to protecting expressive and religious liberties.[127] We ought not to reflexively rule out certain innovations or changed perspectives that may result from transnational engagement, even if these things relate to First Amendment liberties.[128] At a minimum, insofar as possible First Amendment exclusivity and exceptionalism ought to be justified on grounds that are persuasive not only to domestic officials and citizens but also to international audiences.

Colonial-era Americans exhibited a healthy cosmopolitan curiosity, and respect for the opinions of mankind. Contemporary Americans ought similarly to be open to alternative ways of thinking about expressive and religious liberties.[129]

Global Export

Finally, cosmopolitanism requires that we reconsider the extent to which the United States can or should export the First Amendment to other nations. In this context, the objects being exported consist of constitutional standards as well as expressive and religious norms and practices.

First Amendment exceptionalism severely limits the extent to which American expressive and religious liberty standards can be exported and transplanted abroad. Although American-style rights protections have proliferated across the globe, most of the world has rejected the First Amendment's exceptional protections for speech, press, privacy, and religion. In both substance and practice, exceptionalism severely limits America's ability to transplant the First Amendment abroad.

This is just as well. Most nations demonstrate some regard for expressive and religious liberties. However, no single regime or standard is likely to emerge with respect to such rights. With regard to global constitutional liberties, heterogeneity, rather than homogeneity, is most likely to be the norm.

This does not mean American officials must abandon efforts to export First Amendment principles, norms, and practices. However, this will be accomplished, if at all, through a combination of encouragement, persuasion, and facilitation rather than insistence or compulsion.[130] As it seeks to export democratic culture and democratic practices, the United States will need to focus on shared values, rather than exportation of specific American doctrines or models.

Exportation of norms and practices conducive to expressive and religious liberties can result from a variety of actions. U.S. officials can start, as I suggested earlier, by showing respect for First Amendment limitations abroad and thus leading by positive example. Further, they can encourage the spread of expressive and religious freedoms through both multilateral diplomacy and unilateral actions. They can participate in international activities and programs including cultural exchanges, educational initiatives, and informal transnational processes. In addition, the United States can also export or spread First Amendment–like freedoms through trade and subsidization policies. In particular, it can export new technologies that enable foreign citizens to resist political suppression by authoritarian regimes. Finally, U.S. legislators and regulators can approach the Internet as a global resource with the potential to spread democratic practices and freedoms across the world.

In the export context, the most important cosmopolitan principles are respect and humility. The United States ought to respect the diversity of approaches that nations have taken with regard to expressive and religious liberties. It ought to approach global forums with an understanding that these liberties are the product of cultural, political, and constitutional histories that differ – sometimes markedly – from our own. As Kwame Appiah has observed, "As cosmopolitans, we should ... defend the right of others to live in democratic states with rich possibilities of association within and across their borders, states of which they can be patriotic citizens. And, as cosmopolitans, we can claim that right for ourselves."[131]

We ought not to insist that the First Amendment serve as a universal model for all of the citizens of the world. Instead, the United States ought to ensure that foreign political institutions are respecting basic human rights such as freedom of speech and freedom of religion. At the same time, it ought to recognize that nations differ with regard to the specific content of those rights.

PART II CONVERSATION AND COMMINGLING

3 MOBILITY AND EXPRESSIVE LIBERTIES

In 1962, Louis Zemel, an American citizen and holder of a U.S. passport, applied to the U.S. State Department to have his passport validated for travel to Cuba. Then as now, federal laws and regulations limited U.S. citizens' travel to Cuba as part of an economic embargo. Zemel wanted to go to Cuba "to satisfy [his] curiosity about the state of affairs in Cuba and to make [him] a better informed citizen."[1] Specifically, he wanted to acquaint himself with "the effects abroad of our Government's policies, foreign and domestic, and with conditions abroad which might affect such policies."[2] Zemel's passport application was denied. He litigated his case to the Supreme Court of the United States, which ultimately concluded that it could not "accept the contention of appellant that it is a First Amendment right which is involved."[3] This was so, said the Court, even though the Cuba travel restrictions undeniably reduced "the flow of information" concerning Cuba.[4] The Court characterized the passport denial as "an inhibition of action" rather than expression, comparing it to a prohibition on physical access to the White House.[5] "The right to speak and publish," proclaimed the Court, "does not carry with it the unrestrained right to gather information."[6]

In 2004, Tariq Ramadan, a prominent Swiss philosopher, poet, and writer, sought to enter the United States to accept an academic post at Notre Dame University. Ramadan is an expert in the interpretation of Islamic texts and preaches, among other things, the virtues of inclusivity and integration for Muslims. After he obtained a nonimmigrant visa, the State Department informed Ramadan that the visa had been revoked, allegedly on the ground that he "espoused or endorsed" terrorism – advocacy that was forbidden under the USA PATRIOT

Act. Ramadan eventually resigned his appointment with Notre Dame. When he later applied for a visa to enter the United States, for the purpose of participating in various conferences and academic events, the State Department alleged that Ramadan's visa application was denied on the ground that he had provided material support, in the form of charitable contributions, to designated foreign terrorist groups. The government defended the visa application denial, in part on the ground that it had the authority to deny entry to aliens, even if based solely on ideological or associational grounds.[7] After many years of litigation, that specific assertion was never judicially resolved. Secretary of State Hillary Clinton eventually lifted the ban on Ramadan's entry, thereby allowing him to visit the United States and to participate in academic conferences and lectures.

This chapter begins the assessment of the First Amendment's transborder dimension by examining the intersection between the cross-border movement of persons and rights of speech and association.[8] The ability to control the movement of persons and things across territorial borders is a core aspect of national sovereignty.[9] It would, of course, be untenable and unwise to insist that U.S. borders be fully open in terms of exit and entry. However, personal mobility warrants more careful First Amendment consideration than courts and scholars have generally provided. Movement across borders is an economic, political, and *constitutional* phenomenon.[10] I do not claim that all restrictions on cross-border movement raise First Amendment concerns. However, the cross-border movement of persons does often implicate First Amendment liberties. In order to fully understand and appreciate the First Amendment's transborder dimension, we need to recover the connection between freedom of movement and freedom of expression.

Even in a digital era when information is widely distributed, migration remains critical to many forms of cross-border conversation and commingling. Each year, millions of U.S. citizens travel abroad. Some do so in order to gather information about other cultures; engage face-to-face with aliens in scholarly, religious, artistic, educational, and other endeavors; and even participate in political protests abroad. Contrary to *Zemel*'s broad assertion, when these and other activities are restricted or burdened, a First Amendment right is often affected. Similarly, when aliens seek entry to the United States for expressive and associative reasons, the First Amendment ought to apply with full force to the claims of citizens who wish to hear and assemble with the alien speaker as I argue in Chapter 6, and to the alien's own liberty claims. Finally, under a cosmopolitan approach the First Amendment would prohibit the U.S. government from expelling or removing lawfully resident aliens for any reason that would otherwise violate the First Amendment if applied to citizens. As I explain in the text that follows, current federal law suggests that Congress has a greater appreciation of the First Amendment aspects of cross-border movement than does the executive or judicial branch. It is vitally important that all three departments fully recognize and support this important aspect of the First Amendment's transborder dimension.

FOREIGN TRAVEL AND THE FIRST AMENDMENT

Restrictions on foreign travel take different forms, from traditional embargoes and licensing schemes to more contemporary "watch lists" and other travel restrictions. As *Zemel* demonstrates, the Supreme Court long ago concluded that travel restrictions do not generally implicate the First Amendment. As we shall see, in its initial encounters with passport restrictions, the Court was more receptive to the claim that foreign travel was closely tied to expressive liberties. Over the years, Congress has liberalized some federal laws regulating foreign travel. Although some Cold War–era restrictions have been eliminated, terrorist watch lists and other contemporary measures raise similar cross-border travel concerns.

Historical Background

Americans today most likely take for granted their ability to board an airline or ship and travel about the world. Such freedom of movement has not always been the norm. Indeed, throughout American history, legislators and executive officials have limited citizens' foreign travel both during wartime and in times of peace.

Prior to World War I, the United States did not have a formal passport system. Officials regulated international travel pursuant to a set of ad hoc and informal practices. The State Department essentially exercised plenary authority to grant or deny foreign travel applications.[11] In 1918, during World War I, Congress enacted the first law prohibiting foreign travel without a valid passport.[12] The State Department later imposed certain geographic limits on foreign travel with U.S. passports.[13]

As the nation entered the Cold War in the 1950s, the U.S. passport system remained an ad hoc enterprise. Indeed, a single official within the State Department bureaucracy, Mrs. Ruth Shipley, exercised what was essentially unreviewable discretion in granting or denying citizens' passport applications.[14] During Shipley's tenure, citizens were routinely denied the ability to travel abroad based on ideological, associational, or religious grounds.[15] Throughout the Cold War, U.S. officials frequently prevented American communists from traveling abroad. Prominent Americans who were denied passports during the McCarthy era included Arthur Miller, Paul Robeson, and Linus Pauling.

In decisions during the 1950s and 1960s, the Supreme Court ruled that Congress had not granted the executive branch the statutory authority to deny passports to American citizens based solely on ideology or belief.[16] As discussed later, these decisions were based primarily on principles of statutory interpretation. However, First Amendment concerns relating to ideological passport denials undoubtedly influenced the Court's construction of the passport laws. Indeed, some justices explicitly addressed the First Amendment values associated with foreign travel.

Congress later shifted its approach from narrow, ideological passport denials to broader proscriptions on citizens' foreign travel. Federal laws and regulations imposed economic sanctions and trade embargoes with regard to certain nations. For example, in the 1980s, the Reagan Treasury Department promulgated regulations that treated a host of expenditures related to travel to Cuba as prohibited economic transactions and required that citizens receive either general or specific licenses to visit there.[17] Such schemes effectively created a travel ban with respect to certain foreign nations. Insofar as citizens and resident aliens wish to travel abroad for journalistic, academic, or other expressive purposes, travel embargoes significantly affect First Amendment activities and interests.

Although they have been amended in many respects, some of these trade laws and licensure regulations remain in place today. In addition, although Congress has limited executive authority to impose travel restrictions with regard to certain areas of the world, presidents are still authorized to impose such restrictions during officially declared emergencies.[18] For example, in 2003, President George W. Bush imposed emergency travel restrictions with regard to travel to Iraq.

Recently, federal officials have used computerized "watch lists," including the so-called "No Fly List," to regulate foreign travel.[19] Under this system, travelers have their names checked against a federal database and can be denied exit (or entry) if found to be on a terrorist watch list. Civil libertarians have claimed that, for purely ideological reasons, political protesters and activists have been placed on restricted travel lists. The claim has been difficult to assess, owing to a lack of transparency regarding the processes by which the lists are compiled and enforced.

Quasi-Recognition

Although it has acknowledged that foreign travel and free speech are related, the Supreme Court has never recognized a First Amendment right to exit the country. As I noted earlier, the Court has invalidated certain egress restrictions on statutory grounds. It has also indicated that citizens have a liberty interest in foreign travel under the Fifth Amendment's Due Process Clause. The Court has characterized restrictions on foreign travel as limits on conduct that do not raise serious First Amendment concerns. In sum, the ability to travel abroad has, at most, been granted a qualified, quasi-recognized constitutional status by the courts.

In 1958, the Supreme Court held in *Kent v. Dulles* that the Secretary of State lacked the statutory authority to deny passports to communists or others wishing to travel abroad for the purpose of furthering communist ideals or causes.[20] As discussed in more detail later, Justice Douglas's opinion for the Court emphasized the close connection between foreign travel and activities such as cross-border information-gathering and association.[21] Ultimately, however, the Court based its decision largely on statutory grounds. With regard to the constitutional claims, the Court merely recognized that the right to participate in foreign travel was part of the liberty protected by the Fifth Amendment's Due Process Clause.[22]

Similarly, in its 1964 decision in *Aptheker v. Secretary of State*, the Court invalidated a federal statute making it unlawful for a Communist Party member to apply for a U.S. passport.[23] The Court held that a citizen's ability to travel abroad could not be conditioned on renunciation of political associations.[24] Once again, however, the Court emphasized that citizens possess only a Fifth Amendment interest in foreign travel, rather than a First Amendment right to venture beyond U.S. borders.

In 1965, the Supreme Court further clarified the connection between foreign travel and the First Amendment. As noted earlier, in *Zemel v. Rusk*, the Court upheld the denial of Louis Zemel's application to travel to Cuba.[25] Recall that Zemel sought to travel to Cuba to acquaint himself with "the effects abroad of our Government's policies, foreign and domestic, and with conditions abroad which might affect such policies."[26] The Court held that Zemel had failed to raise a First Amendment claim.[27] *Zemel* characterized travel, regardless of its purpose, as a form of conduct.[28]

Three years later, in *United States v. O'Brien*, the Court announced a general First Amendment standard applicable to laws that are unrelated to the suppression of expression but nevertheless incidentally burden speech.[29] *O'Brien* held that such laws are subject to an intermediate form of First Amendment scrutiny. Thus, *O'Brien* indicated that insofar as passport denials or revocations indirectly burdened speech, they would be subject to at least some First Amendment scrutiny.

However, in *Haig v. Agee*, decided in 1981, the Court did not apply *O'Brien*'s standard to a passport revocation.[30] Agee's U.S. passport was revoked while he was residing abroad, on the ground that he had imperiled U.S. national security when he revealed the names of undercover CIA operatives working in foreign nations and protested CIA programs and activities abroad. The Court assumed that, as a citizen, Agee enjoyed some Free Speech Clause protection even when located abroad.[31] But it avoided the First Amendment implications of the passport revocation, in part by characterizing Agee's speech as an unprotected attempt to obstruct intelligence operations.[32] According to the

Court, this was action, not speech, and thus Agee was not entitled to First Amendment balancing or any other free speech protection.[33] The Court then went on to clarify that the Fifth Amendment *"freedom to travel outside the United States"* was not as robust as the *"right* to travel within the United States."[34] According to the Court, although the right to domestic travel was considered "virtually unqualified," the freedom to travel abroad was "no more than an aspect of 'liberty' protected by the Due Process Clause."[35]

After *Zemel* and *Haig*, the seemingly close connection between foreign travel and First Amendment concerns suggested in decisions such as *Kent* and *Aptheker* seemed to have been forgotten. According to these later decisions, a passport denial or revocation does not implicate the First Amendment – even if the applicant seeks to travel abroad for the express purpose of information-gathering, association, protest, or worship. So long as minimal due process protections are afforded, any constitutional requirements would seem to be met. Following this approach, federal courts have consistently rejected First Amendment challenges to a wide variety of restrictions on foreign travel.[36]

Recovering a First Amendment Right to Travel Abroad

Foreign travel is one aspect of a more general intersection between the First Amendment and cross-border activities. Part of my cosmopolitan project is to recover the relationship between foreign travel and the First Amendment. This would not grant citizens an absolute right to exit the country, regardless of national interests. However, recovery of the First Amendment right to travel might aid legal challenges to some travel restrictions, including watchlists and future limits on foreign travel. It could, as discussed later, also hasten the repeal of existing travel embargoes and the liberalization of existing licensing requirements that inhibit travel to some nations.

In essence, my claim is that the Supreme Court was on the right track in the 1950s and 1960s when it acknowledged the close connection between foreign travel and the First Amendment. The Court made a critical error in the 1970s and 1980s, however, when it minimized this relationship and characterized foreign travel as merely a quasi-recognized due process interest. To reverse this constitutional error, we must first recover the substantive First Amendment justifications for recognizing a right to engage in foreign travel.

First Amendment Justifications for a Right to Travel

Scholars and judges were more receptive to the notion that foreign travel was a fundamental right in the middle part of the twentieth century. Foreign travel was becoming more common, and had the potential to significantly increase and facilitate cross-border trade and exchange. Perhaps the most eloquent articulation of the position that a U.S. citizen's freedom to travel abroad is a fundamental right was authored in 1956 by Zechariah Chafee.[37] Chafee, who served as the lead U.S. representative during the negotiation of the principal United Nations covenants on freedom of speech, press, and belief, adopted a cosmopolitan view of the connection between cross-border movement and constitutional liberty. Indeed, he argued that the right to travel abroad was a basic human right that was inscribed in the original Constitution of 1787. According to Chafee, personal mobility was one of the original rights protected under the Constitution.[38]

Chafee wrote his book before the jurisprudential heyday of the First Amendment in the Supreme Court. However, First Amendment principles and values undoubtedly influenced his conception of, and regard for, the constitutional right to travel abroad. Freedom to travel abroad was important, Chafee wrote, to "foreign correspondents and lecturers of public affairs" who required first-hand access to information.[39] Further, Chafee recognized the importance of foreign travel to scientists, scholars, and academic pursuits. He wrote: "Scientists and scholars gain greatly from consultations with colleagues in other countries. Students equip themselves for more fruitful careers in the United States by instruction in foreign universities."[40] Chafee also recognized the importance of foreign travel to "reuniting families," an interest that relates to the First Amendment concept of "intimate" association.[41]

Chafee's defense of the fundamental right to cross international borders rested substantially on what are now core First Amendment justifications. No stranger to international travel himself, Chafee recognized the autonomy concerns that attended the freedom to cross international borders. Ultimately, he noted, "Our nation has thrived on the principle that, outside areas of plainly harmful conduct, every

American is left to shape his own life as he thinks best, do what he pleases, go where he pleases."[42]

Chafee considered the right to travel abroad to be especially critical to citizens' self-governance. He contended that the right to travel abroad helped U.S. citizens to become well-informed on the domestic issues of the day, and to understand that people like themselves live abroad.[43] The ability to go abroad and to literally see things for themselves meant that American citizens were not limited to government-provided information or material collected by only a few, select correspondents. Even as the nation was in the grip of an emotional campaign to root out Communism and other foreign ideologies, Chafee insisted that Americans ought to be active participants in cross-border exchanges and activities. He believed that "views on domestic questions are enriched by seeing how foreigners are trying to solve similar problems."[44] Chafee contended that contacts abroad "contribute to sounder decisions at home."[45]

On the Supreme Court, Justice Douglas adopted a similar worldview with regard to the relationship between foreign travel and First Amendment expressive liberties. In his opinion for the Court in *Kent*, which as discussed earlier invalidated ideological passport denials principally on statutory grounds, Douglas quoted at length from Chafee's book.[46] In later concurring and dissenting opinions, Douglas argued that foreign travel was critical to citizens' ability to engage in self-governance. Arguing against passport restrictions, he wrote that the "ability to understand this pluralistic world, filled with clashing ideologies, is a prerequisite of citizenship."[47] In addition, Douglas claimed that the freedom to travel abroad served other cosmopolitan values. In his concurring opinion in *Aptheker*, Douglas wrote that cross-border travel was important not just for self-governance purposes, but for a variety of "cultural, political, and social activities – for *all the commingling which gregarious man enjoys*."[48]

In supporting a right to engage in foreign travel, Justice Douglas was more explicit than was Chafee in terms of his reliance on the First Amendment. Thus, he described the right to exit as "kin to the right of assembly and the right of association."[49] Dissenting in *Zemel*, Justice Douglas acknowledged the critical importance of granting First Amendment protection to foreign fact-gathering and conversation:

"The right to know, to converse with others, to consult with them, to observe social, physical, political and other phenomena abroad as well as at home gives meaning and substance to freedom of expression and freedom of the press."[50] In sum, Douglas argued that the right to leave the country was both an independent First Amendment right and a freedom that facilitated other rights, such as freedom of speech and of the press.

Although writing well before the decline of territorial sovereignty, Justice Douglas clearly recognized that the world was becoming more interconnected. In response to critics who argued that limiting the government's power to restrict citizens' territorial egress would somehow diminish U.S. sovereignty, Douglas wrote: "America is of course sovereign; but her sovereignty is woven in an international web that makes her one of the family of nations."[51] Articulating some of the themes and characteristics of globalization, Douglas observed: "The ties with all the continents are close – commercially, as well as culturally. Our concerns are planetary, beyond sunrises and sunsets. Citizenship implicates us in those problems and perplexities, as well as in domestic ones."[52] Thus, Douglas recognized that the United States was a member in the community of nations. He acknowledged that, although we are citizens of a nation, we share common concerns with the peoples of the world. Douglas viewed First Amendment guarantees, including the right to travel abroad, as critically important to discussion and resolution of global problems.

Somehow, we seem to have lost sight of these important connections. Americans likely take for granted that they are free to leave the country at any time. Millions of U.S. passports are issued each year, and millions of Americans travel to overseas destinations. Most of these travelers likely assume that the Constitution strongly protects their ability to do so, as a fundamental right. Many Americans still view themselves as mobile explorers and pioneers. However, this self-perception does not square with the manner in which cross-border mobility has been treated under the Constitution in general or the First Amendment in particular.

We need to focus more specifically, as Chafee and Douglas did, on why travel abroad ought to be considered a fundamental right. As they observed, traditional First Amendment justifications such as self-governance and the search for truth apply in cross-border as well as domestic contexts.[53] As Chafee and Douglas recognized, foreign travel facilitates global fact-gathering and domestic decision making, creates opportunities to associate with others across the world, supports a robust global free press, and increases the transparency of governmental activity that takes place beyond U.S. shores. As I explained in Chapter 2, these activities are deeply rooted in the Constitution's own cosmopolitan origins. Early Americans engaged in cross-border travel for precisely these reasons.

Chafee and Douglas also pointed to more explicitly cosmopolitan justifications for treating foreign travel as a fundamental – and, in Douglas's case, an explicit First Amendment – right. Travel abroad breaks down physical and cultural barriers. It creates channels for global conversation and commingling where common concerns can be identified, discussed, and analyzed directly rather than through official intermediaries. These conversations are not limited to matters of politics or public policy, but rather extend, in Justice Douglas's artful phrasing, to "all the commingling which gregarious man enjoys."[54]

As Chafee argued, the right to travel abroad was enshrined, as one of the original human rights, in the Constitution of 1787. The values and benefits associated with cross-border movement confirm that the right to travel abroad is properly recognized as a central aspect of the First Amendment. Moreover, personal mobility is an expressly recognized right under international human rights laws and agreements. Under the Helsinki Accords and other international instruments to which the United States is a signatory, freedom of movement "without regard to frontiers" is considered a fundamental right. This reflects a growing international consensus that personal mobility facilitates important economic, political, and constitutional interests.

U.S. citizens ought to be able to participate fully and confidently in global debates and endeavors. To do this, they will require access to foreign persons, information, and ideas. In the twenty-first century, virtual access and exchange will obviously be critical aspects of this cross-border exchange. Indeed, some might argue that access to the Internet eliminates any need for special constitutional protection for a right to travel abroad. However, digital communication does not eliminate the need for more personalized conversation and commingling.[55] Nor can it replace political protest and other forms of group activity that rely on tangible forums and means of expression. Some portion of gregarious man's speech and association will always be done face-to-face. Further, certain kinds of information-gathering by the press and others simply cannot be done virtually. The collection and verification of factual and other information often requires physical presence.

The ability to exit the United States ought not to be treated as an anemic personal "freedom," which is protected by only the most minimal of due process requirements. Rather, foreign travel ought to be conceptualized as a fundamental First Amendment right that facilitates activities such as cross-border information-gathering, cultural exchange, and association. In ruling otherwise, the Supreme Court disconnected foreign travel from its First Amendment roots, ignored the cosmopolitan heritage of expressive liberties, and essentially relegated foreign travel to a form of nonexpressive conduct.

The Substance of the Right

There is, then, a First Amendment foundation for a right to foreign travel. But what does it mean, in terms of substance, to speak of a First Amendment right to exit?

There are several ways in which such a First Amendment right might be characterized or defined. In the broadest sense, we might, as one scholar has proposed, treat traveling abroad as an expressive act.[56] This argument sweeps too broadly. Simply boarding a flight to France is no more distinctly expressive than a decision to take a bus from California to New York. Such interstate travel is appropriately protected under structural principles of federalism and interstate harmony. Some commentators have argued that international travel is similarly protected, as an aspect of U.S. citizenship and structural constitutional principles.[57] This is one way to strengthen constitutional protection for foreign travel.

For travel restrictions to be subject to First Amendment review, however, a more specific expressive interest or activity must be identified. One can readily imagine such cases. For example, a citizen's decision to expatriate or repatriate constitutes an expressive act. Changing national allegiance is a powerful means of expressing one's sentiments concerning such things as patriotism, community, and loyalty.

A substantial burden on the act of expressing or changing allegiance, for example, a retaliatory passport revocation or restriction, would give rise to a colorable First Amendment claim. Further, the government might restrict foreign travel based on the content of a citizen's expression. A restriction might be imposed in response to a citizen's announcement that he intends to travel to a foreign nation for the specific purpose of engaging in a protest of U.S. foreign policy. Or a citizen might be placed on the travel "watchlist" as a result of specific statements or associations. Such travel restrictions raise serious First Amendment concerns.

What, though, of a case such as *Zemel*, in which a U.S. citizen avers that he wants to travel abroad for the purpose of engaging in foreign fact-gathering and other identified expressive activity? Here, too, the act of travel arguably has an expressive purpose or component. In *Zemel* and *Agee*, the Court erred in ignoring or discounting the expressive aspect of the travel in question. In such circumstances, travel restrictions and passport regulations ought to receive a form of intermediate First Amendment scrutiny.

A few commentators have defended a right to foreign travel on First Amendment grounds – specifically, on the ground that travel abroad facilitates foreign inquiry and information-gathering.[58] For example, Barry McDonald would extend a right to gather information abroad to circumstances in which (1) the putative recipient intends to broadly disseminate the information gathered inside the United States; (2) the information pertains to a matter of political concern within the United States; and (3) the information is sought by a member of some group whose function is to obtain such information for the purpose of public dissemination.[59]

McDonald's proposal would extend some First Amendment protection to cross-border travel for the purpose of information-gathering. However, the protection his approach would afford is very narrow. Under McDonald's formulation, the U.S. institutional press, when reporting to domestic audiences on matters relating to the policies or activities of the U.S. government, would have the strongest – indeed, based on the third proposed limitation in the preceding paragraph, apparently the only – claim to First Amendment protection.

As McDonald notes, there are sound reasons to proceed with caution when recognizing something as broad as a right to travel to foreign
nations for the purpose of gathering and disseminating information.
Nevertheless, if we are going to recognize a First Amendment right in
this context, it ought to serve First Amendment values as broadly and
effectively as possible. Moreover, it ought to account for things such
as modern communications technologies and the general manner in
which global information flow actually occurs.

Under McDonald's proposal, a U.S. citizen who wishes to invoke
a First Amendment right with regard to foreign travel must intend to
disseminate information broadly within the United States in order to
claim First Amendment protection. Thus, citizens who intend to travel
abroad and to report their findings and experiences on Facebook or
some other medium to either a small group of fellow citizens in the
United States, or to foreign audiences, or perhaps to a mixed local and
global audience, would not be protected. However, it is not clear why
the size of the audience, its location, or its makeup ought to be dispositive in terms of granting or denying First Amendment protection. In
the digital era, the information-gatherer has a First Amendment interest in sharing her findings, experiences, and impressions with mixed
audiences of variable sizes across the world.

McDonald's proposal is based on several assumptions regarding
the strict separation of foreign and domestic information marketplaces,
the composition of global audiences, and the scope of self-governance.
If the dissemination occurs online, its scope may be local, global, or
something in-between. Even if it is disseminated by the press, the
information will likely reach mixed audiences comprised of citizens
and aliens. Some U.S. citizens in the intended audience may be living
abroad. Further, McDonald's proposed right appears to be grounded
on a traditional conception of domestic self-governance under which
information is protected only insofar as it pertains to a matter of public
or political concern within the United States. However, as I argued in
Chapter 2, this narrow justification for protecting information flow
is not well suited to a digitized era in which communications transcend borders and matters of public concern are no longer defined
in strictly territorial terms. Global inquiry, conversation, and commingling pertain to a wide range of artistic, scientific, cultural, and

academic concerns that have little or nothing to do with domestic politics. Moreover, within domestic political communities, sometimes the most pressing matters of public concern relate to global or international issues.

Finally, why ought a First Amendment right to travel for purposes of information-gathering to be limited to individuals or organizations whose primary function is to gather and disseminate information? Why, in other words, are press credentials required in order to assert such a right?

The institutional press has no monopoly on information-gathering or dissemination, whether foreign or domestic. The Supreme Court has not generally granted the press any special or unique First Amendment rights. What is needed in this context is a broader protection for citizens' ability to seek out information and cultivate cross-border relationships by going directly and in person to foreign locations and sources. This protection ought to extend to bloggers, artists, educators, religious figures, and other citizens who participate in global marketplaces and the process of cross-border information flow. Of course, it is clear that the proposed right would disproportionately benefit the institutional press, which has the greatest incentives and resources to travel to remote locations for the purpose of reporting on foreign events. However, the right to travel abroad for the purpose of information-gathering and information-sharing ought to be considered a fundamental First Amendment right possessed by all citizens.

McDonald narrowed his proposed right in part owing to enforcement and other pragmatic concerns. However, merely acknowledging that foreign travel sometimes has an expressive element will not generally interfere with federal authority to regulate cross-border movement. Nor will it result in would-be travelers routinely prevailing in First Amendment challenges to a host of general embargo, licensing, or other travel regulations. Recovering the expressive element of foreign travel would not create a broad constitutional right to go anywhere one pleases, regardless of governmental interests.

Content-based travel restrictions would be subject to heightened scrutiny and thus frequently invalidated. But content-neutral restrictions would be subject to a form of intermediate scrutiny, under which the government would likely prevail in many cases.[60] In cases

like *Zemel*, the government's diplomatic and other interests in imposing the travel restrictions are unrelated to expression, may be considered substantial, and could pass the necessary tailoring requirement.
The point is that courts ought to ask such questions, rather than
avoid or assume answers to them or incorrectly characterize foreign
travel as a form of conduct regardless of its purpose or function. As
discussed in the text that follows, recovering the First Amendment
roots of foreign travel could also lead to substantial payoffs in both
the legislative and administrative realms.

Legislative and Administrative Barriers to Foreign Travel

It seems unlikely that the Supreme Court will revisit or overrule *Zemel*
and its other foreign travel precedents. However, recovering the intersection between the First Amendment and foreign travel might influence legislative and executive officials who have primary responsibility
for regulating foreign travel.

In contrast to federal courts, U.S. policymakers have long considered and balanced interests concerning territorial sovereignty, cross-
border movement, and international diplomacy. As I have noted, the
political branches have already liberalized many federal laws and regulations relating to international travel. For example, in 1991, Congress
amended U.S. passport laws to eliminate explicitly ideological bases for
denials or revocations. The law now specifies as impermissible bases for
passport denial, revocation, or restriction "any speech, activity, belief,
affiliation, or membership, within or outside the United States, which,
if held or conducted within the United States, would be protected by
the first amendment."[61]

Further, in recent decades, the U.S. government has not placed
significant formal restrictions on foreign travel. A federal ban on travel
to Libya was lifted in 2004. Current federal embargo regulations relating to Cuba are more liberal than they were a few decades ago. In
particular, the regulations allow for the issuance of general or specific travel licenses for scholars, journalists, and scientists.[62] Specific
licenses may also be granted for travel relating to familial obligations,
religious activities, humanitarian projects, and cultural performances
or exhibitions.[63] As a result, some cultural, artistic, academic, and other

exchanges between Cuban and American citizens can now take place. These are all positive developments insofar as the cosmopolitan First Amendment is concerned.

Various forces and events led to these legal and policy changes. Economic concerns played a significant role. Policymakers have also been motivated, at least in some instances, by international obligations. Specifically, with regard to travel restrictions, U.S. legislators and executive officials responded to the Helsinki Accords and other international agreements that require signatories to facilitate movement across international borders. There was also some limited consideration of First Amendment concerns.

The First Amendment ought to play a more prominent role in debates regarding the limits of foreign travel. This could lead to further liberalization of embargoes and other restrictions.[64] Thus, federal regulations continue to provide that the Secretary of State retains broad authority to deny or revoke a passport if she determines "that the applicant's activities abroad are causing or are likely to cause serious damage to the national security or foreign policy of the United States."[65] Further, although the list of travelers eligible for general or specific licenses to Cuba has expanded, the regulations still restrict travel by many Americans who wish to travel abroad, some for purposes similar to those averred by Louis Zemel. Moreover, even with regard to academic, political, and scientific exchanges, U.S. citizens must still obtain specific licenses to travel abroad. Licensure requirements for foreign travel impose burdensome prior restraints on cross-border commingling and exchange. Congress and executive agencies ought to understand that when they provide for and protect citizens' cross-border movement, they are facilitating the exercise of fundamental constitutional rights.

Recently, bipartisan proposals have been introduced in the House of Representatives that would eliminate most if not all remaining licensure requirements for travel to Cuba.[66] Further, the Obama administration granted a general license for travel to Cuba to all U.S. citizens with "close relatives" there.[67] This important policy change recognizes the significant burden that embargo laws and regulations place on the right of intimate, familial association. A more cosmopolitan perspective on First Amendment rights as they relate to foreign travel may provide further impetus for liberalization and elimination of barriers to cross-border movement.

ALIEN EXCLUSION AND REMOVAL

Restrictions on alien entry and federal laws providing for alien removal can also raise First Amendment concerns. The ability to see, to hear, and to associate with a foreign speaker on U.S. soil, in person, depends on the speaker's ability to lawfully gain entry to and residency status within the United States. Exclusion and removal of aliens on ideological grounds offends basic First Amendment values. Just as citizens must have the ability to exit the country and travel abroad, so too must they be able to participate in conversation and commingling involving resident aliens. Further, lawful foreign visitors ought to be entitled to engage in political and other discussions without fear of removal. In these basic respects, alien mobility is an important aspect of the free cross-border trade in ideas.

Alien Mobility – Background

In many countries, including some Western democracies, it is relatively common for speakers to be denied entry or removed based solely on the content of their communications or their ties to certain individuals or groups. Nations typically cite concerns regarding national security and other broad public interests as the bases for exclusion or removal. For example, Britain, Canada, and South Africa have refused entry to speakers based on their public statements regarding, respectively, Islam, terrorist organizations, and Tibet. British officials actually publish a master list of those excluded from entering the country each year, to demonstrate to the world the country's "values and standards."[68]

Despite the First Amendment's free speech and association protections, throughout its history the United States has engaged in similar behavior. Early U.S. immigration laws imposed blanket exclusions on entire classes of aliens who espoused or were believed to have adopted certain ideologies, or who were members of disfavored groups.[69]

The United States also has a long history of engaging in expulsion or removal of aliens on ideological grounds.[70] The Alien and Sedition Acts of 1798, which reflected a deep-seated and provincial fear of foreign ideas and influences, authorized the president to remove any alien considered dangerous to the peace and safety of the United States.[71] Many aliens were removed under these laws solely for their public statements, beliefs, or associations.

From World War I through the end of the Cold War, Congress authorized visa denials, immigration exclusions, and deportations of anarchists, Communists, and other persons who conveyed ideas that were deemed a threat to the interests and security of the United States.[72] During the Cold War, federal laws authorized exclusion of aliens based solely on the content of their speech or associations. Section 212(a) (27) of the McCarran-Walter Act,[73] enacted in 1952 over President Truman's veto, authorized exclusion of aliens who sought to enter the United States "solely, principally, or incidentally to engage in activities which would be prejudicial to the public interest, or endanger the welfare, safety, or security of the United States."[74] Section 212(a) (28) of the Act specifically authorized exclusions of "anarchists" and communist affiliates.[75] From 1952 through the late 1970s, thousands of aliens were deemed excludable under section 212(a)(28), forcing them to seek waivers from the Attorney General in order to enter the country.[76] During this period, State Department and immigration officials excluded numerous foreign scholars, artists, and musicians. This policy adversely affected academic, cultural, and other types of cross-border exchange.[77]

In the late 1970s, Congress repealed some of the most blatant ideological bases for alien exclusion. The McGovern Amendment,[78] enacted in 1977, restricted the government's ability to exclude suspected Communists or anarchists under section 212(a)(28) of the McCarran–Walter Act.[79] Years later, Congress concluded that the executive branch had misused this section to exclude noncitizens based solely on their statements or ideologies.[80] In the 1980s, the Reagan administration turned to section 212(a)(27) of the Act which, as noted, allowed for exclusion when aliens' activities in the United States would be "prejudicial to the public interest."[81] Many foreign officials and scholars were subject to visa restrictions under this provision.[82]

In 1990, owing in part to international pressure, Congress passed the Moynihan–Frank Amendment,[83] which expressly prohibited the exclusion or deportation of noncitizens "because of the alien's past, current, or expected beliefs, statements, or associations, if such beliefs, statements, or associations would be lawful within the United States."[84] Further, in the 1990s, amendments to U.S. immigration laws sought to limit excludable offenses primarily to conduct rather than speech or ideology.[85]

Despite these amendments, federal laws and regulations may continue to permit ideological exclusion and removal. U.S. immigration laws and regulations allow for the exclusion of aliens based on "potentially serious adverse foreign policy consequences."[86] Further, the president has broad authority to remove citizens of enemy nations, without even conducting a pre-removal hearing, on national security grounds.[87]

In response to the threat of terrorism, Congress has enacted additional alien exclusion provisions. In 1996, Congress delegated to the U.S. State Department the authority to exclude "representative[s]" and "member[s]" of terrorist organizations.[88] Shortly after the September 11, 2001 attacks, Congress imposed additional restrictions on entry, including exclusions of aliens affiliated with terrorist causes and groups.[89] A provision of the USA PATRIOT Act permits the Department of Homeland Security to bar from the United States any alien who has used a "position of prominence within any country to endorse or espouse terrorist activity."[90] The State Department has interpreted this "endorse or espouse" provision to authorize exclusion of aliens based on "irresponsible expressions of opinion by prominent aliens who are able to influence the actions of others."[91] Finally, the REAL ID Act of 2005 rendered aliens excludable on the same substantive grounds as the USA PATRIOT Act, but without regard to whether they held a "position of prominence" in their home countries.[92]

The extent to which federal officials have relied on these terrorism-based laws and regulations is unclear. It is difficult to know how often, or on what specific grounds, federal agents deny entry to aliens based on their speech activities. However, every now and then, exclusions do come to the public's attention. In one recent instance, two British tourists were denied entry to the United States after joking on

Twitter that they were going to "destroy America" and "dig up Marilyn Monroe."[93]

The exclusion of Tariq Ramadan, mentioned at the beginning of the chapter, is not unique. Many prominent foreign academics have alleged that they have been denied visas under the terrorism laws.[94] Civil libertarians claim that in recent years, dozens of scholars, journalists, and other putative speakers have been excluded solely for ideological reasons.[95] In some cases it may be difficult, if not impossible, to discern the basis for an alien's exclusion.[96] The government may provide no reason at all for the exclusion or it may assert as it did in Ramadan's case, that the alien was barred under laws prohibiting entry for reasons other than ideology or association.[97]

This assumes, of course, that the government must provide some content-neutral reason for exclusion. The executive has consistently asserted that the United States has the power, owing to its authority over immigration and foreign affairs, to exclude aliens based solely on ideological or associational grounds. An appellate brief filed by the George W. Bush administration claimed that Congress may constitutionally exclude persons based solely on ideology, beliefs, or memberships.[98] Although the Obama administration was urged to renounce and disclaim any such argument, or one based on inherent presidential authority, it declined to do so.

Entry, Removal, and the First Amendment

The First Amendment generally forbids content discrimination and, thus, would seem clearly to condemn governmental decision-making on ideological grounds, even in the immigration context. The notion that the U.S. government is authorized to discriminate against speakers or speech in order to express "national values" is flatly inconsistent with core First Amendment principles and values. However, the strict prohibition on content discrimination has not been applied with full force in transborder contexts, including immigration proceedings.

The Supreme Court has characterized admission to the United States as "a privilege granted by the sovereign."[99] Despite having opportunities to do so, the Court has never held that the First Amendment forbids ideological exclusion. It has also suggested, in precedents that have not been overruled, that aliens may be removable solely on ideological grounds.[100] The notion that an alien's ability to enter or remain in the United States implicates a mere privilege, which may be denied based on constitutionally protected expressive activities, rests on provincial principles. These include traditionally narrow conceptions of constitutional community, territorial sovereignty, and First Amendment domain.

Despite a very long history of alien exclusion, we have no clear answer with regard to whether the First Amendment itself constrains such governmental decisions. *Kleindienst v. Mandel,* decided in 1972, is the principal guiding precedent.[101] In *Mandel,* a Belgian journalist and self-described "revolutionary Marxist," sought a visa to enter the United States for a limited period to participate with American scholars in academic conferences and other discussions. The visa application was denied – for ideological reasons, according to the academics who issued the invitation, and for reasons relating to Mandel's conduct on earlier trips to the United States, according to the government.

The Supreme Court held that aliens have no First Amendment right to enter the country to convey ideas or information or to associate with U.S. citizens or institutions.[102] However, the Court held that audiences within the United States do have a First Amendment right to receive information from foreign speakers.[103] That includes, said the Court, the right "'to have the alien enter and to hear him explain and seek to defend his views.'"[104] In its decision, the Court explicitly noted the importance of protecting face-to-face interaction. In particular, it concluded that the possibility of communication by telephone or other technological means did not resolve the specific First Amendment concerns relating to alien exclusion.[105]

Although it recognized domestic audiences' right to hear or receive information from foreign sources in person, *Mandel* did not offer any specific justification for protecting citizens' right to speak to and associate with aliens. Indeed, it strongly suggested that any First Amendment interest was insubstantial and could easily be outweighed by governmental interests.

In making this determination, the Court did not follow established First Amendment doctrines or methods. It did not balance the audience's interest in hearing the alien's ideas in person against the government's interest in denying the visa or apply ordinary First Amendment standards to the exclusion order. Instead, the Court required only that the government provide a "facially legitimate and bona fide reason" for the exclusion.[106] Once the government met this minimal burden, the Court indicated that courts were not authorized to engage in further scrutiny of the government's explanation.[107] According to the Court, this deferential approach acknowledged the government's plenary authority with regard to immigration and entry into the United States.[108]

Some scholars have observed that *Mandel* "raises as many questions as it answers."[109] As several court decisions from the 1980s demonstrated, the phrase "facially legitimate and bona fide reason" is not particularly helpful to lower courts.[110] The standard suggests that American audiences have an unusually weak First Amendment interest in receiving foreign visitors. It does appear that the government is required to at least provide some basis or explanation for exclusion – although even that may be debatable.[111]

Mandel's exclusion was ultimately upheld on the ground that he overstayed a prior visa and thus engaged in an excludable offense. Thus, it remains unclear whether the First Amendment prohibits the government from excluding an alien from the United States based solely on statements he has made, ideological beliefs he has adopted or espoused, or associations he has joined.

Aliens who have successfully entered the United States enjoy at least some degree of First Amendment protection.[112] Thus, with regard to the First Amendment, the government cannot impose criminal or civil liability on lawfully resident aliens based solely on what would otherwise be protected expressive activity if engaged in by a citizen in the United States.[113] As noted earlier, however, it is less clear whether these protections apply in the immigration context – that is, whether lawfully resident aliens can be removed or deported based solely on their expressive activities.

One of the leading cases on the issue, which upheld the removal of an alien on the ground that he was a member of the Communist Party, was decided in 1952.[114] The Supreme Court's holding, which rested in part on the proposition that the First Amendment did not protect membership in the Communist Party, has been undermined by subsequent decisions.[115] However, lower courts have disagreed as to whether the government can deny naturalization to and ultimately deport a lawful resident alien based solely on his expression or expressive activity.[116] The Supreme Court has not addressed this question in any recent case. However, it has held that a legally resident alien cannot challenge an otherwise lawful deportation on the ground that the government selectively enforced the immigration laws against him because of protected speech.[117]

The lack of clarity regarding resident aliens' First Amendment rights is hardly unusual. Indeed, the scope of resident aliens' constitutional rights has long been the subject of controversy and conflicting precedents. As David Cole has observed, "The difficulty of the question is reflected in the deeply ambivalent approach of the Supreme Court, an ambivalence matched only by the alternately xenophobic and xenophilic attitude of the American public toward immigrants."[118]

The First Amendment and Alien Visitors

Like citizens' ability to exit the country, alien mobility is an important aspect of the First Amendment's transborder dimension. The free cross-border flow of persons supports and facilitates not just global commerce and recreation, but also the free exchange of ideas and various forms of international association. The First Amendment ought to preclude exclusion of alien visitors based on lawful speech they have communicated abroad or that they intend to communicate once they reach U.S. shores. It ought also to protect any lawful foreign visitors from forced removal based on speech or associational activities.

First Amendment Values and Alien Visitation

Zechariah Chafee extolled the expressive benefits of alien visitation. Although he was writing at a time when fear of communism was rampant and ideological exclusions were rather common, Chafee nevertheless recognized the benefits of this mode of international exchange. He argued that, despite domestic strife and concerns over communist infiltration, there was still "plenty of room … for temporary visitors from abroad to land, look around, talk, learn, and let us learn from them."[119] Chafee viewed foreign visitors as sources of information and important contact points connecting U.S. citizens and the community of nations beyond their shores.

Chafee appreciated the significant loss to American society from viewing and treating foreign visitors as potential threats to national security and public order. He specifically lamented that, in the 1950s, many scholars and lecturers had "refused invitations to lecture or attend conferences because they would not go through scores of humiliating questions and endless delays."[120] As a result, he argued, the system of alien exclusion chilled and suppressed a variety of academic and cultural pursuits. It also affected U.S. credibility with regard to human rights relating to speech and association. Ideological exclusion signaled to aliens and foreign audiences, including foreign governments, that the United States was not the open society it purported to be in international circles.

Chafee also explained, in more general terms, why aliens ought not to be denied entry based on mere differences in outlook or ideology. "Indeed," he wrote, "differences in outlook may have advantages when our purpose is to build up mutual understanding as a basis for trust and friendship and to increase our knowledge from what foreign travelers tell us."[121] This is the critical flip side of the First Amendment right to travel abroad. Chafee's focus on "differences in outlook," "mutual understanding," and "trust" implicates some of the core First Amendment values relating to cross-border movement.

By engaging with aliens abroad and at home, citizens can join an international marketplace of ideas. They can learn more about what divides and connects the peoples of the world. They can converse and commingle with aliens, gather information, and work toward solving mutual problems. In these and other respects, alien visitors contribute to the supply of knowledge required for Americans to effectively engage in self-governance in an interconnected world. Excluding or removing aliens based on what they have said or with whom they have associated offends fundamental First Amendment principles as well as international agreements that protect freedom of expression "without regard to frontiers". These ideological barriers interfere with the most personal and intimate forms of cross-border conversation and commingling.[122]

In *Mandel*, the Supreme Court devoted little attention to these First Amendment concerns. It did not even mention any of the foregoing benefits or values associated with cross-border mobility and citizen–alien exchange. Indeed, the Court has never placed cross-border movement in First Amendment perspective. This is unfortunate, and not only because it renders the law uncertain. A future Supreme Court decision that recognizes the connection between alien mobility and expression, forcefully rejects ideological exclusion, and endorses a robust First Amendment right to receive foreign visitors would protect citizens' core expressive liberties. Perhaps as importantly, such a decision would send a strong message to the rest of the world that the ability to visit the United States is not subject to ideological litmus tests.

In substance, *Mandel* recognized only the weakest form of First Amendment interest in foreign exchange. Of course, it is appropriate to deny entry to aliens who pose a clear danger to public safety.[123] However, temporary visitors armed only with words and ideas pose no such imminent danger. The "facially valid and bona fide" standard is a stranger to First Amendment doctrine. It is a product of the extraordinary deference with which courts have reviewed immigration policies. As Gerald Neuman has argued, the idea that courts are somehow disabled from reviewing First Amendment claims in the context of alien exclusion does not withstand scrutiny.[124] As Neuman has observed, "The indiscriminate suspension of normal standards of judicial review of immigration policy endangers not only the rights of aliens, but also the rights of citizens."[125]

Even if the Supreme Court fails to deliver, the political branches can act on their own to facilitate cross-border exchange between citizens and foreign visitors. As discussed earlier, at the conclusion of the Cold War, Congress liberalized some visa and exclusion laws. Unfortunately, the Moynihan–Frank Amendment and other laws did not eradicate the danger or practice of ideological exclusion. To an uncertain degree, earlier congressional liberalization of exclusion laws has been undermined by recent terrorism-based restrictions.

Insofar as they permit purely ideological rather than specific conduct-based exclusions, these restrictions ought to be repealed. Like the Court, Congress and the president have a responsibility to interpret and protect First Amendment rights. Entry bans based solely on speech, ideology, or association rest on the notion that importation of ideas is itself dangerous to American society. As noted, such restrictions prevent American audiences from receiving information and from associating or assembling with foreign visitors who wish to come to the United States.[126] If the Supreme Court will not do so, then Congress ought to clarify that ideological exclusions are invalid regardless of context. The State Department and other executive agencies ought to abandon the notion that "irresponsible expressions of opinion by prominent aliens who are able to influence the actions of others" provide an independent basis for alien exclusion.[127]

Ideological exclusions are not the only relevant concern when it comes to cross-border mobility. In a broader sense, U.S. officials ought to carefully review any barriers that exclude foreign visitors. All such laws may have significant First Amendment consequences. For example, in 2009, the Obama administration lifted a twenty-two-year ban on entry into the United States of HIV-positive individuals. The ban was based on health, rather than speech, concerns. Nevertheless, it affected important First Amendment interests relating to academic inquiry and association. Among other things, the lifting of the entry ban allows international AIDS researchers and activists to meet in the United States. It allows U.S. scientists, institutions, and activists to host and take a leading role in global conversations regarding pressing international public health issues.

We need, at long last, to recover the intersection between cross-border movement and our First Amendment values. Just as foreign travel is not merely a luxurious pastime enjoyed by America's leisure class, ideological exclusion of aliens is not merely the concern of a handful of academics who wish to engage with foreign visitors. In a globalized world where ideological divisions spark international debate and violent reaction, mobility is more important than ever to the development of mutual respect and understanding. To be sure, ideological exclusions do not deny American citizens of access to the writings and thoughts of excluded aliens. However, First Amendment rights cannot be denied based solely on the claim that information may be available from some alternative source. In any event, alien exclusions cut off forms of conversation and commingling that cannot be replicated through digital domains. As the Supreme Court recognized in *Mandel*, audiences have a First Amendment interest in face-to-face interaction.

Alien Visitors, Expressive Liberties, and
International Hospitality

Finally, the United States ought to adopt the position that legally resident aliens are entitled to full First Amendment protections while they are within its borders. This means that as a constitutional principle, noncitizens ought not to be denied citizenship or removed from the country based on ideological or associative activities that would be protected if engaged in by citizens. Like alien exclusions, these sorts of restrictions on migration and mobility implicate important First Amendment concerns.

Enforcement of First Amendment limitations in connection with naturalization and removal decisions rests on a solid constitutional foundation. The Supreme Court has indicated that the First Amendment itself does not acknowledge any distinction between citizens and resident aliens.[128] With regard to core First Amendment values and justifications, many resident aliens have been in the United States for long periods of time. Thus, they have strong connections to local political communities, are often actively engaged with the local citizenry, and participate in conversations regarding matters of public concern. Foreign visitors may thus contribute to domestic debates and conversations in a more expansive and direct way than aliens who intend to remain in the United States only for a short time. As David Cole has observed: "In classrooms, courts, workplaces, private associations, and town hall meetings, noncitizens and citizens routinely find themselves side-by-side. If noncitizens did not have the same First Amendment rights to express themselves as citizens, the conversations in each of these settings would be considerably less free."[129]

Domestic constitutional principles are not the only relevant source of obligations to lawfully resident aliens. Protecting aliens' First Amendment rights is an international custom or obligation. By protecting the expressive rights of alien visitors, the United States extends a form of cosmopolitan hospitality to them.[130] Hospitality protects "the right of a stranger not to be treated in a hostile manner by another upon arrival on the other's territory."[131] Granting First Amendment rights to non-citizens is consistent with international human rights law. As David Cole has observed, "[h]uman rights treaties, including those that the United States has signed and ratified, uniformly provide that the rights of due process, political freedoms, and equal protection are owed to all persons, regardless of nationality."[132] For example, the Universal Declaration of Human Rights and the International Covenant on Civil and Political Rights extend free speech and association rights to all noncitizens residing within a nation.

Of course, the Constitution is not a suicide pact. If the United States has evidence that a lawful resident alien is involved in terrorist activities, has violated U.S. laws, or is engaging in incitement of other unlawful expression, then it may exclude or remove the alien on these specific grounds. However, basing adverse immigration decisions on protected First Amendment activity harms the functioning of domestic political communities, denies enforcement of basic human rights, and diminishes America's standing in the world community.

4 CROSS-BORDER COMMUNICATION AND ASSOCIATION

Corliss Lamont was the son of a wealthy New York financier, a professor of philosophy, a civil rights activist, and the proprietor of Basic Pamphlets. In the 1960s, Lamont published and distributed within the United States pamphlets and other literature concerning a variety of subjects of public interest including civil liberties, foreign relations, and war and peace. In July 1963, Lamont received a form notice from the Post Office Department in San Francisco, California, informing him that it was holding certain "communist political propaganda" addressed to Basic Pamphlets. The material in question, a pamphlet entitled "Peking Review," had been detained at one of eleven screening points set up across the United States to search unsealed mail that originated abroad.[1] Under postal laws and regulations, Lamont could receive the material only by notifying the Post Office of his desire to receive foreign political propaganda. Fearing that compliance with the law would result in his name being placed on a list of citizens affirmatively requesting receipt of communist propaganda, Lamont refused to respond. Instead, he commenced a lawsuit challenging the constitutionality of the postal scheme under the First Amendment. In *Lamont v. Postmaster General*, the Supreme Court invalidated the postal law, ruling that it violated Lamont's right to receive information.[2] The decision marked the first time the Court had ever invalidated a federal statute on First Amendment grounds.

In the 1990s, the Humanitarian Law Project (HLP), a human rights organization based in Los Angeles, was working with the Kurdistan Workers' Party (PKK) in Turkey, encouraging it to resolve its disputes with the Turkish government through peaceful, lawful means.

It taught the PKK how to file human rights complaints before the United Nations and helped it file complaints, assisted it in peace overtures to the Turkish government, and advocated in coordination with PKK for Kurdish human rights. A federal law enacted in 1996 makes it a crime to provide "material support," including expert advice or assistance, to groups the U.S. State Department has labeled "foreign terrorist organizations." In 1977, the secretary of state had designated the PKK a "foreign terrorist organization," which appeared to make HLP's activities a criminal offense. HLP and others filed suit, claiming that the material support law violated its First Amendment speech and association rights. In *Holder v. Humanitarian Law Project*, the Supreme Court upheld the material support laws as applied to HLP's otherwise lawful and peaceful expressive activities.[3] This decision was also a first – the first time a Supreme Court majority had ever upheld a content-based regulation of speech and association.

Lamont and *Humanitarian Law Project* raise fundamental questions regarding the First Amendment and cross-border expressive activities: To what extent do citizens have a right to send and receive communications and materials across international borders? Are communications that originate within the United States but cross international borders fully protected by the First Amendment? What is the nature and scope of the First Amendment right to associate with aliens, whether located in the United States or abroad?

The answers to these and other questions relating to cross-border speech and association are surprisingly unclear. We have leapt headlong into a globalized and digitized era in which speech and association traverse, and indeed sometimes seem to transcend, territorial borders. Most Americans probably assume that the First Amendment protects their right to receive information from foreign sources and to send communications and materials abroad. However, these rights have never been clearly or firmly established in American constitutional law. Some courts and commentators have advocated extending full First Amendment protection to communications and associations that cross international borders or have assumed that such protection applies. Others, including some prominent First Amendment scholars, have adopted a more provincial view – namely, that the First Amendment protects expressive and associational liberties within the

U.S. constitutional community, as defined by its territorial borders, and does not apply fully if at all to cross-border expressive activities. Further, it is a mistake to assume that the now technologically enhanced ability to communicate across borders somehow creates or implies a constitutional right to do so.[4] Neither *Lamont* nor any other Supreme Court decision provides clear justifications for protecting cross-border conversation and commingling.

This chapter argues in favor of granting robust First Amendment protection to cross-border expressive activities, including speech and association. As in other transborder contexts, we must weigh the benefits of cross-border conversation and commingling against the national security and foreign affairs concerns that sometimes arise at international borders. In Chapter 5, I examine some of the most difficult cases in this regard, including cross-border incitement and enemy-aiding speech. This chapter, like the last, focuses more generally on the relationship between territorial borders and expressive liberties. As we shall see, that relationship is critically important not only to the individual speaker or international activist, but also more generally to the free cross-border flow of information.

REGULATION OF CROSS-BORDER COMMUNICATION

Like other nations, the United States regulates cross-border communication and information flow. As described below, U.S. laws and regulations restrict the cross-border distribution of commercial, cultural, scientific, and political content. Federal law criminalizes certain direct communications by Americans to foreign governments, foreign officials, or foreign organizations. U.S. laws have until very recently limited citizens' access to all propaganda and other materials distributed by the U.S. government abroad. Although Congress has loosened a number of laws restricting cross-border speech and association, the principle that the First Amendment speaks in a muted or different voice at the territorial borders remains firmly entrenched in U.S. laws, regulations, judicial decisions, and legal commentary. As the Supreme Court observed in a decision upholding the seizure of allegedly obscene films by customs agents, "Import restrictions and searches of persons or packages at the national borders rest on different considerations and different rules of constitutional law from domestic regulations."[5] As we shall see, this principle remains in force and affects cross-border information flow in the current digital era. Although digitization has altered the means of cross-border exchange, it has not eradicated territorial sovereignty, territorial borders, or territorial regulation.[6]

Cultural and Commercial Expression

For more than a century, U.S. customs laws and regulations have restricted or prohibited the import and export of a broad array of informational materials that would otherwise be entitled to First Amendment protection. These laws have significantly affected the cross-border flow of cultural, artistic, and commercial information.[7]

Educational and Artistic Materials

U.S. laws have long prohibited or restricted cross-border exchange of a variety of materials, including books, magazines, and artwork. Not surprisingly, restrictions on cross-border information flow have been most prevalent during wartime. Under the Trading With the Enemy Act (TWEA), enacted in 1917, the United States banned or restricted the import and export of various books, films, periodicals, and other expressive material.[8] During the Vietnam War, executive officials invoked TWEA to seize books and newspapers produced in North Vietnam and China and refused to allow their entry into the United States, until the addressees obtained import licenses and demonstrated that the country of origin would obtain no financial benefit from importation.[9] Aggressive enforcement of TWEA continued during the Cold War. Thus, for example, in the 1980s, the U.S. Office of Foreign Asset Control (OFAC) seized a variety of books and magazines imported from Cuba.[10]

Other federal laws regulate cross-border commercial and cultural exchange. Under the Tariff Act of 1930, U.S. customs and immigration officials have broad authority to conduct border searches and to seize any unauthorized items of commerce.[11] The Tariff Act's drafters apparently sought to track First Amendment doctrine. Thus, the Act purports to distinguish between protected and unprotected expression.

Among other things, the Tariff Act bans the import or export of materials that incite insurrection, convey a true threat, constitute obscenity, might be used to procure an unlawful abortion, or advertise a lottery.

Under the Tariff Act's authority, U.S. customs agents have seized a wide variety of books, newspapers, and other materials that constitute protected speech.[12] The Act still prohibits the importation of certain "immoral" articles of commerce.[13] Moreover, it permits the treasury secretary alone to determine whether certain materials ought to be excluded. For example, the secretary is authorized to permit importation of otherwise banned books so long as he is satisfied that the item is one of "the so-called classics or books of recognized and established literary or scientific merit."[14] Under federal regulations, the secretary has been granted similar authority with regard to potentially obscene materials.[15]

Other U.S. laws and regulations govern the cross-border sharing of music, books, films, and other artistic works. In 1949, the United States signed the Beirut Agreement, a multilateral treaty intended to facilitate international dissemination of films and other audiovisual materials of an educational, scientific, and cultural character.[16] Under the agreement, qualifying materials were exempt from customs duties, import licenses, special rates, quantitative restrictions, and other costs. For many domestic film distributors, these costs substantially restrict the ability to distribute in foreign markets.

To receive the benefits provided under the Beirut Agreement, distributors must obtain a certificate from the appropriate governmental agency in the country of the material's origin attesting to the item's educational, scientific, or cultural merits. At one point, federal regulations provided that the approving agency would not certify any material for exemption if it attempted to "influence opinion, conviction, or policy," "espouse a cause," "attack a particular persuasion," or if it "may lend itself to misinterpretation, or misinterpretation of the United States or other countries."[17] A federal appeals court invalidated these regulations on First Amendment grounds.[18] However, current regulations still allow for some content review by agency officials, mainly to ensure compliance with the terms of the Beirut Agreement.

On its own initiative, Congress has relaxed some cross-border restrictions. In response to aggressive federal enforcement activities under TWEA, Congress enacted two laws that were intended to facilitate the exchange of information with foreign nations – including those subject to economic embargoes. The Berman Amendment, enacted in 1988, bars the Executive Branch from applying TWEA and other customs laws in a manner that interferes with the import or export of lawful "informational materials."[19] Federal regulations broadly define "informational materials" to include, without regard to format or medium, "[p]ublications, films, posters, phonograph records, photographs, microfilms, microfiche, tapes, compact discs, CD ROMs, artworks, and news wire feeds."[20]

Although the Berman Amendment appeared to exempt a variety of expressive materials from U.S. import and export controls, OFAC and other federal agencies have sometimes interpreted the law narrowly. For example, in the 1980s, OFAC opined that the informational materials exemption did not apply to original artwork.[21] OFAC also ruled that the 1991 broadcast of the Pan American Games from Cuba was not within the "informational materials" exemption.[22] In 1994, Congress enacted the Free Trade in Ideas Act,[23] which essentially reiterated the broad regulatory exemption under the Berman Amendment and implementing regulations. Nevertheless, as some commentators have noted, OFAC has continued to adopt narrow interpretations of the informational materials exemption.[24]

New methods of cross-border exchange have raised unique questions. For example, it is not clear whether TWEA and federal export regulations apply to the range of social media that have altered the global communications landscape. If these laws apply, American companies offering such services might in some cases be required to block access to users in certain foreign countries. Owing to the prevalence of social media, application of the regulations could significantly affect the free cross-border flow of information.

Scientific, Technical, and Sensitive Materials

A number of federal laws and regulations govern the cross-border exchange of scientific, technical, and sensitive information, including materials that potentially implicate national security. The Export Administration Act of 1979 (EAA), a successor to earlier and much more stringent Cold War export control laws, imposes export controls on certain materials and technologies that have civilian or dual civilian–military applications.[25] Export control laws and regulations require an export license for any materials, information, and items that could have military applications.[26] A few thousand such items appear on what is known as the Commerce Control List, which is compiled by federal regulators pursuant to the EAA and successor laws.

Under federal Export Administration Regulations (EAR), a person may not share, without an export license, "information and know-how ... that can be used to design, produce, manufacture, utilize, or reconstruct goods, including computer software and technical data."[27] Owing to their potential dual-use functions, computers, computer code, and technological data have been of particular concern. While it seems that most license applications are ultimately approved, federal regulators do not maintain data regarding which particular applications have been denied.[28] Nor is it possible to know how many would-be exporters of information decided not to apply for an export license under the EAR owing to its strict requirements.

To date, there have been relatively few First Amendment challenges to export licensing regulations. Some challenges relating to computer source code have been successful.[29] In response to these challenges and to international market conditions, in which computer source code has become a significant export commodity, federal officials have amended the EAR to more broadly permit cross-border publication and sharing of computer source code, encryption products, and other computer technology.[30] This has eased somewhat the free speech concerns raised by broad restrictions on cross-border code-sharing.

To be covered under the EAR, it is not always necessary that information physically cross U.S. borders. A so-called "deemed export license" is required whenever sensitive information or technology is shared by a U.S. business or research institution with certain foreign nationals in their employ.[31] Under these circumstances, the information is *deemed* to have been exported to the foreign national's home country. The apparent national security concern is that the foreign national may return home and reproduce or otherwise share the information with a foreign government or aliens living abroad. No court has ever squarely addressed, in a published opinion, whether the "deemed export" licensing regulations violate the Free Speech Clause.

Cross-Border Political Expression

Political content and materials are also subject to some cross-border regulations. Despite congressional liberalization or repeal of some export and import laws, the United States still restricts cross-border political speech.

Direct Communications with Foreign Officials and Agents

As discussed in Chapter 2, fear of foreign influence was a central concern at the nation's founding. Although many framers adopted a cosmopolitan perspective, some early American laws sought to limit or prevent foreign influence by restricting contacts with foreign powers.

For example, the Logan Act of 1799 makes it a crime for any American citizen to engage in unauthorized "correspondence or intercourse with any foreign government or any officer or agent thereof" with the intention of influencing the foreign affairs of the United States.[32] The Logan Act remains on the books, but has rarely been invoked or enforced. Under its literal terms, a citizen concerned about nuclear proliferation would be subject to criminal prosecution for sending a letter or e-mail to the Kremlin urging Russian officials to resist U.S. efforts to place strategic missile defense systems in neighboring countries.[33]

Although obscure, the Logan Act raises important questions regarding the contemporary scope of cross-border expressive liberties. Whether the Act violates the First Amendment, or is otherwise unconstitutional, remains an open question. If the Logan Act is valid, then Congress could presumably enact a law prohibiting U.S. citizens from communicating with aliens with the intent to advocate, encourage, or merely espouse terrorist acts against the United States. Further, if communications with foreign persons and agents can be broadly restricted or even banned, then perhaps governmental surveillance and interception of those communications would not implicate or violate the First Amendment.[34] Indeed, if the First Amendment does not apply to citizens' cross-border communications, then federal officials would presumably be free to gather or restrict any such communications based on their content.

Foreign Political Propaganda

The chapter began with a discussion of *Lamont v. Postmaster General*, which invalidated a postal prior restraint on receipt of foreign political propaganda.[35] These materials have long been subject to legal prohibition and sanction in the United States. In the 1940s and 1950s, the federal government set up centers across the United States, at which unsealed mail originating abroad was searched and frequently seized.[36] The intended recipients were required to fill out a reply card and affirmatively request delivery of the offending materials. In *Lamont*, the Supreme Court held that the U.S. Postal Service could not impose this sort of prior restraint on receipt of material that reached the postal stream.[37]

Although the prior restraint provision was repealed, other portions of the statute challenged in *Lamont* have remained in force. The law resurfaced two decades later in the Supreme Court, in a case involving dissemination of foreign political propaganda within the United States. The Foreign Agent Registration Act (FARA) of 1938, which was enacted in response to the threat of Nazi propaganda, requires any "agent of a foreign principal" residing in the United States to register with the Attorney General and to comply with certain filing and disclosure requirements prior to distributing "foreign political propaganda" within the United States.[38] The disclosure provisions specifically require that foreign political propaganda must be labeled such that it conveys to the recipient that the distributor of the materials is an agent of a foreign principal and has registered as such with the attorney general. The provisions also require that the distributor state that registration does not indicate approval of the material by the U.S. government.

The disclosure requirements were upheld by the Supreme Court in *Meese v. Keene*,[39] a case decided in 1987. Barry Keene, a California attorney and member of the state senate, sought to distribute three Canadian films in the United States. The films had been identified by the Department of Justice as foreign political propaganda. The subject of two of the films was acid rain and the third dealt with nuclear war. Keene argued that the registration and labeling requirements would chill his distribution of the films in the United States and would adversely affect his personal, professional, and political reputations.

The Court rejected Keene's claims. It reasoned that "propaganda" had two distinct meanings. According to the Court, one of the meanings was pejorative; however, it concluded that the more germane definition was neutral and conveyed only that the information was being distributed with the intent of influencing public opinion. The Court also distinguished the provision invalidated in *Lamont*, which required that the foreign materials actually be detained until a recipient came forward to claim them. In contrast, the Court concluded that the FARA disclosure provisions "simply required the disseminators of such material to make additional disclosures that would better enable the public to evaluate the import of the propaganda."[40] Finally, the Court concluded that there was no evidence that the label "political propaganda" had any chilling effect on distribution of foreign materials in the United States.[41]

The United States also creates its own political propaganda for foreign distribution. U.S. laws and regulations authorize the federal government to appropriate and spend tax dollars to disseminate positive messages about America to various foreign audiences.[42] Although certain materials and recipients were exempted, since World War II U.S. law has generally banned the receipt and dissemination of these communications within the United States.[43] This effectively imposed a cross-border speech restriction on U.S. political propaganda. A federal district court rejected a First Amendment challenge to the dissemination ban brought by members of the print press and a state senator.[44] The court relied substantially on the Supreme Court's reasoning in *Zemel v. Rusk* which, as discussed in Chapter 3, upheld foreign travel restrictions and broadly concluded that the First Amendment does not grant citizens an "unrestrained right to gather information" about their government.[45] Without fanfare or much in the way of public discussion, Congress recently repealed part of the dissemination ban.[46] Thus, for the first time in decades, U.S. citizens will be able to obtain certain U.S. State Department communications and listen to certain overseas broadcasts funded by the United States government. Other forms of U.S. foreign propaganda remain subject to the dissemination ban.

Political Participation by Foreign Nationals

Some cross-border political speech restrictions apply specifically to aliens. For example, U.S. laws ban certain kinds of political participation by foreign nationals in U.S. elections. Federal election laws prohibit foreign nationals, whether residing in the United States or located abroad, from contributing funds or other campaign resources in any U.S. election.[47] This ban was enacted to protect U.S. elections and

domestic policymaking from foreign influence – a problem first identified during hearings conducted by Senator Fulbright in 1966.[48]

In *Citizens United v. FEC*, a majority of the Supreme Court reserved
the question whether the ban on alien political contributions violates
the First Amendment.[49] Only Justice Stevens, who authored a dissent,
addressed the issue. He argued that the ban on foreign nationals' contributions would likely survive First Amendment scrutiny, owing in
part to traditional distinctions between citizens and aliens in U.S. campaign and other laws.[50]

Congress has recently considered a number of proposals that would
further restrict political contributions and other forms of participation
by foreign nationals in U.S. elections. Owing to the uncertainty regarding the First Amendment rights of aliens, whether these laws would
withstand judicial scrutiny is unclear.

The First Amendment Status of Cross-Border Communication

The Berman Amendment, the Free Trade in Ideas Act, and other laws
loosening cross-border speech restrictions demonstrate that U.S. lawmakers understand the importance of these exchanges to international
commerce, international relations, and perhaps constitutional liberties.
However, courts and scholars have disagreed regarding whether cross-
border communication is indeed protected by the First Amendment.
We still lack an explicit and definitive account of the First Amendment
status of cross-border communication.

Lamont v. Postmaster General established that citizens have a right to
receive communications that extends to materials originating overseas.
This First Amendment right to receive was relied on in *Kleindienst v.
Mandel* which, as discussed in Chapter 3, recognized that citizens have
an interest in receiving alien visitors in the United States. However,
neither these nor any other decisions stand for the broad proposition
that Americans have a fundamental First Amendment right to receive
information from abroad.[51]

Lamont may have come closest to recognizing such a right. However,
the result in *Lamont* arguably turned more on the effect of the prior
restraint, as applied to material already in the U.S. postal stream, than

on the origin or content of the information detained. As the Court stated, "We rest on the narrow ground that the addressee in order to receive his mail must request in writing that it be delivered."[52] Indeed, one scholar who has closely studied *Lamont* argues that the decision hinged not on the First Amendment, but rather on the unique institutional characteristics of the U.S. Postal Service.[53]

In any event, *Lamont* did not set forth any affirmative First Amendment justification for protecting the receipt of foreign political or other information. The majority opinion did not mention any connection between foreign political speech and domestic self-governance. Nor did it appear to rest on the Holmesian notion that citizens had nothing to fear from foreign ideas or ideologies. Moreover, the Court made clear that its decision left undisturbed U.S. officials' broad authority to search and seize materials at the border. Indeed, long after *Lamont* was decided, customs and border officials were still seizing political and other protected material at international borders. Some lower courts upheld these seizures.[54] Finally, in subsequent cases, the Court has itself distinguished or failed to rely on *Lamont.* In its recent decision in *Holder v. Humanitarian Law Project,* for example, the Court upheld restrictions on cross-border speech and association without so much as mentioning or even citing *Lamont.*

As I have noted, courts have occasionally entertained First Amendment claims relating to the *export* of certain types of information. However, these decisions similarly fail to offer strong support for a First Amendment right to engage in cross-border communication. Whether the First Amendment protects the rights of American citizens to communicate, by whatever means, with audiences located beyond U.S. shores has received surprisingly little judicial consideration. As one federal appeals court addressing restrictions on cross-border Internet speech recently stated, "The extent of First Amendment protection of speech accessible solely by those outside the United States is a difficult and, to some degree, unresolved issue" and "the extent – indeed the very existence – of such an extraterritorial right under the First Amendment is uncertain."[55] The relatively few courts that have ruled on challenges to export control laws and regulations have typically *assumed* that the First Amendment applies.[56] As in *Lamont,* these courts have offered little or no justification for applying the First Amendment to cross-border communication and information flow.[57]

The most explicit and extensive consideration of this issue appears in the district court's decision in *Bullfrog Films, Inc. v. Wick*, which invalidated federal regulations, promulgated under the Beirut Agreement, concerning the exportation of films.[58] The court rejected several arguments by the federal government to the effect that citizens have no First Amendment right to communicate across international borders. It rejected the argument that, "when United States citizens direct their speech to foreign audiences, the government may regulate such speech on the basis of content."[59] The district court also rejected the contention that the constitutional grant of foreign affairs powers to Congress and the president authorized suppression of speech directed to foreign audiences.[60] It concluded that, "in the absence of some overriding governmental interest such as national security, the First Amendment protects communications with foreign audiences to the same extent as communications within our borders."[61] Finally, the court rejected the government's argument that "the world at large is not a 'First Amendment forum.'"[62] On appeal, the Ninth Circuit Court of Appeals did not reach or address these specific arguments.

What neither the *Bullfrog Films* court, nor any since, has explained is why or to what extent the First Amendment justifies protection for cross-border communication. Although some commentators have contended that the First Amendment protects cross-border speech,[63] other scholars have expressed doubts that the Free Speech Clause applies with equal force to domestic and cross-border communications. Although these scholars have not generally disclaimed all protection for cross-border expression, they have not fully embraced this aspect of the First Amendment's transborder dimension.

Robert Kamenshine, writing specifically about some of the export controls discussed earlier, questioned whether the First Amendment could be interpreted to "justify a concern over restriction on the flow of information and ideas out of the country."[64] He argued that traditional First Amendment justifications do not generally extend to speech directed to a foreign audience – at least one that is composed entirely of aliens.[65] Kamenshine claimed that "[n]o first amendment self-governance interest exists in informing foreign nationals" of debates regarding U.S. politics or foreign policy; that "[a]ssisting foreign nationals to find truth ... is not a first amendment goal"; and that the self-fulfillment or autonomy rationale "does not provide a persuasive basis for affording protection to the purely foreign dissemination of information."[66]

William Van Alstyne has also expressed doubts regarding the First Amendment's applicability in cross-border contexts. He suggested that a hypothetical U.S. law banning citizen war propaganda directed to aliens abroad would likely not give rise to any cognizable free speech claim.[67] Van Alstyne reasoned, in part, that "such speech is not addressed to our public forum, to sear *our* consciences."[68]

Similarly, Cass Sunstein has argued that the earlier-mentioned "deemed export" licensing rule, which would give rise to significant free speech concerns if applied to domestic communications between citizens and aliens, does not implicate the Free Speech Clause. Sunstein reasoned that the licensure scheme does not restrict domestic political discussion and thus does not implicate central First Amendment concerns.[69]

A number of other scholars have adopted a similar orientation regarding cross-border communications. In general, they have reasoned, the Free Speech Clause protects only or primarily *domestic* exchanges.[70]

In sum, neither the right to receive foreign communications nor the right of citizens to communicate with audiences located abroad currently rests on solid First Amendment ground. It seems to be an open question whether export controls, trade laws, and other restrictions on cross-border communication implicate, let alone violate, the First Amendment.

Digitization and Cross-Border Communication

In light of the digitization of expression, some might wonder why it matters whether the First Amendment applies to cross-border communications. It seems that any speaker who is intent on communicating with aliens abroad can simply use available technologies to bypass U.S. laws and regulations.[71] Put another way, the Internet seems to essentially moot the question of First Amendment protection for cross-border communications.

Digitization has made cross-border communication much cheaper and easier. It has also made governmental regulation of cross-border speech and information flow far more difficult. In a digitized era, speakers will sometimes be able to bypass border restrictions in order to communicate with aliens abroad. Digitization is also producing other effects. For example, even prior to the repeal of the ban on access to and distribution of U.S. foreign propaganda, access to the Internet allowed U.S. citizens to gain access to and distribute propaganda messages communicated by the United States in foreign nations. Digitization makes such bans more difficult to enforce.[72] Digitization may also defeat efforts to cabin or limit free speech protections to communications directed solely to domestic audiences. In the digital era, audiences are increasingly composed of a mixture of citizens and aliens.

However, digitization will not eliminate the need to determine whether the First Amendment protects cross-border communication. For many years, Internet exceptionalists have contended that digitization will eliminate governmental control of cross-border information flow.[73] But the Internet has not created a borderless world where communications are effectively immunized from legal sanction. As Jack Goldsmith and Tim Wu have argued, far from being a borderless space, the Internet has developed such that geography and place remain critically important to the regulation of cross-border expression, trade, and other activities.

Goldsmith and Wu's central claim is that, even in the digital age, governments exercise territorial control with regard to cross-border speech and information flow. What has changed, according to Goldsmith and Wu, are the enforcement methods by which governments regulate cross-border exchange.[74] Rather than attempt to intercept communications at the border, the U.S. government now focuses its regulatory energy on individual speakers and domestic intermediaries – Internet service providers, search engines, and browsers – that are present within the United States and thus subject to its jurisdiction.[75]

Goldsmith and Wu concede that a domestic enforcement strategy focusing on some combination of individuals and intermediaries cannot prevent all harmful or illegal digitized communications from crossing international borders.[76] However, they argue that domestic enforcement strategies will "succeed ... by lowering the incidence of prohibited activities to an acceptable degree."[77] These strategies supplement, and in some cases support, enforcement of laws and regulations restricting cross-border communications. U.S. trade, customs, national security, and other laws do not exempt digital communications from licensure schemes and other restrictions. Further, as I noted earlier, recent revelations show that digital cross-border communications are subject to widespread surveillance and may be intercepted by government agents. Finally, as I discuss in Chapter 5, digital communications that cross international borders may be subject to criminal penalties under federal incitement, provision of material support to terrorists, or treason laws.

The digitization of speech has enabled a virtual revolution in cross-border communication and information flow. However, like other nations, the United States continues to exercise a significant degree of what some commentators call "interdependence sovereignty" – the ability "to regulate the flow of goods, persons, pollutants, diseases, and ideas across territorial boundaries."[78] The bottom line is that the mere fact that content is communicated on the Internet does not immunize it from the many laws and regulations that restrict cross-border exchange.

CROSS-BORDER ASSOCIATION

U.S. citizens frequently participate in relationships with aliens and organizations located abroad. The extent to which citizens enjoy a First Amendment right to enter into lawful associations with aliens and foreign entities located beyond U.S. shores remains an intriguing, and relatively unsettled, transborder issue.

As I discussed in Chapter 3, entry and exit restrictions can significantly affect citizens' ability to participate in cross-border associations. We learned that citizens have a First Amendment interest in inviting aliens located abroad to the United States. We also learned that, according to the Supreme Court, aliens themselves have no cognizable First Amendment speech or associational rights. In *Kleindienst v. Mandel*, the Court held that federal officials may exclude aliens for any asserted "facially valid and bona fide" reason. Moreover, the Court has characterized and treated citizens' ability to travel abroad, whether for the purpose of speaking or associating with others, as a weak "freedom" rather than a fundamental First Amendment right.

Although *Mandel* and *Lamont* suggest that citizens have some First Amendment interest in participating in cross-border associations, reported decisions offer only limited First Amendment recognition of such activity. In one case, a federal appeals court upheld the secretary of state's order closing a foreign mission in the United States.[79] The court reasoned that operating such a mission was a form of pure conduct rather than speech. It also held that citizens have only a minimal First Amendment interest in associating with a foreign entity and, in any event, have no "right to represent a foreign entity on American soil."[80] In reaching these conclusions, the appeals court relied heavily on the fact that the association in question involved participants on both sides of the international border. This fact, the court observed, implicated the federal government's broad foreign affairs powers.[81]

The same appeals court also rejected a challenge to federal funding conditions relating to abortion services that restricted cross-border speech and association.[82] Again, the court treated as significant the fact that the associational activities crossed international borders. It concluded that *Mandel*, the alien exclusion case, stood for the proposition that cross-border associations stood on a weaker footing than purely domestic ones. It also reasoned, contrary to prior case law, that two organizations do not have a First Amendment right to associate with one another.[83] The court did not explain why *Mandel*, which involved exercise of the federal immigration power, even applied in the context of cross-border expressive associations involving the provision of abortion counseling and services.

These decisions suggest, although they do not hold, that cross-border association is not a fundamental First Amendment right. What is clear, however, is that courts do not analyze domestic associations this way. In the domestic context, courts do not treat the day-to-day operations of expressive associations as pure conduct; characterize the targeted closure of an organization (including the cessation of operations and the sale of all of its assets) as an indirect and incidental interference with expressive and associational rights; characterize associational partners who are reluctant to comply with what they view as invalid legal restrictions as "fair-weather ... associates;"[84] treat inapposite or marginally relevant precedents as nearly dispositive; or suggest novel doctrinal limits on associational rights. As I discussed in Chapter 2, these are all characteristics associated with a form of judicial quasi-recognition of transborder First Amendment liberties.

The Supreme Court most recently addressed the issue of cross-border association in *Holder v. Humanitarian Law Project*.[85] As noted earlier, in that case the Court held that federal laws barring the provision of "material support" to groups the U.S. State Department has labeled "foreign terrorist organizations" do not violate the First Amendment's freedom of speech and freedom of association guarantees, either facially or as applied to citizens' lawful speech that is "coordinated" with such groups (as opposed to forms of "independent" advocacy).[86]

The specific expression at issue in *Humanitarian Law Project* consisted of advising and training foreign groups such as the Kurdistan Workers' Party and the Tamil Tigers regarding peaceful and lawful means of resolving their political grievances.[87] Among other things, U.S. citizens wished to work with such groups to teach them how to file petitions with the United Nations.[88] The U.S. government charged that these groups were actively involved in terrorist activities, and evidence from government affidavits and other sources supported this allegation. The question presented was whether forms of expressive support, such as filing briefs in court on behalf of groups with an historical connection to terrorism and violence, could be criminally proscribed under federal law.

According to the Court, so long as citizens' expression is "coordinated" with such disfavored groups, the government may constitutionally proscribe it under the material support provisions – even if the speakers did not specifically intend to further the organizations' illegal and violent enterprises.[89] Notably, the Court rejected the government's contention that the material support provisions regulated pure conduct rather than speech.[90] It even purported to apply heightened scrutiny to the law's provisions. However, the Court found the government's interest in combating terrorism to be "an urgent objective of the highest order."[91] Further, applying substantial deference to the government's views regarding the harms associated with speech that is "coordinated" with foreign terrorist organizations, the Court found that the material support provisions were narrowly tailored to combat terrorism and to serve other national interests.

Having thus held that *coordinated speech*, which of course is itself a form of association, could be criminalized under the law, the Court spent very little time analyzing the separate associational claims. It noted that the material support provisions did not preclude citizens from joining the designated foreign terrorist organizations as members, but only proscribed the separate act of providing them with material support in the form of coordinated advocacy or assistance.[92]

Apparently, citizens are allowed to join a foreign organization so long as they do nothing to actually lend support or legitimacy to it. As David Cole has noted, this reasoning recognizes an "empty" right of association that is essentially "limited to holding a membership card."[93] The Court also suggested, without explanation, that the defendants' speech and associational claims might have been decided differently had they involved purely domestic activities and associations.[94] Thus, as suggested by some lower court precedents, domestic political associations appear to operate at the First Amendment's core, while cross-border associations reside at its periphery.

In sum, according to reported decisions U.S. citizens appear to have a limited, quasi-recognized First Amendment right to associate with foreign persons and entities beyond American shores. If the Supreme Court's decision in *Humanitarian Law Project* is any indication, cross-border association stands on notably weak constitutional footing, at least relative to domestic associational activity.

COSMOPOLITANISM AND CROSS-BORDER INFORMATION FLOW

Throughout American history, cross-border communication has been an important political and social activity. As I discussed in Chapter 2, the early "republic of letters," which crossed vast oceans, forged cross-border channels of communication linking Americans to others within the community of nations. However, cross-border communication and information flow have not been fully embraced as part of the First Amendment system of free expression. Cross-border communication and information flow properly belong closer to the First Amendment's core than to its periphery. Indeed, in a globalized and digitized world, ensuring the continued free flow of information across international borders ought to be a national priority.

Information Flow Without Regard to Frontiers

Case law and constitutional scholarship have largely neglected cross-border information flow as a distinct First Amendment concern. Some early work is now outdated. Scholars such as Kamenshine and Van Alstyne, who expressed doubts concerning the First Amendment's protection of cross-border communication, wrote before the end of the Cold War and before globalization and digitization created much tighter international connections.

Cross-border channels, whether they are physical or digital in nature, facilitate communication of a broad range of information, materials, and ideas. Today, the Internet is developing into a twenty-first century version of the republic of letters. In this sphere, although it cannot escape regulation entirely information flow readily traverses territorial borders. Individuals are able to share thoughts and ideas efficiently and cheaply over vast geographic spaces, and to communicate in new and innovative ways.

Scholars such as Kamenshine and Van Alstyne also wrote during a period when First Amendment self-governance justifications were dominant themes in free speech doctrine and jurisprudence. Thus, it may well have seemed to these scholars, and many courts as well, that cross-border communication was not properly considered a core First Amendment concern. Speech directed outward, beyond U.S. shores, did not address domestic political concerns in a way that suggested full First Amendment protection was appropriate. Instead, to some scholars and courts, cross-border communication seemed more like a privilege or quasi-liberty that government could restrict as it deemed necessary.

However, traditional conceptions of self-governance are ill suited to a digital era in which speech readily traverses territorial borders. The First Amendment does not protect cross-border communication solely because it contributes to local or domestic political conversations – although it may certainly do so. Ensuring protection for cross-border information flow ensures that citizens can be informed and engaged with regard to matters of international or global concern, better able to participate in global dialogues and debates, free to explore foreign cultures, and immersed in international commerce. It permits, and even invites, foreign information and ideas to enter, mingle with, and perhaps even challenge domestic truths.

Indeed, particularly in this century is it important that none of the conventional First Amendment justifications be given narrow, provincial interpretations. We ought not to treat territorial borders as formally restrictive boundaries with regard to citizens' self-governance, the search for truth, individual autonomy, fact-gathering and dissemination, and personal collaboration. Rather, we ought to recognize explicitly that cross-border communication and information flow facilitate global conversation and commingling.[95] These activities allow citizens to connect across borders, communicate with strangers in foreign lands, disseminate information across vast distances, and share cultural norms with distant and diverse audiences. Cross-border information flow allows Americans to connect with the rest of the world and to expand their social and political fields of vision. It demonstrates that despite many important cultural and political differences, Americans share much in common with other members of the world community. It creates a potential channel for empathy and understanding through conversation.

Of course, allowing information to flow freely across borders can also highlight national differences and lead to conflicts. Like domestic expression, cross-border communications can lead to misunderstandings and much worse. Passion may lead to violence and bloodshed, and international debate may lead to stalemate. However, even contentious conversation can serve cosmopolitan First Amendment purposes. It arouses passions, instigates international debates, and may cause speakers and audiences to question their long-held positions, prejudices, and commitments. These are the same benefits typically cited in defense of domestic freedom of speech. As I discuss in Chapter 5, we are now facing similar challenges and dilemmas in an emerging global theater.

It is significant that none of these values or justifications for protecting cross-border expression was even mentioned in *Lamont, Mandel, Humanitarian Law Project*, or other judicial decisions implicating transborder expression and association. Although Congress has at times seemed to recognize the values inherent in cross-border information flow, courts and scholars have not fully justified or explained its First Amendment status.

In a recent book about contemporary press freedoms, Lee Bollinger suggests that we need an affirmative judicial statement that shifts the discussion "from the constitutional paradigm of a national public forum to a global one."[96] He argues that we need a *New York Times v. Sullivan* for the twenty-first century. Bollinger appears to envision a landmark decision that recognizes the need to facilitate and protect transborder press rights in emerging global forums.[97]

Bollinger's thesis and proposal move in the direction I am suggesting. He focuses outward and addresses an important gap in traditional understandings of freedom of the press. We tend to think of the press as a domestic institution. However, freedom of the press is essential to cross-border information flow. Americans rely on the press to report on distant and fast-breaking stories and to investigate international events and issues that affect domestic politics. In the absence of a well-financed and active press that is engaged in cross-border information-gathering and distribution, Americans would have to rely more often on foreign news outlets. These institutions may have fewer incentives to doggedly pursue information relating to U.S. officials, actions, and policies in international contexts. Conceiving of the press as a global institution also sheds new light on the dangers associated with restrictions on cross-border information flow. For example, warrantless surveillance of cross-border communications by U.S. national security agencies may hamper the formation of confidential relationships between journalists and their foreign sources.

The vital concerns Bollinger identifies extend beyond freedom of the press. They apply more generally to cross-border information flow. A Supreme Court decision connecting First Amendment free press concerns to cross-border information flow would be valuable and welcome. However, what we really need is a *Lamont v. Postmaster General* for the twenty-first century. The landmark decision would expressly state, for the first time, that the First Amendment fully protects cross-border communication and information flow. It would rely on both traditional and cosmopolitan values and justifications to support extending First Amendment protection to cross-border conversation.

In addition to my earlier observations regarding traditional free speech justifications, there are other useful materials at hand. The Court could begin with Justice Marshall's observation, in his dissenting opinion in *Mandel*, that "[t]he progress of knowledge is an international venture."[98] Other, more recent, statements suggest that international connectivity is a core First Amendment value. For example, in *Reno v. ACLU*, the Court described the Internet as "a unique and wholly new medium of worldwide human communication" and a "new marketplace of ideas" containing "vast democratic forums" from which "any person with a phone line can become a town crier with a voice that resonates farther than it could from any soapbox."[99] *Reno* is an essential building block for situating cross-border expressive liberties closer to the First Amendment's core. It recognizes the Internet's potential to open cross-border lines of communication and to share information in global forums. It values this activity regardless of whether the ultimate payoff runs to domestic self-governance or local politics.

Further, a twenty-first century *Lamont* would acknowledge U.S. commitments under international law to facilitate the free cross-border flow of information. As discussed in Chapter 1, the United States has entered treaties and international agreements under which it is obligated to facilitate the free flow of information "*without regard to frontiers*." By entering into these agreements, the United States has recognized that cross-border information flow is part of the system of international human rights. International law reflects what Saskia Sassen has referred to as "a growing consensus in the community of states to lift border controls for the flow of capital, information, and services and, more broadly, to further globalization."[100] Contemporary understandings of the First Amendment ought to recognize and reflect this emerging global consensus.

A Supreme Court decision along the foregoing lines would be highly symbolic but also substantively meaningful. Outdated and repressive laws that are ripe for invalidation or repeal include the Logan Act and the FARA provisions regulating distribution of foreign political propaganda within the United States. These statutory relics are antithetical to First Amendment values and conflict with international commitments to the free flow of information without regard to frontiers. A more contemporary example of the sort of laws and practices that would be suspect under this approach would be U.S. surveillance of citizens' and journalists' cross-border communications. At the very least, we ought to be clear as to whether, and if so why, these communications are fully protected under the First Amendment. That aspect of the surveillance story has thus far been absent in both public and academic debates.

Indeed, once we commit to recognizing cross-border information flow as a central First Amendment concern, other existing legal restrictions also become suspect. For example, the so-called "deemed export" rule restricts the distribution of information to foreign nationals based, it would appear, on the assumption that they will export and use the information for illegal purposes. The dangers associated with dissemination of sensitive and technical information are obviously quite serious. However, imposing a prior restraint and licensure scheme on U.S. institutions is a heavy-handed and constitutionally suspect means of addressing these risks. The approach is inconsistent with a robust commitment to the cross-border exchange of scientific and educational information. Background checks for all employees and other internal controls on access to sensitive information would serve the government's interests just as well, without treating the sharing of information with foreign nationals as a per se violation of export controls.

Limits on aliens' access to information and participation in domestic politics might also warrant greater constitutional scrutiny. The ban on political contributions by foreign nationals presents a close question. The law assumes that foreign nationals have no cognizable interest in domestic politics or the outcome of U.S. elections and that their participation threatens the legitimacy of the domestic political process. As some scholars have observed, in a globalized era, it is no longer clearly the case that foreign nationals have no legitimate interest in domestic elections.[101] Moreover, the strong presumption that cross-border donations and support will only produce nefarious or harmful results ignores the many possible benefits of cross-border conversation. Aliens' participation might lead to different perspectives on domestic and international policies. It could teach us something about our own system of electoral politics. In any event, we ought not to assume that foreign contributions and other forms of political participation will necessarily corrupt or pollute the American democratic process. At the very least, we ought to ensure that any restriction on participation by foreign nationals is narrowly tailored to the government's actual concerns. Contribution limits or disclosure requirements may be sufficient to protect against foreign danger or corruption.[102]

Like cross-border mobility, cross-border information flow is a critically important aspect of the First Amendment system of free expression. Under a more cosmopolitan interpretation or perspective it is crucial that, to the extent possible, information be freely shared among the peoples of the world "without regard to frontiers."

A Global Information Policy for the Twenty-First Century

We now live in a world where domestic and foreign speech marketplaces are tightly interconnected. The First Amendment does not reach or govern all of those marketplaces. However, as U.S. officials develop national and international information policies for the twenty-first century, they need to adopt a more cosmopolitan perspective. They ought to proceed with the understanding that they are actively shaping the contours of not only the First Amendment's transborder dimension but of the global communicative infrastructure.

As a general matter, a cosmopolitan approach counsels that the United States should develop policies that facilitate global interconnectivity and information flow. This obviously does not mean that U.S. borders ought to be thrown open to import and export of all information and materials. As mentioned earlier, some forms of cross-border conversation and commingling directly threaten national interests. However, as noted, policymakers can further ease U.S. laws and regulations restricting cross-border exchange. They can also continue to cooperate with other nations to ensure the free flow of information across the world's territorial borders.

I have argued that the courts can play a role in encouraging and producing this result. However, as Jack Balkin has observed, future debates regarding global information policy are likely to focus less on judicial interpretations of the First Amendment or traditional regulatory methods than on regulatory policies concerning new technologies, Internet access, intellectual property, and the sharing of data and other information.[103] As we move deeper into the twenty-first century, U.S. officials must develop information policies that take into account modern conditions under which information flows across international borders.

Balkin provides some helpful theoretical guidance for these debates, particularly in terms of updating First Amendment concerns and justifications. He encourages legislators and regulators to adopt policies that facilitate technological collaboration, which Balkin argues will allow people to participate in the construction of "democratic cultures" and institutions.[104] He urges policymakers to focus on creating a free expression infrastructure that preserves the Internet's open architecture and features. In more concrete terms, Balkin supports policies such as network neutrality and broad immunity for Internet service providers on the grounds that they encourage the free flow of information and encourage innovation.

Balkin's democratic culture theory is cosmopolitan and outward-oriented. It is premised on the reality that modern forms of communication frequently transcend the nation-state.[105] As he observes, "we need a free speech theory that recognizes that technological changes have made it possible for large numbers of people to broadcast and publish to audiences around the world, to be speakers as well as audiences, to be active producers of information content, not just recipients or consumers."[106] In First Amendment terms, Balkin argues that officials must "protect the development of knowledge and opinion through securing the freedom of speech, press, petition and assembly, and through policies designed to promote the growth of-and access to-knowledge."[107]

Note that these are international and global, rather than solely domestic, concerns. Much of the innovation and connectivity Balkin envisions will take place across territorial borders, rather than within a single territory. Thus, it is important to recognize that laws and regulations enacted in and by the United States will have domestic as well as cross-border and global effects. In part, this is attributable to the fact that the Internet is a global resource that cuts across jurisdictions. Thus, when U.S. policymakers consider exercising authority over the Internet, they need to consider the cross-border and global effects of proposed regulations. And when they assert U.S. power to regulate harmful conduct abroad, they must consider the possibility that unintended consequences could result both extraterritorially as well as within the United States.

These concerns were highlighted when Congress recently proposed measures to combat foreign copyright and trademark infringement on the Internet. One of the main objections to the proposed bills, the Stop Online Piracy Act (SOPA) and the Protect IP Act (PIPA), was that these measures posed threats to global online freedom of expression and innovation. Thus, for example, provisions in the bills that required the blacklisting of foreign sites suspected of hosting pirated intellectual property would have denied U.S. users access to foreign and domestic sites. Further, SOPA and PIPA would have effectively denied any legal process to foreign sites that were accused of piracy.[108] U.S. sites hosting suspect content would have been shut down based solely on an interested party's unilateral allegation that a site was hosting illegal content. Opponents of the bills argued that the prospect of being cut off from advertising and other funding would deter websites across the globe from adopting innovative approaches to linking to third party content.

SOPA and PIPA are case studies in the sorts of concerns highlighted by a more cosmopolitan First Amendment perspective. In seeking to address an admittedly serious global problem, Congress threatened the interconnectivity and innovation that have facilitated the Internet's rapid development. SOPA and PIPA were controversial departures from a growing consensus that information policies ought to support a unified, open Internet. Governmental entities, technology companies, and civil society organizations came together to ensure that information laws and policies continue to protect and advance cross-border free speech, press, privacy, and associational rights in the digital era.

Rather than work against these various interests and institutions, U.S. officials ought to consult with them to develop global information policies for the twenty-first century. Organizations such as the Global Network Initiative and the Organization for Economic Co-operation and Development have developed some basic principles that emphasize the need to promote and protect the global free flow of information and the open, distributed, and interconnected nature of the Internet. U.S. policymakers should engage with these and similar groups when developing Internet and other global communications policies.

Another aspect of information policy that U.S. officials need to consider carefully is the use of "soft power" censorship.[109] Private censorship has become a significant and growing concern, especially with regard to digital content. Many social media sites and other private content providers allow governments and others to request that material be removed based on the companies' own internal speech standards. Private censors are not state actors and are thus not constrained by the First Amendment. U.S. officials have pressured private intermediaries to deny services to certain speakers and to ban content from their sites.[110] This sort of informal pressure is not a new phenomenon.[111] However, in a networked system that depends substantially on private intermediaries to host and communicate content across the globe, the threat is unique and magnified.

Harder forms of censorship such as prior restraints and criminal prohibitions pose the greatest threat to cross-border information flow. Although it poses a lesser danger to cross-border communication and information flow, soft power is a growing threat. The United States has been among world leaders in terms of requesting that social media and other websites remove what it considers offensive or harmful content. The U.S. government has also pressured private intermediaries to refuse to carry content or provide services to speakers and information providers. I suggest in Chapter 5 that there may be situations when soft forms of censorship can prevent international violence. However, should it be used frequently and without compelling justification, soft censorship could create an informal system of cross-border information suppression.

There may be some private remedies for soft censorship. Yochai Benkler has suggested the possibility of private law contract and tort actions against intermediaries for wrongful denial of service.[112] Courts could also apply more flexible state action rules in cases where public officials are involved in producing the service denial. However, these claims are longshots under current law. The goal, as Benkler has observed, is to protect "a right to communicate and not to be unreasonably excluded from services critical to achieving that end."[113] U.S. policymakers are in the best position to ensure that the right to communicate in global forums is protected and that online content is not censored or suppressed through the exercise of soft power except in the most extraordinary circumstances.

Owing to First Amendment and international principles of free expression, U.S. officials ought to promote and facilitate the global free flow of information. As they do so, officials must understand that the infrastructure erected in one part of the world's interconnected system of marketplaces will not be hermetically contained within a single nation's borders. Rather, changes to this infrastructure will affect the free flow of information across many nations' territorial borders. As Secretary of State Hillary Clinton has observed, "The new iconic infrastructure of our age is the Internet. Instead of division, it stands for connection." U.S. policymakers ought to focus on preserving and facilitating this connection.

DOMESTICATING CROSS-BORDER ASSOCIATION

Americans participate in common causes with aliens around the world. For many of the same reasons, discussed earlier, for protecting cross-border communication, citizens ought to enjoy full First Amendment rights to associate and collaborate with aliens located abroad. The ability to commingle across international borders is a central First Amendment concern and an integral aspect of emerging norms of global citizenship.

As noted earlier, courts have not embraced this view of cross-border association. I will present a fuller critique of *Humanitarian Law Project*, in particular its treatment of enemy-aiding speech, in Chapter 5. Here I want to focus on the Supreme Court's rather minimal treatment of the freedom of association.

As I noted earlier, the Court appropriately rejected the government's contention that associating with members of a designated foreign terrorist organization for the purpose of advising and assisting the organization was a form of pure conduct. To that extent, the Court rejected the methodology of judicial quasi-recognition of cross-border First Amendment liberties. However, although the Court purported to apply strict scrutiny to the material support laws, it deferred substantially to asserted governmental national security and foreign affairs interests and departed from settled First Amendment doctrine regarding the criminalization of mere association. Indeed, the decision rests on a principle of guilt-by-association. The Court held that coordinated activities could be criminalized even if the participants did not embrace or specifically intend to further the foreign terrorist organizations' alleged criminal ends.

The "membership card" version of cross-border association recognized by the Court in *Humanitarian Law Project* is a denuded variant of the domestic freedom of association. As I observed earlier, the Court strongly suggested that the government could not impose similar burdens on *domestic* association rights. Although cross-border association does raise some distinct regulatory challenges, there is no compelling justification for categorically placing cross-border association at the First Amendment's periphery.

David Cole, who represented the respondents in *Humanitarian Law Project*, has offered some possible justifications for the Court's suggestion that domestic and cross-border associations occupy different First Amendment positions.[114] Cole's central purpose in doing so was not to defend the Court's decision, but rather to ensure that *Humanitarian Law Project* remained limited in scope and did not substantially restrict domestic speech and associational liberties. Despite his efforts, I argue that the foreign-domestic distinction does not survive close scrutiny.

Cole first observes that the government has imposed special restrictions on foreign entities and has even limited citizens' travel and access to alien speakers.[115] Although it is true that the government has burdened citizens' access to aliens and cross-border association, for reasons I have already suggested these limits are themselves suspect.

Cole also notes that treating domestic associations differently from "foreign" ones might reconcile *Humanitarian Law Project* and Supreme Court precedents invalidating restrictions on "domestic" Communist Party membership.[116] But referring to these associations as "foreign" ignores their important cross-border character. What the government is actually restricting is citizens' ability to participate in otherwise lawful associations with aliens who happen to be located abroad. Nor is the characterization of the Communist Party as a "domestic" organization clearly correct. Congress certainly viewed the communist threat as one emanating, in the first instance, from abroad. In any event, the Communist Party precedents did not invoke any foreign–domestic distinction.

Cole offers three other reasons why the purported foreign–domestic distinction suggested in *Humanitarian Law Project* may withstand scrutiny and serve to support granting greater protection to domestic associations. First, he suggests that enforcement of the material support laws might be analogized to diplomatic sanctions.[117] This is a variation of one of the government's arguments – namely, that enforcement of the material support laws would serve foreign affairs and diplomatic interests. However, the material support laws do not actually regulate *diplomacy* with a foreign nation. Instead, they directly restrict the ability of citizens to associate with private parties who, again, happen to be located beyond U.S. borders.[118]

Second, Cole argues that cross-border association lies closer to the periphery than to the core of the First Amendment's concern with self-government.[119] For the reasons I have discussed in this and previous chapters, the focus on domestic self-governance is too narrow in a digitized and globalized era. Cross-border association and commingling serve many of the same First Amendment functions as cross-border speech. We ought not to base differential treatment of cross-border association on provincial conceptions of self-governance.

Third, Cole posits that the risk of governmental censorship of political speech is greatest where domestic associations are regulated.[120] Again, the focus on domestic political expression is unduly narrow. In any event, the United States has a long and unfortunate history of censoring foreign persons, ideas, and associations. Thus, there is in fact a very real danger of political censorship in cross-border contexts. Indeed, any time the government is allowed to target disfavored groups for the purpose of making them radioactive or untouchable, the specter of political censorship is present. Preventing citizens from engaging in political or other dialogue with aliens beyond U.S. shores is a form of political censorship.

Finally, Cole suggests that the foreign–domestic distinction might be defended on the ground that foreign organizations are generally more difficult to regulate because they operate beyond U.S. jurisdiction and do not have domestic assets that can be seized.[121] Although the regulatory challenges are certainly more acute with regard to foreign organizations, this does not justify criminalization of citizens' overtures to and contacts with them. First Amendment protection for domestic association is not justified by the availability of other means for controlling local organizations, including seizure of their assets. Rather, it is premised on the importance of the activity of associating with others in furtherance of common causes. An increasing number of these causes and associations now cross territorial borders.

In sum, the suggested distinctions between domestic and cross-border associations mischaracterize the nature of the collaborations at issue and are based on provincial assumptions regarding the First Amendment's core and periphery.[122] I share Cole's desire to preserve domestic association rights in the wake of *Humanitarian Law Project.* However, instead of singling out cross-border associations for special disadvantages, we ought to domesticate freedom of association such that it protects the widest possible variety of associations and organizations. The First Amendment ought to be interpreted in a manner that facilitates meaningful cross-border associations, not hollow membership-card relationships.

5   FALSELY SHOUTING FIRE IN A GLOBAL THEATER

Justice Oliver Wendell Holmes, Jr. once wrote that "the most stringent protection of free speech would not protect a man in falsely shouting fire in a theater and causing a panic."[1] Primarily as a result of the Internet and its emerging virtual spaces, a new global theater has emerged. The geographic contours of this theater extend far beyond U.S. territorial borders. Indeed, owing to globalization and the digitization of communication, the global soapbox the Supreme Court referred to in 1999, when striking down Congress's first attempt to restrict speech on the Internet, has now largely materialized.[2] Speakers' voices and the effects of an increasing number of expressive activities now frequently traverse territorial borders, entering a global theater that spans vast portions of the globe.[3]

Some of the expressive activity in the global theater is dangerous or potentially harmful. Pastor Terry Jones of Gainesville, Florida, helped to ignite riots in Afghanistan when he put the Koran "on trial" and burned a copy of the holy book. Just a few years later, an American filmmaker ignited riots across the Middle East when he distributed on the Internet a movie trailer for *Innocence of Muslims*, which harshly denigrated Mohammed. Tarek Mehanna, a Sudbury, Massachusetts pharmacist, was convicted of providing material support to terrorists, primarily for posting translations of Al Qaeda materials on the Internet. A cartoonist in the United States was forced to go into hiding after she posted a comment on a website encouraging readers to participate in "Draw Mohammed Day." Anwar al-Awlaki, a Yemeni-American, was killed by a drone strike in Yemen on the order of President Obama based in part on the charge that he incited terrorist activity in the

United States and abroad. After Julian Assange, the publisher of the foreign website WikiLeaks, shared with several Western news outlets and posted on the Internet classified documents concerning American military operations in Iraq and Afghanistan and a trove of diplomatic cables, U.S. officials suggested that he should be treated as a terrorist or prosecuted under the Espionage Act of 1917.[4]

In Chapter 4, I argued that the First Amendment applies to and ought to protect fully various forms of cross-border conversation and commingling. There, I focused primarily on the virtues and benefits of cross-border conversation and commingling. However, hateful speech, enemy-aiding speech, and other forms of potentially harmful expression also increasingly traverse international borders. This chapter focuses on the more dangerous aspects of transborder conversation and commingling. In light of the emergence of the global theater, we need to revisit the relationship between the First Amendment's protection of expressive liberties and traditional governmental concerns regarding public disorder, incitement to unlawful actions, the provision of support to foreign enemies, and disclosure of official secrets. Does the First Amendment protect a speaker who falsely shouts fire in a global theater or offends citizens of foreign nations?

Does it permit prosecution of speakers who aid the enemy through speech activities? Does it apply to foreign-based websites that disclose U.S. secrets? In the global theater, maintaining robust protection for potentially harmful expression will affect audiences, cultures, and nations beyond U.S. shores. Whether, and to what extent, the First Amendment protects dangerous or potentially harmful expression in the global theater will have a significant effect on the extent of expressive freedom, not just in the United States, but across the globe as well. In considering whether it will retain exceptional protection for such expression, U.S. officials and citizens will be pressed to think more globally. They will need to consider the emerging global theater – a common space where conversation and commingling among the peoples of the world will become the norm. In most cases, I argue, a cosmopolitan perspective supports retention of First Amendment doctrines relating to potentially dangerous communications. However, the nature of the debate concerning the scope of and justification for expressive liberties in the twentieth century is changing. As I discuss in

Chapter 9, the United States faces an increasingly skeptical and rest-less world community that does not share its views regarding expres-sive liberties. In this century, Americans will need to mount a more effective defense of these exceptional views. That case can be made, but to this point it has not been adequately articulated by officials, courts, or commentators.

THE GLOBAL THEATER

A combination of factors has created a global theater where traditional lines between domestic and foreign speech marketplaces have blurred or begun to disappear.[5] These factors include expanded access to global communications networks; the development of technologies that allow end users easily and inexpensively to store, link to, and distribute digi-tized material; the proliferation of media outlets; and the characteristics of modern media and news cycles – in particular the tendency to focus intensely on the most controversial statements or events. The global the-ater offers all of the benefits of a shared conversational space. However, it has also created a distinct space in which new forms of global conflict and unique threats to the state have begun to materialize.

Digitization and Interconnectivity

As discussed in Chapter 4, global channels of speech and association have become tightly interconnected.[6] Indeed, global interconnectiv-ity is a signature characteristic of freedom of speech, association, and press in the twenty-first century.[7]

Digitization has facilitated interconnectivity, which has fundamen-tally changed the manner in which communication and information are disseminated. In the global theater, a speaker who intends to, or appears to be, addressing a discrete local community is often actually speaking to a global audience. Of course, cross-border communication flows in the opposite direction as well. Increasingly, foreign speech reaches the United States with the same relative ease and through the same or similar channels of communication.

This connectivity is often touted as a positive characteristic of the contemporary marketplace of ideas – and indeed it is. Global interconnectivity facilitates cosmopolitan First Amendment values. It facilitates self-governance on a global scale and contributes to transborder innovation and collaboration. As Jack Balkin has observed, because interconnectivity expands opportunities for public participation in creative and other endeavors, it leads to participation in and the spread of "democratic culture."[8] It also helps to expose Americans to distant cultures; broadens political, scientific, and cultural fields of inquiry and debate; and expands opportunities for transborder commingling.

These are all positive developments. However, interconnectivity can also produce serious dangers and harms. In the global theater, hateful and offensive expression flows freely across, and sometimes causes harm well beyond U.S. borders.[9] Some domestic expression may also aid or give comfort to U.S. enemies abroad. Citizens and aliens may be able to disseminate harmful information from distant locations. Conspiracies and other harmful associations may cross borders just as easily as humanitarian and other beneficial forms of commingling.

The digitization of communication complicates regulation of these and other types of potentially harmful expression and association. In many cases, speakers will be able to hide their locations and identities from authorities. Further, nations differ with regard to the extent of protection they afford to content such as hate speech and incitement.[10] Harmful expression that crosses the border from a nation where it is constitutionally protected cannot always be intercepted or suppressed in a receiving nation that does not afford the expression any constitutional or other protection.[11] Thus, for example, protected hate speech hosted on a U.S. website may also be available in France and Germany, where the distribution of such material is prohibited.[12] Such conflicts are part of a broader set of concerns relating to the intersection between the First Amendment and foreign expressive and religious laws or models.[13]

In sum, interconnectivity has helped to create a global theater or agora where citizens of various nations communicate with one another with relative ease. This shared space acts as a kind of digital "republic of letters" that crosses international borders.[14] However, some of this conversation will offend, incite, or otherwise negatively affect foreign audiences. In an increasing number of cases, it will lead to conflicts among cultures and nations that do not share the exceptional American perspective with regard to protecting certain harmful or offensive communications.

The Compression of Space and Time

In the global theater, the elements of communicative space and time are far more compressed than they are in traditional communication forums. Whereas it used to take days, weeks, or even longer for a local event or statement to have any impact beyond U.S. borders, in the global theater exposure and reaction occur quickly, sometimes instantaneously, across the world.

Owing to the existence of interconnected and compressed channels of communication, seemingly local and parochial concerns can instantly become subjects of global conflict. Thus, Pastor Jones's Koran burning produced not just local and national, but also robust international debate regarding tolerance for offensive and hateful expression. So did distribution of the *Innocence of Muslims* trailer, which generated worldwide controversy and some foreign riots. Similarly, opposition to the proposed construction of an Islamic center blocks from Ground Zero in Manhattan (the so-called "Ground Zero Mosque") was reported and commented on not only by news outlets in New York City and across the United States, but also by sources around the world.

As these examples show, in the global theater's transnational media echo chamber, local events may garner a level of attention that is out of all proportion to their actual significance. Further, although aliens located abroad may have little or no tangible or political connection to an event within the United States, local expression may quickly become a matter of concern to diverse global audiences and affect public order and security in distant nations.

Again, insofar as such conditions encourage and facilitate global dialogue and understanding, they ought to be celebrated. However, spatial and time compression may also lead to serious misunderstandings and global conflicts. Many recipients and audiences live in places that do not embrace America's exceptional First Amendment protection for hateful, offensive, and other harmful materials. Further, although many speakers and audiences share a common language, the danger of mistranslation and misunderstanding in the emerging global theater is quite real. Depending to some degree on the nature of national and international media coverage, foreign audiences might mistakenly assume that noisy domestic opposition to something like a proposed Islamic center communicates the sentiments of the public at large or even the U.S. government.

Compression of space and time may also lead to more tangible harms. In the digital era, audiences need not be physically present to be instantly aware of, or even psychologically affected or inflamed by, domestic communications. Audience members located in distant places and cultures across the world may experience physical and psychological effects as a result of communications within the United States. Thus, armed with nothing but an Internet connection, a U.S. speaker may be able to incite riots or other breaches of the peace thousands of miles away. In this environment, local expression may lead to physical injury, property damage, and even death in geographically dispersed locations throughout the world.

The State and De-Territorialized Speech

As I have observed, in the global theater even the most localized expression can produce global conflict, provoke foreign audiences, and cause distant harms. De-territorialized speech can also affect vital government interests relating to national security, foreign affairs, and diplomacy. This emerging reality will affect the manner in which governments perceive and seek to regulate expression in the global theater.

In the United States, pundits and commentators on both sides of the political spectrum regularly suggest that domestic protest and other speech will embolden U.S. enemies abroad, harm American troops, undermine national interests, or legitimize terrorism. Some commentators and politicians press this point even further and argue that some forms of domestic political dissent and protest are treasonous. Most, if not all, such claims are rightly dismissed as pure political rhetoric or hyperbole. Overblown and baseless charges of treason are nothing new in American politics.

Throughout U.S. history, domestic protest and offensive speech have posed some remote and indeterminate threat to foreign military operations and foreign relations. In the pre-global theater era, the claim that domestic political speech would actually provide some concrete or meaningful assistance to foreign enemies generally seemed farfetched.

However, in the digital era, such claims may be more difficult to dismiss. For example, in an extraordinary (perhaps unprecedented) gesture, President Obama publicly warned that Terry Jones's plan to burn a copy of the Koran, which was clearly protected in the United States by the First Amendment's Free Speech Clause, would nevertheless be a "recruitment bonanza" for Al Qaeda and indeed could "greatly endanger our young men and women in uniform who are in Iraq, who are in Afghanistan."[15]

On what basis might Jones's offensive speech be considered a real threat to U.S. national security or military operations abroad? As noted, communications in the global theater traverse international borders with relative ease. Moreover, these communications are not only more likely to reach terrorists and other enemies abroad, but to reach them in forms that are useful to violent causes. A video file of a Koran burning, or of a domestic protest in the United States, can easily become a hyperlink on a foreign terrorist's website. In terms of recruitment and propaganda, the link could provide a form of immediate aid. Similarly, a digitized file of confidential information that is made available on the Internet could be instantly downloaded by enemy forces on foreign battlefields. Access to this information could increase the potential for harm to U.S. troops and military assets abroad.

Americans frequently associate and collaborate with foreign-based organizations and institutions. The United States has sought to criminalize certain forms of contact between American citizens and foreign organizations with suspected links to terrorism. According to the U.S. government, speech that merely puts such organizations in a positive light could embolden foreign enemies and threaten national security.[16] The Internet creates new opportunities for citizens to communicate supportive messages or information about such groups. Some of these communications may pose distinct threats to national security.

Further, in the global theater, even local communications could conceivably affect foreign relations. In the context of support for foreign terrorist organizations, the American government voiced concerns about how foreign allies might react were the United States to allow its citizens to interact with such groups. Federal officials have also weighed in on domestic conflicts with international implications. In addition to speaking out publicly concerning Pastor Jones, President

Obama also voiced public support for a developer's right to build an Islamic center in Manhattan.[17] These statements were directed not merely or primarily to domestic audiences, but also to foreign audiences who were paying close attention, in real time, to events in lower Manhattan.

From the state's perspective, communications in the emerging global theater will create new regulatory and rule of law challenges. In responding to new threats, officials will not always be able to rely on traditional regulatory methods. Government officials may increasingly be tempted to rely on extrajudicial regulatory mechanisms, such as mass surveillance, private censorship, and perhaps more lethal methods such as targeted killing. But in some instances, owing to the existence of a vast distributed and interconnected network, both traditional and newer methods of restricting dissemination of secret or harmful expression may prove futile.

BREACHES OF PEACE IN THE GLOBAL THEATER

First Amendment doctrines relating to breaches of peace and public disorder were developed in domestic forums, where speakers and audiences shared both physical spaces and cultural norms. We must now decide what perspective or orientation to adopt with regard to offensive and potentially harmful speech that is disseminated in a global theater. Specifically, in this new environment how, if at all, ought speakers, courts, and government officials to take foreign effects and reactions into account?

Global Incitement

Suppose that an American speaker specifically intends to incite violence or unlawful activity beyond U.S. borders. Suppose, further, that the speech does not fall under the statutory definition of "material support" provided to designated foreign terrorist organizations, as discussed later. Whether a speaker can be punished for nonproximate, indeed extraterritorial, incitement is an unresolved First Amendment question. How that question is answered may affect the extent to which political and other forms of speech can be conveyed both in the United States and in the global theater.

Under First Amendment doctrine, the categorical treatment of "incitement" as unprotected expression mediates a basic tension between allowing speakers to express political viewpoints and the power of the state to protect citizens, and the state itself, from violence and unlawful actions.[18] Under the incitement standard, speech advocating violence or other criminal action cannot be suppressed unless it is "directed to inciting or producing imminent lawless action and is likely to incite or produce such action."[19] Relative to the laws of other nations, this is an extraordinarily speech-protective standard. Whether it can or will remain so in the global theater is a critical question.

How might the incitement standard apply in this distinct theater? Under the incitement doctrine, as a speaker comes ever closer to steeling an audience to actual violence, the state's interest in regulation becomes correspondingly stronger. As the Supreme Court once observed, the state is not required to wait for the "putsch" to actually occur.[20] Rather, it may take action to secure its assets, interests, and institutions prior to the first shot being fired or the first act in furtherance of a riot or other unlawful act. In other words, speakers do not have a First Amendment right to expressly encourage imminent harm or violence where it is likely to occur. To paraphrase Justice Holmes, a speaker who falsely shouts fire in a theater, causing a potential riot or other disturbance, is not entitled to First Amendment protection.[21]

From the early twentieth century to the present, the violence and unlawful activity in incitement cases decided by the Supreme Court was relatively close at hand. Under twentieth-century sedition, antiradicalism, and other national security laws, federal and state officials generally sought to control expression that was intended to arouse a local and physically proximate audience to unlawful conduct or violence. To be sure, in some early wartime incitement cases, the potential for disruption of military operations and threats to execution of U.S. objectives and missions abroad were key considerations. However, the overriding concern was not with remote deserters, foreign communists, or radical terrorist cells operating in foreign nations. The assets, interests, and institutions threatened by antiwar and communist propaganda were typically located inside the United States.[22] The proximate and "imminent" threats related to the orderly conduct of the domestic draft, continued production of domestic munitions, and the survival of state and local governments.

Suppose that the harm is likely to occur, if at all, only in some distant location thousands of miles from U.S. shores. Does the incitement doctrine apply to expression that is intended to and likely will produce such effects? Could a speaker located in the United States be prosecuted for inciting violence or unlawful acts halfway around the world? What effect would this sort of liability have on the development of the Internet and the global theater?

These questions made little sense in a world where communication traveled slowly, if at all, across territorial borders. However, owing to interconnectivity and the compression of space and time, whether a speaker could be prosecuted and punished for something we might call global incitement is now both a relevant and, it turns out, a close question.[23]

In the digital era, it might be possible to treat some expression disseminated across interconnected global networks as a form of unlawful incitement. As a result of digitization, it is more difficult to draw clear lines between purely domestic or proximate, and foreign or distant, threats to public order. Moreover, digitized expression now includes not only text, but also images and sophisticated forms of videography. In the global theater, seemingly distant threats may be clearer and more vividly and realistically present – despite their considerable distance from the speaker – and more proximate in terms of space and time.

Thus, assuming the speaker intends by express advocacy to incite a foreign audience to unlawful action and that such action can indeed be shown by the government to be both imminent and likely to occur, U.S. authorities could restrict or prevent the communications in an effort to prevent foreign riots, disturbances, damages, or unlawful acts likely to harm U.S. assets, personnel, or interests abroad.[24] This means that, in some cases, a speaker located within the United States could be punished under an incitement theory for communicating certain information or materials on the Internet.[25]

However, under the current incitement standard, such prosecutions are likely to be rare. The requirements of imminence and likelihood of harm impose serious constraints on governmental regulation of incitement in domestic forums.[26] Where the target audience and

danger are located abroad, authorities would have to engage in preci-
sion surveillance and have nearly impeccable timing. To demonstrate
imminent harm, the domestic speaker who intends to incite violence in
Afghanistan or Yemen may have to be apprehended at the moment or
just before he clicks "send." A perhaps more serious challenge would
be proving that foreign recipients were ready to participate in imminent violence or unlawful activity once the expression was communicated abroad. Interconnectivity makes it easier to communicate across
international borders. However, the requirements of imminence and
likelihood of harm pose serious obstacles to prosecuting digitally facilitated global incitement.

Thus, under the current incitement standard, charges and convictions would not likely have much effect on speech in domestic forums
or in the global theater. However, some jurists and academics have
questioned whether the traditional incitement standard is workable
in the digital era, particularly in light of the threats posed by online
terrorist expression.[27] The potential physical and diplomatic harms
associated with extraterritorial incitement could provide additional
impetus for challenging or altering the incitement standard. U.S. legislators could enact a broader proscription on advocacy of unlawful
action on the Internet, and courts might ultimately be convinced to
uphold such a law.

It is no secret that other nations deplore the U.S. incitement standard and that many would cheer such a result. The laws of other nations
take a different approach to incitement. Governments in many nations
have more latitude to restrict terrorist advocacy. Many view the incitement standard as creating a haven for global hate speech. This charge
cannot be easily dismissed. Indeed, a more cosmopolitan perspective regarding First Amendment rights forces us to acknowledge the
adverse global effects of American free speech exceptionalism.

Terrorism itself is a shared, global threat. Accordingly, some have
urged U.S. cooperation in developing a unitary incitement standard.
The difficulty, as other scholars have noted, is that it is not at all clear
that the problem of terrorist advocacy can be resolved by unilateral
changes in U.S. speech standards and doctrines. Even if the United
States weakened its incitement standard, the distinct problem of online
terrorist speech would not be magically eradicated.[28] Indeed, nothing

short of an international treaty or other agreement is likely to be effective in terms of reducing global extremist expression.[29] The likelihood that even established democratic nations can or would eventually agree on a single standard for incitement is not great.

All of this assumes that the incitement standard is indefensible in the global theater. It will no longer do for Americans to rest on assumptions. It is possible to state a convincing case that on balance, the incitement standard will contribute to more open cross-border conversation and dialogue in that theater. The First Amendment incitement standard was specifically calibrated to protect criticism of government and advocacy of unpopular viewpoints, particularly during times of global conflict and turmoil.[30] The United States, like other nations, is facing new "fighting faiths" in an unprecedented global war.[31] The implications for political speech are similar to those Americans addressed in the early and mid-twentieth century. When considering a broad proscription of online terrorist rhetoric and advocacy, the United States ought to draw on its historical experience and the lessons of a long history of governmental efforts to suppress mere advocacy.

Americans know, from experience, that a broad proscription on Internet or other forms of advocacy would diminish speakers' ability to participate in global conversations regarding their own and foreign governments, religious creeds and doctrines, war, and a variety of other matters of global public concern. It would also diminish domestic and cross-border conversation and information flow. During formative twentieth century American free speech conflicts, citizens' ability to participate in self-governance and engage with foreign persons and ideologies was sharply restricted. American officials are rightly hesitant to impose such restrictions in the still-developing global theater.

Just as the initial development of the incitement standard shaped the contours of domestic and, to some degree, international speech rights, how the United States responds to online advocacy will significantly influence the scope of political freedoms in the global theater. Thus, despite the refuge it provides for some terrorist advocacy, the preservation of the First Amendment incitement standard is arguably critical to the development of a free and robust global theater. Without it, or something like it, the Internet and the larger global theater would be subject to controls that have not applied in traditional theaters. This is a dangerous experiment to undertake, given the relatively recent emergence of a global theater.

If it is going to defend and explain retention of its exceptional incitement standard, the United States ought to address the matter in global rather than purely domestic terms. Rather than insisting on exceptionalism for its own sake or as a matter of national sovereignty, the United States ought to defend this choice in more universal or global terms. The argument, in general terms, would proceed as follows: The incitement standard creates much-needed digital breathing space for the distribution of political speech across international borders. We know from experience that this is more likely than repressive foreign and international standards to facilitate global information flow. We still do not know precisely what the Internet will become. Until we do, however, we ought to preserve something like *Brandenburg*'s speech-protective incitement standard.

Global Offense and Insult

Breaches of global peace might arise in other contexts. As noted earlier, in the global theater, local conversations and concerns will increasingly become flashpoints for global conflicts. In some cases, these conflicts will produce harmful, perhaps even deadly, extraterritorial effects. Many foreign audiences will be deeply offended, even psychologically harmed, by speech originating in the United States. How, if at all, ought we to take these foreign effects and reactions into account?

Speakers, private actors, and nation-states are just beginning to address some of the complexities that arise when offensive and insulting speech enters a common space where a multitude of speech standards apply. In Chapter 9, I address these conflicts in greater detail. Here, I will offer general and preliminary observations concerning the regulation of offensive and insulting speech in the global theater.

U.S. speakers sometimes specifically intend to court global controversy and cause international offense. Consider again Pastor Jones's Koran burning, or the posting of the *Innocence of Muslims* trailer. Both incidents were linked to international rioting. In both instances, the content was subject to criminal prosecution, even punishment of death, in many nations. In contrast, under settled First Amendment doctrine, the burning of religious items and insults to religion are protected speech.[32] Under the First Amendment, speech does not lose its protection merely because an audience reacts negatively or even violently to it.[33] Nor, under current First Amendment standards, can offensive domestic expression be restricted or suppressed on the grounds that it will upset international leaders or complicate foreign affairs.[34] Offense and hurt feelings, whether experienced by domestic or foreign audiences, are simply not sufficient to outweigh the right to free speech. Instead, Americans have long relied primarily on counter-speech as the preferred means of dealing with offensive and insulting content.

Of course, the United States could reduce or even eliminate legal protection for offensive and insulting expression. For example, the United States could, as many nations have suggested, criminalize certain kinds of deeply insulting expression. The case for doing so is not as weak as sometimes assumed. As with incitement, we can no longer simply pretend that First Amendment exceptionalism has no effect on the rest of the world. From the perspective of many foreign audiences, First Amendment standards fail to show proper respect for cultural, racial, religious, and other core human characteristics. Citizens and officials in foreign nations complain, with some justification, that the First Amendment's exceptional protection for hateful and insulting expression has created a haven for hate groups, who broadcast and communicate their messages with impunity from within the United States.[35] The chorus of foreign criticism has been echoed by some American legal scholars, who argue that free speech doctrine overvalues speaker autonomy at the expense of human dignity and other important values.[36]

American citizens and officials must seriously engage these arguments. They need to ask what, if any, justifications exist for retaining robust protection for offensive and insulting expression in a global theater where speakers share a common space and speech routinely traverses territorial boundaries. Again, as Americans think about this question, they ought to think not only of the impact on their own domestic speech rights, but also about the future contours and characteristics of the global theater.

Allowing a foreign heckler or some distant hostile audience to suppress offensive domestic expression would significantly diminish speakers' ability to convey emotional appeals and to arouse passions among audiences in the global theater. Suppressing local speech based on foreign audiences' negative reactions would also limit, perhaps severely, the ability to convey political messages in this emerging theater. It would allow foreign hecklers to impose the most restrictive speech standards on the rest of the world.[37]

In the global theater, there is no shortage of counter-speech outlets available to the aggrieved and insulted. Protection for offensive and insulting expression can facilitate multicultural conversation and exchange. To be sure, owing to differences in cultural and legal norms, conversations and encounters in the global theater will sometimes be tense and unpleasant. As in local forums, difference and diversity can lead to misunderstanding, conflict, and even occasional fits of violence. However, these things can also lead to transnational understanding and even a degree of empathy.

Thus, for example, American communities witnessed the deeply felt reactions to the Koran burning across the world. At the same time, foreign audiences observed the manner in which counter-speech in the United States marginalized, condemned, and eventually ostracized offensive speakers without the necessity of legal sanction or resort to mob violence. The conversation that ensued in the wake of this incident revealed an international consensus that the symbolic act had little social value.

The Koran controversy also demonstrated the different processes by which communities regulate things such as offense and psychic harm. Even if no community is ever convinced to adopt the other's approach, there will at least have been opportunity for dialog regarding freedom of speech and comparative constitutional values. Suppressing offensive speech in the United States would ignore deeply ingrained cultural differences. It would also drive expressive diversity, which allows for experimentation, comparison, and learning, out of the global theater.

Assuming, as is almost certain, that the United States will retain its exceptional protections for offensive and insulting speech content, it is important that its citizens and officials explain these justifications clearly, carefully, and with respect, to the rest of the world. For too long, this has not been the American approach. For much of its history, the United States has not felt obligated at all to explain or defend free speech exceptionalism to global audiences. However, this obligation follows directly from the harm that can ensue in the global theater from certain kinds of expression emanating from the United States. It follows, as well, from the fact that, in the global theater, no nation's law regarding harmful speech reigns supreme.

The First Amendment is a unique part of our law, but it is not the law of the global theater. We cannot insist that other nations simply accept American free speech standards and the harms they sometimes produce. However, the United States does have the unique advantage of more than two hundred years of experience in terms of responding to and regulating various forms of harmful expression. Thus, the most important function of the First Amendment as it concerns the global theater may be educative – that is, what it can teach the world about things such as tolerance, transparency, and self-governance. With regard to offensive and insulting expression, the central value it teaches is respect for pluralism. That value is critically important in an emerging global space where forbearance, tolerance, and respect for a diversity of speech laws and cultures will be necessary to preserve global peace.

In an address to the United Nations following the *Innocence of Muslims* controversy, President Obama offered at least a partial defense of American free speech exceptionalism. He explained to the assembled world leaders that, "in a diverse society, efforts to restrict speech can become a tool to silence critics, or oppress minorities."[38] These, he explained, are universal concerns. Moreover, as the president explained, "when anyone with a cell phone can spread offensive views around the world with the click of a button, the notion that we can control the flow of information is obsolete."[39] President Obama overstates this point, particularly in terms of the obsolescence of state control over information flow. However, his general sentiments capture the core costs of suppressing potentially harmful content in the global theater.

In the interest of world peace and security, we must find ways to manage global conflict stemming from offensive and insulting expression. One potential nonstate solution is for entities such as social media sites, which now provide and to some degree control the channels of global communication, to selectively block access to offending content. Foreign officials have asked social media sites such as Twitter, Facebook, and YouTube to block offensive material that is not in compliance with their speech laws. Twitter has granted requests by German

officials to block access to Nazi feeds. YouTube has blocked access to
blasphemous materials, including the *Innocence of Muslims* trailer, in
certain Islamic nations.

In Chapter 4, I noted that site blocking and other soft means of
censorship are becoming more prevalent and that frequent and unjus-
tified resort to this form of suppression poses an emerging challenge
to global information flow. The simple fact is that in situations where
offensive speech is transmitted in the global theater, private intermediaries will shoulder more of the burden when it comes to regulating
global information flow and maintaining global peace. If exercised in
a tailored and responsible manner and without governmental command or undue pressure, private blocking could ease some tensions
in the global theater. In certain instances, including the *Innocence of
Muslims* episode, private intermediaries have shown that they can help
reduce international conflicts by selectively blocking access to offensive communications.

However, this is a partial and imperfect solution. Among other things,
it places responsibility for protecting freedom of speech and press almost
exclusively in the hands of private intermediaries. These businesses are
not currently bound by constitutional requirements and often make
blocking decisions based on very broad and vague standards. Moreover,
if private censorship is not limited or regulated in some way, it could be
used to censor criticism of government officials. This is an acute danger
in authoritarian nations. However, it remains a legitimate concern even
in liberal democracies including the United States.

Selective suppression by private U.S.-based intermediaries will not
eliminate the dissemination of offensive material to nations that do not
wish to receive it. Nevertheless, it does provide an imperfect means of
retaining U.S. speech protections while still showing some respect for
the disparate laws and cultures of other nations. Despite its dangers,
private censorship could help to preserve global peace during periods
of especially high tension. At certain times, it may reduce the potential
for violence and other social harms. If used sparingly and judiciously,
limited private suppression may be preferable to hard forms of government censorship.

Internet intermediaries are not the only critical private parties in
the new global theatre. Some of the burden of reducing or avoiding

conflict in the global theater will fall on speakers themselves. Speakers located in the United States must be aware that, in the digital age, their words and actions will more frequently be conveyed to worldwide audiences. Communications transmitted on the Internet may be intentionally broadcast across the globe. However, even speech and symbolic activity that may initially be intended only for local consumption might be transmitted through various media outlets into the global theater.

American speakers must understand that they are participating in a different kind of global dialog. Thus, they must consider the possibility that local expression will reach and offend foreign audiences. Regardless of whether such speech remains protected under U.S. laws, this new reality could affect the content and form of domestic communications.

In traditional speech contexts, a speaker communicates with the knowledge that relevant audiences share certain legal and cultural norms. She typically chooses her forum and audience. She is usually able to see, hear, or at least envision audiences, and to gauge their characteristics and likely reactions. By contrast, in the global theater, speakers will generally lack such contextual cues. In many cases, it will be difficult or impossible to gauge how a message will or is likely to be received.

As a result, speakers who address controversial matters in the global theater will speak with an added measure of uncertainty regarding hostile foreign reaction. Among other things, they may be concerned about threats to personal safety emanating from abroad. Recall in this regard the American cartoonist who was forced into hiding when she received threats for encouraging others to post drawings of the Prophet Mohammed on the Internet.

Where domestic speakers face specific and tangible threats from abroad, American officials ought to offer some form of protection against physical harm from hostile audiences.[40] However, because officials cannot generally provide protection from hostile foreign audiences, speakers will sometimes face difficult decisions regarding what to convey in the global theater. Speaking in the global theater may require either an added degree of fortitude or, in some cases, a different calculus regarding whether to convey certain highly offensive messages.

Just as it is appropriate and necessary for speakers to consider the nature of local audiences, so too might they now have to account for diverse global listeners. These audiences do not generally share a commitment to protecting blasphemous and other forms of insulting or hateful expression. American speakers are not currently required to alter the content of their speech in response to potential global reactions or threats. However, in the global theater, they may feel increased pressure or even a sense of obligation to do so. In the interest of respecting foreign cultures or avoiding international insult, a more cosmopolitan perspective on the exercise of free speech rights could lead to a degree of forbearance or message alteration.

ENEMY-AIDING EXPRESSION

In the global theater, it will be easier for speakers, from both domestic and foreign locations, to assist, aid, or lend legitimacy to terrorists and other U.S. enemies. In the text that follows I examine a category of communication, *enemy-aiding expression*, that raises some unique challenges in the global theater. I define the category as follows: Any expression by a U.S. citizen that (1) aids or furthers the causes of enemies of the state[41] by (2) (a) lending legitimacy to enemy causes or organizations; (b) materially assisting enemies in carrying out their objectives; or (c) providing enemies with treasonous "Aid and Comfort."[42] As I explain in the sections that follow, this category includes domestic rhetoric and political dissent, the provision of material support to foreign terrorists, cyber-treason, and remote forms of incitement and terrorist advocacy.

Domestic Dissent

Especially during wartime or other national emergencies, domestic dissent, incendiary rhetoric, and even praise for national enemies and their causes could conceivably assist U.S. enemies abroad. Recall, for example, that according to President Obama and other high-level cabinet and military officials, Pastor Jones's plan to burn a copy of the Koran was likely to serve as a "recruitment bonanza" for Al Qaeda and other U.S. enemies.

In the global theater, domestic dissent could assist, embolden, or legitimize foreign enemies in some unique ways. Speeches by antiwar political candidates, statements denigrating Islam as a corrupt or violent faith, and editorials that defend the basic rights of enemy combatants or foreign terrorist groups all can be broadcast around the globe in a matter of seconds. This content can reach global audiences, including foreign enemies, in forms that can be put to instant propaganda or other harmful uses.

Under settled First Amendment principles, government does not have the authority to suppress domestic political expression on the ground that it might indirectly provide aid to the nation's enemies.[43] Indeed, this is the case even if a domestic speaker specifically intends by his rhetoric, dissent, or symbolic act to undermine American foreign or domestic interests.[44] As Eugene Volokh has observed, under the First Amendment, "much speech that does help the enemy must remain constitutionally protected."[45]

In the global theater, there is an increased risk that domestic speech may be useful to foreign enemies. However, this marginally greater risk is not sufficient to reduce or eliminate First Amendment protection for domestic political dissent.

Indeed, protection for domestic political dissent and rhetoric is as important in the global theater as it is in traditional domestic forums. Citizens are increasingly communicating in virtual spaces that are readily accessible to global audiences, often with the intent that those audiences be part of the exchange. Thus, domestic dissent may inform not just domestic debates but global ones as well.

Further, as in domestic forums, U.S. citizens ought to be permitted to criticize their officials and debate international issues such as war, religion, and terrorism in the global theater, without fear of reprisal. Insofar as American officials are concerned that domestic dissent will feed anti-American sentiment and aid enemies abroad, they can readily address global audiences, clarify U.S. policy, and use other measures short of suppression to assuage such concerns.

Providing "Material Support" to Foreign Terrorists

As discussed in Chapter 4, U.S. citizens interact with aliens beyond American borders in various political, humanitarian, religious, cultural, and other endeavors. I have argued that a First Amendment right to engage in cross-border association ought to be fully recognized and enforced. Of course, this right is not absolute. For example, cross-border criminal conspiracies and other illegal forms of commingling can be suppressed and punished.

Some cross-border relationships will involve persons or groups that the U.S. government considers a threat to national security. Under federal law, the United States designates certain groups "foreign terrorist organizations." It is current U.S. policy to render such groups radioactive, or essentially untouchable.

In *Holder v. Humanitarian Law Project*, the Supreme Court upheld federal laws barring the provision of "material support," including expert advice and assistance, to such groups. The Court held that these provisions do not violate the First Amendment's freedom of speech or freedom of association guarantees, either facially or as applied to speech that is "coordinated" with such groups.[46] This was so, the Court held, even if the speakers do not specifically intend to further the organizations' illegal and violent enterprises.

The speech and association at issue in *Humanitarian Law Project* consisted of advising and training foreign groups, including the Kurdistan Workers' Party and the Tamil Tigers, regarding peaceful and lawful means of resolving their political grievances.[47] For example, a group of U.S. citizens wanted to teach such groups how to file petitions with the United Nations.[48]

Humanitarian Law Project is a troubling precedent.[49] It does not even mention *Brandenburg's* speech-protective incitement standard, thus rendering this standard irrelevant to at least one class or category of cross-border communications. The decision is also in conflict with traditional First Amendment justifications, which emphasize a commitment to protecting peaceful political speech in the interest of self-governance and the search for truth.[50] Further, a long line of precedents prohibits the government from imposing content-based restrictions on citizens' relations with officially disfavored persons or groups or criminalizing mere association.[51] Yet *Humanitarian Law Project* places no burden on the government to demonstrate that citizens are actively and intentionally engaged in a joint venture with enemies of the state whose purpose is to inflict harm or produce violent conduct. Transformative twentieth century free speech battles, which tested restrictions on radical, socialist, and communist speech and association, taught that foreign ideologies ought to be met with robust counter-speech rather than governmental suppression. By contrast, *Humanitarian Law Project* effectively allows Congress to criminalize core political expression and association.

Moreover, the Court's application of a nonstandard form of deferential, but nominally heightened, scrutiny is inconsistent with the First Amendment's demanding incitement standard.[52] As noted earlier, the incitement standard creates a narrow category of speech that can be suppressed based on the speaker's intent to cause an imminent breach of the peace and the likelihood that the breach will occur. The organizations at issue had engaged in violent terrorist activity in the past. However, the speech at issue in *Humanitarian Law Project* did not advocate, nor did the speakers intend to produce, any criminal or violent act. Rather, as the government conceded and the Court acknowledged, defendants were engaged in otherwise lawful political discussion. The Court has held that such expression cannot be criminalized merely because it might aid a group in furtherance of its unlawful ends.[53] The speaker must have knowledge of the unlawful activity and intend to participate in it. *Humanitarian Law Project* does not require this sort of knowledge or specific intent.

Also troubling was the Court's conclusion that mere words could be treated as the functional equivalent of more tangible forms of assistance, such as the provision of funds or weapons.[54] Under this fungibility principle, the Court reasoned that speakers who provide assistance in the form of legal instruction or petition-filing are enabling foreign groups to channel organizational resources to more violent activities.[55] The operative assumption, as alleged by the government, is that terrorist organizations do not segregate their funds.[56] Thus, teaching the members of such organizations how to navigate international law and processes is essentially the functional equivalent of making a contribution to the organization's violent activities fund.[57] The Court also accepted the government's contention that designated foreign terrorist organizations working with American partners are typically engaged in tactical and opportunistic behavior. In other words, the groups engage in speech and associational activities that appear to advance lawful causes at the United Nations "as a means of buying time to recover from short-term setbacks, lulling opponents into complacency, and ultimately preparing for new attacks."[58]

The Court's analysis is inconsistent with the First Amendment's broad protection for potentially harmful expression. Expression and association have traditionally been treated as means of persuasion, rather than as potentially dangerous commodities some audience might use to violent ends. By treating words themselves as a form of material support, the Court further blurred the distinction between conduct and expression.[59] Under that distinction, while the government may freely regulate the tangible effects of harmful conduct, it must tread more carefully insofar as words and other expressive forms are concerned.[60] Further, the Court's analysis is inconsistent with the principle that speech may not be restricted or suppressed solely on the ground that an audience might use it for some improper purpose – including, presumably, for obfuscation or delay.[61]

Humanitarian Law Project rests on other disconcerting principles that could negatively affect cross-border expression and association. The Court concluded that peaceful and lawful political expression, when coordinated with a foreign terrorist organization, can be criminalized in part owing to its supposed tendency to lend "legitimacy" to terrorist causes.[62] However, it is difficult to distinguish criminally legitimating expression from some of the earlier-discussed domestic speech that praises, supports, or lends credence to the causes of national enemies. Indeed, the Court's legitimacy concern threatens to sweep in a large swath of otherwise protected political expression.[63] Like other aspects of the Court's analysis, it is inconsistent with precedents that forbid government from criminalizing speech on the ground that it might legitimize the causes of some disfavored group.[64]

As other scholars have noted, the distinctions the Court sought to draw between protected political speech and "material support" are rather thin and ultimately unconvincing.[65] The Court stressed that the material support prohibition did not apply to so-called "independent" political speech.[66] However, it failed to identify any clear limiting principle that would protect even the ordinary domestic enemy-aiding expression discussed earlier. As I noted previously, a substantial amount of domestic dissent and contention might be quite useful to foreign terrorist and other enemies. A video file of an American citizen burning the Koran could prove far more useful to Al Qaeda than a brief filed on its behalf in a U.S. court or a petition filed on its behalf at the United Nations.

Finally, the Court relied on broad foreign affairs and diplomacy justifications. It observed that United States allies might "react sharply" if the government were to permit citizens to collaborate in even peaceful endeavors with common enemies.[67] One might think of this as a cosmopolitan consideration, a demonstration of concern or sensitivity regarding international opinion. A more careful reading suggests that the Supreme Court has taken a step toward recognizing a foreign affairs exception to the First Amendment.[68] As I explained earlier, foreign offense is not generally a valid basis for criminalizing domestic political speech. Nor is the mere fact that citizens' communications or associations with designated foreign terrorists might to some indeterminate degree complicate U.S. diplomacy a proper basis for suppressing speech based on its content.

In many respects, *Humanitarian Law Project* is a provincial First Amendment decision. It departs from fundamental doctrines, principles, and precedents that are fully applicable in domestic forums. While purporting to apply strict scrutiny, it defers to the government's national security and foreign relations concerns. The Court also posits a foreign–domestic distinction with respect to First Amendment freedoms that suggests full constitutional protection applies only to intraterritorial communications and associations. Further, the decision essentially adopts Congress's skeptical perspective that exchange with certain foreign groups is generally dangerous or, in any event, not "all to the good."[69] Indeed, the Court goes much further, treating speech that is coordinated with foreign organizations as the very sort of danger that the framers of the Constitution sought to protect against.[70] If interpreted and applied broadly, *Humanitarian Law Project* may discourage a variety of peaceful and otherwise lawful efforts to engage with foreign persons and groups in the global theater.

The decision could also have a broader effect on online and other communications in the global theater.[71] U.S. authorities have arrested and prosecuted citizens under the material support laws for engaging in online expression that the government contends is coordinated with and aids terrorists located abroad. In the beginning of this chapter, I briefly described the case of Tarek Mehanna, the Massachusetts pharmacist who was tried and convicted for conspiring to violate the material support laws. In significant part, Mehanna's conviction was premised on the overt act of translating videos and publications that promoted violent jihad.

As discussed in the next section, convictions for treasonous expression are very difficult to obtain. However, under the material support laws, prosecutors need not satisfy the strict requirements for proving treason. Instead, they may police and restrict online expression by alleging that a speaker has "coordinated" posts and other expressive activities with foreign terrorists, provided "services" such as translation and distribution of materials, and legitimized terrorist causes by disseminating information about their grievances, claims, and agendas.

Of course, in the global theater, any digital soapbox orator can lend credibility to terrorists or their causes by posting flattering or laudatory videos and other information on the Internet. As Mehanna's case demonstrates, the line between protected political advocacy and unprotected material support is not clear. The case also shows the flexibility, or some might charge ambiguity, of the Court's requirement that speech be "coordinated" with foreign terrorists. It suggests that mere advocacy of or support for terrorist causes may result in convictions or guilty pleas under the material support laws.

It is critically important that the channels of communication between citizens and aliens, including even hostile aliens, remain as open as possible.[72] Of course, this does not mean that restrictions on such contacts are never appropriate or that cross-border conversation and commingling are always "to the good." However, any restrictions ought to be narrowly tailored to prevent only intentional efforts to further violent ends. Expansive interpretation and enforcement of the material support laws could chill online expression on matters of global concern. More generally, it would walk us backwards to a time in our First Amendment history when mere advocacy of controversial dogmas and claims was sufficient grounds for conviction and imposition of lengthy prison terms. Under a broad reading of the material support laws, citizens who did nothing more than translate and post Arabic materials, or praise the methods or goals of foreign terrorist organizations online, could be subject to arrest and conviction.

Even if, as some have urged, the Court will not limit the material support laws by applying *Brandenburg*'s speech-protective incitement standard and other time-tested First Amendment principles, Congress can take steps to preserve peaceful forms of cross-border conversation and commingling. First, legislators can adopt a clear standard with respect to "coordinated" expression. The standard ought to require some form of agency or other close working relationship between citizens and designated foreign terrorist groups. This would clarify which types of relationships or associations are covered, narrow the scope of the prohibition to the most dangerous and harmful joint enterprises, and ensure that "independent" domestic political expression is indeed not proscribed. Second, Congress ought to legislate an intent standard that would criminalize otherwise protected speech and association only when "the defendant knows or intends that those activities will assist the organization's unlawful terrorist actions."[73]

These amendments would bring the material support provisions more closely into line with longstanding First Amendment principles. As importantly, they would help to ensure that the global theater's channels of communication remain as open as possible, despite the real threat that terrorism poses to the global community.

Cyber-Treason

Treasonous speech is perhaps the quintessential form of enemy-aiding expression. Under the U.S. Constitution and federal law, any person owing allegiance to the United States who "adheres" to the enemy and through some "overt act" provides it with "Aid and Comfort" may be found guilty of treason.[74] Certain forms of speech favoring, or associations with, U.S. enemies may demonstrate treasonous adherence and/ or the provision of aid and comfort to the enemy.[75]

Treasonous expression might take many forms, including pure speech and symbolic acts. For example, a speaker who reveals state secrets to a foreign agent could be found guilty of treason.[76] A U.S. citizen who travels abroad and meets with foreign enemies, with the intent to harm U.S. interests at home or abroad, could be prosecuted for conspiracy to commit treason.[77] A citizen who travels abroad for the purpose of acting as a "human shield," and who interferes with a U.S. military campaign while doing so, may also be charged with treason.[78] These activities all arguably involve forms of conduct and material aid to state enemies.

In the digital age, federal treason laws could also be applied to Internet propaganda and other communications that lend support or aid to foreign enemies. Such communications might include posting or linking to speeches by terrorist groups and their leaders, distributing messages or information that support foreign enemies' violent or non-violent causes, and defending terrorists from criticism in Web postings or other communications.[79] The personal computer can be a uniquely effective propaganda tool. It allows the speaker to reach wide and dispersed audiences across the globe.

We have thus entered an era in which online treason, or cyber-treason, might be criminalized. The notion that a treason prosecution might be brought in such circumstances is not as far-fetched as it might sound.[80] During the World War II era, courts either held or strongly suggested that propaganda and other expression conveyed on behalf of U.S. enemies could support a treason conviction.[81] Under these precedents, a defendant's expression or expressive acts could demonstrate "adherence" to the enemy and constitute an "overt act" providing "aid and comfort."[82] *Humanitarian Law Project* lends additional support to the argument that even pure speech, if coordinated with U.S. enemies, could lay the foundation for a treason indictment.

Here, again, we confront a situation in which the state could respond to online activity by broadening criminal prohibitions on enemy-aiding speech. However, where the underlying overt act consists solely of speech that is favorable with regard to or legitimizes a foreign enemy, the United States ought not to bring, or even threaten to initiate, treason prosecutions. Several reasons support forbearance.

First, as constitutional scholars have observed, punishing pure speech or association as treason is inconsistent with the original understanding of the Treason Clause.[83] The framers and ratifiers of the Constitution clearly viewed the clause as a shield against prosecution for political expression. That protection remains vitally important not only in domestic forums, but also in the emerging global theater.

Second, modern interpretation of the crime of treason ought to reflect the arc of twentieth-century free speech precedents and doctrines. In particular, the comparatively speech-restrictive "clear and present danger" standard applied in the World War II–era treason cases has been replaced by a far more speech-protective incitement standard.[84] That standard, which requires that the government prove a speaker intended to cause imminent harm, does not permit prosecutions that are based on Internet or other communications that merely express support for foreign enemies.[85] In cases based on overt acts of expression, contemporary incitement doctrine ought to limit the scope of the Treason Clause.

Third, and more broadly, from the postwar period to the present, Supreme Court precedents have emphasized the need to protect citizens' freedom to criticize government and to engage in robust political debate.[86] Like other restrictions on potentially harmful expression, treason laws could have a significant effect on both domestic political expression and global information flow. Indeed, given the severe penalties associated with treason, this potential liability could chill vast amounts of online and other speech relating to foreign enemies, foreign affairs, and national security.[87]

It is true that, throughout American history, speech protection has been less robust during wartime.[88] However, this fact does not counsel in favor of criminalizing a broad category of cyber-propaganda or cyber-advocacy. The combination of the unconventional nature of the global war against terrorism and modern communications technologies poses a distinct threat to political expression. If we are going to preserve and protect political debate in the global theater, application of the treason laws, like application of the material support laws, must be based on something more than a speaker's expression of sympathy for enemies or the possibility that speech might aid their causes.

The principal objective is to avoid punishing pure speech and expressive associations that facilitate discussion regarding matters of domestic, international, and global concern. The best way to accomplish this objective is for courts to interpret the treason laws as applicable only when the government demonstrates a close, agency-type relationship between the defendant speaker and the foreign enemy.

Scholars disagree regarding the extent to which a speaker must be affiliated with an enemy of the state, such that prosecution for treason would satisfy First Amendment standards.[89] Global terrorist networks do not operate on a strict bureaucratic basis.[90] Thus, it may be difficult to determine who is aligned with or adhering to them. However, the factual predicates in the World War II–era cases provide a useful baseline. In those cases, speakers were involved in some kind of employment or agency relationships with enemy forces.[91] These relationships typically involved traveling to foreign countries, using enemy broadcast equipment, and taking specific instructions from foreign enemies.

In the digital era, propagandists need not travel abroad to aid foreign enemies. However, prosecutors should have to prove some overt act of employment or agency other than the posting of enemy-aiding speech on the Internet, independent translation of enemy messages, or the communication of statements that either advocate or praise terrorism. For example, the requisite relationship might be present where the speaker establishes a website at the request of an enemy organization or government, provides technical support for enemy propaganda efforts, or posts messages as specifically instructed by the enemy organization. These acts, which more closely resemble conduct – the provision of tangible assistance and material resources – than pure speech, could be used to establish the requisite collaboration between speaker and enemy. Speech in furtherance of the relationship, including the transmission of operational plans and technological and other information concerning bomb making, could also be considered as evidence of treasonous intent.

Under no circumstance, however, would speech that merely favors, praises, or offers ideological support for foreign enemies come within the domain of federal treason laws. Cross-border channels of communication facilitate self-governance and the global pursuit of knowledge. The mere fact that expression that criticizes government or praises enemies has been distributed across territorial borders provides further reason to protect such communications, rather than justification for extending U.S. treason laws to online political speech.

Remote Propagandizing and Incitement

Digitization makes it possible to communicate potentially harmful materials from anywhere in the world. Earlier, I discussed the U.S.-based speaker who intends to cause an imminent breach of peace abroad. Suppose instead that the speaker, a citizen, is located abroad.[92] From his remote and undisclosed location, the speaker distributes materials on the Internet, in which he advocates terrorist attacks on the United States and praises its enemies. Assuming, as I argue in Chapter 6, that the speaker may raise free speech claims even though his speech activities took place beyond U.S. borders, how ought U.S. officials to respond to this sort of enemy-aiding expression?

Officials could turn to traditional legal remedies. For example, in the case of a citizen who wishes to return to the United States at some point, it might be possible to revoke or threaten to revoke the speaker's passport.[93] Assuming the speaker could be captured, he could be prosecuted for incitement, material support, or some other crime. The problem with these options is that they assume the exercise of jurisdiction and control over the speaker. However, in the global theater, speakers can lob incendiary speech from afar and can often conceal their identities and locations.

Consider the case of Anwar al-Awlaki, who held dual Yemeni and U.S. citizenship. Al-Awlaki, who resided in Yemen, was accused by the U.S. government of inciting violence against American domestic and foreign interests. According to the information disclosed by the U.S. government, al-Awlaki posted videos and other materials on the Internet in which he advocated violence against the United States. Although the government claimed that al-Awlaki had provided more tangible forms of material aid to terrorists in the United States and abroad, those claims were never presented or proven before any judicial or other legal tribunal. Based on intelligence never shared with anyone outside the U.S. national security apparatus, the Obama Administration targeted al-Awlaki for execution. In a U.S. drone strike carried out in Yemen, al-Awlaki (along with another U.S. citizen against whom no criminal allegations had been made) was killed.

Al-Awlaki's killing raises a number of legal issues. Scholars have debated whether, with or without congressional approval, a president can issue such orders with respect to citizens. Targeted killings also raise Fifth Amendment due process concerns. Al-Awlaki was deprived of life without being afforded an opportunity to contest the charges in a criminal or military court. Further, it is not clear what standard the executive branch applies in determining whether to issue a targeted killing order. Finally, drone strikes on foreign soil also raise issues under the laws of armed conflict and international law.

Although they have received less attention, we ought to be mindful that targeted killings could raise First Amendment concerns. In cases involving terrorist advocacy, as opposed to more tangible forms of aid or conspiratorial conduct, it is not clear whether the requirements for unlawful incitement or some other proscribed category of speech apply or must be met. Whether issuance of an executive order directing the killing of a U.S. citizen living abroad for merely advocating violence in Internet postings violates the First Amendment is a question no court has ever faced and no scholar has specifically addressed.

It is true that the United States could attack a propaganda facility run by an enemy force in a war or other armed conflict. But al-Awlaki's alleged conduct does not seem to fit this scenario. It is not clear whether, during something like the war on terrorism, an intentional effort by the government to silence a citizen who is merely advocating terrorism from a remote location would violate the First Amendment.

In light of the substantial due process and free speech concerns involved, steps ought to be taken to limit the possibility that any citizen will be subject to extrajudicial killing based on incendiary expression or expressive activity that would be deemed lawful in the United States. Although there are obvious national security limits, the process ought to be as transparent as possible. The government ought to ensure that there is a basis, independent of the communication of what would otherwise be protected expression, for killing citizens located abroad. The government might also consider leveraging digitization in a manner that provides for some rudimentary process for the accused. Perhaps this could take the form of a virtual hearing in which the target can present some basic defense without appearing or submitting to American custody. Finally, in the case of terrorist advocacy, the United States ought to resort to targeted killing only after it has exhausted all other options, including efforts to remove any dangerous expression from servers and websites – a process that, as noted earlier, raises its own free speech concerns but is certainly less troublesome, in terms of constitutional, international, and human rights, than extrajudicial killing.

In the global theater, the United States will need to strike a delicate balance that protects the expressive rights of citizens, preserves national security, and respects the rule of law (including international law). The circumstances surrounding the killing of Anwar al-Awlaki show that American officials have not adequately resolved the manner in which such interests ought to be balanced. With regard to remote drone killings rule of law, due process, and free speech concerns must be further examined and transparently resolved.

THE "NETWORKED FOURTH ESTATE"

As many of the examples discussed so far indicate, in the global theater, governmental efforts to control transnational information flow will be complicated or in some instances even futile. The recent controversy surrounding WikiLeaks most clearly demonstrates this point. As that controversy shows, in the global theater states will have to deal with a distinct form of global press.

Yochai Benkler has referred to this new entity as the "networked fourth estate."[94] The networked fourth estate operates on a global scale, mostly in virtual spaces. It is not subject to a single set of laws or constrained by any code of journalistic ethics. It leverages interconnectivity and new forms of digital activism to thwart governmental efforts to control information flow.

As Benkler has observed, the development of a twentieth century networked press requires that we "ask how comfortable we are with the actual shape of democratization created by the Internet."[95] In the global theater, nations will not be powerless to protect state secrets and other confidential information. Thus, the United States can prosecute Americans who disclose such information under espionage, confidentiality, and other national security laws.[96] However, information in the hands of foreign distributors using computer networks will be more difficult to regulate and control.

As in other contexts, how the United States and other nations respond to this challenge will influence the development and exercise of global press freedoms. Benkler and other scholars have emphasized the need to think of the press in global terms, both in terms of the challenges it faces and the functions it will serve in the twenty-first century.[97] U.S. officials will need to think about how to respond to the challenges posed by an entity operating beyond its borders that presses or surpasses legal boundaries with regard to distribution of national secrets and confidences.

The WikiLeaks controversy is an early case study. Since its disclosures, the United States has publicly expressed its intention to prosecute WikiLeaks and its founder, Julian Assange, under the Espionage Act or other national security laws.[98] The national security and foreign affairs interests of the United States are clearly significant. However, for several reasons, prosecuting foreign information distributors such as Assange and WikiLeaks would disserve the First Amendment in general and, more specifically, would suppress global information flow.

First, the prosecution itself may violate the First Amendment. An alien brought to the United States to face trial under federal criminal laws would likely be entitled to raise First Amendment free speech and free press defenses.[99] Insofar as Assange and WikiLeaks acted to inform the global public regarding U.S. military and foreign policy, they would have a strong basis for claiming free speech and press protections. The United States has never tried anyone (other than a government employee), under the Espionage Act or other federal law, for merely receiving or disseminating confidential information. In *New York Times v. United States* (the Pentagon Papers Case),[100] some Supreme Court justices noted that Congress may have authorized prosecution of recipients and disseminators under the Espionage Act.[101] However, in neither that case, nor any since, has the government prosecuted a newspaper or other recipient of confidential information. Indeed, the Supreme Court has strongly suggested that, where the recipient of information of public concern has not engaged in informational theft or other wrongdoing, he cannot be prosecuted for publishing it "absent a need of the highest order."[102] The Court has emphasized that the appropriate step in this context is to ensure that sanctions for theft and misconduct are made more severe and properly enforced.[103] In sum, prosecution of Assange or other global information recipients and distributors would rest on shaky constitutional ground.[104]

Second, imposing criminal liability on foreign distributors could damage domestic press freedoms. Insofar as any prosecution would be based primarily on knowing receipt and publication of confidential information, there would be little to distinguish *The New York Times* or *The Washington Post* from WikiLeaks. The damage to the domestic press could be substantial. Receipt and distribution of embarrassing governmental secrets are core, fundamental, press functions. If liability were threatened, government whistleblowers might be reluctant to come forward. Newspapers and other media might be reluctant to report government secrets, even if they had no role in obtaining them. As I have emphasized, in the global theater, domestic and foreign spheres cannot be neatly separated or distinguished. In this context, limits placed on foreign distributors may cut back on core press freedoms at home. Limiting domestic press freedoms would restrict both the domestic and the global flow of information.

Third, a repressive U.S. response could compromise the nation's credibility and its efforts to facilitate global information flow. The United States has encouraged the use of new technologies to promote self-government in foreign nations, to facilitate information-sharing in global marketplaces, and to ensure worldwide transparency with regard to authoritarian governments. Many in the world community would likely (and correctly) view aggressive U.S. prosecution of foreign information recipients and distributors as fundamentally inconsistent with these commitments.

Fourth, with regard to the dissemination of government secrets, there is a certain futility in efforts to suppress digital information after the fact. Once the information enters the global theater, it is often impossible to prevent its further dissemination. Mirror sites and instantaneous worldwide distribution over interconnected networks will ensure that the information remains in the global theater. Moreover, efforts to prosecute distributors will simply draw greater attention to the leaked information.

We do not yet know what the networked fourth estate will become, how it will function, or how it will interact with existing press entities and governments. America's long experience with a free press suggests that the "networked fourth estate" will challenge governments in a way that prompts repressive measures. In the global theater, governments do not have to tolerate leaked secrets or the free flow of harmful diplomatic or national security information. However, it will be more important than ever that they safeguard information and prevent thefts. A networked fourth estate will be less organized, more geographically dispersed, and perhaps, owing to the complexities of digitized distribution, a more powerful agent of transparency than the world has yet seen. Whether it takes this or some other form will depend on regulatory and enforcement decisions made in the near term. U.S. officials would be well advised to take the long view, rather than to institute unprecedented prosecutions of the emerging networked global press.

6 EXPRESSIVE LIBERTIES BEYOND U.S. BORDERS

U.S. citizens frequently engage in speech, association, and press activities while abroad. They speak on matters of public concern, associate with aliens, engage in protest activities, distribute information, attend American universities, and report from foreign locations. Aliens' speech and associational activities can also be affected by U.S. laws and official acts outside the United States. Owing to the reach of American laws and the geographic expansion of U.S. authority, the First Amendment's geographic scope or domain has become a concern of increasing importance.[1] This chapter discusses the expressive aspects of the extraterritorial First Amendment. Chapter 7 discusses the extraterritorial application of the First Amendment's religion clauses.

Courts and commentators have long struggled to analyze and define the Constitution's extraterritorial domain. The First Amendment's text does not generally address matters of domain or geographic scope. It is unclear whether or to what extent expressive guarantees, including freedom of speech and press, limit the U.S. government when it acts abroad. The Supreme Court has never definitively resolved whether the First Amendment's speech, association, press, or petition guarantees apply beyond U.S. shores. The issue continues to attract robust scholarly debate. The detention of alleged enemy combatants in the global war on terrorism has focused renewed judicial, scholarly, and public attention on extraterritorial constitutional rights, including free speech.[2]

In this chapter, I argue that citizens' free speech and other expressive rights are presumptively portable, which means that the U.S. government must recognize and respect them regardless of geographic location. I present both traditional and cosmopolitan justifications for this conception of the First Amendment's domain. Moreover, I argue that in certain circumstances, aliens abroad also enjoy limited First Amendment protection. I do not advocate universal First Amendment protection for aliens' speech and other interests. However, where the United States demands obedience from aliens to its own laws, it ought to extend First Amendment protections to them. Under this "mutuality of legal obligation" approach, in some instances the First Amendment's domain would extend to aliens located abroad.

DEFINING CONSTITUTIONAL DOMAIN

Before considering the First Amendment's extraterritorial domain, it is useful to summarize the extent to which the Constitution is presently deemed to apply beyond U.S. borders as well as the various approaches courts and scholars have applied in analyzing constitutional domain. The Constitution's territorial domain has expanded since the founding. Among other things, the acquisition of American territories and the exercise of American power abroad have led to more expansive conceptions of constitutional domain. However, the extent of that expansion remains an open and controversial question. Courts and scholars continue to debate the extent to which citizens and aliens enjoy constitutional protections beyond U.S. shores.

Citizens and Constitutional Domain – From Territoriality to Pragmatism

From 1891 to the middle of the twentieth century, a strict territorial approach to constitutional domain prevailed. As the Supreme Court said in *In re Ross* (1891), "[t]he Constitution can have no operation in another country."[3] This formal territorial approach was grounded in traditional conceptions of national sovereignty.

Even with respect to U.S. citizens, under the territorial approach the Constitution's domain was strictly limited to territories over which the United States exercised legal sovereignty. This domain included only some territories acquired by the United States that were inhabited by both citizens and non-citizens. In the *Insular Cases*, which were decided in the early part of the twentieth century, the Supreme Court refused to extend full constitutional protection to inhabitants of acquired territories including Florida, Hawaii, the Philippines, and Puerto Rico.[4] However, the Court strongly suggested that the inhabitants of these territories possessed certain fundamental constitutional rights, among them the First Amendment's freedom of speech.[5]

Gradually, as the United States became a superpower and exercised authority beyond its national borders, the strict territorial approach fell out of favor.[6] As Kal Raustiala observed in his comprehensive study of constitutional rights and territoriality, during the twentieth century the "legal spatiality" approach, under which rights varied with a person's location, ceased to apply in a variety of legal contexts.[7] The move away from legal spatiality opened the door to more universal interpretations of constitutional domain.

In its 1957 decision in *Reid v. Covert*,[8] the Supreme Court appeared to reject the strict territorial approach to constitutional domain. In a case involving the wife of a U.S. serviceman accused of murder and subjected to court-martial in England, the Court held that the Fifth and Sixth Amendment due process and jury trial provisions were applicable.[9] A plurality of justices adopted a universal perspective regarding citizens and constitutional domain. They observed that "[t]he United States is entirely a creature of the Constitution" and "can only act in accordance with all the limitations imposed by the Constitution."[10] According to Justice Black, who wrote for the plurality: "When the Government reaches out to punish a citizen who is abroad, the shield which the Bill of Rights and other parts of the Constitution provide to protect his life and liberty should not be stripped away because he happens to be in another land."[11] Justice Black dismissed the strict territorial interpretation of constitutional domain adopted in *In re Ross* as "a relic from a different era."[12]

Despite the *Reid* plurality's endorsement of a de-territorialized approach to constitutional domain, the Supreme Court did not hold that the entire Bill of Rights, much less the entire Constitution, applied to citizens located abroad. Justices Frankfurter and Harlan, who wrote separate concurrences in *Reid*, adopted a more selective approach under which only certain fundamental constitutional rights would apply

beyond U.S. borders.[13] Frankfurter and Harlan based their analysis of
constitutional domain on practical concerns, such as "the particular
circumstances, the practical necessities, and the possible alternatives
which Congress had before it."[14] Although they disagreed on the theory
of constitutional domain, the justices agreed that the Bill of Rights (and,
presumably, other constitutional provisions) might not apply with the
same force when citizens are located beyond U.S. borders. Thus, Fifth
and Sixth Amendment guarantees might apply less robustly, or more
contingently, depending on the defendant's location.

With regard to constitutional domain and the rights of U.S. citizens,
Reid remains the Supreme Court precedent most directly on point.
Although some justices reasoned in universal terms, the holding of
the case is somewhat narrower. Thus, even insofar as U.S. citizens are
concerned, the Court has not expressly adopted a universal approach
to constitutional domain.

The Constitution and Aliens Abroad

Reid v. Covert addressed the extraterritorial constitutional rights of citizens. The extent to which the Constitution applies to foreign nationals
who are located abroad was not at issue. Insofar as aliens are concerned, the Supreme Court has similarly failed to articulate a clear
approach to constitutional domain.

In *United States v. Verdugo-Urquidez*, the Court held that the Fourth
Amendment's warrant requirement did not apply to the search of a
Mexican citizen's property in Mexico.[15] The Court concluded that aliens
located abroad "can derive no comfort from the *Reid* holding."[16] A plurality in *Verdugo-Urquidez* emphasized that the Fourth Amendment's
text refers to "the people," language that was interpreted to exclude
aliens located abroad.[17] However, this membership or social compact
approach did not garner the support of a majority. Indeed, in his con-
currence in *Verdugo-Urquidez*, Justice Kennedy expressly rejected the
membership approach.[18] Instead, he relied on a functional approach to
constitutional domain similar to that adopted by Justices Frankfurter
and Harlan in *Reid v. Covert*.[19]

In his dissent, Justice Brennan relied on "basic notions of mutuality"
to support extension of the Fourth Amendment's warrant requirement

to the extraterritorial search.[20] According to Brennan, Verdugo-Urquidez was entitled to the protections of the warrant requirement because the U.S. government, by investigating him and applying U.S. criminal laws to his conduct, had essentially treated him as a member of the national political community.[21]

As noted earlier, U.S. detention policies implemented in connection with the global war on terrorism have raised new questions regarding constitutional domain. In *Boumediene v. Bush*, the Supreme Court held that aliens detained at the U.S. Naval facility at Guantanamo Bay, Cuba, were entitled to the protection of the writ of habeas corpus.[22] Justice Kennedy, writing for the Court, wrote that when the U.S. government acts abroad, its powers are not "'absolute and unlimited'" but rather are subject "'to such restrictions as are expressed in the Constitution.'"[23]

In *Boumediene*, the Court applied a pragmatic and contextual approach to constitutional domain.[24] Under this approach, which was foreshadowed in the concurring opinions of Justice Harlan and Justice Frankfurter in *Reid*, practical concerns largely dictate constitutional domain.[25] Thus, according to the Court, with respect to the writ of habeas corpus, the most important considerations are the nature and degree of control the U.S. exercises over the territory in question, the importance of the writ itself, the status of the detainees, the location of the arrests and detentions, and any practical obstacles to administration of the writ beyond U.S. borders.[26]

If *Boumediene* announces a new governing standard with regard to constitutional domain, then extraterritorial application of the Constitution to citizens and aliens alike may generally turn on pragmatic and policy considerations. Because the Court has not yet applied this approach to other constitutional provisions, its effect on constitutional domain, including the First Amendment's geographic reach, is unclear.

General Approaches to Constitutional Domain

In response to the decisions discussed in the preceding section, legal commentators have described and developed various approaches to constitutional domain.[27] Some of these approaches would apply the

Constitution in general, and Bill of Rights guarantees in particular, *only* to U.S. citizens located abroad.[28] Others would extend at least some, and perhaps all, constitutional protections to aliens located abroad. A review of the extensive literature addressing constitutional domain is beyond the scope of this chapter. However, in general, after *Boumediene* there are four principal approaches.[29]

One approach is to apply the Constitution and the Bill of Rights in foreign territories only to U.S. citizens and not foreign nationals, on the ground that only citizens have entered into a social compact and are members of the constitutional community. As noted earlier, this membership approach garnered the support of a plurality in *Verdugo-Urquidez* but was not applied in *Boumediene*.

A second approach is to treat U.S. constitutional guarantees as universal rights applicable wherever the U.S. government exercises power and as capable of being invoked by both citizens and aliens regardless of location.[30] Although a few Supreme Court justices and legal scholars have expressed support for this approach, it does not have any precedential support.[31]

A third approach, which is sometimes referred to as a "mutuality of legal obligation" approach, requires that U.S. officials comply with constitutional limits whenever citizens or aliens located abroad are within U.S. custody "or when the nation attempts to exact obedience to its laws."[32] This more limited form of domain would extend constitutional protection abroad in a narrower set of contexts, such as detention or criminal prosecution.

Finally, under the contextual approach adopted in *Boumediene*, constitutional domain is defined with reference to practical and pragmatic considerations. As I have observed, the extent to which *Boumediene* represents the new governing standard for constitutional domain is not clear.

Under these general approaches, there appears to be a consensus that U.S. citizens ought to enjoy at least some constitutional protections against government actions regardless of location. With regard to the rights of aliens, courts and most commentators have not embraced any form of universalism.[33] The mutuality of obligation approach has been advanced by some scholars, but has not enjoyed significant support among the Justices of the Supreme Court.[34] Finally, depending on context and circumstances, the functional and pragmatic approach applied in *Boumediene* may offer aliens located abroad some constitutional protection.

CITIZENS AND EXTRATERRITORIAL EXPRESSIVE RIGHTS

The First Amendment's extraterritorial dimension has received relatively little judicial or academic attention. Previous chapters have touched on certain extraterritorial concerns. Chapter 3 discussed the relationship between cross-border travel and First Amendment freedoms of speech, association, and press. Chapter 5 touched briefly on potential extraterritorial speech concerns, including the U.S. approach to citizens and aliens who are disseminating harmful speech from foreign locations. This chapter more specifically addresses citizens' rights to speak, associate, assemble, petition the government for redress of grievances, and engage in press activities when they are physically located beyond U.S. shores. The question, in general, is whether the First Amendment follows the flag or the government and hence applies to regulations of U.S. citizens' expressive activity in foreign nations.

Speech, Association, Assembly, and Petition

U.S. citizens frequently travel abroad for specific expressive purposes. They do so to communicate with foreign audiences, to protest their own government's actions and foreign policies, and to associate with aliens located abroad. Whether the First Amendment, in particular, applies to Americans overseas is an issue that has never been definitively resolved.[35] Courts and scholars have taken different views on the matter.

In *Haig v. Agee*, the Supreme Court upheld the revocation of a citizen's passport on the ground that, while in Germany, he had disseminated sensitive information and threatened to expose Central Intelligence Agency operatives.[36] In *Agee*, the Court assumed, but did not expressly decide, that the Free Speech Clause applied to efforts to regulate or restrict citizens' expressive liberties beyond U.S. borders.[37] Because it ultimately held that Agee's statements were not protected speech, the Court did not consider or adopt any specific approach to defining the First Amendment's extraterritorial domain.[38]

Like the Supreme Court, some lower courts have assumed that the First Amendment applies where the federal government seeks to restrict the speech of U.S. citizens abroad. For example, in one case, the D.C. Circuit Court of Appeals applied the Free Speech Clause to the pamphleteering activities of U.S. soldiers stationed abroad.[39] As in *Agee*, the court did not discuss *Reid v. Covert* or adopt a specific approach to constitutional domain. The Ninth Circuit has similarly assumed that the First Amendment applies to citizens' communications in Mexico, but again the court did not take a specific position regarding constitutional domain.[40]

Courts have also entertained First Amendment claims by citizens who have traveled abroad to protest and serve as "human shields."[41] Human shields protest U.S. policies by traveling to foreign nations and taking up positions that make it more difficult for the U.S. to carry out bombing and other military campaigns. In the shield cases, the principal issue has been whether federal travel restrictions enforced against the protesters violate the First Amendment. The courts have thus devoted scant attention to the question whether the First Amendment applies to the extraterritorial symbolic conduct itself. Instead, the cases have generally been disposed of on the assumption that they involve regulation of cross-border movement. As a result, the foreign protest decisions do not specifically address the First Amendment's extraterritorial domain.

In one case involving application of U.S. customs regulations to the cross-border shipment of films, a U.S. district court purported to address the extraterritorial speech rights of the distributor.[42] As discussed in Chapter 4, although the court purported to justify extending full protection to citizens' expressive activities abroad, its analysis contained several inaccurate statements. First, the court mistakenly reasoned that "the Bill of Rights applies abroad."[43] As noted earlier, this is not an accurate statement of the Supreme Court's approach to constitutional domain. The Court has not held that the Bill of Rights is applicable in toto beyond U.S. shores. Second, in response to the government's contention that the First Amendment does not apply to speech directed across territorial borders, the court stated that *the entire world* is a "First Amendment forum."[44] That, too, is an overstatement – it is not supported by any constitutional precedent or other authority.

Although it was not technically addressing a beyond-border speech restriction, the district court did make an intriguing statement regarding the First Amendment's extraterritorial domain. It rejected the government's argument that the communication or information must relate to matters of domestic public concern in order to be protected by the Free Speech Clause. The court rejected that rule on the ground that "matters occurring abroad, e.g., government 'news leaks' to the foreign press, are likely to find their way into this country and become a part of our domestic political debate."[45] Thus, even assuming that self-governance is the principal justification for protecting free speech, the court reasoned that speech disseminated abroad might still be relevant to domestic political debate.

In contrast, other decisions have suggested that the Free Speech Clause does *not* always apply to citizens' speech activities abroad.[46] For example, in *Desai v. Hersh*, the district court stated that "first amendment protections do not apply to all extraterritorial publications by persons under the protections of the Constitution."[47] *Desai* involved an Indian citizen who brought a defamation suit in a U.S. federal court against an American author, Seymour Hersh, who had written a book about U.S. foreign policy during the Nixon administration.[48] The book was published in both India and the United States, and the plaintiff sought recovery under both Indian and U.S. defamation law.[49]

One of the issues was whether the court could apply Indian defamation law, which affords less protection to speakers than First Amendment defamation doctrine, to speech that is distributed abroad by a U.S. citizen.[50] The court held that U.S. libel law applied. However, it noted:

> ...[h]ad defendant written a book and published it solely in India concerning plaintiff's activities as a public official in the government of India, but minimally related to a matter of public concern in [the United States], the need for protection of first amendment interests would be greatly lessened, if not entirely absent.[51]

Desai raises an interesting issue regarding the resolution of conflicts between U.S. defamation law and the defamation laws of other nations. Even if a speaker abroad is protected by the Free Speech Clause, it is not necessarily the case that U.S. constitutional law applies. I examine conflicts issues in Chapter 9. I focus here on the court's general approach to extraterritorial application of the Free Speech Clause.

In *Desai*, the court stated that the First Amendment "shields the actions of speakers for the benefit of their audience."[52] Under this reasoning, if the speech or publication does not affect the free flow of information inside the United States or address a matter of public concern within its borders, then the speaker is not entitled to protection under the First Amendment. The court also stated that a citizen could *waive* free speech protection if he "intentionally published the speech in the foreign country in a manner sufficient to indicate abandonment of first amendment protection."[53]

Thus, although the court was resolving a choice of law issue, in a broader sense, its analysis suggests that American citizens may have limited expressive rights abroad. To be sure, *Desai* acknowledged that failing to grant First Amendment protection to speech published abroad might chill speech both inside the United States and abroad.[54] The court noted: "Our world is shrinking every day as a result of improvements in mass communications and travel."[55] But despite these observations, the court was unwilling to grant automatic protection to materials that citizens deliberately publish abroad.[56] This suggests that the First Amendment does not automatically follow the government. Moreover, the court added that citizens can waive free speech and free press rights when they speak or publish abroad.

What about the right to receive information? *Lamont v. Postmaster General* held, for the first time, that the First Amendment protects a right to receive information.[57] The information at issue in *Lamont* originated in China. Regardless of whether they have extraterritorial rights to convey or publish information, it is not clear whether U.S. citizens located abroad have a First Amendment right to receive information from either citizens at home or aliens abroad. As the Ninth Circuit Court of Appeals stated in *Yahoo! Inc. v. La Ligue Contre le Racisme et l'Antisemitisme*, a case involving enforcement of a French injunction against speech originating in the United States and posted on the Internet, "[t]he extent of First Amendment protection of speech accessible solely by those outside the United States is a difficult and, to some degree, unresolved issue."[58]

In *Yahoo!*, the issue of direct regulation of citizens' right to receive information abroad was not clearly implicated or addressed. Insofar as extraterritorial speech rights were at issue, the court did not clarify whether the foreign audience at issue consisted solely of aliens or some mixture of aliens and citizens. Nor was it entirely clear whether the court was concerned about the speaker's right to distribute information to foreign audiences or the rights of recipients abroad to obtain the materials. The court merely observed that, insofar as it required some restriction on access to the material in question, the French court's order might require a determination "whether the First Amendment has extraterritorial application."[59] Ultimately, the decision did not address whether U.S. citizens (or, for that matter, aliens) located abroad have a First Amendment right to receive information that originates within the United States.[60]

In sum, a number of speech issues relating to citizens' extraterritorial expressive rights have not been resolved. In addition, several other First Amendment questions have not been addressed in any published judicial decision or in scholarly work. Thus, it is not clear whether the following extraterritorial rights of citizens are recognized: (1) the right to receive information that is published by a fellow citizen abroad; (2) the right to associate for expressive purposes with fellow citizens or aliens located abroad; (3) the right to "peaceably assemble" in foreign locations; and (4) the right to petition government for a redress of grievances beyond U.S. shores. To be sure, these questions may not arise with frequency in the courts. However, because the U.S. government acts and regulates expressive activities across the globe, we ought to know whether these rights are within the First Amendment's extraterritorial domain.

Freedom of the Press in Foreign Locations

The American press has sought access to foreign battle zones, detention facilities, and American operations in foreign lands. In the wartime context, the issue of extraterritorial press rights has arisen most recently in connection with strict limitations imposed by the George W. Bush and Obama administrations on access to military tribunal proceedings at Guantanamo Bay, Cuba.[61] The concern with extraterritorial press freedoms extends beyond these access restrictions. For example, some accounts of the Pentagon's manipulation of American journalists during the Iraq and Afghanistan conflicts suggest that content-based regulation of the press may have occurred in those nations.[62]

Extraterritorial press freedoms are also vitally important outside the wartime context. The American press gathers and disseminates a variety of information abroad, not only about the United States and its policies but also about the governments and cultures of other nations. The audiences for contemporary press and media outlets are geographically diverse and are composed of both citizens and foreign nationals.

As a general matter, the Supreme Court has held that the press enjoys no special or unique First Amendment status or rights.[63] However, as a function of resources and institutional position, the press is in a unique position to report on foreign affairs, wars, and other events that take place abroad. The press's ability to gain access to foreign sites and American personnel abroad is critical to this reporting.

Federal courts have assumed, again with little comment or analysis, that the First Amendment likely applies to the press while they are operating beyond U.S. shores.[64] However, no court appears to have ever upheld an extraterritorial First Amendment claim by a member of the American press.[65] As one commentator has written, "So far as existing case law is concerned, there appears to be nothing to prevent the Pentagon from eliminating on-scene coverage of military operations, detention facilities, military hospitals, and other auxiliaries of war."[66]

As I indicated in Chapter 2, a number of transborder First Amendment rights have what might be called a "quasi-recognized" status. Press rights are clearly among them. A few judicial decisions suggest that a plausible argument might be made, in an appropriate case, for enforcing press rights abroad; but again, no court has ever accepted such an argument or actually enforced extraterritorial press rights.

ALIENS AND EXTRATERRITORIAL EXPRESSIVE RIGHTS

As discussed earlier, whether the Bill of Rights applies to aliens located abroad remains an open question. In *Verdugo-Urquidez*, the Supreme Court held that the Fourth Amendment's protections did not apply to a search of an alien's property abroad. However, in *Boumediene* the Supreme Court held that alien detainees at Guantanamo are entitled to habeas corpus protection. It is worth noting that even *within* the United States foreign nationals' First Amendment rights are not entirely clear or secure.[67]

In general, courts and commentators have not accepted or advanced arguments that aliens are entitled to extraterritorial First Amendment protection. The Supreme Court has held that aliens have no First Amendment right to enter the United States for purposes of speaking to or associating with U.S. citizens.[68] In *Johnson v. Eisentrager*, which was decided six decades prior to *Boumediene*, the Court ridiculed the idea that "during military occupation irreconcilable enemy elements, guerrilla fighters, and 'werewolves' could require the American Judiciary to assure them freedom of speech, press, and assembly as in the First Amendment."[69] Thus, at least during wartime, *Eisentrager* suggests that aliens located abroad in areas occupied or controlled by the United States have no free speech or other First Amendment rights.

Some lower courts have held that aliens lack standing to challenge U.S. funding conditions that substantially affect their speech activities abroad.[70] For example, the United States has sometimes imposed a global gag rule with respect to abortion counseling by foreign nongovernmental organizations and others who receive U.S. funding. The gag rule has prohibited foreign recipients from using even their own funds for such counseling – a condition that would ordinarily violate the First Amendment if imposed on domestic speakers.[71] Further, in one rather unusual case, a U.S. district court held that the First Amendment did not prohibit it from ordering alien defendants subject to the court's jurisdiction from petitioning or otherwise communicating with their *own* governments abroad, on the ground that aliens have no First Amendment rights beyond U.S. territorial borders.[72]

Commentators have also been skeptical of assertions that aliens located abroad possess First Amendment rights. Thus, Kermit Roosevelt has argued that, although communications in foreign countries between aliens and U.S. citizens might deserve some limited protection, none of the traditional justifications for protecting freedom of speech, including self-governance and self-actualization, support extending First Amendment protection to alien-to-alien communications.[73] Other commentators have argued that enemy aliens, including those who have been detained abroad by the United States, are not entitled to assert free speech defenses.[74]

In a response to Roosevelt, Gerald Neuman agreed that self-governance principles are of limited relevance in the context of alien speech abroad.[75] He also conceded that the United States has no obligation to facilitate aliens' self-actualization.[76] However, Neuman asked, "is it so clear that no First Amendment concerns are raised when the [U.S.] government reaches out to crush aliens' self-actualization abroad?"[77] Neuman argued that aliens could assert some speech rights under the "mutuality of legal obligation" approach and, perhaps, under the pragmatic approach adopted in *Boumediene*.[78] Under either approach, not all free speech protections would apply to aliens located abroad. However, foreign speakers who are held in U.S. detention facilities or who are taken into U.S. custody and prosecuted based on their communications might be entitled to some degree of protection under the Free Speech Clause, depending in part on the practicability of extending such protection.[79]

In sum, the relatively few reported decisions and limited academic commentary strongly suggest that First Amendment guarantees do not generally apply extraterritorially to aliens. However, as noted earlier, the Supreme Court has not yet been asked to apply *Boumediene*'s approach to constitutional domain in other contexts or to otherwise clarify the extent of First Amendment protections available to aliens abroad.

A COSMOPOLITAN FIRST AMENDMENT DOMAIN

Although granting universal First Amendment protection to citizens and aliens regardless of location is not a feasible approach, we ought to conceive of the domain of free speech and other expressive guarantees as broadly as possible. U.S. citizens ought to enjoy protection for free speech, press, assembly, and petition rights without regard to frontiers or borders and without regard to whether the expressive activity serves domestic interests in self-governance. Treating expressive rights as portable will facilitate citizens' participation in global conversation and commingling. Moreover, freedom of expression and freedom of press are international human rights that the United States is obligated to protect regardless of location. The First Amendment's expressive protections thus ought also to be available to aliens, whenever the U.S. government directly regulates the expressive activities of foreign nationals beyond its borders. Under this approach, no foreign speech laws or standards would be displaced. Further, the approach stops well short of First Amendment universalism or imposition of an affirmative duty on the United States to further the expressive liberties of aliens in foreign lands.[80] Rather, it requires that aliens who are subjected to direct regulatory control by the United States in their own or other foreign lands be entitled to the same First Amendment benefits and defenses as U.S. citizens.

Territoriality and First Amendment Domain

The provincial account of the First Amendment's domain assumes that if a communication or activity does not occur inside our borders, does not relate to a matter of public concern in that territory, or involves aliens beyond U.S. borders, then the First Amendment generally does not apply. This account or perspective rests on traditional conceptions of territorial sovereignty and constitutional domain. Provincialism is manifested in various aspects of the current conception of First Amendment domain: The Supreme Court's grudging assumption that U.S. citizens *might* enjoy some free speech and other First Amendment protections while traveling or residing in foreign lands; the persistent confusion regarding whether citizens' speech published abroad is within the First Amendment's domain; judicial reluctance to recognize and enforce American expressive rights abroad; and the principle that aliens, as community outsiders, possess no extraterritorial First Amendment rights.

As I have argued throughout this book, as a legal, jurisdictional, and constitutional principle, territoriality's influence has steadily declined.[81] As the plurality stated in *Reid*, the idea that the Constitution has no force beyond U.S borders, even with respect to citizens, is truly a "relic from a different era." Although theories and approaches to domain differ, the notion that the U.S. government acts without constitutional constraints abroad has been firmly rejected.

With regard specifically to citizens' expressive rights, the old territorial conception of domain is inconsistent with the emergence of new global marketplaces of ideas. Globalization, digitization, and contemporary governance have all challenged or undermined the traditional distinction between foreign and domestic forums. Thus, a refusal by U.S. courts to grant First Amendment protection to citizens' publications or press activities in foreign countries may indeed substantially affect the domestic marketplace of ideas. Similarly, U.S. conditions imposed on foreign grant recipients' expression in their native lands may substantially affect expressive liberties both at home and abroad. In a more general sense, regulatory decisions made in the United States with regard to Internet access, domain names, or online intellectual property will typically produce both domestic and foreign effects.

In a world with increasingly interconnected channels of communication, it is becoming more difficult for governments to isolate foreign and domestic marketplaces. Our conception of the First Amendment's domain must acknowledge that territorial borders no longer mark or define clear boundaries with regard to citizens' interests, connections, and concerns. As Lee Bollinger has observed, globalization and digitization are "tightening connections among open markets and systems of communication and helping us to perceive issues and problems as transcending national borders."[82]

As discussed in prior chapters, speakers can now communicate with worldwide audiences regardless of location. What once were considered "domestic" disputes or conflicts can now quickly become matters of public concern around the world. Although some would deny First Amendment protection to citizens' speech that is distributed to alien audiences abroad, audiences in the digital age now frequently comprise a diverse mixture of aliens and citizens. A global press distributes information to worldwide audiences. American universities are becoming more active participants in global educational endeavors. In an increasing number of contexts, it has become difficult if not impossible to speak in terms of purely domestic or purely foreign marketplaces, audiences, or effects.

The decline of territoriality has certainly not eliminated the effective exercise of sovereign authority over cross-border activities. Governments retain the power and means to protect citizens against the domestic effects of activities beyond their borders.[83] Moreover, territoriality's decline as a marker of constitutional domain does not necessarily mean that aliens abroad enjoy all First Amendment or other constitutional rights. However, the emergence of something like global marketplaces suggests that we need to reconsider both traditional justifications for protecting expressive activities and previously articulated grounds for denying First Amendment protections to speakers beyond U.S. borders.

The Portability of Citizens' First Amendment Rights

We ought to treat American citizens' rights to engage in speech, assembly, petition, and press as fully portable. There are various justifications for adopting this conception of the First Amendment's domain.

Perhaps, as one court suggested, at least insofar as citizens' rights are concerned we ought to view the entire world as a "First Amendment forum." This approach has some rhetorical appeal. But as I have noted, it ignores the fact that there are many places abroad that are not open for discussion, assembly, and other expressive activities. International assemblies, diplomatic missions, and active battlefields are but a few examples. The global public forum conception or metaphor seems both too broad and too narrow. It sweeps too broadly in terms of place, while at the same time limiting protection to matters of narrow domestic concern. As well, the global forum concept does not provide any substantive or instrumental justification for protecting citizens' speech abroad.

We could define the First Amendment's domain with reference to basic self-governance values. Under this approach, citizens' expressive activities abroad would be protected insofar as they contributed to domestic political discussion or to other debates regarding matters of public concern. However, as Jack Balkin has observed, a focus on self-governance is "too narrow in the age of the Internet."[84] As Balkin notes, many expressive activities transcend territorial borders. Indeed, as noted earlier, in a world where information readily traverses territorial borders and marketplaces of ideas intersect and overlap, it has become increasingly difficult to identify a discrete domestic sphere of self-governance. Thus, we ought not to condition protection for extraterritorial speech on its distinct contribution to domestic political debate.

The Supreme Court has rejected strict territorial and social compact approaches to constitutional domain. Instead, the Court has adopted an approach to constitutional domain that is rights-specific and functional.[85] The justifications for protecting citizens' expressive rights beyond U.S. borders run much deeper than membership or social compact principles. A strong basis for extraterritorial protection can be found in several sources.

We can start with the text of the First Amendment, which contains no geographical limitation. It states simply that "Congress shall make no law," not that Congress "shall make no law applicable to citizens located within the United States." The drafters of this language were acutely aware of the importance of extraterritorial conversation and commingling. Further, like the Fifth and Sixth Amendment rights at issue in *Reid v. Covert*, expressive liberties are undoubtedly fundamental. Political rights such as free speech and press are so central to ordered liberty that they deserve recognition and protection regardless of where they are exercised. There is no general functional or practical reason why the United States cannot recognize, and enforce, citizens' First Amendment rights abroad.

As I have suggested in previous chapters, traditional First Amendment justifications have considerable force in transborder contexts. In many cases, recognizing citizens' expressive rights abroad would facilitate self-governance, truth-seeking, and individual autonomy. In the modern era, citizenship has become a more fluid concept, matters of public concern are no longer defined strictly by territorial borders, the search for truth does not end at the water's edge, and citizens routinely engage in expressive activities abroad.[86] These new realities point toward a more expansive conception of First Amendment domain.

Traditional free press justifications also support extraterritorial protection for access, information-gathering, and other interests. U.S. power transcends territorial borders. Extraterritorial abuses of that power are as important as, or in some cases perhaps more important than, domestic scandals and incidents. American history has demonstrated the need for governmental transparency and power-checking beyond U.S. shores.[87] Assured of rights portability, American press members would be able to confidently assert access and other rights in foreign locations. This would include detention facilities and other U.S. installations located beyond U.S. borders.[88] As some scholars have recognized, the ability to gather information abroad is a core aspect of the First Amendment freedom of the press.[89]

There are also more cosmopolitan justifications for conceptualizing the First Amendment's domain broadly. Citizens' extraterritorial expressive rights ought to be recognized and protected in order to facilitate participation in cosmopolitan conversation and commingling. American military and diplomatic personnel, protesters, students, faculty, aid workers, press members, and others ought not to fear that they have waived or otherwise lost First Amendment protection by traveling abroad, publishing information in foreign countries, or criticizing American officials in a manner that causes embarrassment in foreign relations.[90] Lack of protection could inhibit transnational engagements, lead U.S. publishers to limit distribution of information solely to domestic forums, restrict citizens' access to information abroad, or stifle debate on American campuses in foreign nations. These effects would all be inconsistent with the First Amendment's commitment to wide-open and robust debate on matters of public concern.

Moreover, protecting citizens' First Amendment rights in foreign lands may, as Jack Balkin has suggested, facilitate the spread of "democratic culture."[91] Democratic practices may spread not only through transnational digital channels, but also through real-space contacts and collaboration in foreign locations. Extending First Amendment protections to citizens abroad would set an example for the rest of the world. It would demonstrate America's commitment to things such as academic and press freedoms.

Consider, for example, an American public university branch campus located in the United Arab Emirates (UAE). Let us assume that, when they are located off campus property, students and faculty would be required to respect and comply with the speech laws of the UAE. However, the First Amendment ought to govern on the campus itself. Providing students and faculty on campus with free speech protections that are otherwise not available in the UAE would send a powerful message concerning freedom of speech. Similarly, the United States, which frequently emphasizes the importance of press freedoms in its interactions with foreign leaders, could reap both symbolic and diplomatic benefits were it to recognize and enforce the rights of the American press without regard to location.[92]

The campus and press examples raise some important points regarding recognition and enforceability of extraterritorial First Amendment rights. These questions relate to U.S. obligations to respect, and the practicality of enforcing, extraterritorial speech rights in locations under U.S. control.

Owing to the mission of most American educational institutions to provide a space for free inquiry and debate, recognition and enforcement of free speech rights in these places is a compelling and overriding commitment. This central mission ought, in most cases, to outweigh concerns raised by the foreign sovereign with regard to speech on campus. This means that a student whose free speech rights are violated on the UAE campus ought to have recourse against campus officials in U.S. courts. Of course, students also have an obligation to pay due respect to the laws of the host nation. When the student ventures beyond campus and engages with the larger community, she is required to comply with UAE speech laws. In a similar manner, she is required to obey the general laws of a local community when she ventures beyond a campus located in the United States.

With regard to the press, there are obvious national security and foreign affairs concerns when members seek access to military and other installations abroad. As a few courts have recognized, this is not grounds for denying recognition to extraterritorial press freedoms altogether. As I have noted, courts have been reluctant to enforce press rights abroad. However, in many cases enforcement of basic press rights would not be impractical. The same is true with respect to protest activities. Of course, as American peace activists in Pakistan and elsewhere around the world have discovered, conditions on the ground and foreign military intervention may impede or even prevent expressive activities. However, absent the most compelling countervailing interests, American officials ought to avoid taking actions that directly restrict such activities. Indeed, they ought whenever and wherever possible to recognize and enforce citizens' right to protest and communicate in foreign territories.

These examples also raise the question whether American officials have any affirmative legal or constitutional obligation to facilitate extraterritorial expressive activities. As a formal constitutional matter, the answer is no. However, merely recognizing First Amendment rights abroad will not be adequate to guarantee their effective exercise.

Thus, Lee Bollinger has persuasively argued that the United States ought to provide greater funding to the international press corps so that it can effectively report on foreign affairs and other international matters. Similarly, administrators of American campuses abroad may be faced with calls for protection of students or faculty who run afoul of restrictive foreign speech laws. Perhaps they ought to assist or defend students and faculty who are subject to prosecution under such laws. More generally, they ought to consider educating not just the campus but the larger community regarding expressive and religious liberties. In similar fashion, American military and diplomatic personnel have a responsibility to protect and facilitate citizens' protest and other activities abroad. These obligations go beyond matters of constitutional right and judicial enforcement. However, they too are critical to enjoyment of First Amendment liberties abroad.

Support for extraterritorial protection of citizens' expressive liberties is not limited to domestic sources such as constitutional text and free speech theories. The international community has recognized that free speech and other expressive liberties are central to human dignity. Indeed, in many parts of the world they are recognized as universal human rights. The United States has a deep and longstanding commitment to global freedoms of speech, press, and information flow. It is formally committed to protecting expressive liberties without regard to location or geography. The United States was the driving force behind adoption of the Universal Declaration of Human Rights and has ratified the International Covenant on Civil and Political Rights. These and other instruments protect the right to seek, receive, and impart information "regardless of frontiers."[93] These international commitments provide additional grounds for imposing an obligation on U.S. officials to avoid directly restricting or suppressing the expressive freedoms of their own citizens while they are abroad.

In sum, I have proposed a conception of First Amendment domain that recognizes citizens' extraterritorial rights to the fullest extent possible. The normative foundation for this approach is based on textual, functional, traditional, and cosmopolitan justifications. If the United

States is truly committed to freedoms of speech, association, and press without regard to frontiers, it ought at least to resolve in the affirmative the question whether its own citizens enjoy First Amendment expressive liberties wherever they happen to be in the world.

The First Amendment and Aliens Abroad

Does this expansive conception of domain suggest that the United States ought also to extend First Amendment protections to foreign nationals abroad? As other scholars have noted, there are strong justifications for granting foreign nationals within the United States full First Amendment rights.[94] If territory and membership no longer strictly determine constitutional domain, and assuming the United States is committed to protecting expressive liberties across the globe, might there be a basis for extending First Amendment protection to aliens regardless of location?

In this context, there are a number of grounds for caution and limits. First, within the United States, the First Amendment is the presumptive constitutional standard. Thus, it is appropriate to apply that standard to both citizens and aliens alike. In foreign nations, however, aliens are subject to the host nation's speech and other laws. We thus ought to be mindful of the need to respect and not displace foreign speech laws.

Second, extending expressive guarantees to aliens abroad raises some serious pragmatic concerns. As Gerald Neuman has observed, "the requirements of religious and ideological neutrality read out of the speech and religion clauses of the First Amendment cannot be applied to all contexts of human interaction."[95] Thus, Neuman contends, an alien ought not to be able to bring a First Amendment challenge to U.S. funding or other support that discriminates in favor of a pro-American political party in a foreign election.[96] The concern is that imposing free speech, press, and other constraints abroad with respect to aliens would "overburden the government by attempting to enforce in the broader context constraints chosen for the narrower one."[97]

Third, Neuman has also expressed a concern that any limits imposed abroad may filter back to domestic contexts "to undermine the original core."[98] Thus, we ought to be mindful of the concern that extension of the First Amendment's domain to foreign nationals and foreign locations could dilute free speech and other expressive liberties in the United States.

These are all valid concerns. However, as Neuman himself acknowledges, they do not lead inevitably to the proposition that the United States is free to disregard entirely First Amendment considerations in its dealings with aliens abroad. Indeed, some of Neuman's concerns might also counsel against extending First Amendment rights to *citizens* abroad.

In particular, we must be careful not to dilute what Neuman calls the "original core" of expressive rights. We must then have some confidence that courts can draw contextual distinctions between domestic and foreign applications of First Amendment rights. Given the numerous contextual distinctions courts already manage under First Amendment doctrine, it seems reasonable to suppose that they can make the territorial distinctions required to preserve domestic rights. As they apply the free speech guarantee in schools, libraries, public parks, and other places, courts can adapt its principles based on geographic concerns. Note that this adaptation goes to enforcement, not recognition, of extraterritorial speech rights.

Here as elsewhere, universal application of the First Amendment is and ought not to be the goal. At the same time, we must recognize that the United States acts globally. U.S. laws and practices can have a significant effect on foreign speakers and expressive marketplaces. The fundamental question is when, if ever, the United States is bound to respect the First Amendment in its interactions with foreign nationals abroad.

The mutuality of legal obligation approach, which was discussed earlier, provides the most plausible answer to this question and one that is consistent with cosmopolitan principles. As Neuman has explained, this approach can be described as "identifying a sphere in which a nation's law operates, which was once defined in geographical terms but now is viewed more broadly."[99] Under the mutuality approach, aliens "are within the sphere either when they are within the nation's territory or on specific occasions when the nation attempts to extract obedience to its laws."[100] This approach would extend First Amendment protections to aliens abroad only when the United States exercises custody and control over them or otherwise demands from them obedience to U.S. laws.

The mutuality approach has various cosmopolitan features and benefits. First, it recognizes a limited obligation to extend constitutional protection to foreign nationals and thus to facilitate expressive liberties regardless of location. It expands the First Amendment's domain, if only to a limited degree. At a minimum, it requires that U.S. officials refrain from things such as direct suppression of alien speakers and censorship of foreign presses. Application of these bedrock First Amendment constraints poses no risk of dilution of First Amendment rights back home.

Second, by limiting the regulatory power of the United States in foreign nations, the mutuality approach to First Amendment domain "protects the ability of individuals to participate in the culture in which they live and promotes the development of a culture that is more democratic and participatory."[101] This too is consistent with core First Amendment principles, as well as longstanding American diplomatic goals.

Third, the mutuality approach is consistent with international standards regarding sovereign jurisdiction. These standards focus on a government's effective control of areas and persons.[102] The approach is also consistent with the various international agreements and compacts mentioned earlier, which express support for freedom of speech and other rights "without regard to frontiers."

To be sure, unlike territorial or universal approaches to constitutional domain, the mutuality of obligation approach does not adopt a bright-line rule. Thus, it may pose some difficult questions in terms of applicability. In some cases, it might not be clear whether the United States is obligated to respect the First Amendment rights of aliens. What constitutes a demand for obedience to U.S. law, or an effective exercise of sovereignty with regard to an alien speaker or press member? Is a visa application sufficient to trigger constitutional limits? Are foreign aid grantees subject to otherwise unconstitutional conditions sufficiently constrained so as to come within the First Amendment's domain? Is a speaker who is extradited to the United States and who otherwise has no contacts with the nation entitled to First Amendment protection? Is there an exception for enemy combatants in military custody?

There are no easy answers to these questions. They will require the sort of contextual and practical analysis the Supreme Court employed in cases like *Boumediene*. As Gerald Neuman has suggested, after *Boumediene*, a court faced with a question whether an alien may assert extraterritorial speech rights may have to consider factors such as "where the speech originated, where its intended audience was, and the location of detention and trial" in order to determine the extent to which First Amendment standards and doctrines apply.[103]

However, as a general matter, the mutuality approach would allow alien speakers who are detained and prosecuted for expressive activities to assert First Amendment defenses.[104] This means that the enemy propagandist and the foreign website operator would be entitled to the protections of the First Amendment, insofar as the U.S. government is prosecuting them for crimes under U.S. laws relating to speech or the distribution of information. Mutuality principles would also extend to foreign journalists working on behalf of the U.S. press abroad. This is an important extension of free speech and free press rights. During the Iraq War, several foreign journalists working for American press outlets were arrested and taken into U.S. custody, where some remained for months.[105]

Particularly in criminal prosecutions, where the penalty is sometimes life imprisonment or death, foreign nationals ought to be able to raise constitutional limitations on governmental power – including the First Amendment's protections against punishing persons for their speech or beliefs. The question is not what rights a foreign national has in Yemen or Saudi Arabia. Rather, what is at issue is the extent to which U.S. officials and courts can punish aliens haled into American legal processes for political and other forms of protected speech.

In these cases, it is clear that the United States has exercised effective control over the foreign national and demanded obedience to its laws. It may seem incongruous, or simply wrong, to allow aliens who are criminal defendants to invoke the First Amendment. It may offend some to even suggest that aliens who are alleged to be aligned with U.S. enemies ought to receive First Amendment protections. But as the Supreme Court's precedents show, the burden rests on those who would argue that government officials are permitted to simply disregard the expressive liberties of foreign nationals located in foreign territories.

To be sure, First Amendment defenses may be unsuccessful in many cases involving aliens abroad. They would be particularly difficult to assert, perhaps, in cases involving enemy combatants tried by military commissions. However, insofar as our government is insisting that foreign nationals comply with U.S. laws, the protections of the First Amendment ought generally to be available to those facing prosecution. Even in foreign locations, the military and other U.S. institutions ought not to be allowed to censor press outlets or punish negative or unfavorable press coverage.

The mutuality approach would also allow aliens who are subject to the jurisdiction of U.S. courts to raise First Amendment claims with regard to restrictions imposed by those courts on their expressive rights in their native countries. In one unusual case I mentioned earlier, a court ordered foreign nationals before it as defendants in a civil lawsuit not to contact their own governments while abroad.[106] The extraterritorial speech rights of aliens subject to legal process in the United States are within the First Amendment's domain. U.S. courts have no power to restrict the otherwise lawful speech of foreign nationals in this manner, even if the speech occurs beyond U.S. borders.

Other claims will be more difficult to assess under mutuality principles. For example, are aliens entitled to raise First Amendment challenges to their exclusion from the United States on ideological grounds?[107] To be sure, American audiences may be prepared to assert First Amendment claims in such cases. But where an alien is accused of violating criminal or civil proscriptions on terrorist advocacy, and this is the ground for denial of a visa, the alien has at that juncture been subject to U.S. law and ought to be entitled to raise his own First Amendment claim.

Similarly, foreign organizations that receive U.S. grant monies ought to be allowed to contest unconstitutional conditions on First Amendment free speech grounds.[108] Here, again, U.S. laws have been applied and obedience to their conditions required. In the funding context, American spending conditions have been used to profoundly alter dialogue in foreign nations regarding issues such as reproductive rights.[109] Foreign aid recipients, like domestic ones, are not entitled to federal funding. And the government can expend funds to convey its own distinctive message in foreign nations. But aliens who are otherwise eligible for U.S. aid ought to enjoy the same protection against conditions that bar the use of *private* funding to disseminate critical information to foreign audiences. In this and other contexts, citizens and aliens are engaged in cross-border, cooperative endeavors. Allowing aliens to assert First Amendment claims thus facilitates cosmopolitan conversation and commingling involving Amercian citizens.

Of course, insofar as enforcement of aliens' rights is concerned there are a multitude of complications. These include jurisdictional complexities, the limited relief that may be available even if such claims are successful, and pragmatic concerns regarding the standards to be applied to aliens' claims. My claim is simply that there are grounds for expanding the First Amendment's domain such that aliens abroad enjoy some limited expressive rights protections.

In sum, we ought to recognize some claims by aliens located in foreign nations to freedom of speech and other First Amendment protections. The mutuality of legal obligation approach is a limited but meaningful cosmopolitan implementation of the United States' obligation to respect expressive liberties without regard to borders.

Limits on Extraterritorial Domain

The approach to First Amendment domain I have proposed would entail recognition of citizens' expressive rights abroad and would recognize aliens' expressive rights under the limited circumstances of the mutuality of legal obligation approach. However, as the Supreme Court has emphasized, constitutional domain is grounded in pragmatic concerns. In operation, the extraterritorial First Amendment would be subject to a variety of limitations.

For a number of reasons, expressive guarantees might not be as robust in foreign locations as they are at home. As Justices Harlan and Frankfurter noted in *Reid*, constitutional liberties might not apply with the same force or in the same manner abroad as they do in the United States. In determining how such liberties were to be enforced in foreign locations, courts would have to consider carefully the government's foreign affairs and national security interests. For example, human shield protests and press access claims involving military installations or battlefields obviously raise safety and security concerns. First Amendment time, place, and manner standards and information-gathering principles developed in the press context would need to be applied in a manner that is sensitive to such interests. This is consistent with the general character of First Amendment enforcement, which again tends to be highly contextual.

Certain claims may not be cognizable on justiciability and other grounds. For example, given the special nature of their missions, diplomats and military personnel working abroad may not be able to challenge disciplinary measures taken against them even if based on statements regarding matters of public concern.[110] Further, as discussed in more detail in Chapter 8, the U.S. government has broad authority to define and distribute messages in international forums. Neither citizens nor aliens would be able to challenge governmental propaganda and other forms of extraterritorial government speech on First Amendment grounds.[111]

Practical obstacles to litigation would also limit certain First Amendment claims. For example, citizens located abroad may be reluctant to sue their American protectors and handlers for alleged constitutional or legal violations. As well, legal processes and forums may not be available for adjudication of certain extraterritorial claims.

Insofar as foreign nationals located abroad are concerned, the mutuality approach itself imposes significant limitations on First Amendment claims. Recall that it is only in cases where the U.S. is insisting on obedience to its laws that the First Amendment is triggered. There are limits even within this narrow domain. For example, First Amendment claims would not be cognizable in the context of military operations carried out on the battlefield. Thus, for example, no alien could challenge on First Amendment grounds the U.S. government's decision to destroy enemy telecommunications assets or its surveillance of telephone conversations or other communications (insofar as these take place abroad).[112]

Moreover, like some citizens, many aliens could have difficulty gaining access to meaningful legal process. Although they might gain entry to the United States or obtain an injunction against unconstitutional funding conditions, aliens will still face remedial hurdles. They will generally not be able to file legal actions to stop the U.S. government from taking certain actions abroad. In prosecutions involving national security or foreign relations concerns, the government may well satisfy even a strict scrutiny standard.[113] Further, aliens generally cannot

rely on any enforcement mechanisms under
as these are notoriously weak.[114] The agreen
inside the U.S. absent statutory consent, whic
granted.

Finally, despite the recognition of some Fi
tion for aliens, the mutuality approach does no
obligation on U.S. officials to facilitate the expr
abroad.[115] Foreign nationals who reside in autho
regimes cannot claim a First Amendment right _____ance with
regard to censorship and other expressive restrictions imposed by their
own governments, any more than a U.S. citizen can insist on governmental assistance in disseminating a message to the public. Of course,
the United States could decide, as a matter of foreign policy, to take
measures to support free speech rights beyond its borders. Indeed,
as I discuss in Chapter 10, the United States has a long and laudable
history of doing so. However, no foreign national abroad could insist
that it do so.

In sum, adopting a more expansive conception of the First
Amendment's domain would provide important substantive protections to both citizen and alien speakers and distributors. However,
extraterritorial enforcement of those rights would raise some distinct
and in some cases insurmountable limitations.

7 TRANSBORDER RELIGIOUS LIBERTIES

Although this book is primarily about expressive liberties, the First Amendment's religion clauses – the Free Exercise Clause and the Establishment Clause – also have a distinct and important transborder dimension. In previous chapters, I have touched briefly on the subject of religious freedom. In Chapter 3, I discussed visa denials involving, among others, foreign religious leaders and scholars. In Chapter 5, I examined the regulation of speech in the emerging global theater that is offensive to religion. In subsequent chapters, I discuss other topics relating to religious liberties, including application of the Establishment Clause in international foreign affairs forums (Chapter 8) and official U.S. engagement with foreign faiths and religious laws (Chapter 9).

This chapter focuses specifically on the cross-border and extra-territorial exercise of First Amendment religious liberties. Throughout American history, the practice and enjoyment of religious freedoms have traversed territorial borders. As a result of digitization and global-ization, various forms of transborder religious conversation and com-mingling have flourished. The intersection of religious freedom and territorial sovereignty has given rise to both longstanding and unique contemporary problems relating to the exercise of religious freedoms. These include the tension between protecting robust religious expres-sion and global concerns regarding terrorism; possible threats arising from cross-border commingling between citizens and foreign religious scholars, leaders, and officials; and U.S. government support for sec-tarian institutions and projects in foreign nations.

As I have regarding First Amendment freedoms of speech, press, petition, and association, in this chapter, I argue that religious free exercise must be fully protected against restrictions at and beyond U.S. borders. I also argue that the Establishment Clause places some limits on U.S. government activities abroad. Here, as elsewhere, I am not arguing in favor of universal application of First Amendment doctrines or standards. Nor, as I discuss further in Chapter 9, do I envision displacement of domestic religious liberties by foreign laws or religious liberty standards. My perspective and proposals are more limited in nature. I argue in favor of a conception of the First Amendment's religion clauses that will facilitate cross-border conversation and commingling, and adopt a more expansive conception of constitutional scope or domain insofar as religious liberties are concerned. As I explain, respect for foreign religious laws, practices, and cultures is an important element of this approach to religious freedoms. Core principles of First Amendment religious freedom must be preserved and protected. However, we must also sometimes account for and accommodate the diverse religious histories, conditions, and cultures that exist across the globe.

THE RELIGION CLAUSES IN TRANSBORDER PERSPECTIVE

For some, envisioning the religion clauses from a cosmopolitan perspective might be difficult. Even if one accepts that freedoms of speech and press, for example, have a distinct transborder dimension, the Free Exercise Clause and the Establishment Clause may appear to some to relate solely to domestic concerns regarding the relationship between religion and the state. In fact, however, the religion clauses have cosmopolitan roots and have long protected important transborder activities and relationships. In addition, both U.S. and international law expressly recognize religious liberties as universal human rights. Despite significant differences in terms of specific legal and constitutional protections, in most parts of the world religious freedoms of belief, worship, and association are considered fundamental human rights.

Cosmopolitan Roots

U.S. scholars and judges have frequently noted the difficulties with divining the meaning and scope of the First Amendment's religion

clauses.[1] The ratification history does not include discussion of the
cross-border or extraterritorial scope of the religion clauses. The framers were quite understandably occupied with more immediate domestic concerns. At least as a matter of originalist interpretation, it is not
possible to say whether the framers or ratifiers of the religion clauses
anticipated or broadly understood that they would apply in transborder situations. However, as I noted in Chapter 2, this does not mean
that the religion clauses must or ought to be viewed as narrow provincial protections. The clauses have notable cosmopolitan attributes and
historical roots.

Although the First Amendment was adopted primarily to protect
the domestic freedom to practice one's religion free from (national
and, later, state) governmental coercion, the text itself contains no
geographic limitation.[2] It states that "Congress shall make no law
respecting an establishment of religion, or prohibiting the free exercise
thereof." Nor do the religion clauses contain any restriction relating to
political or constitutional membership. The text does not in any way
limit protection to "the people" or to American citizens. Instead, it
speaks generally to legislative competency rather than to location or
membership.

Beginning in the eighteenth century, wave after wave of immigrants
imported religious beliefs and practices to American colonies. Thus,
from the beginning, there was a robust transborder trade in religious
ideas and ideologies. Further, we know that the American colonists
were eager to escape religious persecution in foreign lands. As a result
of their experiences abroad, the colonists looked with great disfavor on
established churches such as the Church of England. They were also
acutely aware of efforts by other foreign governments to compel citizens' religious observances. Thus, at the very least, the colonists' experience in foreign lands shaped their views regarding the church–state
relationship and the importance of religious liberty more generally.

In addition to being influenced by global events and conditions,
the framers were also influenced by European thought regarding religious freedom. Among the more influential thinkers of the day was
Thomas Paine, an English-American political theorist and author, who
argued for a strict separation between church and state. That position gained favor with both James Madison and Thomas Jefferson, the

chief architects and most important early American interpreters of the Establishment Clause.

The religion clauses were drafted and adopted at a time when religious persecution was a global concern. As discussed in Chapter 2, the framers drafted the Constitution and Bill of Rights with an eye toward recognition of the United States as a member of the community of nations. They were surely aware of developing international law principles relating to freedoms of conscience, belief, and worship. They understood that no nation worthy of recognition in the community of nations denied these basic freedoms to its people. Although they developed a unique approach to matters of church and state, in part as a result of early experiences abroad, the framers also sought to convince the community of nations that they respected religious freedoms more broadly.

Thus, although they were surely focused on domestic applications, it seems unlikely that the framers and ratifiers of the First Amendment understood the religion clauses to be wholly inoperative at and beyond U.S. borders. Americans' concern with religious establishments and freedom to worship related principally to efforts by the new national government to establish a recognized church in the United States and efforts to ban or compel certain kinds of worship. However, there is reason to believe that early Americans were committed to anti-establishment principles without regard to where a church was founded. For example, they presumably would have objected to attempts by their newly formed government to spend tax revenues to support the establishment of churches or other religious institutions in foreign lands.

To be sure, as we shall see, some early federal practices suggest some ambiguity regarding the scope or domain of the Establishment Clause. But over time, the United States has generally adhered to religious neutrality principles in its dealings with foreign powers and on foreign soil. Thus, for example, in the 1797 Treaty of Tripoli the United States sought to assure signatories that it was not founded as a "Christian nation" and was not in any way hostile to the Muslim faith.

Although there appears to have been no discussion of the matter in the ratification debates, it also seems plausible to conclude that early Americans would have objected to the denial of free exercise rights regardless of territorial location. This follows from both the importance of religious liberty to the framing generation and the then-recent history of religious persecution in foreign territories.

Judicial pronouncements on the domain of the religion clauses are sparse. In 1878, the Supreme Court held that the Free Exercise Clause applied in all contiguous U.S. territories.[3] The Court has never decided a case involving extraterritorial application of the religion clauses. As discussed later, only one federal court of appeals has addressed whether the Establishment Clause applies abroad.

To be clear, I do not claim that the religion clauses were intended, as a matter of original constitutional construction, to apply to or address transborder concerns. However, like the First Amendment's expressive liberty guarantees, the religion clauses were not adopted in a domestic vacuum. They were drafted and ratified, in part, as a result of international experience and intellectual influences from beyond U.S. shores. Ultimately, however, the ratification history does not definitively support either a provincial or a more cosmopolitan conception of the religion clauses.

Transborder Religious Activities

Whatever the ratifiers and adopters may have intended, in terms of actual practice, the religion clauses have a significant transborder dimension. Americans' religious interests and activities have long intersected with and extended far beyond U.S. territorial borders.

People of faith have long engaged in transborder activities for the purpose of discussing, enhancing, or advancing religious beliefs and projects. Americans have participated in religious and charitable activities that traverse international borders. They have entered into cross-border associations involving foreign religious persons and institutions. Of course, there has always been a robust cross-border exchange of religious ideas. Recently, aided by digitization, churches and people of faith have harnessed the Web to facilitate cross-border proselytizing, preaching, worship, and a variety of other religious activities.

The general and specific U.S. laws discussed in Chapters 3, 4, and 5 have affected some of these religious activities. Thus, for example, American officials have denied visas to foreign religious leaders and limited foreign travel by citizens on religious grounds. Restrictions on cross-border information flow have restricted the export and receipt of religious literature. U.S. officials have recently focused on restricting certain kinds of religious expression in the global theater. To combat radical religious expression, they have adopted and enforced restrictions on supporting terrorism.

Although I have addressed these disputes in terms of freedom of speech, they intersect as well with religious liberties. Restrictions on cross-border religious association and other activities raise distinct and as-yet unanswered questions regarding the transborder dimension of religious liberties. Do the Free Exercise Clause and U.S. religious liberty laws protect such exchanges? Do these legal protections prohibit laws that single out certain forms of cross-border religious exchange? How does religious free exercise relate to cross-border conversation and commingling?

Of course, religion itself has never been defined or limited by territorial borders. Many U.S-based churches operate transnationally. Their followers are located throughout the world. U.S. citizens have long served as religious workers and missionaries in foreign nations.[4] Aliens, including alleged enemy combatants, have claimed that their religious liberties were violated in encounters with American military and other personnel abroad. It is not clear whether the First Amendment's Free Exercise Clause or federal laws protecting religious freedom apply beyond U.S. borders, to either citizens or aliens.

Finally, U.S. aid decisions and foreign policy initiatives increasingly rely on diplomatic and other forms of engagement with religious leaders and communities abroad. As discussed further in Chapter 8, U.S. diplomats and other government officials converse and cooperate with religious leaders and sectarian communities across the world. In addition, the United States expends substantial sums of money on foreign aid. Some of this support funds foreign sectarian projects and institutions. The extent to which the Establishment Clause applies to foreign sectarian aid and other forms of extraterritorial religious cooperation remains unclear.

Courts and scholars have not paid much attention to cross-border and beyond-border religious activities. Particularly as religion and religious concerns become an increasingly important part of global conflict, dialogue, and international relations, American officials and courts will need to consider and address such concerns. In general, we ought to have a better sense of how the core concepts enshrined in the First Amendment's religion clauses relate to and intersect with international borders.

U.S. Commitments to Global Religious Freedom

The United States has taken an official position concerning the global importance of religious liberties. In international agreements, commitments, and policies, the United States has articulated the view that religious freedoms are fundamental human rights.

Of course, this does not mean that First Amendment standards are universally applicable. Nor does it mean that foreign standards regarding religious liberties, many of which differ significantly from First Amendment doctrines, are to apply in the United States. Rather, in a more general sense, American support for global religious freedoms is an aspect of national foreign policy that advocates protection for fundamental liberties including religious belief and practice.

Thus, the United States supports Article 18 of the Universal Declaration of Human Rights, which recognizes that "[e]veryone has the right to freedom of thought, conscience, and religion."[5] The scope of this freedom includes the right to teach, practice, and observe religion or belief in public or private contexts.[6] As explained in Chapter 1, the United States supports Article 18 with certain reservations – that is, only insofar as it is consistent with domestic First Amendment protection for such activities.

U.S. law also indicates strong support for international religious freedoms. Congress appropriates and the executive spends substantial funds to facilitate global religious freedom. In addition, in 1988, Congress enacted and President Clinton signed into law the International Religious Freedom Act (IRFA). Among other things, IRFA requires that the United States "oppose violations of religious freedom that are or have been engaged in or tolerated by the governments of foreign countries" and to "promote the right to freedom of religion in those countries."[7] IRFA provides a menu of possible sanctions for the president to invoke in the event of violations of religious freedom by other nations.

For many decades now, ensuring universal protection for religious freedoms has been an official plank of U.S. foreign policy. Thus, the United States officially supports protection for religious liberties regardless of frontiers or borders.

THE FREE EXERCISE OF RELIGION ACROSS BORDERS

The relationship between the First Amendment's free exercise guarantee and territorial borders is not well developed. This is so for a variety of reasons, including limits on the justiciability of free exercise claims and the substance of First Amendment doctrine. However, a variety of laws and regulations, many of which have been discussed in previous chapters, can restrict or even suppress cross-border religious free exercise. To gain a more complete understanding of the First Amendment's transborder dimension, it is important that we understand how free exercise principles and concerns intersect with international borders.

Current Interpretations, Understandings, and Ambiguities

In the past few decades, U.S. free exercise doctrine has changed rather dramatically. In 1990, the Supreme Court held in *Employment Division v. Smith* that application of neutral laws of general applicability to religious practices does not generally violate the Free Exercise Clause.[8] Under current doctrine, the Free Exercise Clause is not offended unless government officials single out certain religious practices for discriminatory treatment.[9]

Smith was not the last word on the subject of free exercise rights. Congress responded to the decision by enacting the Religious Freedom Restoration Act (RFRA), which requires that government officials demonstrate a compelling interest for imposing substantial burdens on religious practices and provides that the restriction must be narrowly tailored to that interest.[10] RFRA was invalidated insofar as it applied to the states, but it continues to apply with regard to federal acts and policies.[11] In addition, other federal civil rights laws, including employment discrimination laws, provide general protections and exemptions pertaining to religious free exercise.

Although these free exercise standards and protections clearly apply within the United States, it is not clear whether they protect cross-border activities. Export and import restrictions, travel bans, and federal laws restricting the provision of material support to terrorists can all be properly characterized as generally applicable laws. However, insofar as they impose substantial burdens on religious practices, they could be subject to review under RFRA's more demanding standard. Moreover, other federal statutes and regulations provide at least some free exercise protection for cross-border activities. For example, current federal laws and regulations prohibit denials or revocations of U.S. passports and exclusion of aliens on religious grounds and would also appear to exempt most religious informational materials from import and export restrictions.

Thus, some federal laws protect aspects of the cross-border free exercise of religion. Whether these or other protections for cross-border free exercise are constitutionally mandated remains an open question. No federal court has ever directly ruled on the constitutionality of foreign travel restrictions or visa denials that are based solely on religion. As one scholar has noted, "There is no clear authority on the question of the government's power to exclude people from this country on the ground of religion or to exclude them when the result would be a serious burden on religion."[12]

In one infamous case involving a federal penalty imposed on a church for entering into an employment contract with an alien minister, the Supreme Court suggested that, owing to America's Christian and religious nature, it could not imagine that Congress would intentionally exclude Catholic ministers.[13] In other cases, however, some justices have not ruled out the existence of a governmental power to exclude aliens based on religious grounds. For example, Justice Frankfurter opined in a deportation case that Congress and the president plainly had the authority to exclude individuals on *any* ground – including, he claimed, anti-Semitism or anti-Catholicism.[14] In *Kleindienst v. Mandel*, which upheld exclusion of aliens so long as the federal government offered a facially plausible justification, Justice Douglas wondered in his dissent whether under the majority's view the government could exclude an alien on the basis of his or her belief about Christ.[15] It is of course possible that singling a person out for exclusion on religious grounds would violate the Free Exercise Clause or RFRA. On the other hand, owing to *Mandel*'s refusal to broadly hold that content-based exclusions violate the Free Speech Clause or other protections, the issue cannot be considered settled.

Nor have courts addressed the constitutionality, or validity under RFRA, of other cross-border restrictions that could substantially interfere with the free exercise of religion. As discussed in Chapter 3, the Supreme Court has recognized a First Amendment right under the Free Speech Clause to receive information from abroad.[16] Although courts have not addressed such a claim, presumably that right would extend to religious materials, at least insofar as they constitute protected speech and are subject to some form of prior restraint. Further, the U.S. government has taken some steps to restrict the cross-border flow of religious expression and materials that are deemed to raise national security concerns. Thus, foreign distributors and domestic recipients of religious sermons or Islamic translations could be subject to prosecution under U.S. laws prohibiting the provision of material support to terrorist organizations.

It is not entirely clear whether the distribution or communication of religious information by U.S. citizens to foreign audiences is protected by the Free Exercise Clause.[17] Only one reported case addresses the application of U.S. export laws to religious materials.[18] In *Welch v. Kennedy*, a Quaker claimed that enforcement of a trade embargo affecting distribution of funds and materials to North and South Vietnam violated his free exercise rights.[19] He argued that the government did not have the power to regulate the provision of humanitarian relief that is motivated by religious conscience.[20] The district court, without analysis, assumed that the Free Exercise Clause applied to the cross-border distribution of religiously motivated humanitarian aid. However, the court dismissed the claim on the ground that the trade laws imposed only an incidental burden on religious practices and beliefs.[21] Today, the embargo law might be treated as a generally applicable law under *Smith*. If a court were to determine that the export ban imposed only an incidental burden on religious free exercise, the claim would also fail under RFRA.[22]

The *Welch* court simply assumed that the Free Exercise Clause applies to the cross-border provision of religious aid or materials.

But if, as discussed in Chapter 4, it is not clear whether the First Amendment's Free Speech Clause protects cross-border communications with foreign audiences, this might not be so clear cut. If a religious practice does not speak to or address matters of faith that are of concern to the domestic polity, does it still fall within the scope of the Free Exercise Clause? Or are religious liberties different in terms of their expected territorial scope?

Cross-border association for specific religious purposes has similarly received scant judicial or scholarly attention. In Chapter 4, I discussed the manner in which courts have reviewed First Amendment cross-border association claims in general. As noted there, courts have relied on a broad conception of the foreign affairs power, extended immigration and other inapposite precedents to these claims, altered basic free speech doctrines such as the speech–conduct distinction, and come perilously close to adopting a long-discredited principle of guilt-by-association.

In *Holder v. Humanitarian Law Project*, the Supreme Court rejected a First Amendment right of association claim brought by American citizens who worked with designated foreign terrorist organizations on peaceful dispute resolution and other projects.[23] The Court said, in essence, that the citizens were permitted to join the organization but not to provide it with any form of actual assistance. *Humanitarian Law Project* did not address whether spiritual forms of support or assistance, such as prayer and other forms of ministry, would also run afoul of the material support ban.

The material support statute contains a specific exemption for certain religious materials.[24] However, if pure speech activities could violate the material support ban, perhaps prayer and ministry might as well. Participating in coordinated religious events or activities would surely lend legitimacy and support to foreign terrorist organizations, which was one of the Court's concerns. On the other hand, recall that part of the Court's rationale for upholding the material support ban as applied to speech was that terrorists' resources were not segregated, and thus even advocacy on their behalf could free up resources for violent activities. It is not clear whether this rationale would extend to coordinated religious services, activities, or associations. If it does, and the material support ban is generally enforced in such contexts,

Humanitarian Law Project may jeopardize substantial cross-border collaborations that are organized and run by religious groups. At the very least, it will expose donors to charitable organizations that are also designated foreign terrorist organizations to criminal liability – even if, as the decision made clear, they lack any intent to further the organization's allegedly unlawful ends.

In addition to this potential limitation, cross-border religious associations have also been negatively and, some argue, disproportionately affected by federal terrorism financing laws. U.S.-based Muslim charities, in particular, have been burdened by federal laws that provide for the seizure and freezing of assets held by designated terrorist organizations.[25] Charitable giving, or *zakat*, is one of the "five pillars" of Islam and is considered a religious obligation of all observant Muslims. Many of the preferred beneficiaries of *zakat* are located in foreign nations. Federal terrorism financing laws can chill, limit, or prevent both domestic and cross-border charitable giving, imposing a substantial burden on Muslims' religious practices.

Further, the closure of domestic religious charities can burden American Muslims' "freedom to associate with Muslim religious and community organizations, including mosques, Islamic schools, Arab and Muslim advocacy organizations, and Muslim charities."[26] This burden stems not only from the enforcement actions themselves, but also from the climate of fear created by policies targeting Muslim charitable giving. Finally, application of U.S. terrorism financing laws and regulations may adversely affect foreign-based religious entities that have First Amendment rights owing to their substantial connections to the United States.[27]

For a variety of reasons, neither courts nor scholars have developed a clear approach to cross-border free exercise issues. With regard to religious expression, the likely supposition is that the Free Speech Clause provides all the protection that is needed. However, as I have observed throughout Part II, the cross-border aspects of freedom of speech have themselves never been fully and adequately developed. With regard to activities such as travel and distribution of religious materials, current federal laws and regulations do provide some protection for cross-border free exercise. Further, as least in the modern era, direct interferences with cross-border religious association have been relatively rare. Finally, some may interpret *Smith* as generally foreclosing free exercise challenges to generally applicable travel, export, and other laws (although RFRA may still provide an avenue for relief in some cases, and so-called "hybrid" claims based on both free speech and free exercise rights may also provide an avenue of constitutional relief).

These reasons ought not to deter closer inquiry regarding the constitutional foundation for cross-border free exercise of religion. Freedom relating to religious practices raises distinct constitutional concerns. In the cross-border context, as in other circumstances, the free speech framework is not an adequate substitute for specific consideration of free exercise concerns.

For example, as discussed in Chapter 3, the Supreme Court has recognized only a weak "freedom" to travel abroad under the Fifth Amendment's Due Process Clause. Whereas in free speech cases courts have been able to avoid First Amendment concerns in part by characterizing the speaker's activity as conduct rather than speech, that argument has no force in the free exercise context.[28] The Free Exercise Clause protects both belief *and* conduct. Thus, we cannot so readily dismiss a minister's or missionary's challenge to generally applicable travel restrictions on the ground that the government has restricted only conduct and nothing more.

Further, as *Humanitarian Law Project* shows, contemporary restrictions on cross-border exchange and association may impose unique restrictions on religious free exercise. Finally, more explicit consideration of cross-border concerns may provide further insight into the merits and demerits of First Amendment provincialism as well as contemporary interpretations of the Free Exercise Clause.[29]

Protecting Cross-Border Religious Conversation and Commingling

The central concerns with regard to cross-border free exercise are the facilitation of cross-border religious exchange and protection for association that is based on faith or religious belief. It is vitally important that we view these concerns as fundamental aspects of the First Amendment's Free Exercise Clause.

Justifications

The First Amendment justifications for protecting cross-border free exercise are similar to, but in some important respects distinct from, those advanced in Chapters 3 and 4 in support of protecting activities such as cross-border movement, speech, and association. As in expressive contexts, the ability to reach across borders has become increasingly important in a globalized society. With regard to religion, in particular, global conflict and misunderstanding call for robust and nondiscriminatory protection for cross-border religious conversation and commingling. Without these freedoms, important opportunities for dialogue, exchange, and understanding will be lost.

Countless recent examples of religious conflict across the globe have demonstrated that cross-border and cross-cultural religious dialog is critically important. Global conflict relating to religious beliefs stems in large part from fundamental misunderstandings regarding the diverse faith traditions and tenets that are practiced across the globe. Protecting free exercise of religion from cross-border restrictions, including even some generally applicable laws and regulations, serves the broader goal of encouraging global religious conversation and commingling.

This does not mean that any and all forms of religious practice would be treated the same. The government surely has compelling reasons for restricting those religious practices that threaten national security or interfere with military operations abroad. However, at least insofar as proselytizing, the provision of materials, and participation in charitable activities are concerned, core aspects of citizens' cross-border free exercise rights are implicated.

Extending constitutional and statutory protections to cross-border religious free exercise would facilitate the global flow of information, theological and other ideas, and religious materials, and would also protect cross-border charitable activities that are based specifically on faith or religion. This approach would protect citizens' ability to engage with domestic and foreign religious communities. As the illustrations in the next subsection demonstrate, this must include participation in foreign religious cultures – even if those cultures have characteristics that our own political and constitutional communities find deeply offensive. Thus, American citizens ought to be free to travel abroad for the purpose of transporting American religious practices and beliefs to foreign nations, as well as to participate in foreign religious cultures.

Protecting cross-border free exercise would also meet American obligations under international and domestic laws relating to religious freedoms. As a state party to the International Covenant on Civil and Political Rights (ICCPR) and the Convention on the Elimination of All Forms of Racial Discrimination, the United States is obligated to respect freedom of religious belief, practice, observance, and worship, and must not discriminate in providing protection for freedom of religion and association. International human rights law expressly protects the freedom to manifest one's beliefs through acts of charity, including charitable donations. Finally, on the domestic front, IRFA expressly recognizes the fundamental and global character of religious freedoms.

Illustrations

To help clarify the extent to which cross-border activities are an important dimension of religious free exercise, I want first to focus on two hypothetical scenarios described by John Mansfield in his work on the religion clauses and foreign relations.[30] Mansfield offered these hypotheticals in the course of articulating his own cosmopolitan approach to transborder religious liberties. His examples and analysis address some of the still-open constitutional issues regarding cross-border free exercise discussed above.

In Mansfield's first hypothetical, American evangelists wish to travel to Indonesia for the purpose of converting people from Islam, Hinduism, and other religions to fundamentalist Protestantism. The Indonesian government objects to what it sees as "a neocolonialist attack on the culture of its country and a threat to the political and religious status quo there."[31] The United States, fearing the possible political and cultural unrest that the evangelists may cause abroad, makes it a crime to travel to Indonesia for the purpose of making religious conversions and denies the passport applications. As Mansfield notes, "Here we have a square conflict between a strong tradition of religious liberty – the right and duty to carry the Gospel to foreign lands – and respect for the wishes of the government of another country."[32]

How ought this conflict to be resolved under the First Amendment? As I have noted, as a matter of current free exercise interpretation, the answer is not clear. Given that religious practices have been explicitly singled out, the hypothetical may be beyond the rule of *Smith* or subject to review under RFRA. Even so, the government may posit a compelling foreign relations interest and argue that its prohibition is narrowly tailored to address the specific conflict that has arisen in Indonesia.

As discussed in Chapter 3, the Supreme Court has recognized only a weak freedom to engage in foreign travel. Moreover, in several foreign travel cases, the Court has deferred substantially to the foreign policy interests of the U.S. government. In addition, in *Humanitarian Law Project*, the Court explicitly relied on the federal government's concerns that certain U.S. allies might be upset if American citizens were allowed to provide certain services to foreign terrorist organizations. As in that case, the question that is raised by Mansfield's first hypothetical is whether respect for the laws and sensibilities of a foreign nation can diminish or even cancel out core First Amendment liberties.

Mansfield contends that even in the areas of foreign affairs and relations, the First Amendment must protect an "irreducible core" of religious liberty, and that this core cannot be violated or encroached on except in the face of "foreign policy considerations of the gravest sort."[33] He does not specifically define this First Amendment core. But certainly it must include the ability to reach across borders to discuss matters of religion and, particularly when this is considered a religious duty, to persuade others to join one's faith.

Foreign policy considerations such as those Mansfield posits are not an adequate basis for requiring that American citizens shed their free exercise rights at the border. The restriction on foreign travel in the example would prevent citizens from engaging with foreign religious communities. It would restrict their participation in an intimate form of religious dialogue. Although international human rights laws do not formally restrict domestic laws relating to cross-border travel and free exercise, the passport denial would also be inconsistent with U.S. obligations to protect freedom of religion without regard to frontiers.

What, though, of respect for Indonesian law and culture? In Chapter 9, I argue that consideration and respect for the laws and cultural norms of other nations is an important aspect of the First Amendment's transborder dimension. The First Amendment is distinct from, and increasingly conflicts with, the expressive and religious liberty regimes of other nations. I argue that American officials and citizens must respectfully engage with foreign laws and avoid all forms of rights imperialism. As I discuss, in some cases, this could mean that foreign speech and other laws will be enforced within the United States. More generally, I argue that in international forums and discourse with other nations, the United States ought to act less provincially and be more aware that it operates within a community of nations with diverse laws and principles relating to expressive and religious liberties.

In Mansfield's hypothetical, the United States is not being asked to enforce foreign laws relating to religious liberty within its own borders. Nor is it seeking to export First Amendment free exercise principles to a foreign nation or to displace local religious laws or principles. Rather, the government has limited the cross-border liberties of its own citizens owing to a political objection lodged by a foreign government. Indonesia may enforce its own laws against U.S. citizens and others who travel into its territory.[34] American citizens can be warned that this may be the consequence of their free exercise and that the First Amendment will not protect them from the necessity of compliance with foreign laws while abroad. However, the First Amendment ought to bar the United States from restricting citizens' foreign travel on the ground that their religious practices would upset a foreign nation or its inhabitants.

In Mansfield's second hypothetical, a Muslim-American applies for a passport for the purpose of traveling to an Islamic country "to participate in a way of life there that includes some discrimination on the ground of religion and a church-state system that would be prohibited in the United States."[35] Here, the citizen does not seek to proselytize or convert foreign citizens, but rather to join a foreign religious culture. The United States defends the denial of the passport on the ground that it believes Islam "creates hostility among other religious groups" and because it wishes to promote freedom of belief and separation of church and state across the globe.[36]

This passport denial restricts citizens' ability to practice a religion whose basic tenets conflict with American commitments to religious equality and church–state separation. In essence, the U.S. government seeks to prevent American citizens from engaging in a form of cosmopolitan free exercise. In the example, the government singles out Islam, a particular religious faith. Thus, the rule announced in *Smith* does not apply. Here, too, the provincial justifications offered by the government are not sufficient to outweigh the citizens' free exercise rights. A central part of the "irreducible core" Mansfield mentions is the right to choose which beliefs to adopt and which religious faiths to practice. In the context presented, both domestic and international law support recognition of such core rights. As Mansfield argues:

> [I]f the ways of the foreign country are not implicitly absolutely condemned by the Constitution, wherever engaged in – as would be the case with slavery or torture – but instead are among those ways of other peoples to which respect is due, there seems no justification for distinguishing between the alien and the citizen, and while affirming the alien's right in the foreign country to live in accordance with these customs, prohibiting the citizen from participating in them as well.[37]

This second cross-border example highlights a fundamental aspect of religious free exercise. The Free Exercise Clause prohibits the government from standardizing citizens' faith. It bars government from restricting the practice of disfavored religions, and it does so regardless of where the religious practice occurs. Just as the Free Exercise Clause prohibits the government from abridging citizens' religious freedoms based on the objections of foreign governments, it bars the government from restricting citizens' free exercise rights based on its determination that religious beliefs or regimes do not ascribe to American values. The United States is free to communicate its views with regard to Islam and other religions in diplomatic and other venues; it is not permitted to do so by restricting the free exercise rights of American citizens. Indeed, the United States ought to demonstrate its commitment to religious liberty and pluralism by vigorously protecting the rights of its own citizens to join whatever faith communities they choose.

Mansfield's hypothetical restrictions are, of course, merely illustrative. Current federal laws prohibit religious discrimination in passport administration. As citizens, we expect those laws to be respected and enforced. However, as the alien exclusion context demonstrates, legislative minds and federal policies could change in response to new threats and challenges abroad. The contours of First Amendment protection in the immigration and foreign affairs contexts remain sufficiently uncertain such that Mansfield's hypothetical problems raise real concerns. Even if they are merely hypothetical at the moment, it is important that we clarify the metes and bounds of the Free Exercise Clause.

Other illustrations reinforce the need to protect core cross-border religious activities and practices. Religion and religious practices cross international borders in a variety of ways. They do so in the form of persons, informational materials, and religious affiliations. In the twenty-first century, we will likely witness the growth of cross-border faith communities. Religious institutions have begun to harness the Internet and digital forums to expand their faith communities. Digitization will facilitate cross-border religious conversation and commingling. However, U.S. laws and enforcement policies will pose some tangible and direct challenges to cross-border free exercise.

In particular, as I noted earlier, U.S. antiterrorism laws may target or have a disparate effect on certain forms of cross-border free exercise. Federal material support laws ought not to be applied to religious activities such as prayer and religious worship, even if these activities involve designated foreign terrorist organizations. Just as peaceful and otherwise lawful speech and association ought not generally to give rise to criminal liability under antiterrorism laws, peaceful forms of religious expression and association ought to be protected in this context. Congress ought to amend the material support laws to make this clear as explicit as possible.

Other forms of religious practice and affiliation, including *zakat* or charitable giving, raise far more difficult questions under the material support and terrorism financing laws.[38] With regard to actual terrorist organizations, *zakat* directly conflicts with the compelling U.S. goal of denying funds to terrorist organizations. As the D.C. Circuit stated in response to a RFRA claim brought by a Muslim organization, "[t]here is no free exercise right to fund terrorists."[39] Even if a court were to accept that donors had a free exercise interest in participating in *zakat*, that interest would likely be outweighed by the government's compelling national security concerns.

Still, as President Obama acknowledged in a 2009 speech in Cairo, Egypt, U.S. "rules on charitable giving have made it harder for Muslims to fulfill their religious obligation."[40] The president stated that the United States was "committed to working with American Muslims to ensure that they can fulfill *zakat*."[41] The challenge, of course, is to restrict only those organizations and donors that actually pose a threat to national security.

International religious communities depend on the free flow of humanitarian and charitable funds. Aggressive enforcement of over-broad terrorism financing laws will disparately affect cross-border religious association. The United States ought to protect the rights of citizens to engage religious schools, charities, hospitals, and other organizations that are part of growing cross-border faith communities. It can do this by, among other things, working with domestic religious organizations to ensure that guidelines for charitable giving are clear, designations of terrorist organizations are accurate, and enforcement of terrorism financing laws does not chill religious affiliations and practices.[42]

As the discussion indicates, providing protection for cross-border religious giving is not solely a civil liberties concern. National security, diplomatic, and foreign affairs justifications also support adopting a more respectful and protective orientation with regard to cross-border free exercise. Chilling the cross-border free exercise rights of Muslim-Americans or others based on religion undermines U.S. goodwill and reputation in the world community. Further, insofar as American anti-terrorism policies denote a lack of respect for foreign religious cultures, this may decrease the incentives of religious communities both at home and abroad to assist authorities in fighting global terrorism.

THE RELIGION CLAUSES ABROAD

In Chapter 6, I argued that the First Amendment's free speech, press, petition, and association guarantees generally apply to U.S. governmental actions abroad. I also argued that, in certain contexts, aliens may also have limited extraterritorial First Amendment rights. Do the religion clauses similarly follow the flag or the government? If so, how ought they to apply beyond U.S. borders?

Free Exercise

There are several circumstances in which extraterritorial free exercise claims might arise. U.S. officials might restrict the activities of American missionaries and other citizens abroad. The United States could enact laws forbidding citizens to engage in any form of religious discrimination abroad.[43] Statutory and constitutional claims might also arise when U.S. citizens employed abroad by government or private entities claim they have been subjected to religious discrimination.[44] Finally, U.S. officials could subject aliens located abroad, including U.S. military detainees, to religious discrimination.[45] Although the justifications and degrees of protection differ with regard to citizens and aliens, the scope or domain of the Free Exercise Clause ought generally to follow the U.S. government as it asserts power across the globe.

Citizens Abroad

The Supreme Court has not addressed the extent to which the Free Exercise Clause protects citizens abroad and the question has not received sustained attention elsewhere. As I have noted, the text of the Free Exercise Clause contains no geographic limitation. Some limited support for extending free exercise protection beyond U.S. borders can be found in the Supreme Court's decision in *Reynolds v. United States*, which held that the Free Exercise Clause applies in U.S. territories that are on the path to statehood.[46] However, given the territories in question, one might argue that this relates more to intraterritorial than extraterritorial constitutional domain. In addition, the precolonial history of religious persecution in foreign nations might lend some limited support to universal protection of citizens' free exercise rights. Having escaped persecution abroad and established free exercise as a fundamental right, it would be odd to then interpret the Free Exercise Clause to permit religious discrimination by U.S. officials when they act abroad.

In addition to these textual, precedential, and historical arguments, general approaches to constitutional domain all seem to support recognition of citizens' free exercise rights abroad. I discussed these general approaches in Chapter 6.

As I explained, the United States has rejected a pure territorial model in which constitutional rights are available only to those within its territory. The Supreme Court's precedents have strongly suggested that the Constitution follows the government as it regulates citizens. The various approaches to constitutional domain indicate that citizens enjoy First Amendment free exercise rights regardless of location. Under a membership or social compact model, citizens would enjoy constitutional protections, regardless of location, simply by virtue of their status as citizens. As I noted in Chapter 6, however, membership is not an attractive approach to First Amendment domain, owing in part to the implication that aliens may not enjoy certain liberties even when they are located within the United States.

Under what has been referred to as a "mutuality of legal obligation" approach, citizens would possess free exercise rights abroad whenever the U.S. government has control over or applies specific laws to them. Pursuant to this approach, domain would be determined by the nature of the restriction and the degree of control exercised by U.S. officials. The scope of the Free Exercise Clause would be less certain, and perhaps somewhat narrower, under the mutuality approach than under the membership model.

Under the functional approach that has been articulated in some Supreme Court cases, the primary question, as Justice Harlan stated in his concurring opinion in *Reid v. Covert*, is whether recognition of the right in question would be "impracticable and anomalous."[47] This approach requires consideration of a variety of factors including location and practical obstacles to recognition.[48] In some contexts, such as active battlefields or the day-to-day conduct of foreign relations, free exercise rights are likely unenforceable. However, as a general matter, recognition of citizens' free exercise claims would not be "impractical and anomalous." There is no overriding pragmatic reason to exempt the U.S. government from free exercise constraints when domestic legislation directly restricts citizens' free exercise rights overseas or when officials act abroad in a manner that targets or discriminates against citizens based on their religious beliefs.

As discussed in Chapter 6, none of the general approaches to constitutional domain adequately captures the central importance of transborder First Amendment liberties. At least with regard to citizens, free exercise rights, like free speech, press, and association rights, ought to be deemed portable and thus globally recognized and enforced.

Cosmopolitan justifications support this conclusion. Free exercise rights follow the government owing, in part, to what one scholar calls "conscience" justifications.[49] That is, respect for free exercise values ought to be considered universal because the United States has itself formally committed to the principle of global religious freedom. The United States ought to lead by example. It cannot simultaneously claim to support universal religious freedoms while denying free exercise rights to its own citizens when they are abroad. It can support universal religious liberties most directly by protecting the free exercise rights of its own citizens regardless of where they happen to be located.

American citizens ought not to fear that protection against religious discrimination by their own government will dissipate or diminish when they cross international borders. As noted earlier, the Free Exercise Clause facilitates cross-border religious conversation and commingling. Some of that cross-border activity may lead to forms of religious affiliation that occur beyond U.S. borders. A refusal to recognize citizens' extraterritorial free exercise rights could restrict Americans' ability to participate in fundamental religious practices beyond U.S. borders. Mansfield's second hypothetical, which was discussed earlier, shows that the failure to recognize free exercise rights abroad could restrict citizens' ability to interact with, and even to join, religious institutions and faith communities located abroad. Such decisions lie at the core of the free exercise guarantee.

Under the conscience and cosmopolitan approach, the government would be prohibited from violating free exercise rights wherever in the world it is operating. The real question is how, specifically, free exercise doctrines and principles would apply in foreign contexts. Extending free exercise protections beyond U.S. shores could lead to conflicts with foreign religious laws and practices. Here, as elsewhere, we must situate the First Amendment in a community of nations that has not in all instances adopted its specific values. More specifically, the United States must determine how much respect it is prepared to give to the laws and religious cultures of foreign nations when it operates and regulates abroad.

For example, John Mansfield posits a hypothetical facility operated by the United States in Saudi Arabia.[50] The Saudi government insists that only Muslims be employed at the facility. The United States acquiesces to this condition, primarily on the ground that the facility is critical to national defense but, let us assume, also to demonstrate respect for local religious laws and norms. As a result, some otherwise qualified non-Muslim Americans are denied an opportunity to work at the facility. Let us assume that along with U.S. taxpayers, these putative applicants object to the discriminatory nature of the employment qualifications.

According to Mansfield, these employment decisions do not violate the Free Exercise Clause or federal laws that prohibit discrimination based on religion.[51] He observes that "[t]he national security interest is great ... and the value of respect for another [religious] culture is present."[52] Although showing respect for the foreign culture will restrict the employment opportunities of some Americans, it will benefit American Muslims who wish to live and work as Muslims in an Islamic country. Thus, on balance, Mansfield concludes that this form of employment discrimination does not "implicate the core value of religious freedom in the first amendment."[53]

I find this case somewhat more difficult than Mansfield does. We agree that the free exercise guarantee applies to citizens located abroad. As I have argued, it is critically important that the American government not prevent citizens from traveling abroad and participating in foreign religious communities and cultures.

The discriminatory hiring policy does facilitate the cosmopolitan pursuits of some Muslim-Americans. However, there is something unsettling about direct participation by the U.S. government in such a blatantly discriminatory employment program. This is especially true when the program singles out a particular faith, a practice that implicates not only free exercise rights, but also a core concern of the Establishment Clause. Certainly, viewed from the perspective of the excluded applicants, the discriminatory hiring policy implicates interests at the core of the Free Exercise Clause.

Showing respect for foreign religious laws and norms is generally an appropriate consideration in extraterritorial contexts. However, as I have indicated in the free speech context, this respect must have some limits. Consider a different hypothetical in which employment at the same facility is conditioned on a signed statement of loyalty to Islam or Shari'a law. Assume that this sort of requirement is common in the foreign country in question and that some American applicants object to the requirement. Are we prepared to allow the federal government to impose a loyalty requirement on American citizens in deference to foreign religious law or practice, so long as it serves U.S. national security interests to do so? Would free exercise and free speech principles forbid this infringement on personal conscience? Mansfield correctly observes that the key consideration must be to protect citizens' core free exercise rights. However, the definition of that core is contested and uncertain.

Suppose, to take another example Mansfield discusses, that a company incorporated in the United States hires an American citizen to fly helicopters in Saudi Arabia.[54] The job requires flying a pilgrimage route to Mecca – specifically, the transport of emergency service personnel who would maintain order among the pilgrims and attend to their safety. Saudi Arabian law makes the presence of non-Muslims in the Mecca region a crime punishable by death. The American citizen, a Baptist, initially agrees to convert to Islam and receives religious training. He later changes his mind and sues under U.S. federal employment discrimination laws. A U.S. court rules that being a Muslim is a bona fide occupational qualification and dismisses the suit.[55]

The balance in this case is a delicate one. The private employer is subject to antidiscrimination laws even when operating abroad, and the citizen retains free exercise protections even though the employment takes place beyond U.S. shores. However, the court's decision seems more defensible than the restrictions on employment at the hypothetical U.S. facility located abroad. In this case, the federal government is not mandating or otherwise coercing any religious conversion. The Free Exercise Clause protects citizens' voluntary choices to participate in foreign religious cultures. The employee consented to a religious conversion so that he could participate in that culture and only later changed his mind. To operate in the specific foreign territory, the employer must comply with Saudi religious laws. Rather than asserting the universal primacy of First Amendment free exercise principles, the court's ruling demonstrates a degree of respect for foreign laws.[56]

These are all difficult examples. Some may view them as evidence of the impracticability of extending free exercise protections to citizens across the globe. As noted in both previous and subsequent chapters, these sorts of conflicts will inevitably arise when governments act beyond their own territorial borders and diverse liberty regimes intersect.

However, courts will not be overburdened by extraterritorial free exercise claims brought by American citizens.[57] When such cases do arise, courts will need to decide how to preserve core free exercise rights in foreign territories that are governed by religious laws and values that differ markedly from those in the United States. In some cases, it may be that core free exercise rights and foreign religious laws can both be respected and enforced. In other cases, there may be an irreconcilable conflict between these interests. In balancing enforcement of core free exercise rights with the government's ability to pursue foreign policy and foreign relations initiatives, courts and officials will need to think carefully about how much respect to show host nations' religious laws and norms. In adjudicating such claims they must generally be careful to preserve the fundamental core of free exercise guarantees. In all but the rarest cases, this means invalidating U.S. discrimination against citizens' particular faiths or religious practices.

Aliens and Extraterritorial Free Exercise

In Chapter 6, I discussed the extent to which First Amendment expressive guarantees applied to aliens located abroad. I concluded that, under a "mutuality of legal obligation" approach, in certain limited circumstances aliens ought to be entitled to assert free speech and other First Amendment protections. For similar reasons, in limited contexts aliens located in the United States or abroad ought to be entitled to assert free exercise rights.

The text of the Free Exercise Clause does not limit either the geographic scope or the class of beneficiaries who are entitled to protection. The history and core principles of religious free exercise condemn all forms of religious discrimination and persecution, whether they occur within the United States or beyond its borders. Finally, as noted earlier, the United States has expressed its commitment to universal protection of religious belief and practice.

With regard to aliens, the Supreme Court has rejected a strict territorial approach to constitutional domain. Further, as discussed in Chapter 6, while some Supreme Court justices have advocated a membership or social compact-based approach under which aliens would not be entitled to constitutional protections, that approach has never commanded a majority. Instead, as the Court recently emphasized, when the U.S. government acts abroad, its powers are not "'absolute and unlimited'" but rather are subject "'to such restrictions as are expressed in the Constitution.'"[58]

The Court has adopted a functional approach to determining constitutional domain that emphasizes the nature and degree of control the United States exercises over the territory in question, the importance of the constitutional guarantee, the status of the claimant, the location of the governmental action, and any practical obstacles to administration of the right beyond U.S. borders.[59] Under this functional approach, in some circumstances, aliens located abroad would be entitled to assert free exercise claims. For example, under the functional approach, it would appear that the Free Exercise Clause and perhaps federal laws regarding religious discrimination apply to alien detainees held at Guantanamo Bay.[60]

Thus, the Supreme Court has itself adopted a more cosmopolitan approach to constitutional domain. Under this approach, aliens are not absolutely precluded from asserting free exercise claims. The functional approach does not provide a central or overarching justification for extending protection to aliens. The reasons to do so, insofar as free exercise is concerned, are again both conscience-based and cosmopolitan. The United States cannot claim to be committed to universal protection for free exercise and other religious liberties yet, at the same time, deny these rights to aliens under its custody or control. This is so whether the aliens are located within or beyond the United States. When the government discriminates against aliens on religious grounds, it has violated a guarantee that transcends borders.

Extraterritorial alien free exercise claims are also not likely to arise with frequency. Under a mutuality of legal obligation approach, aliens would be entitled to free exercise protection when (1) they are located within the United States, (2) the U.S. government has demanded obedience from aliens to its laws, or (3) the United States has detained aliens in territory that lies beyond U.S. shores but is under the control of American authorities.[61] As with free speech and other expressive claims, we must ensure that recognizing such claims abroad will not lead to the dilution of domestic free exercise rights.[62]

Thus, an alien who is threatened with deportation based on religious grounds could assert a viable free exercise claim. An alien excluded from the United States on religious grounds would be entitled to pursue a free exercise claim.[63] As noted earlier, alien detainees held at the Guantanamo Bay detention facilities may be entitled to raise constitutional and statutory free exercise claims.[64] Of course, the United States could extend statutory and constitutional protections beyond this narrow realm. It could, for example, choose to grant free exercise protection to alien employees working overseas.[65]

The United States has an obligation to facilitate and to protect the free exercise rights of its own citizens regardless of location. It ought also to be prohibited from discriminating on religious grounds against aliens over whom it exercises control and from whom it demands legal obedience. In both instances, the class of individuals likely to be affected will be quite small. Conflicts between U.S. and foreign religious laws and values could arise in this class of cases. Despite the difficulties extraterritorial free exercise claims pose, it is critically important that the United States recognize and protect religious free exercise wherever in the world it asserts its power and authority.

Extraterritorial Establishment

Like many other questions relating to the First Amendment's transborder dimension, whether the Establishment Clause applies extraterritorially has not been definitively settled. As the United States pursues foreign policy objectives in the Middle East and elsewhere around the world, Establishment Clause concerns will likely arise with increasing frequency. In Chapter 8 I discuss anti-establishment principles as they relate to the conduct of U.S. foreign affairs. Here I address the more specific and antecedent question of the Establishment Clause's geographic domain.

The United States spends substantial sums of money abroad and maintains diplomatic and other properties in many foreign nations. Some U.S. funds have supported religious institutions and communities abroad. This support has included construction of mosques and other religious institutions, as well as funding of sectarian educational programs.[66] Whether the Establishment Clause applies beyond U.S. territorial borders remains an open question specific and antecedent.

The *Restatement (Third) of Foreign Relations* declares that "the right not to be subject to an establishment of religion [is] protected against infringement in the exercise of foreign relations power as in domestic affairs."[67] Under the Restatement view, the Establishment Clause operates as a structural or separation of powers provision rather than as a guarantee of individual rights. On that basis, the Establishment Clause would apply wherever the U.S. government acts. As a structural protection, the prohibition on establishment of religion would apply to all federal legislation in the same manner as the requirement that funds be properly appropriated by the legislature in order to be expended by the executive. The establishment prohibition would presumably also extend to government-sponsored religious displays and other activities that support religion or specific sects. Thus, in general, the requirement of religious neutrality would apply at U.S. educational, military, and other institutions abroad.[68] The *Restatement* approach is consistent with the cosmopolitan conception of constitutional domain that I have been advancing. It provides for an expansive anti-establishment domain.

The limited judicial treatment of Establishment Clause domain also supports extraterritorial application. To date, only two courts have considered whether the Establishment Clause applies abroad. In *Dickson v. Ford*, the Fifth Circuit dismissed an establishment claim challenging the appropriation of funds for emergency military assistance to the state of Israel, on the ground that it was a political question implicating the balance of power in the Middle East.[69] In *Lamont v. Woods*, the Second Circuit reached the merits and held that the Establishment Clause applied to the expenditure of U.S. funds abroad.[70] As *Dickson* shows, taxpayer plaintiffs face significant hurdles in bringing claims under the Establishment Clause. In general, the Supreme Court has restricted constitutional standing in Establishment Clause cases.[71] Its standing precedents could sharply limit review of administrative actions in foreign nations.

As the only precedent to address the merits of extraterritorial establishment, *Woods* deserves close attention. In *Woods*, Corliss Lamont (who, as discussed in Chapter 4, successfully challenged a federal law restricting receipt of foreign propaganda) and other taxpayers challenged federal grants to twenty foreign religiously affiliated schools. Eleven of these schools were Israeli and nine were affiliated with the Roman Catholic Church. The schools were located in various U.S. territories and foreign countries. They received grants under the American Schools and Hospitals Abroad (ASHA) program, which was authorized by the Foreign Assistance Act.[72] The grants were made to individuals or groups inside the United States for the benefit of the foreign schools. The U.S. sponsors were responsible for transferring the funds to the schools abroad and had virtually no contact with the foreign affiliates.[73] Agency guidance specifically proscribed the use of ASHA grants to train persons for religious pursuits or to construct buildings or other facilities intended for worship or religious instruction.[74]

The *Woods* court observed that the Establishment Clause clearly applied to the ASHA grants to *domestic* recipients because the funding decisions were made in the United States.[75] However, to determine whether the Establishment Clause limited U.S. government actions abroad, the court utilized the analytical framework from *United States v. Verdugo-Urquidez*.[76] As discussed in Chapter 6, in *Verdugo-Urquidez*, the Supreme Court held that the Fourth Amendment's probable cause and warrant requirements did not apply to a search by U.S. law enforcement officials of a nonresident alien's residence in Mexico. Following the analytical approach taken in *Verdugo-Urquidez*, the *Woods* court examined the First Amendment's text, the operation of the Establishment Clause domestically and abroad, the history of the Establishment Clause, the extent to which support for religion overseas relates to and benefits religious institutions in the United States, and policy considerations relating to extraterritorial application of the anti-establishment principle.[77]

As the court noted, the Establishment Clause "contains no limiting language."[78] With regard to history, the court acknowledged that the original understanding of the Constitution's framers with regard to extraterritorial application could not be determined. However, it rejected the government's claim that the Establishment Clause was principally intended to prevent the federal government from establishing a domestic national religion. After reviewing the drafting records and ratification debates, as well as Madison's "Memorial and Remonstrance against Religious Assessments," the court concluded that the Establishment Clause was more broadly intended to prohibit the national government from using taxpayer funds to directly support religion – regardless of context or location.[79]

With regard to the harm that flowed from extraterritorial support for religion or religious institutions, the court noted that, in contrast to an unconstitutional search, which takes place at the time of execution, "any alleged Establishment Clause violations in this case, if established, would have occurred in the United States – i.e., at the time that appellants granted money to United States entities for the benefit of foreign sectarian institutions – and not abroad – i.e., at the time the money was received or expended."[80] The court also emphasized the transnational character of religions and religious institutions. It observed that "because religion transcends national boundaries, [U.S.] aid to a Catholic school in the Philippines may strengthen not only that school, but also the Catholic Church worldwide[.]"[81] Thus, according to the court, U.S. taxpayers were indeed injured by the grants to foreign religious schools.

Finally, the court concluded that no significant policy considerations weighed against applying the Establishment Clause's prohibition on direct funding of religion abroad. Again comparing the application of non-establishment principles to the Fourth Amendment requirements addressed in *Verdugo-Urquidez*, the court concluded that no class of aliens would have standing to challenge U.S. funding programs, Establishment Clause doctrines were "flexible enough to accommodate any special circumstances created by the foreign situs of the expenditures," the expenditures being challenged had no connection to national security, and invalidation of the foreign aid would have no deleterious effects on U.S. foreign aid programs or foreign policies.[82] In sum, the court determined that under an essentially functional and contextual approach to constitutional domain the Establishment Clause's limitations followed the funds.

Woods offers a more complex route to extraterritorial application of the Establishment Clause than does the *Restatement*'s basic structural approach. The opinion has a few technical flaws and ambiguities.[83] Further, it has been criticized on the merits by some commentators, who question whether the court's reasoning has been eroded by domestic jurisprudential developments allowing for sectarian participation in general funding programs and who also contend that U.S. officials may be entitled to broad foreign affairs–type deference when funding sectarian programs abroad.[84]

Despite these flaws and criticisms, *Woods* provides a convincing cosmopolitan account of the Establishment Clause's domain. The court refused to declare plaintiffs' claims nonjusticiable merely because they related in some sense to foreign affairs. It relied on the fact that neither the constitutional text nor history supported a territorial approach to Establishment Clause domain. The court also recognized the transnational character of religion and religious organizations, and thus the futility of relying on a sharp domestic–foreign divide in determining constitutional domain. Ultimately, it adopted the same principle as the *Restatement* – namely, that the U.S. government is bound by Establishment Clause limitations regardless of where it exercises authority. *Woods* provides a plausible alternative justification for applying non-establishment principles beyond U.S. borders, one that is consistent with past and more recent Supreme Court precedents addressing constitutional domain.

Of course, the conclusion that the Establishment Clause applies abroad is only the first step. Once domain has been established, the question is *how* the Establishment Clause ought to be applied abroad. Although there are some similarities, this is a more complex issue than that raised by extraterritorial application of the Free Exercise Clause. As in the free exercise context, when applying the establishment prohibition we must decide how much respect to accord foreign religious norms and cultures. In other words, we will need to situate the Establishment Clause within a community of nations that adopts approaches to church–state relations that differ from those applicable within the United States. In addition, a number of specific doctrinal questions would arise.[85]

One bright-line approach would be to allow U.S. support for sectarian institutions and activities abroad so long as this activity does not violate the laws or constitution of the foreign regime.[86] However, this would sacrifice the core principles of the Establishment Clause to foreign religious laws and cultures.

As he did concerning the Free Exercise Clause, John Mansfield proposed a more balanced and cosmopolitan approach to enforcement

of the Establishment Clause abroad. Writing before the *Woods* decision, Mansfield imagined a hypothetical program in which some portion of U.S. aid was channeled to science education in Malaysia.[87] The
purpose of the funding was to promote economic development in
Malaysia, which the United States hoped would lead to a more peaceful Southeast Asia. Mansfield hypothesized that the only schools in
Malaysia that were eligible for U.S. aid were operated by the government, which insisted that Islamic instruction be provided.

As Mansfield observed, if it were provided in the United States,
this sort of direct assistance would plainly violate the Establishment
Clause. It would have the direct effect of advancing, promoting, or
endorsing Islam.[88] However, Mansfield argued that the provision of
aid in his hypothetical would not violate the Establishment Clause. His
primary concerns were twofold – first, to protect an irreducible core
of protection under the religion clauses and second, to show appropriate respect for foreign religious laws and cultures. With respect to the
Malaysian aid, Mansfield reasoned that the U.S interests in providing
the funds were important, that the aid accorded with the wishes of the
Malaysian government and thus demonstrated "respect for the ways of
other nations," and the burden on religious minorities in Malaysia and
on taxpayers in the United States was not sufficient to threaten core
non-establishment principles.[89]

Relying in part on Mansfield's work, the *Woods* court adopted a
similar flexible approach to extraterritorial establishment. The court
started with the premise that it would be inappropriate and impractical to apply a "mechanical" anti-establishment approach in the foreign
aid context.[90] It noted that respect for foreign church–state models or
cultures might dictate reversal of the usual presumption of establishment in cases involving direct funding for pervasively sectarian institutions.[91] Thus, if the U.S. government could demonstrate a compelling
reason for providing the aid – for example, if the grantee is the *only*
practically available channel for the aid, or "a given country has no
secular educational system at all" – then the grant may not violate the
Establishment Clause.[92]

There are limits to this contextual approach. For example, Mansfield
proposed another hypothetical in which U.S. aid is directed not to science education in a foreign nation but to "the teaching of a moderate

version of Islam, on the theory that it will provide a bulwark against both Communism and Iranian-style Islamic fundamentalism."[93] As he observed, notwithstanding respect for foreign religious norms and weighty national security concerns, such aid might still conflict with core non-establishment values.[94] The same might be said were the U.S. government to directly fund the building of mosques in Islamic nations, even if were to do so for reasons related to foreign relations or national security.

The interpretation of extraterritorial establishment adopted by Mansfield, and by the court in *Woods*, preserves core anti-establishment principles while showing respect for the foreign religious cultures in which U.S. funding and other activities take place. U.S. citizens are entitled to protection from government establishments wherever they might occur. At the same time, the Establishment Clause must be applied in a manner that takes local context into account.

This approach to domain will sometimes require that courts have a basic knowledge of foreign religious laws and cultures. Courts can obtain this information through the assistance of the parties, *amici*, the U.S. State Department, and publicly available information. They must ensure that the circumstances in which U.S. aid directly supports religious endeavors abroad are truly extraordinary and well justified. This approach to Establishment Clause domain will not license broad-based federal aid to religious institutions or projects. Nor will it supplant or dilute domestic anti-establishment standards or principles.[95] As I argued earlier, courts are generally competent to distinguish foreign and domestic contexts for purposes of determining whether the Establishment Clause's core values have been violated.

The approach adopted by the *Restatement*, in *Woods*, and by Mansfield "endorses neither heavy-handed cultural imperialism nor complete cultural relativism, but while insisting on certain fundamentals, also gives recognition to the many paths by which humanity makes its way."[96] To be sure, conflicts and complications will arise as courts apply and uphold religious neutrality principles abroad. However, in addition to preserving and protecting the religious liberties of citizens and certain aliens, extraterritorial application of the religion clauses in foreign contexts could be an educational and otherwise beneficial exercise for Americans. As Mansfield wrote:

It is possibly to our interest that societies with ideas quite different from our own, including ideas about the proper relation between government and religion, should exist. For the answers we have for ourselves are not so certainly correct that we can afford to be without the light that comes from other very different ways.[97]

PART III   THE COMMUNITY OF NATIONS

8 THE FIRST AMENDMENT IN INTERNATIONAL FORUMS

Part II focused primarily on the protection of transborder First Amendment liberties, and in particular individuals' ability to converse and commingle across and beyond territorial borders. Part III addresses broader concerns relating to the First Amendment's status and operation in the global community. Expressive and religious liberties are only part of the concern. In the discussion that follows, I widen the scope to consider more carefully and systematically the manner in which the First Amendment intersects with foreign affairs, transnational diplomacy, and international relations.

This chapter addresses the manner in which the First Amendment applies, operates, and guides governmental activities in what I refer to as international forums. U.S. policies are developed, conveyed, and executed within formal governance institutions, through diplomatic and foreign affairs negotiations, and by means of domestic legislation that affects U.S. relations with other members of the community of nations. In these forums, U.S. diplomacy and foreign relations are conducted primarily through the communications of federal officials, agencies, diplomats, and transnational institutions.

In these areas, constitutional guidance is even scarcer than in the transborder contexts discussed in Part II. Constitutional text, history, custom, and precedent all contemplate that the U.S. government will communicate in international forums through diplomatic messages, official policies, programs, and propaganda.[1] Through these channels, the United States communicates with other states in the community of nations, as well as with foreign citizens across the world. However, there is little concrete guidance regarding the scope of this authority – and, specifically, whether and to what extent the First Amendment's expressive and religious liberty guarantees might apply in or affect international forums.

The federal government has principal responsibility for conducting the nation's foreign relations. However, subnational governments and private speakers also increasingly have substantial interests in various matters of global concern. A locality may wish to express its displeasure concerning alleged human rights violations taking place in Darfur or Syria. A U.S. citizen concerned about the proliferation of nuclear arms may want to send a letter or an e-mail to the Kremlin, urging officials not to scuttle a proposed arms reduction agreement with the United States. Multinational corporations such as Google must sometimes communicate directly with certain foreign regimes regarding business operations and conditions abroad. U.S. citizens have a strong interest in being informed regarding what messages their national leaders and representatives are conveying in foreign lands.

The Supreme Court has stated that in international forums, "the President alone has the power to speak or listen as a representative of the nation."[2] Broad authority granted under foreign affairs, diplomacy, and government speech principles leaves relatively little breathing space for the communication of diverse views and participation by citizens, subnational governments, and others. However, we might instead envision international forums in which a variety of subnational and private speakers participate in more open and dynamic conversations. In these forums, the U.S. government may represent the views of the nation but can still be encouraged to facilitate dialogue or at least avoid suppression of relevant viewpoints. Even if the First Amendment is not formally applicable in international forums collaborative, marketplace, and other free speech principles could inform and guide the exercise of U.S. power there.

In international forums, the First Amendment's prohibition on religious establishment raises some distinct concerns. In Chapter 7, I argued that the First Amendment's Establishment Clause imposes some extraterritorial limits on U.S. governmental authority. As I noted, owing to the character of certain foreign religious cultures and pragmatic concerns, difficult application questions could arise in international contexts. These concerns are magnified by the need for federal officials to act with dispatch and flexibility regarding matters of foreign relations and national security. However, as the United States becomes more deeply involved with religious leaders and institutions abroad, religious neutrality concerns will become more acute. There is little judicial or other guidance regarding the extent to which the First Amendment limits official engagement with religious leaders or communities in international forums. In international forums, the U.S. obviously must be able to engage with foreign religious figures and communities. However, even in international forums, I will contend that in some cases it ought to be required or at least encouraged to respect core religious neutrality principles.

PARTICIPATION IN INTERNATIONAL FORUMS

Participation in international forums takes a variety of forms. These include direct government-to-government communications in formal processes; public diplomacy carried out by the U.S. State Department in foreign nations; broadcasts by the Voice of America and other U.S. media outlets; distribution of U.S. propaganda materials in foreign nations; and participation by subnational governments, corporations, nongovernmental organizations, and individuals in debates regarding matters of international or global concern. The Constitution expressly assigns certain foreign affairs functions. However, participation in international forums is not generally governed by a set of formal rules; rather, its dynamics are largely a product of historical understanding and customary practices. The First Amendment is rarely invoked in international forums, either in terms of imposing formal restrictions on governmental activity or acting as a form of guidance for U.S. officials. My central claim in this chapter is that the First Amendment can play a useful and significant role even in such forums.

The Federal "Voice"

As a matter of constitutional design, the president and Congress share the nation's foreign affairs powers. This includes the critical prerogative to form and communicate the nation's foreign affairs messages. As

Louis Henkin has said, the president is the "sole organ" of the nation in its external relations and its sole representative with respect to foreign nations.[3] As Henkin has put it, the president is the "spokesman" of the nation.[4] Thus, with regard to foreign governments, the president is expressly and impliedly authorized "to make and receive communications on behalf of the United States."[5]

The president's "monopoly of communication with foreign governments" derives in part from his power to appoint and receive "Ambassadors, other public Ministers and Consuls," subject to Senate approval.[6] He also receives heads of state, foreign ministers, and special envoys. The appointment power carries with it the power to instruct appointees with regard to what, where, and how they shall communicate.[7] As Henkin has observed, "That the President is the sole organ of official communication by and to the United States has not been questioned and has not been a source of significant controversy."[8]

The president conducts the nation's day-to-day foreign diplomacy in a variety of international forums. Among the executive's many expressive acts are recognition of foreign governments, proclamations of solidarity with allies, communication of the nation's positions and policies regarding foreign conflicts and international disagreements, participation in treaty-making and negotiation of international agreements, and speaking on behalf of the United States "in the subtle process by which customary international law is formed."[9] The president also defends the nation's interests in diplomatic exchanges and international and multinational tribunals, and frequently calls nations to account for alleged violations of treaties or human rights obligations. In international forums, the president and his representatives engage in various collaborative projects with a variety of secular and sectarian foreign constituencies. In sum, the president is an active, vocal, and powerful participant in international forums.

Although the president is considered the "sole organ" in terms of international diplomacy, Congress directly influences and participates in foreign relations. Congress has been granted various express lawmaking powers with regard to foreign relations, including the power to regulate commerce with foreign nations, to define and punish crimes committed abroad, and to declare war.[10] Like the president, Congress also possesses unenumerated foreign affairs powers.[11] Among other things,, these powers authorize Congress to enact immigration and exclusion laws and to regulate the activities of U.S. nationals abroad.

Like the president, Congress communicates foreign policy messages and objectives. Sometimes it does so through its enumerated legislative powers. Some of the laws and regulations discussed in previous chapters restrict or prohibit certain activities in part to project a message or viewpoint. For example, laws relating to foreign commerce, including the economic embargoes discussed in Chapter 3, help to convey America's policies with regard to foreign regimes. Similarly, federal immigration laws communicate the definition and scope of the American political community. In addition, national security laws denounce or disfavor certain groups and associations in order to counteract their activities or messages. Thus, federal agencies, including the U.S. State Department, are authorized to designate or label certain organizations "federal terrorist organizations." Finally, U.S. laws require that certain incoming materials be labeled "foreign political propaganda." This communicates something about the source of origin and content of these materials to American audiences.

Congress also exercises substantial political influence in the foreign affairs realm. Here, too, it acts through a variety of expressive mechanisms. These include nonlegislative riders, sense resolutions, committee investigations, and, of course, overseas travel and other foreign policy activities by individual members. Members of Congress frequently make speeches about foreign policy, conduct investigations and hearings, attend international conferences, and communicate with aliens and foreign officials abroad. In sum, like the president, Congress is a vocal participant in the conduct of foreign relations in international forums.

As in the domestic sphere, the U.S. also speaks through its purse in international forums. The government spends substantial amounts of money to spread American messages and viewpoints to every corner of the world. When it funds speech, including speech in foreign nations, the federal government often conditions that funding on compliance with restrictions that facilitate dissemination of its own messages abroad. For example, under various presidential administrations, federal law has placed restrictions on domestic and foreign funding recipients' ability to communicate information concerning abortion.

Congress has wide, although not unlimited, latitude under conditional spending programs to disseminate and control American foreign policy messages.[12] Where the federal government adopts a policy and communicates it as speaker, the Court has held that its conditional funding decisions are generally beyond First Amendment scrutiny.[13]

Federal agencies and institutions, including the U.S. State Department and the Broadcast Board of Governors, also transmit messages to foreign audiences. As part of international diplomacy, government agencies and officials facilitate transnational associations and exchanges through which they communicate positive messages regarding the United States.

At least since World War I, the executive and legislative branches have participated in more specific informational or propaganda efforts in foreign nations. Like other nations, the United States disseminates information across the world through radio, satellite, and other technologies. In furtherance of U.S. national security and other objectives, the federal government uses covert military and other clandestine operations as vehicles for distributing information and materials abroad. Some of this information constitutes propaganda that, according to one source, "consists of manipulation of mass communication to influence the attitudes and behaviour of audiences."[14]

Finally, even U.S. courts sometimes communicate in international forums. The "judicial power" extends to cases arising under federal laws and treaties and cases involving foreign ambassadors, as well as to controversies "between a state, or the citizens thereof, and foreign states, citizens, or subjects."[15] Courts interpret federal laws and sometimes issue decisions that affect the claims of aliens and foreign regimes. Indeed, as a result of globalization and jurisdictional expansion, federal courts now frequently operate and communicate in international forums.

Subnational Voices

The Constitution expressly limits the foreign affairs powers of the states.[16] Yet states and localities are part of an interconnected world where local, national, and international concerns frequently overlap. Today, legal resident aliens constitute a substantial and growing segment of subnational political communities. Further, state and local economic and other interests extend far beyond local territorial boundaries.

Neither express nor so-called "dormant" foreign affairs limitations have generally prevented states or other subnational governmental units from engaging in significant activities in the global arena.[17] Subnational governments have long expressed their views regarding matters of international and global concern. Indeed, one constitutional scholar has traced state and local speech in international forums as far back as 1798.[18] The list of subjects on which states and localities have weighed in is long and diverse. For example, through legislation and regulation, states and localities have expressed opinions relating to communism, apartheid, the Arab boycott of Israel, the death penalty, racial equality, and human rights. They have enacted measures condemning conditions, events, and even governmental regimes in South Africa, Switzerland, Northern Ireland, the Soviet Union, and Cuba. None of this expressive activity was authorized or invited by Congress or the president.

Recent enactments relating to human rights violations in Myanmar, genocide in Darfur, and Iranian disarmament confirm that state and local governments are deeply affected by and interested in global events. As discussed later, most recently, at the express invitation of Congress, states and localities enacted Sudanese divestiture measures as a means of protesting genocidal events in Darfur. Finally, several states have become vocal participants in the national debate over immigration policy – a matter that lies at least partially in the foreign affairs realm.

The character and effect of state and local enactments concerning foreign affairs concerns have varied.[19] Some of the subnational measures have taken the form of direct regulations. Subnational enactments have taxed or otherwise penalized local businesses or individuals who have done business with disfavored regimes. Other state and local measures have merely instituted state divestment or encouraged private divestment and economic boycotts. Still others have simply expressed the "sense" of the subnational body with regard to foreign affairs concerns. Finally, like the federal courts, state courts increasingly must read, construe, and apply the laws of foreign nations. Their interpretations and opinions might offend a foreign regime or have other foreign affairs or foreign policy ramifications.

In sum, despite the "sole organ" or "sole voice" principle, many of the aforementioned measures communicate subnational positions regarding foreign policy and foreign affairs. Just as federal laws communicate policy preferences and goals, subnational enactments may express the collective will of state and local political communities.

States and localities have enacted measures for various reasons. Enactments have articulated dissent and disapproval of foreign regimes, sought to persuade national lawmakers to adopt particular foreign policy positions, expressed moral outrage to audiences at home and abroad, or signaled disassociation from human rights violations or other global atrocities. Some of the acts, such as local "sense" resolutions, constitute pure political speech. Others, such as those that couple moral statements with regulatory requirements, might be thought of as a form of symbolic conduct. Still others, such as judicial decisions, may contain statements regarding foreign laws and regimes that might be deemed offensive to officials in the relevant nations.

In sum, although the federal government's voice is undoubtedly the loudest and most forceful one in the foreign affairs arena, it is plainly not the only one that is heard in international forums.[20] States and localities have been frequent and active participants in these forums.

Private Voices

As the discussion in previous chapters has shown, private speech, press, and association often touch on foreign affairs concerns. Like the speech of subnational governments, the speech of individuals, nongovernmental organizations, multinational corporations, and members of the press sometimes addresses or implicates foreign affairs. Previous chapters criticized a number of restrictions on private cross-border and beyond-border expressive and religious activities and addressed the problem of domestic speech that incites violence abroad. I do not revisit those subjects here. Rather, I want to focus more directly on how private voices sometimes enter and affect foreign affairs debates in international forums.

U.S. citizens and corporations speak and associate in the foreign affairs realm in a variety of ways. A substantial amount of domestic expression – speech that originates in the United States – relates specifically to foreign affairs subjects and concerns. The First Amendment protects citizens' rights to address these issues – on blogs, in newspaper letters to the editor, in news reports, in correspondence with their representatives, and so forth. Speakers can freely associate with others to express their views regarding foreign affairs. They can also protest at foreign embassies.[21]

However, some forms of private speech and association more directly implicate foreign affairs. For example, an American citizen might send a letter or other communication that addresses foreign affairs concerns directly to a foreign government or its agents. U.S. citizens might seek to distribute information or messages abroad that foment dissent in foreign lands or incite aliens to revolution in their home nations.

Further, private citizens sometimes weigh in on foreign policy debates when they travel abroad. For example, in the 1960s Stokely Carmichael traveled to Vietnam to directly observe the effects of U.S. foreign policy. When he returned to the United States, Carmichael publicly criticized U.S. foreign policy with respect to Vietnam. Similarly, American public figures such as Jesse Jackson and Louis Farrakhan have traveled abroad in an effort to resolve foreign policy disputes. Presidential administrations have sometimes authorized private citizens to assist in tense foreign affairs situations. As the recent overseas activities of former Presidents Carter, Clinton, and George H. Bush and international celebrities such as Bono demonstrate, private citizens are sometimes informally deputized to act as overseas ambassadors.

U.S. citizens also enter the foreign affairs realm when they invite alien scholars, artists, and others to visit the United States. Chapter 2 examined the First Amendment implications of immigration exclusions. Citizens' desires to hear what an alien speaker has to say in person may sometimes conflict with U.S. foreign policies. U.S. citizens also seek to collaborate with foreign partners on a variety of projects involving subjects ranging from education, to peaceful dispute resolution, to reproductive services. As discussed in Chapter 4, they operate and associate with foreign missions inside and outside the United

States. Domestic activists also collaborate with foreign organizations on human rights and other projects, both at home and abroad. As we have already seen, some of these collaborative ventures may intersect with U.S. foreign affairs and national security concerns.[22]

In international forums, multinational corporations are increasingly involved in communications and collaborations that intersect with foreign affairs. Internet conglomerates like Google and Yahoo! have been involved in direct disputes with foreign governments. Google has been involved in an ongoing, public dispute with Chinese officials regarding China's demand that the company censor access to certain content. This dispute implicates important U.S. foreign affairs objectives and foreign relations concerns. Yahoo! Inc. was involved in a tense conflict with French courts involving application of French hate speech laws within the United States. Owing to globalization and digitization, the frequency of transborder contacts and conflicts between U.S. corporations and foreign regimes is likely to increase.

Finally, the U.S. press also contributes to the marketplace of ideas regarding foreign policy concerns. Press members working abroad frequently report on and editorialize regarding issues pertaining to foreign affairs and relations. As one would expect, while some of this coverage is favorable with regard to U.S. foreign policies, a substantial portion of it is critical. Like other private voices, American press institutions contribute to conversations and dialogues in international forums.

FOREIGN AFFAIRS AND FREEDOM OF SPEECH

In international forums, the free speech interests of various parties intersect with the federal government's foreign affairs authority. This area has generally been governed by a single-voice principle. This principle is based on the "sole organ" concept mentioned earlier. It rests on the provincial idea that the foreign and domestic realms can and ought to be sharply divided. Under the single-voice principle, the federal voice preempts subnational voices and private participation in international dialogue, and conversation is distinctly and sometimes sharply limited by structural constitutional principles. Notwithstanding the compelling interests in federal control, it is possible to envision a more marketplace-based approach in which dialog and cooperation are encouraged in international forums. This approach would maintain ultimate federal control, but would acknowledge the significant subnational and private interests in conversations that take place in international forums.

Foreign Relations and Policymaking

As is the case with other powers, Bill of Rights guarantees apply to and limit the exercise of national foreign affairs authority. Nevertheless, insofar as the day-to-day conduct of foreign relations is concerned, the First Amendment does not impose any readily discernible limits on federal officials. For example, no entity or person (including a member of the press) would have an enforceable First Amendment right to access or attend a meeting between the president and a foreign ambassador who is received at the White House. Moreover, even assuming citizens have First Amendment rights abroad, they have no right to participate in international negotiations or other diplomatic processes. In general, notwithstanding any First Amendment interests claimed by private speakers, the federal government can control the conditions under which it conducts foreign relations.

Putting aside for the moment possible complications raised by the Establishment Clause, the national government also has plenary authority to formulate the specific content of the nation's foreign policy. For example, suppose that the federal government takes a position that is contrary to the views of a majority of the municipalities or citizens of the United States and allocates funds to convey its message across the globe. Mere disagreement with the foreign policy positions taken by the national government would not give rise to a viable First Amendment claim.

Even assuming a plaintiff could surmount standing obstacles, which is quite doubtful, there is no viable First Amendment argument for blocking or suppressing communications made by national officials or their representatives in the conduct of the nation's foreign relations. As discussed later, the articulation of national foreign policy is clearly a form of government speech. As such, it is not clear what, if any, constitutional limits apply to it.[23] But certainly no First Amendment objection would lie.

Finally, to ensure effective dissemination of its foreign policy messages, the national government can act to prevent actual interference with foreign relations. Just as state and local enactments can be expressly preempted if the national government determines that they would actually disrupt relations with foreign governments or harm national security, communications by private individuals that actually threaten foreign policy objectives or harm national security can also be restricted. This is not the same as saying that all private speech that touches on foreign affairs is broadly subject to official suppression or that there is a foreign affairs exception to the First Amendment. However, private speakers have no right to actively insert themselves into, or to interfere directly with, U.S. foreign relations or foreign policymaking.

"Sole Organ" and "Single Voice"

As discussed, under the U.S. Constitution, a longstanding structural principle provides that, in the realm of foreign affairs, the federal government – the president as its "sole organ" and Congress as an important participant – is regarded as the "single voice" of the nation. Simply put, the president plays the lead in foreign affairs. As one commentator has suggested, in the realm of foreign affairs the president has traditionally been considered a "soloist" rather than part of a chorus.[24] Taken literally, this means that in the vast realm of foreign affairs, the national government is not constitutionally required to tolerate the views of any other speaker. It may monopolize the forum. It may do so without regard to ordinary First Amendment rules under which official discrimination based on content is heavily disfavored and generally not allowed.

When Congress expressly preempts state laws, or a state regulatory provision clearly conflicts with a federal law, the Supremacy Clause generally mandates that other voices be silenced.[25] (Whether states and localities might possess First Amendment speech rights is discussed later.) However, Congress and the president rarely speak with such a clear voice. Thus, courts must sometimes determine whether federal pronouncements impliedly preempt subnational initiatives. An even more fundamental question is whether the existence of a "dormant" foreign affairs power preempts *any* state enactment touching on foreign affairs or foreign commerce – whether or not the national government has actually spoken, and whether or not the subnational message conflicts or interferes with any articulated national foreign affairs policy.

Although the Supreme Court has often invoked the sole organ and single-voice principles, its opinions have not charted a consistent path. States and localities have sometimes been permitted to act and, more importantly for purposes of the present discussion, to express their views in situations where foreign affairs are directly implicated. However, in several decisions, the Court has indicated that the sole organ and single-voice principles are potentially broad and strongly preemptive.

For example, in *Zschernig v. Miller*, the Court held that owing to constitutional grants of foreign relations powers to Congress and the president certain offensive state speech touching on foreign affairs was impliedly prohibited. In *Zschernig*, the Court reviewed a state law that required that judges, in ruling on aliens' testamentary claims, determine whether foreign laws contained a reciprocal right that would entitle U.S. citizens to take property.[26] The Court chastised several state courts for negatively characterizing, and in some cases expressly denigrating, foreign regimes in the course of adjudicating aliens' testamentary dispositions. Owing to what the Court referred to as the "great potential for disruption or embarrassment" attending such statements, it was reluctant to place the matter "in the category of diplomatic bagatelle."[27] The Court concluded that under the state escheat and testamentary statutes, judicial criticism of "authoritarian" regimes was both unavoidable and constitutionally problematic. This offensive subnational judicial speech, the Court reasoned, was impliedly preempted because it might adversely affect and interfere with the conduct of foreign relations and the federal government's ability to convey a unified foreign policy.[28]

Zschernig represents the Court's most aggressive statement of the single-voice principle. Although more recent cases have not expressly relied on its reasoning, *Zschernig* has never been overruled. Although they do not go quite as far as *Zschernig*, the approaches taken in more recent Supreme Court decisions could also broadly suppress subnational expressive measures relating to foreign affairs.

In *Crosby v. National Foreign Trade Council*, decided in 2000, the Supreme Court invalidated a Massachusetts law that barred state entities from contracting with companies that did business in Burma on the ground that the provision (and other similar laws) was preempted *sub silentio* by a federal law that imposed economic sanctions on Burma.[29] Massachusetts enacted the divestiture law partly as a means of disassociating itself from Burma's human rights practices. Thus, the Massachusetts law was one means of expressing state disapproval of Burmese officials' conduct. In that respect, the state law shared the overarching goals of condemnation and economic isolation being pursued by the United States. Nevertheless, the Court held that the Massachusetts law violated the single-voice principle and contradicted federal policy. It concluded that the state law was statutorily preempted because it intruded on the president's diplomatic powers, imposed sanctions on foreign entities, and compromised the president's ability to speak for the United States with regard to Burmese policy. Although the Court relied on statutory rather than constitutional preemption principles, as a result of its decision state and regulatory actions intended to disassociate through divestiture were ruled invalid.

Most recently, in *American Insurance Association v. Garamendi*, the Supreme Court held that a California law requiring disclosure of information regarding Holocaust-era insurance policies impermissibly interfered with the president's conduct of foreign affairs.[30] California's law was intended primarily to provide information to Holocaust victims' families residing in the state. It required that insurers make the disclosures, leave the state, or lose their state licenses. Although the Court declined to decide whether, under *Zschernig*, any state enactment touching on Holocaust claims was constitutionally preempted, it indicated this might well be the case where states strayed from what the Court characterized as their "traditional" responsibilities.[31] According to the Court, it was sufficient that California's law conflicted with a federal *policy* emphasizing cooperation rather than sanctions. Thus, the state law was incompatible with the single-voice principle. In essence, the president had proposed a whisper while the states wished to speak in a louder tone.

The apparent breadth of the *Garamendi* decision prompted a strong dissent from Justice Ginsburg, which was joined by Justices Stevens, Scalia, and Thomas. The dissenters were uncomfortable with the broad dormant preemption approach taken by the majority. As they saw it, California was merely attempting to convey critical information to a segment of its population. The dissenters would have required that the president actually speak clearly, preferably through an executive agreement, before considering whether the single-voice principle preempted California's attempt to communicate information to its citizens through the disclosure statute.

As discussed later, these decisions have not entirely prevented states and localities from making their voices heard on matters relating to foreign affairs. However, if applied literally, *Zschernig* and other preemption decisions would substantially limit participation by subnational governments in foreign affairs conversations taking place in international forums. The Supreme Court has indicated that even merely *offensive* subnational government speech may be silenced. It has not required that federal officials articulate a clear message as a prerequisite to preemption. Further, the Court has discovered conflicts with federal prerogatives even where the subnational speaker does not take a dissenting view and no actual disruption or interference occurs.

In sum, Supreme Court precedents retain fairly robust single-organ and single-voice principles. In the vast external realm of international forums, at least as a formal matter the federal government enjoys a constitutional monopoly on expression. Although cases such as *Szchernig*, *Crosby*, and *Garamendi* involved offensive utterances, disassociation activity, and information distribution by states, respectively, First Amendment free speech principles were not raised or discussed in any of the cases.

Private Speech Rights in International Forums

Domestic speech by private speakers on matters relating to foreign affairs is not subject to any general federal preemptive power. However, as discussed in earlier chapters, when individuals and associations seek to participate in transborder conversation and commingling, their

First Amendment rights are certainly regarded as less robust than in domestic settings.

As we have seen, foreign affairs deference is deeply embedded in judicial review of transborder First Amendment claims. The Supreme Court and lower courts have approached regulations of private speech and association touching on foreign affairs with a degree of deference sometimes bordering on the granting of plenary federal powers.

Speech that indirectly implicates foreign relations or foreign affairs concerns has been treated exceptionally. Indeed, the *only* case in which a Supreme Court majority has ever upheld a content-based law involved cross-border speech that raised foreign affairs concerns.[32] In other contexts as well, courts have concluded that citizens' speech and association rights must yield to asserted federal foreign policy and national security interests.[33] As I argued in Chapter 4, the breadth of judicial deference to national power in the foreign affairs realm strongly suggests that there is an implicit foreign affairs exception to the First Amendment.

As discussed in Chapter 4, federal laws also impose special restrictions on access and distribution with regard to certain materials relating to U.S. foreign relations. The Court has held that domestic distributors of "foreign political propaganda" can be compelled to label their materials as such, as a means of conveying information to American audiences regarding the origins and content of the expression.[34] Moreover, until very recently, federal law barred American citizens from obtaining and distributing information relating to certain foreign affairs matters. The Smith–Mundt Act broadly prohibited Americans from accessing and distributing within the United States any propaganda materials distributed by their own government in foreign nations. The law was enacted in part out of concerns that federal agencies would distribute coercive propaganda within the United States. In effect, however, the Smith–Mundt restrictions barred citizens from learning what their own government was saying to foreign audiences. Nevertheless, prior to the recent partial repeal of the domestic dissemination ban, which allows Americans to obtain and listen to at least some foreign propaganda distributed by the federal government, federal courts rejected both First Amendment and freedom of information challenges to the Smith-Mundt restrictions.[35]

Further, as discussed in Chapter 3, it remains unclear whether the federal government can deny entry to aliens based solely on ideological grounds. Current federal immigration law contains broad foreign affairs grounds for exclusion. Federal law permits the secretary of state to exclude aliens when he or she has "reasonable ground to believe" that the alien's entry or proposed activities "would have potentially serious adverse foreign policy consequences."[36] Pursuant to this statutory authority, the government might contend that a domestic audience's desire to hear a high-profile foreign speaker's claim that a nuclear-armed Iran would be a *positive* development for world peace is outweighed by current U.S. foreign policy regarding disarmament.

Finally, under a more direct but rarely enforced restriction, federal law actually codifies a single-voice principle with respect to private speech regarding foreign affairs. The Logan Act of 1799, which criminalizes any unauthorized communication by a U.S. citizen (regardless of location) to a foreign government, is firmly rooted in the single-voice principle. Under the terms of the Logan Act, all private speech directed to foreign governments that has not been expressly authorized by the United States (presumably by the U.S. State Department or some other agency with appropriate jurisdiction and authority) in advance is expressly prohibited and subject to criminal penalties. Stokely Carmichael, Jane Fonda, and other private citizens who have traveled abroad and communicated with foreign governments and agents have technically violated this federal law. At least according to its literal terms, the Logan Act is broadly preemptive of private expression in international forums.

FOREIGN AFFAIRS SPEECH AND FIRST AMENDMENT PRINCIPLES

Rather than view international forums as places where the federal government holds an effective monopoly on speech, we could instead conceive of them as more akin to international free speech marketplaces. The strict foreign–domestic divide on which the preemptive model rests fails to account for the substantial interests of subnational and other speakers in foreign affairs debates – not to mention the reality of their longstanding participation in foreign affairs conversations. It also fails to acknowledge important social factors, such as technological advances, that render restrictions on distribution of and access to diplomatic and foreign affairs materials less effective. We ought to leverage and apply First Amendment marketplace and other free speech principles to construct a different conception of the intersection of free speech and foreign affairs. In the text that follows, I explore several ways that this might be accomplished. These alternatives include recognizing and enforcing the speech rights of subnational governments; adopting a model of free speech federalism that is based on dialogic principles; and creating more breathing space for private voices in international forums. I also propose some First Amendment guidelines for the dissemination of U.S. propaganda in international forums, and provide free speech justifications for permitting domestic access to and circulation of propaganda materials distributed abroad by the United States.

International Marketplaces and Foreign Affairs Dialog

International forums are the physical and virtual places where foreign relations are conducted. They are places of conversation, commingling, message distribution, and dialog involving the United States, foreign governments, and private actors. As I discussed earlier, despite broad constitutional grants of foreign affairs authority to federal actors, a variety of institutions and individuals regularly participate in foreign affairs discussions and debates. International forums are already vibrant, diverse, and dynamic marketplaces of ideas where viewpoints intersect and clash and solutions to international and global problems are sometimes produced through dialog and cooperative action.

To be sure, national governments are the dominant voices in these marketplaces. As a function of international law, constitutional interpretation, and the nature of foreign relations, they will remain so. However, the mere fact that some voices are more prominent than others in international forums does not mean that the speech marketplace metaphor is inapposite. International forums are not perfect marketplaces; but then again, neither are most domestic marketplaces, particularly those in which a few well-heeled voices tend to dominate the discussion. The essential point is that we can conceive of international forums, in physical and metaphysical terms, as marketplaces of ideas.

Although international forums are themselves generally located beyond U.S. shores, the conversations in these marketplaces often implicate domestic self-governance concerns. I have argued throughout the book that the principle of self-governance is not territorially limited or confined. As noted earlier, subnational governments, individuals, and private organizations all have significant stakes in foreign affairs debates and outcomes. As I argue below, a broad debate that includes subnational governments and other speakers can improve the making of U.S. foreign policy. It can also provide an important channel for dissenting views concerning foreign affairs issues. Finally, ensuring that citizens have full access to American foreign propaganda not only improves political debate regarding foreign affairs but also serves as a check on abuse of power in international forums.

The cosmopolitan values discussed in Part II also apply in international forums. In an interconnected world, institutional and individual interests are no longer defined in territorial or geographic terms. The ability to converse and commingle in international forums to at least some degree is critical to governing diverse local communities, forging cross-border connections, obtaining information from distant sources, and facilitating global discourse. A federal monopoly on foreign affairs speech stifles debate on matters of global concern and limits citizens' and organizations' expressive liberties. For citizens who are interested in matters of global concern, international forums are critical sites of autonomous engagement and development.

Challenging or Lowering the Federal Government's Preemptive Voice

Assuming that First Amendment justifications and principles are relevant in international forums, the primary question is how to create breathing space for foreign affairs speech by nonfederal actors while at the same time respecting federal supremacy. I begin with criticism of the single-voice principle, and then consider ways that subnational governments' ability to engage in foreign affairs debates might be protected or enhanced. States and localities could be granted First Amendment free speech rights. However, for reasons I will discuss it is not clear whether this would provide much in the way of formal protection to subnational speech. In the alternative, I propose that the federal government's preemptive voice be lowered through more frequent resort to a process some scholars refer to as "dialogic federalism." Whether or not states and localities possess formal speech rights, this approach recognizes subnational governments' expressive interests in international issues and conversations. Finally, with regard to private individuals and organizations, I reiterate that a strongly preemptive federal monopoly on foreign affairs speech – a foreign affairs "exception" – would violate the First Amendment and thus ought to be rejected.

The Single-Voice "Myth"

Thus far I have assumed that subnational governments speak or engage in expressive activity. As noted in the earlier description of their activities in the foreign affairs realm, states and localities often pass "sense" resolutions in which they take positions on matters of international or global concern. These are clearly expressive acts. Later, I address whether subnational governments have free speech rights. For now, it is sufficient that they communicate their views on matters of global concern in international forums.

Under the broadest interpretation of the single-voice principle, the Constitution impliedly preempts all subnational expression on foreign affairs concerns. In *Zschernig v. Miller*, the Supreme Court held that statements made by judicial officials were impliedly preempted, and thus could be suppressed by the federal government, owing to the *offensiveness* of their content. This holding was not premised on any evidence of actual interference with or disruption of U.S. foreign relations. Rather, the Court based its decision on the mere prospect that foreign governments might react negatively to the judicial opinions.

As I noted earlier, the Supreme Court has not directly relied upon *Zschernig* in its more recent foreign affairs cases. However, it has not overruled the case or suggested that its reasoning is no longer valid. If we want to create some additional breathing space for subnational expression in its purest sense (i.e., sense resolutions and similar enactments), we must reject *Zschernig*'s interpretation of the single-voice principle.[37]

Constitutional scholars have criticized the "single-voice" principle on various grounds. In perhaps the strongest critique, Sarah Cleveland has argued that in terms of constitutional text, history, and realpolitik, the principle is simply a "myth."[38] As described earlier, the president, Congress, and the federal judiciary share the foreign affairs power.

They do not always speak with "one voice."[39] Nor, as noted earlier, have states and localities actually been silent with regard to foreign affairs. Indeed, Cleveland catalogues a long history, beginning in the colonial period, of subnational expression in international forums. The line separating "domestic" from "foreign" concerns has never been as clear as the single-voice principle suggests. As other scholars have observed, that line has blurred considerably as a result of the economic and other aspects of globalization.[40]

This long history of subnational participation in international forums should come as little surprise. As discussed in Chapter 2, the Constitution itself has cosmopolitan origins. From the beginning, citizens and officials have been communicating with each other and with those beyond U.S. borders on matters of international and global concern. What is more, on many occasions, the national government has actually *invited* subnational governments to express their views with regard to foreign affairs concerns. Thus, the idea that the nation has only one speaker in international forums does not comport with American history or the actual conduct of foreign affairs.

Abandoning *Zschernig* would not allow states and localities to interfere with foreign affairs or foreign relations. The concern is that state and local pronouncements could undermine federal prerogatives on the world stage, or create confusion by setting up hundreds of mini departments of state communicating a variety of foreign policy messages. However, at least with regard to subnational sense resolutions and the like, this concern is overstated. In many instances, states and localities communicate messages that are entirely consistent with and support the national position. Further, the federal government has more than adequate constitutional and diplomatic means at its disposal for clarifying and communicating U.S. positions on foreign policy. To the extent that a given state or locality might express a view that is inconsistent with U.S. foreign policy, there is little reason to think that foreign leaders will be unable to discern who speaks for the nation.

Zschernig rests on a vision of speech in international forums that does not comport with either text or historical practice. The Constitution itself does not expressly or impliedly preclude subnational governments from simply stating positions on matters of global concern, or more generally from participating in foreign affairs debates.

Subnational Speech Rights?

The fact that the Constitution itself does not impliedly suppress or censor subnational expression does not mean that Congress might not do so by explicit enactment. In that event, the question whether subnational governments possess First Amendment free speech rights would be directly implicated.

We can start, again, from the premise that the First Amendment limits the exercise of *all* enumerated federal powers, including the foreign affairs powers of the United States. If that is so, and if subnational actors sometimes speak, then we must determine whether their speech rights are protected in some sense from federal regulation in the foreign affairs realm.

To present the matter in specific terms, imagine that Congress enacts the "Unitary Voice Act" (UVA), which provides:

> No state or any governmental subdivision thereof may issue any proclamation, resolution, or other statement that either (1) is inconsistent with or critical of the policy of the federal government with regard to a foreign government, or (2) that may bring into public odium any foreign government, party, or organization, or any officer or officers thereof, or bring into public disrepute political, social, or economic acts, views or purposes of any foreign government, party, or organization.[41]

Note that we are still only considering pure forms of subnational expression – proclamations, resolutions, and statements – rather than regulatory measures that might have some expressive element. Suppose, then, that a state or locality, wishing to issue a resolution on some matter relating to foreign affairs, challenged the UVA on First Amendment grounds.

The Supreme Court has recognized that governmental entities can engage in speech, and has held that government speech is not limited by free speech principles.[42] However, the Court has never decided whether subnational governments possess speech *rights* that can be interposed against national or other forms of regulation. Scholarly and judicial support for granting such rights to subnational governments has been somewhat tepid. A few commentators have argued that courts ought to recognize such rights.[43] A handful of other scholars have invoked free speech values in support of state and local measures, but have stopped short of calling for recognition of First Amendment rights.[44] Courts, too, have generally been reluctant to embrace the notion that states and localities possess formal speech rights.[45]

The case for recognition of subnational free speech rights generally, and in particular in the foreign affairs realm, has some merit.[46] The text of the First Amendment does not expressly prescribe the beneficiaries of the free speech guarantee. Since the colonial era, subnational governments have frequently participated to some extent in foreign affairs debates. Early product boycotts by localities, which were similar to recent subnational divestiture measures, were used to express moral outrage and dissociative sentiments. Moreover, the First Amendment was at least partially envisioned by the founders as a broad structural constraint on federal powers.[47] Thus, its guarantees might be interpreted to shield states and localities from certain forms of federal regulation.

Recent Supreme Court decisions lend additional support to the argument in favor of recognizing subnational speech rights. In *Citizens United v. FEC*, the Court emphasized that speaker *status* cannot be determinative of First Amendment rights.[48] Like corporations, political parties, and other associations, subnational governments collect, channel, and give voice to their members' viewpoints. Further, as noted, the Court has held that local governments are not only capable of speaking, but are also entitled to a kind of First Amendment immunity when they do so.[49]

In terms of First Amendment values, subnational communications serve a number of beneficial purposes. By conveying information to both local and national communities, these measures contribute to both domestic and international marketplaces of ideas concerning foreign affairs. By expressing the collective will of state and local political communities, they can facilitate self-government.[50] In some instances, subnational enactments provide a channel for communicating dissent and for engaging in what constitutional scholars have referred to as "uncooperative federalism."[51]

Contrary to the Court's suggestion in *Garamendi* that states have no legitimate interest in participating in debates outside their "traditional" spheres, in a globalized and multipolar society, "traditional" state and local concerns are not readily identifiable by reference to territorial boundaries. Formal recognition of their speech rights might encourage states and localities to participate in international debates that increasingly affect their and their residents' actual global interests. Recognition would also facilitate the expression of subnational dissent, collective moral outrage, and disassociation, which could result in more effective participation in foreign policy debates.

If states and localities possess speech rights, as a content-based enactment, the UVA presumably would be subject to strict scrutiny. Even granting that the federal government's interests in conducting foreign affairs are compelling, the UVA is an extraordinarily broad restriction on speech and is thus not likely to be viewed as narrowly tailored. Of course, more narrowly drawn restrictions might well satisfy heightened scrutiny.

To be sure, many complications would arise as a result of judicial recognition of subnational First Amendment speech rights, in particular in the foreign affairs area.[52] Thus far, we have been discussing sense resolutions and similar forms of expression. But courts would likely be forced to draw lines among pure speech (sense-of-the-institution measures), pure conduct (subnational tax and regulatory measures), and speech brigaded with action (some divestiture and other measures). As in traditional free speech contexts, these measures might be subject to different First Amendment standards or lie beyond the First Amendment's protections. Outside the category of pure speech, federal limits on state and local measures would likely be upheld.

There are other complications and concerns. The pronouncements of state and local institutions generally will not convey the views of all constituents. Thus, protection of dissenting and minority rights could raise significant concerns. Moreover, states and localities would likely have less robust free speech rights than individuals. For example, they might be forbidden from expressing views that violate or offend the Fourteenth Amendment's Equal Protection Clause, or perhaps other constitutional guarantees.

Finally, we ought to consider the effect on the federal structure and federalism itself. If granted speech rights, states and localities might enjoy some measure of protection against compelled speech, which may be rooted in both First Amendment and anti-commandeering principles.[53] Further, the category of state and local enactments that can plausibly be characterized as expressive, and thus protected by the Free Speech Clause, could be significant. The overall effect on the distribution of power, and federal prerogatives in particular, might be significant.

None of these concerns or complications is necessarily insurmountable. In many cases, courts will have little or no difficulty distinguishing expressive enactments from those that are regulatory. Courts could limit First Amendment protections to sense resolutions and other plainly expressive measures. Whether the subnational institution is "speaking for" a political community may be a difficult question to answer definitively; thus it is important that avenues of dissent remain open to both members of the community and dissenting lawmakers.[54] Constitutional limits on state and local speech, including the Equal Protection Clause, will not likely affect expression on matters relating to foreign affairs. Further, granting states and localities a potential free speech defense to preemption when they express moral outrage or associative preferences in the foreign affairs realm need not portend any major redrawing of state and federal boundaries in domestic arenas. Again, this is certainly the case insofar as courts limit First Amendment protection to purely expressive measures such as sense resolutions.

There is one complication that might prevent even sense resolutions (i.e., "pure speech") from being shielded from broad and implied federal preemption. As I have indicated, the government speech doctrine effectively allows a government speaker to disregard First Amendment limitations. The single-voice principle might be considered a government speech rule in the sense that it essentially provides that the national government need not tolerate other voices in international forums. If this is so, then the federal government can suppress subnational speech, whether on the basis of its content or for any other reason.[55] Under this principle, backed by the force of the Supremacy Clause, subnational speech rights could be broadly preempted.

The foregoing assumes that preemptive government speech principles would apply in the foreign affairs context – a determination the Supreme Court has not yet made.[56] At least as developed thus far, the government speech principle would not seem to support a broad form of implied preemption or something like the UVA. Although it has not imposed precise limitations on government speakers in terms of articulating clear messages, the Supreme Court has never actually applied the government speech doctrine where the government has remained completely silent.[57] In other words, the Court has not yet recognized or articulated a "dormant" government speech doctrine. In the absence of some actual federal message or communication, states and localities would presumably remain free to communicate collective views through sense resolutions and similar enactments.

Permitting subnational speech in the absence of an articulated federal policy would admittedly place some burden on the national government to be more vigilant in terms of monitoring state and local developments. In the case of clear articulation of a federal policy, government speech and supremacy principles likely would lead to preemption of any subnational speech. Courts would have to decide how much clarity is required in this particular context.[58]

Granting subnational governmental entities speech rights could provide some minimal protection for purely expressive measures such as sense resolutions. Although there are meritorious arguments for taking this modest step, courts are likely to remain skeptical and cautious. Among the many doctrinal challenges recognition of subnational speech rights would generate, perhaps none looms larger than application of the government speech principle. Courts may prefer the more traditional ground of structural principles to the uncertainties of the government speech principle. But again, where the government has not said anything and subnational governments have entered a foreign affairs conversation, First Amendment free speech principles, if not formal rights, suggest that their communications ought to receive some protection.

Dialogic Federalism and Free Speech

Even if recognition of subnational speech rights would prevent something like the UVA from being enacted, it is not likely to generate robust subnational participation in foreign affairs debates. At most, it would likely only protect subnational actors against implied constitutional preemption of a small category of foreign affairs pronouncements.

There is an alternative path, based more generally on First Amendment principles and values, for facilitating state and local participation in international forums. Rather than look to the uncertain protections of judicial review, we could focus instead on political processes and venues. Specifically, as some scholars have argued, the concept of "dialogic federalism" presents opportunities for encouraging more diverse participation in foreign affairs debates in international forums.[59]

In essence, rather than conflict and preemption, dialogic federalism envisions "vertical" conversation and cooperation. It recognizes the multipolarity of modern foreign relations and the expressive interests of subnational actors. Dialogic federalism rejects the centralized framework represented in cases such as *Zschernig* and other recent preemption decisions. As the label suggests, the approach is grounded on First Amendment norms and values. It is a mode of federalism that invites speech from a diversity of sources, including subnational actors, nongovernmental organizations, and federal lawmakers. Diversity is encouraged in the hope that it will better serve democratic values than a broadly preemptive, single-speaker, monopolistic model. As scholars have suggested, by opening foreign affairs discussions to multiple speakers, dialogic federalism principles and processes may produce both more democratically legitimate and more effective U.S. foreign policies.[60]

In practice, a free speech federalism based on dialogic principles would look something like the Sudan Accountability and Divestment Act of 2007 (SADA).[61] Within carefully defined limits set forth in SADA, Congress issued an express invitation to states and localities to consider enacting Sudanese divestment measures. Thus, rather than preempt and suppress subnational voices, Congress invited states and localities to participate in an ongoing conversation in an international forum. This allowed the federal government to preserve the essential function of the forum, namely the pursuit of its own foreign policy goals, while encouraging speech by subnational participants with a specific interest in the outcome.

Dialogic free speech federalism would allow states and localities to participate in diverse ways in foreign affairs debates. In contrast to the constitutional path discussed previously, which may provide limited First Amendment protection for sense resolutions and similar enactments, dialogic federalism allows for stronger divestiture and regulatory measures. At the same time, it avoids judicial and other uncertainty by ensuring that foreign policymaking remains the ultimate responsibility of the national government. Although it must sometimes act with centralized dispatch, as SADA demonstrates, the federal government can often proceed by means of cooperation rather than command-and-suppression in international forums.

A dialogic approach does not view subnational voices as obstacles to federal foreign policy objectives. Rather, dialogic federalism conceives of foreign policymaking as a joint venture. Under this conception of free speech federalism, national officials are more likely to view states and localities as participants in the marketplace of ideas relating to foreign affairs concerns. Subnational actors can sometimes assist the national government in conveying a unified message in international forums.

Dialogic processes do not have to proceed by way of federal invitation and central control. In other contexts, through local experimentation, subnational actors may be able to convince federal officials to alter national policies in ways that better reflect the views of the American public. Thus, in some cases, state and local expression and experimentation can lead to bottom-up policymaking. On several occasions, including with respect to South African apartheid, human rights violations in Myanmar, and most recently Iranian nuclear disarmament, national lawmakers responded only *after* states and localities had enacted measures signaling their objection and dissent.[62] The federal government can create space for these measures by lowering its own voice in international forums, thus permitting subnational conversation to add to the marketplace of ideas.

Dialogic federalism has some limitations. Although there will certainly be opportunities for subnational persuasion, the approach works best when the different levels of government agree on a consensus position. Thus, in general, subnational dissent and other forms of "uncooperative federalism" may receive too little protection in dialogic processes. Dialogic federalism is also largely based on the retention of traditional conceptions of centralized governance and international engagement. The federal government may control the terms and contours of the debate. As SADA shows, it can thus prescribe rather strict limits on subnational speech. In all of these respects, dialogic free speech federalism departs considerably from the marketplace model and limits certain forms of subnational self-governance. It sacrifices some free speech values in the interest of centralization and unity of message.

Nevertheless, dialogic federalism represents a far more attractive approach than the preemptive model of *Zschernig* and the single-voice principle more generally. Indeed, either alone or perhaps in combination with some minimal recognition of subnational "pure" speech rights, dialogic federalism would create significant opportunities for states and localities to participate in the crafting of foreign policy. As the federal government becomes more comfortable with the notion that states and localities are policymaking partners rather than meddlesome adversaries, more robust participation in international conversations is likely to follow.[63]

An approach that facilitates more frequent participation by subnational governments in international forums would acknowledge the fact that states and localities have considerable stakes in the manner in which the United States relates to and communicates with members of the community of nations. It would formally recognize that territorial borders and geography do not define distinct spheres of national and subnational concern. And it would demonstrate that First Amendment marketplace and self-government justifications are useful guides in the making of national foreign policy. In short, this approach would view the presumptively federal arena of foreign affairs from a more cosmopolitan perspective.

Private Voices in International Forums

Of course, subnational governments are not the only important non-federal voices addressing foreign affairs. Citizens, from the single blogger to the large multinational corporation, also participate in foreign affairs conversations in international forums. When they do, the First Amendment's free speech and free press guarantees are directly implicated.

In the twenty-first century, multinational corporations and international nongovernmental organizations have become increasingly active in the areas of foreign affairs and foreign relations. These entities do not merely engage in international trade or provide humanitarian relief. They also export cultural goods and engage with foreign regimes. Sometimes, they do so in coordination with the U.S. government, as when the federal government funds democracy initiatives abroad. Increasingly, however, American institutions are charting their own independent foreign policy courses.

For example, as a result of its recent high-profile conflict with China regarding information censorship, Google has begun to develop its own "foreign policy" regarding the global free flow of information.[64] As the Google conflict demonstrates, private speakers engage foreign regimes directly, sometimes with regard to matters of sensitive foreign policy. In developing foreign policy, the federal government may increasingly find itself collaborating not only with subnational governments, but also with domestic companies operating abroad. This change will not significantly threaten the national government's ultimate control over foreign policymaking. However, it will complicate foreign affairs and foreign relations. Regardless of the stance it adopts toward subnational government speech, the U.S. government will clearly not be able to control or suppress all of the private foreign affairs speech in international forums.

Nor should this be the government's goal. Outside the areas of plenary power over foreign relations and the closed forums mentioned earlier, citizens ought to have the widest possible latitude to speak, collaborate, and participate in foreign affairs conversations. However, private speech that touches on foreign affairs matters has either been prohibited by federal law, as in the case of the Logan Act, or subject to something like a foreign affairs trump or exception in the courts. The McCarthy era tactic of criminalizing contacts between U.S. citizens and certain foreign audiences and ideologies ultimately failed. However, cases such as *Holder v. Humanitarian Law Project*, which upheld a content-based antiterrorism law that criminalized speech and association involving foreign organizations, resurrect the notion that the government can suppress even core political speech on foreign affairs grounds.

Part II of the book addressed citizens' liberty to speak and associate across borders. The concept of the international forum helps us to envision a discrete set of foreign affairs marketplaces, and thus to appreciate better the scope of citizens' self-governance interests. Like states and localities, private speakers and audiences have a substantial stake in matters relating to foreign affairs and foreign relations.

In the twenty-first century, the prevalence of global interaction and engagement; the increasing importance of cross-border inquiry and information-gathering; and the need for frequent collaboration with foreigners in endeavors ranging in subject matter from education, to commerce, to religion require protection for private speech and association in international forums.

To create some additional space for private speech in these forums, we can start with low-hanging fruit. The Logan Act purports to suppress private speech on matters of foreign affairs by criminalizing unauthorized communications with foreign governments and their agents. It purports, in essence, to be a Unitary Voice Act for a broad category of private speech that is directed to foreign leaders. The government would lose nothing, except perhaps the threat of prosecution under an almost certainly unconstitutionally vague, overbroad, and content-based law, if the Logan Act were to be repealed. Not a single American has been convicted of violating the Logan Act since its enactment in 1799, and there has been only one reported indictment.[65] The Act is not worthy of the First Amendment principles and tradition that Americans frequently espouse in international forums. In addition to assuring Americans that they are free to communicate lawful content and viewpoints to foreign governments and agents, repeal of the Act would be an important international symbolic gesture.

More generally, American courts should not adopt a foreign affairs exception to the First Amendment. In international forums, courts must, of course, respect and sometimes defer to the foreign policy objectives of the political branches. Active interference with the conduct of foreign relations can obviously be prohibited. However, as I have observed in other chapters, courts have a disturbing tendency to allow the government to overplay its foreign affairs hand.

The mere fact that speech, association, and press activities happen to cross or touch international borders is not a basis for suppression or restriction. Courts ought not to treat every cross-border movement or expressive activity as a "foreign affairs" episode or event, or interpret statutory provisions relating to foreign affairs as conferring unbridled authority on federal officials.

Moreover, as I argue in the next chapter, U.S. courts ought indeed to be more respectful of and engaged with transnational legal sources.

This does not mean that foreign diplomacy ought to serve, as it did in at least a partial way in *Humanitarian Law Project*, as a basis for suppressing citizens' cross-border speech and association. As the world becomes more interconnected, judicial preservation of freedoms of speech, association, and press that touch on matters of international concern will become increasingly important. Courts will play a significant role in ensuring that citizens have access to international forums and can speak as freely as possible in those places.

Political Propaganda in International Forums

As part of its foreign affairs and foreign relations activities, the United States has long engaged in extensive distribution of political propaganda abroad. As well, foreign political propaganda has flowed into U.S. territory. A full treatment of the First Amendment free speech and free press implications of U.S. propagandizing is beyond the scope of this discussion, and I necessarily make only limited observations on this subject. As my former colleague and noted First Amendment scholar William W. Van Alstyne once warned:

> It is too hazardous to generalize about the relevance of freedom of speech under the first amendment to the international law of propaganda, not because the fellow who generalizes takes a risk of being a bigger fool only because he is willing to be wrong about a bigger question, but because "big" questions like this one lack meaning and clarity and so, inevitably, will the answer. The significance of the first amendment necessarily depends upon the context of its involvement.[66]

The United States spends enormous sums each year communicating its positions in foreign nations and other international forums. It is doubtful that there are any enforceable First Amendment limits on this activity. Propaganda is a form of government speech that is conveyed in the context of foreign relations; as such, it does not appear to be subject to ordinary domestic First Amendment limitations. As noted earlier, American citizens would not be able to directly challenge the content of the government's messages in federal court. Any recourse lies in domestic political debate and, ultimately, at the ballot box.

Whether international treaties might limit U.S. propagandizing, and whether the United States could raise First Amendment defenses in international tribunals in response to allegations that it has violated international law regarding propaganda, are interesting but unanswered questions.[67] The United States has not agreed to be bound by international proscriptions on state or nonstate propagandizing. As Van Alstyne has noted, serious constitutional concerns would arise if the United States were ever to agree by treaty or international agreement to restrain the propaganda activities of private citizens in the United States.[68] Owing to its strong commitment to freedom of political speech, it is inconceivable that the United States would agree to place such limits on domestic debate. Nor, despite the relic of the Logan Act, is it likely the United States would prohibit private citizens from disseminating "propaganda" abroad.[69]

This does not end the First Amendment inquiry. Putting to one side any formal international or constitutional obligations, general First Amendment principles still ought to guide the extent to which the United States engages in international propagandizing. Like other nations, the United States is generally empowered and entitled to convey information, diplomatic materials, and national viewpoints to foreign audiences. However, certain forms of coercive propagandizing and informational campaigns might so distort local conversations that they undermine foreign marketplaces of ideas and aliens' effective self-governance.[70] Moreover, as Lee Bollinger has suggested, U.S. international propaganda programs may "harm nascent journalism in societies we care about fostering."[71]

Of course, it is wholly unrealistic to expect the United States to cease communicating positive messages about America and its interests in international forums, or to end specific military and other psychological operations (psyops) programs that are deemed critical to national security. As international law scholars have observed, the point at which instruments of propaganda violate international law is not clear. However, if the United States is going to project support for robust marketplace and self-governance principles in international forums, it would seem that at least some considered self-policing is in order.

In the digital era, the government will be increasingly unable to prevent foreign policy propaganda messages from crossing the border.

As Lee Bollinger observes, "Information anywhere is information everywhere."[72] Bollinger argues that this reality "should lead to grave First Amendment concerns about U.S. disinformation campaigns abroad."[73] The disinformation the United States is actively disseminating in foreign locations today may well find its way into its own citizens' hands, raising First Amendment concerns relating to domestic propagandizing.

Concerns regarding domestic propagandizing are more acute now that the broad Smith-Mundt Act ban on domestic dissemination has been repealed.[74] The repeal is a welcome development insofar as transborder free speech and informational rights are concerned. Americans ought to have access to what their government is saying about itself – and about them – in foreign lands. I do not mean to suggest that the government ought to be permitted to engage in domestic propaganda activity – to target U.S. audiences with governmental messages. However, if the United States is going to engage in such activity abroad, its citizens ought to be able to access statements made on their behalf. Under the repeal legislation, citizens can now lawfully obtain certain State Department materials and can listen to Voice of America and other international broadcasts sponsored by the United States. Although it did not debate or defend the repeal in First Amendment terms, Congress facilitated cross-border free speech when it formally opened this channel of communication and allowed citizens to track foreign policy communications being made on their behalf in international forums.

U.S. propaganda access and distribution restrictions like those in the Smith-Mundt Act fail to account for citizens' strong First Amendment interests in foreign affairs and diplomatic transparency. Recognizing citizens' access rights serves as an important check on government's power to speak coercively or otherwise unlawfully in international forums.[75] This is critical, especially because the First Amendment itself appears to impose no clear limits on government communications abroad and the U.S. has not formally accepted any international obligations to refrain from this activity. The First Amendment protects a right to receive information – including information relating to foreign affairs that is disseminated in international forums. Along with the right to receive foreign political propaganda, American citizens have a First Amendment right to receive foreign propaganda messages distributed by their own government. Although it does not grant sweeping access to American propaganda materials, the Smith-Mundt repeal provision is a step in the right direction.

Of course, much more could be said about legal limitations on state foreign propaganda and disinformation campaigns. As international scholars have recognized, it is permissible for states to seek to influence events beyond their borders by persuasion.[76] Nothing I have said questions this basic principle. But digitization will enhance the power and persuasiveness of government propaganda across the world. In international forums, the First Amendment does not generally apply in a formal sense. But that does not mean its principles and values are irrelevant. The United States ought to be guided, to the extent possible, by free speech and free press principles in these forums. Just as it ought to open marketplaces to diverse participants, the government ought to ensure that its voice does not corrupt or overwhelm international dialogues or international forums.

FOREIGN AFFAIRS AND RELIGIOUS NEUTRALITY

We ought also to think more carefully about how First Amendment principles of religious neutrality relate to foreign affairs. In a globalized world where religion is a significant factor in world affairs, the United States will need to engage on a more frequent and sustained basis with religious leaders and communities. Indeed, under the past three American presidents, religious engagement has been an explicit aspect of American foreign policy. George W. Bush instituted a "faith-based initiative" that distributed funds to domestic and overseas projects. President Clinton signed the International Religious Freedom Act which, among other things, established a U.S. ambassador-at-large for international religious freedom. In a speech he delivered in Cairo in 2009, President Obama suggested that the United States would open a new era of engagement with Muslim communities across the world.

Engagement with religious leaders and communities in the foreign affairs context could raise some difficult Establishment Clause questions. This chapter closes with some thoughts on this still relatively uncharted territory.

In Chapter 7, I argued that the Establishment Clause ought to apply extraterritorially. Thus, as a general matter, when they act abroad, U.S. officials must observe Establishment Clause limitations. As I explained, part of the reason for these extraterritorial limits relates to the domestic effects of foreign engagement. Many religious faiths have a transnational scope or character. Thus, support for religion abroad may benefit religious institutions located within the United States.

More fundamentally, I have argued that the Establishment Clause is a structural limitation on governmental action. As such, it applies regardless of location. Nevertheless, as in domestic contexts, in international forums the First Amendment calls for respect for religious pluralism. Thus, as I have observed, application and enforcement of Establishment Clause doctrine may differ owing to the specific characteristics of the foreign cultures in which the U.S. government operates. In other words, although foreign context is not relevant to the issue of domain, it is relevant in terms of specific applications.

Extraterritorial application of First Amendment non-establishment principles could raise a variety of thorny issues for foreign diplomats and government officials who work closely with religious leaders and communities in foreign nations. Some officials might believe that any effort to work with religious leaders and communities abroad on common ventures could trigger the Establishment Clause. Foreign diplomats and agency personnel who adopted this position might be reluctant to engage with religious institutions and individuals in a variety of contexts. This would be unfortunate because it would hamper U.S. efforts to converse and associate with audiences and organizations that are vitally important to its global foreign affairs and national security objectives.

On the other hand, some might view anti-establishment concerns as out of place in international forums, where church–state relations differ markedly from those in the United States and engagement with religious communities is a critical part of foreign diplomacy and relations. This would leave U.S. officials free to favor and directly support foreign religious institutions and cultures.

Neither the executive branch nor the courts have ever clarified the scope of the Establishment Clause in what I am referring to as international forums.[77] Assuming that it does apply abroad, the Establishment

Clause's prohibition must not be interpreted so broadly that U.S. officials are extensively prohibited from engaging religious communities abroad. Such an interpretation would be inconsistent with a long history of U.S. foreign policy and diplomacy. It is not required by Establishment Clause doctrine or principles. As one prominent task force on religion and foreign policy recently put it, the better view is that the Establishment Clause "does not bar the United States from engaging religious communities abroad in the conduct of foreign policy, though it does impose constraints on the means that the United States may choose to pursue this engagement."[78]

In many instances, U.S. engagement with religious leaders and communities abroad takes place in the context of general initiatives involving both secular and sectarian communities. Inclusion of religious individuals and institutions in medical, educational, political, and legal endeavors does not threaten core First Amendment religious neutrality principles. As in domestic spheres, religion can and indeed ought to be engaged in this manner – in public, across a broad range of secular concerns, and as part of an open and pluralistic conversation. The Establishment Clause ought not to be interpreted to bar or limit this kind of religious engagement. As recent episodes of strife in the Arab world have demonstrated, engagement with religion in international forums is a necessity. It allows the United States to carry out the most effective and inclusive foreign policies.

More difficult questions arise where U.S. officials work closely with foreign sectarian educational institutions and political leaders to develop specific programs or initiatives. Depending on the nature of the mission or the foreign affairs initiative, significant religious effects and entanglement issues may arise.[79] On the other hand, it would be difficult if not impossible to apply something like the domestic "endorsement" test in the foreign policy realm.[80] Questions regarding preferential treatment, relevant cultures or communities, and the identity of the "reasonable observer" would be more difficult to resolve beyond U.S. borders.[81]

These complications do not provide an excuse for lifting the restrictions of the Establishment Clause abroad. However, they do call for greater attention to the special balance in international forums between the conduct of foreign affairs and the religious liberties of American citizens at home. As part of a comprehensive foreign policy initiative concerning transnational religious issues, the executive branch ought to issue guidance on the manner in which diplomats and other officials may engage religion in international forums. That guidance ought to be flexible enough to permit officials to address, and in some cases collaborate, with religious communities abroad while at the same time encouraging them to preserve the core limitations of the Establishment Clause.

The appropriate scope of religious engagement in the foreign affairs context is yet another aspect of the First Amendment's transborder dimension that has not received adequate attention or consideration. The approach to establishment concerns and foreign affairs that I have sketched here, and in Chapter 7, supports global respect for the American church–state separation model as well as recognition of the religious pluralism that exists in international forums. In these forums, the United States need not be completely neutral as to religious concerns. However, when it engages religion, it must avoid the sort of direct and excessive entanglements that the Establishment Clause's core principles condemn.

9 COSMOPOLITAN ENGAGEMENT

Can a French court order a speaker in the United States to cease communicating certain information to French citizens?[1] Should foreign libel judgments, which are not subject to the strict standards imposed under the First Amendment, be enforced in the United States? Can U.S. courts require American publishers to comply with German privacy laws? Can state legislatures ban the recognition and enforcement of Shari'a law and international law? These questions highlight the fact that the First Amendment does not exist in isolation from the larger community of nations. They require that we think carefully about whether, and if so how, the United States ought to engage with foreign laws, ideas, and creeds in the twenty-first century.

In an era marked by interconnectivity and global information flow, First Amendment exceptionalism will be challenged as never before.[2] The challenges will occur in a variety of contexts, including transnational processes and transnational litigation. The cross-border movement of persons, information, and ideas will give rise to conflicts between domestic laws that protect expressive and religious liberties, and foreign laws, principles, and practices that are imported into the United States.

For much of the nation's history, American officials, courts, and legislatures have adopted a parochial orientation with regard to foreign laws and standards relating to expressive liberties. The First Amendment has been treated as a defensive shield against importation of these sources. The overriding concern has been preservation of the First Amendment's exceptional expressive and religious protections. Discrimination against religious faiths deemed foreign to U.S.

communities and practices is also a longstanding and unfortunate aspect of American history and experience. Recent controversies have focused on Islam, which has been singled out and treated as a threat to American constitutional and political orders. Like other faiths before it, Islam is viewed by many Americans as a threat emanating from abroad.

In coming decades, American courts, officials, and citizens will face new challenges from abroad to conform to international and other standards and perspectives. The United States will be pressed as it defends and seeks to adhere to First Amendment principles. As I explain in the text that follows, First Amendment exceptionalism is not in any imminent peril. Its constitutional and cultural roots in the United States are deep and strong, and there are plentiful constitutional and political checks against wholesale importation of foreign models. Nevertheless, it is imperative that as a nation we genuinely come to terms with the fact that the United States is part of a tightly interconnected community of nations where constitutional standards sharply diverge and most nations have taken a path different from our own.

In working through conflicts and disagreements with other members in the world community regarding expressive and religious liberties, the United States ought to refer to and rely on the First Amendment's core principles and commitments. Conversation and commingling can occur not just at the individual level, but also among nation-states. This exchange can lead to understanding and appreciation, not just of differences but also of the many common values nations share with respect to expressive and religious liberties. As a general matter, our First Amendment rejects protectionism and discrimination and promotes dialog and liberal pluralism. Thus, in its encounters with foreign liberty models and foreign belief systems, the United States ought to focus on norms of comity and the educational benefits associated with respectful engagement with transnational legal sources. Further, as we have in past generations, Americans ought to renew our national commitment to cultural and religious pluralism.

As I explain, although it makes room for dialogue and recognition, the cosmopolitan orientation I propose in this chapter does not present any transcendental threat to the First Amendment. Indeed, it is based on a distinctly *American* constitutional pre-commitment to respecting the diverse views of mankind and a First Amendment commitment to engaging with divergent ideas and cultures.

TRANSNATIONALISM AND FREEDOM OF EXPRESSION

Owing to globalization, digitization, and different forms of diplomatic exchange, the First Amendment increasingly intersects and comes into conflict with the free speech regimes of other nations. This intersection occurs in a variety of contexts, some of which pose challenges to the First Amendment's jurisdictional exclusivity and its substantive exceptionalism. In an effort to preserve such things, the United States has generally adopted a provincial posture toward transnational engagement regarding expressive rights. Insofar as expressive liberties are concerned, American courts, legislatures, and executive officials have typically refused to recognize foreign judgments or to seriously engage transnational legal sources.

Territoriality, Exclusivity, and Exceptionalism

The First Amendment provides an exceptional set of expressive guarantees. Relative to other nations' laws and constitutions as well as international standards, the First Amendment has been interpreted to provide far more expansive protection for expressive liberties.[3] As discussed in Chapter 1, examples include First Amendment protections for criticism of government officials, offensive and hateful expression, incitement to unlawful or violent action, commercial speech, freedom of assembly and petition, and freedom of the press.[4]

For many Americans, these exceptional protections are a point of great national pride. Indeed, they are often touted by Americans and government officials as models for the rest of the world. However, it has long been apparent that the community of nations broadly rejects the First Amendment model. As I discussed in Chapter 5, many foreign governments and cultures denounce the protections afforded to American speakers who insult religion, communicate incendiary messages, and advocate violence. Further, some nations view the United States as a haven for hateful ideas that receive limited or no protection elsewhere in the world. More generally, many view as wrongheaded (or worse) the general First Amendment preference for speaker autonomy over individual or communal interests in dignity and reputation.

So long as the acts of citizens and national governments are strictly separated by territorial borders, these divergences do not pose any serious threat of discord or conflict. Americans can be governed exclusively by the exceptional protections of the First Amendment, and foreign nationals can enjoy whatever speech protections their own laws and constitutions provide. In a world composed of separate spheres or territories – particularly one in which foreign laws and judgments receive no legal recognition – transnational constitutional conflict would be rather infrequent.

However, territory no longer defines or restricts legal rights or governmental interests in this manner. As I have emphasized throughout the book, territorial sovereignty has been significantly eroded. In the speech context, certain consequences of that erosion are critically important. First, transnational legal processes, including transnational litigation, have created opportunities for importation of foreign speech standards and judgments. Second, by allowing speakers and publishers to distribute messages and materials across the globe cheaply and efficiently, digitization has increased the points of intersection among various nations' speech and press laws. This has magnified or highlighted First Amendment exceptionalism and caused increased pressure on the United States to modify its approach.

Transnational Legal Processes

Since the postwar era, First Amendment exclusivity and exceptionalism have been vulnerable to diplomatic and other external influences. As it began to engage more frequently with members in the community of nations, the United States was forced to navigate various channels through which other nations could seek to import foreign or international expressive standards. These channels include a variety of transnational processes, such as negotiation of international treaties and agreements, as well as other contacts with foreign officials.

One longstanding concern is that American officials might dilute or even eliminate constitutional protections at home by entering into treaties or other transnational agreements. The Supreme Court sought to quell this fear in *Reid v. Covert*, a case decided in 1957.[5] In *Reid*, a plurality of justices concluded that the Constitution's treaty powers are constrained by the Bill of Rights and other liberty provisions. This means, in essence, that the political branches cannot dilute or bargain away Americans' constitutional liberties by entering into treaties or other international agreements. As discussed later, despite the Court's decision in *Reid*, some Americans continue to view U.S. participation in international treaties and processes as a distinct threat to First Amendment exclusivity and exceptionalism.

International treaties and agreements are part of a larger category of transnational legal processes in which American officials and various private organizations interact with foreign counterparts. These interactions create frequent opportunities for exposure to, and thus possible importation of, transnational legal sources.[6] The concern, again, is that participation in these transnational processes might produce a mandatory international human rights baseline with regard to expressive and/or religious liberties.

For example, as they interact with jurists from other nations, American judges are exposed to foreign speech doctrines, principles, and precedents.[7] This transnational exchange could lead to citation or even adoption of foreign standards by U.S. courts. Less formally, it might exert a more subtle influence on the manner in which American judges interpret the scope of constitutional liberties such as freedom of speech or press. In the United States, insofar as judicial actors are concerned the debate has focused on citation of foreign opinions and precedents.[8] In the death penalty and homosexual rights contexts, mere reference to judicial decisions from foreign tribunals and to foreign laws has been considered by some to be highly controversial.[9]

At least so far, this debate has not addressed interpretation of the First Amendment.[10] Although some Americans routinely urge courts and officials to amend U.S. laws concerning the death penalty and homosexual rights to align them with world opinion, there appears to be little, if any, public support in the United States for doing the same with regard to expressive liberties. Further, although judges in other nations cite and rely on U.S. precedents and standards in adjudicating some free speech and other expressive claims, American judges have not reciprocated by citing transnational sources in First Amendment cases. In this respect, the cross-border flow of ideas is decidedly in one direction.

Transnational litigation is another potential channel for importation of foreign speech and press standards. Foreign plaintiffs who have obtained libel, privacy, and other judgments abroad have sought to enforce those judgments against American citizens in U.S. courts. Most of the public attention has focused on foreign libel judgments. American defendants and public officials have decried what they view as a thriving "libel tourism" industry. They complain that foreign plaintiffs have sought to silence American authors by obtaining libel judgments in the United Kingdom and elsewhere, where jurisdictional and libel standards are not as strict as in the United States, and then seeking to enforce those judgments in the United States (where the defendants' assets are located).

U.S. courts have almost uniformly refused to enforce these judgments on public policy grounds, with many reasoning that judicial recognition of a foreign libel judgment would violate the First Amendment.[11] Constitutional scholars have disagreed as to whether an American court that enforces a foreign libel judgment thereby becomes complicit in violating the First Amendment rights of American speakers.[12] Similar debates have arisen in the context of recognition by U.S. courts of foreign privacy and copyright judgments.[13]

In the United States, legislators ultimately responded to the controversy concerning importation of foreign libel judgments. Several states enacted laws providing that courts need not recognize foreign libel judgments that were entered without the full protections granted under First Amendment doctrine.[14] In 2010, Congress enacted the tellingly entitled Securing the Protection of Our Enduring and Established Constitutional Heritage (SPEECH) Act, which similarly prohibits U.S. courts from enforcing any foreign libel judgment unless the judgment was obtained in accordance with First Amendment–like free speech protections.[15]

Digitization and Importation

As discussed in previous chapters, in the digital era, communications easily cross territorial boundaries. In the absence of a universal speech standard, speech that crosses multiple borders is presumably subject to the laws of multiple sovereigns.[16] In some cases, multiple nations may seek to enforce their domestic laws against speakers who are located far beyond their territorial borders. For example, if an American speaker engages in communication on the Internet that is illegal in France and Germany, he may face civil or even criminal penalties under those nations' speech laws.

Depending on how such transnational conflicts are resolved, they could lead to some importation of foreign expressive standards. A substantial amount of speech that originates in the United States is now accessible across the globe. If French courts can enforce their hate speech laws against U.S. speakers and websites, or German plaintiffs can invoke foreign privacy laws against U.S. publications, then some speech originating inside the United States will effectively be governed by foreign speech standards. Some fear that if this sort of extraterritorial enforcement occurs, it could undermine or even eliminate the First Amendment's exclusive jurisdiction and its exceptional protection for certain speech content. On the other hand, if foreign nations are *not* allowed to enforce their own laws owing to First Amendment concerns, some scholars have expressed concern that American free speech standards will effectively be imposed on the rest of the world.[17]

Thus far, American courts have had limited opportunities to address this sort of digital speech conflict. The most prominent case involved potential enforcement in the United States of a French court judgment, issued pursuant to French hate speech laws, against Yahoo!, Inc., an American website that auctioned Nazi memorabilia on the Internet.[18] A U.S. federal appeals court ultimately declined to decide whether the French judgment was enforceable, and Yahoo! eventually settled the case with French authorities. Notably, in adjudicating the controversy, U.S. courts simply assumed that the First Amendment applied to Yahoo!'s speech, probably owing to its origination within the United States. The courts did not engage in any transnational conflict-of-laws analysis, which would have required some consideration of Yahoo!'s presence in France and France's interest in enforcing its own speech laws.

Along with transnational processes, digitization poses distinct challenges to First Amendment exclusivity and exceptionalism. The United States has not yet adopted a systematic approach to digital speech conflicts.

"Foreign" Religious Laws and Principles

Transnational religious conflicts are less common than those based on speech activity. However, when they occur, these conflicts raise issues that are similar to those relating to recognition and enforcement of foreign speech laws and principles. Recently, controversies have arisen in the United States involving recognition and enforcement of foreign religious laws and principles, in particular those relating to Shari'a law. Other domestic controversies relating to Islam have also highlighted a fundamental tension between resistance to what many view as "foreign" religious norms and practices and the First Amendment's religious neutrality and pluralism principles.

Recently, several American states have enacted legislation or passed referendum provisions that preclude their courts from relying on, referencing, or enforcing international law in general, and Shari'a law in particular.[19] In a constitutional referendum measure referred to as the "Save Our State Amendment," 70 percent of Oklahoma's citizens voted to ban state courts from relying on either international law or what the provision referred to as "Shari'a Law." The Oklahoma amendment states: "The courts shall not look to the legal precepts of other nations or cultures. Specifically, the courts shall not consider international law or Shari'a Law." The amendment defines "Shari'a Law as "Islamic law," which it states is law "based on two principal sources, the Koran and the teaching of Mohammed." The Oklahoma amendment was enacted out of concern that domestic courts would enforce "Shari'a Law" in divorce and other civil actions. This has become a matter of increasing concern in the United States.[20]

The Oklahoma measure and others like it go beyond religious concerns. They are sweeping prohibitions on judicial reference to transnational legal sources. By their terms, such enactments would preclude enforcement of all judgments that are based on foreign law, foreign choice of law provisions in U.S. contracts, foreign marriages, wills that are based on foreign religious principles, and foreign arbitral awards. The measures might even prohibit state courts from citing *Blackstone's Commentaries* – even though Blackstone's work has been relied on in U.S. courts throughout American history. Although a federal court invalidated Oklahoma's "Save Our State" amendment on First Amendment religious liberty grounds, states continue to debate and enact similar measures.[21]

The state anti-Shari'a measures connect religious liberty and transnational concerns in several respects. First, some of the state measures seem to categorize Shari'a law as a type of foreign or international law or an aspect of foreign culture. Just as American courts and legislatures have treated foreign libel judgments as inimical to free speech, Shari'a law has been treated in some jurisdictions as a source of foreign authority that is at odds with American norms of liberty and equality. Second, in some foreign nations, Islam is an officially recognized religion. Thus, its enforcement within the United States arguably raises transnational establishment concerns. Finally, the controversy over Shari'a law is connected to larger American cultural and political debates regarding radical forms of Islam and their connection to international terrorism. In some states, citizens and officials apparently view Shari'a's recognition and enforcement as an existential threat to the American liberal constitutional order. Some Americans have even expressed concerns regarding a supposed plot to replace U.S. constitutional and other domestic laws with Shari'a law. Opposition to Islam has also led to other domestic controversies. These include challenges to the building and location of mosques, and objections to extending public funding of schools to some institutions that offer instruction in Islam.

In the United States, hostility, discrimination, and parochialism with regard to minority or non-mainstream faiths are hardly new perspectives or attitudes. Faiths that are now considered mainstream were once similarly deemed to be outside threats to internal order. Today, in some American communities Shari'a and Islam are viewed through this same parochial prism.

THE FIRST AMENDMENT AND TRANSNATIONAL ENGAGEMENT

Concerns regarding First Amendment exclusivity and exceptionalism cannot be lightly dismissed. Further, some of the tensions between Shari'a principles and domestic constitutional norms are serious. However, these concerns do not justify free speech provincialism or religious parochialism and discrimination. Basic First Amendment principles support engagement with transnational speech laws and other transnational sources. Moreover, in this century's increasingly interconnected world, it is imperative that the U.S. commitment to religious pluralism extend to faiths that are now deemed by some Americans as "foreign." In the discussion that follows, I first address general postures toward transnational laws and constitutional norms. I then explain in several contexts how an approach based on principles of cosmopolitan engagement would apply.

Resistance, Convergence, and Engagement

For reasons that I have already mentioned, in the twenty-first century, constitutional laws and cultures will intersect on a more frequent basis. These regimes are obviously unique, each being the product of distinct historical, political, and social circumstances. As a matter of internal sovereignty, each nation is presumptively entitled to decide which constitutional principles to adopt and enforce.

However, in an era of increased legal and social connectivity, international laws and commitments may influence domestic laws. International treaties and agreements address speech, press, and informational rights. Foreign judicial precedents relating to expressive and religious rights are increasingly accessible to domestic courts. More generally, in a mobile and fluid global environment, models of free speech and religious freedom will connect and collide in various contexts. In sum, it is simply inevitable that the nations of the world will frequently engage in debates regarding the scope of expressive liberties and respect for religious beliefs.

Vicki Jackson has described three general perspectives or postures with regard to the intersection of transnational (i.e., foreign and international) and domestic constitutional laws.[22] She labels these approaches *resistance, convergence,* and *engagement.*[23] Jackson's analysis focuses primarily on the extent to which transnational legal sources might or ought to influence domestic (U.S.) constitutional interpretation. Her typology provides a useful general framework for thinking about receptivity to transnational legal sources and norms in the First Amendment context.

As Jackson notes, *resistance* to transnational law can take various forms. These range from simple indifference to transnational sources to strong objections to treating such sources as relevant in any sense to domestic constitutional interpretation. Owing in part to the First Amendment's exceptional protections for freedom of speech and religion, in the United States, resistance is the dominant orientation regarding transnational expressive and religious laws, standards, and norms.

Perhaps the strongest form of resistance to transnational legal sources is exemplified in the writings of Justice Antonin Scalia.[24] Justice Scalia objects to merely consulting transnational or international law as possible sources of constitutional meaning. His resistance is based primarily on distinctive aspects of U.S. constitutional history and principles of constitutional interpretation. In brief, Justice Scalia maintains that foreign laws are not an appropriate source of domestic constitutional meaning. His strong form of resistance prohibits even reference to foreign precedents and other transnational sources in constitutional cases. Other Supreme Court justices, as well as a number of constitutional scholars, adopt a similar posture of resistance.[25]

Resistance is manifested in other contexts as well. It is exemplified by measures such as the Oklahoma "Save Our State" Amendment which, as noted earlier, would have broadly precluded state courts from referring to or relying on transnational legal or constitutional sources. U.S. treaty reservations, bans on enforcement of foreign libel or copyright judgments that are not predicated upon First Amendment–like protections, and blanket refusals to enforce Islamic judgments or principles are also based on a strong form of resistance to transnational law. With regard to foreign speech and religious judgments, courts and commentators often point to public policy justifications as grounds for resistance. In the case of religiously based judgments, in some cases the concern is that judicial enforcement would be contrary to constitutional equality or other guarantees.[26] The upshot of all this resistance is that foreign laws and judgments are universally rejected in favor of domestic standards, norms, and practices.

In terms of receptivity to transnational legal sources, a *convergence* approach is situated at the opposite end of the spectrum from resistance. Convergence entails embracing transnational law as a significant, even dispositive, source of domestic constitutional law. Like resistance, convergence is a matter of degree. As discussed in Chapter 1, some nations constitutionally mandate consideration of transnational law in domestic constitutional interpretation. Other nations consider these sources to be relevant or persuasive, but not necessarily dispositive.

Insofar as convergence anticipates that nations will agree upon the definition of a category of rights, it is cosmopolitan in a very broad sense – that is, it posits the existence of agreed-on constitutional standards regarding certain universal human rights. Thus, in its strongest form, convergence would require the replacement of exceptional First Amendment expressive and religious protections with more universal standards. In weaker forms, convergence might result only in more modest alterations of domestic First Amendment and other constitutional standards.

Finally, as Jackson explains, *engagement* is a perspective that is generally "founded on commitments to judicial deliberation and open to the possibilities of either harmony or dissonance between national self-understandings and transnational norms."[27] Like resistance and convergence, engagement and openness to transnational legal sources are matters of degree.

In general, engagement views transnational sources as at least being potentially relevant to discussions regarding domestic constitutional meaning. Thus, unlike resistance, engagement does not bar all recognition of foreign judgments, on public policy or other grounds, merely because they are based on foreign constitutional standards. However, as an interpretive approach, in contrast to convergence engagement does not entail an abandonment of domestic standards. Indeed, as Jackson notes, in many instances engagement might ultimately serve to support or reinforce prevailing constitutional interpretations.

Among the various approaches or orientations Jackson identifies, transnational engagement best captures the principles and purposes at the core of the First Amendment itself, including a preference for learning through dialog and respect for pluralism. It is thus an attractive framework for approaching transnational First Amendment issues. Engagement is a cosmopolitan approach in the sense that it is open to consideration of the opinions and approaches of other nations, and in some circumstances extends a degree of comity to their laws and judgments.

In the First Amendment context, the United States ought to reject the strongest forms of transnational resistance. This posture ignores the fact of global interconnectedness and U.S. membership in a global community of nations. It also fails to give due respect to the opinions and interests of other nations. Strong resistance, which forbids even consultation or reference to transnational sources, is anathema to several of the First Amendment's own core commitments – to dialog, the pursuit of education and facilitation of information-gathering, exposure to divergent approaches and ideologies, the search for truth through conversation and clashing viewpoints, tolerance, and pluralism. Resistance "saves" the First Amendment by essentially protecting it from contrary or supposedly dangerous points of view. In doing so, however, resistance rules out the possibility that the United States might learn from other approaches. It also makes it less likely that other nations will look to the American model for standards or constitutional inspiration.

As an approach to First Amendment issues, convergence is also unworkable and unwise. As many recent controversies regarding hate speech and blasphemy show, there is no realistic possibility of universal convergence on controversial matters such as the appropriate degree of protection for offensive expression, the scope of free speech on the Internet, or public displays of religious faith.[28] Nor, in any event, is there any supranational or other final arbiter to determine or enforce such standards.[29] Even if consensus and enforcement mechanisms existed, strong convergence would be an unattractive approach. Although it would reduce conflict, convergence would also suppress cultural differences, eliminate transnational comparisons, and terminate informative debates regarding the proper scope of expressive and religious liberties.

It is important to keep in mind that many nations have achieved a substantial degree of consensus or convergence with regard to protection for expressive and religious liberties. Numerous international agreements express strong commitments to protecting freedom of speech, information, and religious belief. However, convergence with regard to specific constitutional standards is not likely to occur, and may not be an attractive outcome in any event.

In contrast to both resistance and convergence, transnational engagement is predicated on values of pluralism, diversity, and understanding through exchange. Unlike resistance, engagement does not block consideration and recognition of the transnational. Rather, engagement respects diversity; involves assessment of difference and divergence; contemplates the possibility of innovation or change; and encourages domestic officials to keep an open mind with regard to transnational sources. Unlike convergence, engagement does not seek uniformity or global homogeneity with regard to constitutional rights. Rather, a posture of engagement respects a diversity of constitutional approaches – even though it recognizes that diversity complicates enforcement. Transnational engagement anticipates and invites clashing viewpoints in nation-state exchanges.[30]

In its deliberative form, transnational engagement relies on persuasion and reasoning, rather than on the supposed binding force of either domestic or transnational law.[31] Perhaps most importantly, as Jackson notes, it contemplates a "willingness to look outside – for confirmation, for challenge, to check one's own judgment."[32] Thus, for example, engagement with transnational laws regarding hate speech might provide further evidence that the First Amendment standard, which protects most forms of racist and hateful expression, ultimately ought to be retained. Engagement with transnational approaches to libelous speech, or religious liberties, may lead to similar confirmations. On the other hand, engagement could convince U.S. officials and the American public that the First Amendment provides too much protection to psychologically injurious expression; too little protection to reputation, dignity, or religious liberty; or that current protections for confidential information are too weak.

In transnational conversations, the participants will have diverse and often deeply held convictions. U.S. officials and courts ought to approach these discussions with an awareness of and respect for the divergent viewpoints of the community of nations. They ought to be "open to considering the particular legal practices and reasoning of other countries."[33]

As Vicki Jackson explains with regard to the process of judicial interpretation, "Transnational judicial discourse reflects an open deliberative process that draws on a range of sources for challenge and critique of analytical assumptions, for elaboration of common normative values in different institutional settings and for development of understandings of national distinctiveness."[34] As Jackson observes, transnational laws "may be seen as interlocutors, offering a way of testing understanding of one's own traditions and possibilities by examining them in the reflection of others."[35] This observation extends to other transnational experiences and sources, including cultural norms and religious practices. As Justice Stevens has stated, "While the 'American perspective' must always be our focus, ... it is silly – indeed, arrogant – to think we have nothing to learn about liberty from the billions of people beyond our borders."[36]

As I have indicated, transnational engagement will not lead to displacement of the First Amendment or alter most, if indeed any, of its exceptional standards. It would, however, lead to recognition of and engagement with foreign interests, claims, and sources in domestic constitutional adjudication. It could even lead to "some limited recognition of the moral claims of those outside the polity whose interests are affected by domestic constitutional law."[37] Among those with moral claims or other cognizable interests might be foreign plaintiffs, regimes, institutions, or practitioners of certain religious faiths. Recognition of foreign interests and respectful consideration of transnational effects are characteristics of a global constitutional pluralism in which multiple legal orders overlap.[38] More to the point, perhaps, they are characteristics of the First Amendment regime the United States expresses fidelity to in international forums and global conversations.

Adopting a posture of transnational engagement and dialogue would entail a more concerted effort, by U.S. officials and citizens alike, to explain or justify the First Amendment's exceptional standards to members of the community of nations. Jackson refers to the obligation to explain difference to outsiders as "minimal procedural cosmopolitanism."[39] As a member in good standing of the international community, the United States ought to offer clearer and more compelling justifications to outsiders for protecting domestic expression that in some cases crosses international borders and causes harm in the world community. Citizens, elected officials, and judges all ought to be a part of this dialogue concerning constitutional liberties in an interconnected world.

As Jackson observes, engagement rests on a conception of the Constitution "as a form of law that constitutes a country both internally and as a member in a world of nations – that is, as a form of law that by its existence commits its polity to some form of engagement with others, in order to sustain the quality of being a nation in a world of nations."[40] Viewed from this perspective, the Constitution in general, and the First Amendment in particular, can "create an effective interface with other national states."[41]

Treaty-Making and International Diplomacy

American reluctance to engage with transnational standards relates, in part, to the concern that this engagement could result in the dilution or elimination of domestic liberties. The most direct means of importing transnational speech standards into the United States is to impose them through a treaty or other international agreement. If this were to happen, the First Amendment would no longer be the exclusive source of free speech protections within the United States.

As mentioned earlier, in the United States, it is a longstanding and generally accepted principle that treaties cannot override individual rights.[42] However, scholars have questioned whether, in an era marked by globalization and transnationalism, this proposition remains valid. Peter Spiro has argued that, with respect to certain constitutional norms, including freedom of speech, "a case can be made for the international determination of baseline rights."[43]

Professor Spiro challenges what he calls the "doctrine of constitutional hegemony" – the notion that constitutional rights have always prevailed over treaty obligations.[44] Although he concedes that a consensus still exists among American policymakers and judges that treaties cannot override domestic constitutional rights, Spiro claims that constitutional hegemony is not as categorical as many assume it to be. Indeed, he asserts that where a treaty provision conflicts with domestic constitutional law, courts have been more likely to modify constitutional doctrine than to invalidate the treaty.[45] In a world in which territorial borders and national institutions "do not necessarily enjoy normative foundations," Spiro claims, "an international norm against hate speech would supply a basis for prohibiting it, the First Amendment notwithstanding."[46]

If this were a real danger, then American participation in certain transnational dialogues could endanger domestic liberties as we know them. However, as Spiro concedes, "[i]t is unlikely in the extreme that ... treatymakers would undertake such a frontal assault against the supremacy of constitutional rights."[47] In fact, Spiro notes that "it would take a constitutional moment of the highest order to overcome the supremacy norm."[48]

A long history of U.S. treaty negotiation and diplomatic practice supports this conclusion. The United States has consistently demonstrated its unwillingness to bargain away core First Amendment liberties. Indeed, it has been content to risk incurring economic and other costs stemming from its refusal to subordinate domestic First Amendment and other constitutional standards. Even in its presently weakened financial state, there is little evidence that the United States is poised to alter this longstanding international posture of resistance. This is so even in the face of deadly episodes of violence in Libya, Egypt, Afghanistan, and other nations, which may have resulted in part from hateful and blasphemous speech originating in the United States. These episodes have tested but have not even come close to overriding U.S. resolve to maintain exceptional protections for offensive and other forms of presently protected expression.

Thus, it is unrealistic to expect that First Amendment standards will be broadly or generally displaced through the treaty process. Nor, for the reasons I have mentioned, would such a generalized convergence be normatively desirable. Although a more homogenous system would reduce global conflict and reduce the complexity of speech regulation, it would do so only by sacrificing legal and cultural diversity, national experimentation and potential innovation in terms of developing free speech standards, and an important aspect of cross-border information flow. Particularly, as I noted in Chapter 5, when the Internet is still emerging as a global agora or theater, settling on a uniform speech standard could retard or adversely affect development of international marketplaces of ideas.

In the treaty context, the United States has generally responded to concerns regarding the dilution or displacement of domestic liberties by limiting its participation in human rights and other treaties. The Supreme Court has ruled that, absent congressional action, treaties and other international agreements do not create rights or have any legal effect in the United States. Moreover, the United States frequently signs such instruments with reservations, understandings, and declarations that expressly preserve First Amendment free speech standards within the United States.[49]

Although they have been criticized by some commentators, these actions and mechanisms are part of an ongoing dialog regarding universal protection for expressive and religious liberties. Unlike categorical refusals to recognize foreign judgments, which I discuss later, treaty reservations and declarations regarding hate speech or other categories of expression do not reject the broad commitments and components of international agreements. In this context, the United States is not attempting to apply the First Amendment globally. Nor is it denying recognition to the laws of any other nation. In expressive terms, the United States is indicating that although it shares certain common commitments with fellow members of the community of nations, it takes a different view with regard to specific standards. Critical commentary, as well as U.S. defenses, tends to place too much emphasis on points of difference rather than the fact of convergence on basic principles.

There remains an unfortunate tendency to view transnational engagement as presumptively threatening to American free speech standards. Engagement can lead to effective cooperation on international problems. Thus, whenever possible, American officials ought to interpret international agreements and First Amendment standards in a manner that allows the United States to continue to participate. The mere fact that a protocol or agreement tangentially relates to expression is not a reason to refuse to engage, or perhaps even to reserve limits on domestic enforcement. Even when serious First Amendment objections preclude American entry into international agreements and protocols, U.S. officials can and ought to remain involved in the negotiation and proposed implementation of these instruments.[50] American interests are best served by continued involvement in the drafting and negotiation of agreements relating to free speech.

Dialogue regarding shared moral and constitutional commitments is a critical aspect of cosmopolitan engagement. However, the dialogue must be genuine. Too often, the United States reflexively rejects transnational speech models and standards without considering the substance or merits of these approaches. In addition, U.S. officials have sometimes refused to even participate in international conferences, when the agenda includes condemnation of religious bigotry or other speech that is formally protected under the First Amendment. These are missed opportunities to engage with other nations on what is increasingly common ground. Liberal democracies differ in terms of the extent to which they believe certain content ought to be granted legal and constitutional protection. But this disagreement ought to be viewed as an invitation to global dialog, not a reason to disengage.

The United States can condemn religious bigotry without choosing to criminalize it. Explaining that choice, rather than refusing to participate in the dialogue, may not change the minds or policies of world leaders. However, this kind of exchange is critically important for raising and seeking to resolve issues of shared global concern. As a regular dissenting voice in treaty negotiations and international conferences, the United States has many opportunities to explain its free speech principles and norms to global audiences. In terms of genuine dialog, simple boilerplate reservations and declarations will not suffice. Officials need to provide a more robust and informed defense of American free speech doctrines and principles. They need to be capable of making informed, and sometimes nuanced, comparisons between American and transnational liberty models. This requires adequate background knowledge and training with regard not only to First Amendment doctrines and justifications, but also with regard to foreign and international models.

When extolling the merits of First Amendment exeptionalism in international forums, U.S. officials should adopt a more balanced perspective regarding America's own free speech record. As some European scholars have observed, when one considers the complete range of expressive liberties, the narrative of First Amendment exceptionalism appears misleading or even objectively false.[51] Thus, for example, while American officials have derided foreign libel standards as insufficiently protective of free speech, they have granted U.S. citizens far less access to governmental information than some European nations.[52] In short, the American defense of First

Amendment exceptionalism ought to be based on solid fact, not mythology.

In the context of international negotiation and diplomacy, cosmopolitan engagement might begin with a fundamental but important change in posture and tone. Instead of adopting a form of strong resistance, U.S. officials ought to engage fully with transnational free speech and other liberty models. They ought to assess and defend American free speech commitments in more cosmopolitan, and less chauvinistic, terms. And they ought to do so transparently and publicly, so that citizens in nations across the world are likewise engaged in this cosmopolitan conversation.

A recent example of this approach was President Obama's speech to the United Nations, following release by a U.S. producer of a trailer for *Innocence of Muslims*, a film that depicted Mohammed in a disrespectful and offensive way. As discussed in Chapter 5, release of the trailer resulted in riots in some Muslim nations. It was initially linked to a deadly attack on the U.S. Embassy in Benghazi, Libya. A significant portion of President Obama's address concerned the rationale for extending First Amendment protection to offensive speech, such as the film trailer. The President explained:

> It is an insult not only to Muslims, but to America as well – for as the city outside these walls makes clear, we are a country that has welcomed people of every race and religion. We are home to Muslims who worship across our country. We not only respect the freedom of religion – we have laws that protect individuals from being harmed because of how they look or what they believe. We understand why people take offense to this video because millions of our citizens are among them.

> I know there are some who ask why we don't just ban such a video. The answer is enshrined in our laws: our Constitution protects the right to practice free speech. Here in the United States, countless publications provoke offense. Like me, the majority of Americans are Christian, and yet we do not ban blasphemy against our most sacred beliefs. Moreover, as President of our country, and Commander-in-Chief of our military, I accept that people are going to call me awful things every day, and I will always defend their right to do so. Americans have fought and died around the

globe to protect the right of all people to express their views – even views that we disagree with.

We do so not because we support hateful speech, but because our Founders understood that without such protections, the capacity of each individual to express their own views, and practice their own faith, may be threatened. We do so because in a diverse society, efforts to restrict speech can become a tool to silence critics, or oppress minorities. We do so because given the power of faith in our lives, and the passion that religious differences can inflame, the strongest weapon against hateful speech is not repression, it is more speech – the voices of tolerance that rally against bigotry and blasphemy, and lift up the values of understanding and mutual respect.

I know that not all countries in this body share this understanding of the protection of free speech. Yet in 2012, at a time when anyone with a cell phone can spread offensive views around the world with the click of a button, the notion that we can control the flow of information is obsolete. The question, then, is how we respond. And on this we must agree: there is no speech that justifies mindless violence.[53]

As President Obama recognizes, the United States must now convince an increasingly skeptical world that its unique conception of free speech is worth retaining – particularly in contexts where the First Amendment's exceptional ideals produce externalities beyond U.S. borders. That burden rightly rests on the United States, as it often presents itself to the world as the foremost protector of freedom of speech, religion, and other human rights. As I discussed in Chapter 5, U.S. officials need to explain why retaining some protection for hate speech, incitement, and criticism of government officials is necessary for the development of common goods including the Internet. Viewed from this perspective, First Amendment exceptionalism would not be the selfish attitude of an arrogant nation, but rather a principled and intentional choice informed by America's own extensive experience with evils such as authoritarianism, censorship, and discrimination.

Readers may wonder about the tangible benefits likely to be associated with this sort of transnational engagement. After all, no nation is likely to be persuaded to abandon a deeply entrenched constitutional or legal model as a result of (even genuine) international negotiation or conversation. Indeed, following the posting of the *Innocence of Muslims* trailer and President Obama's speech, some nations once again urged the United Nations to consider adopting a universal ban on hate speech and blasphemy.

The notion that no benefits at all will accrue from cosmopolitan engagement overstates the claim. For example, U.S. diplomatic pressure in the wake of concerns about libel tourism may have played some role in speeding or influencing recent changes to British libel law standards. Transnational processes, including pressure by government officials and nongovernment actors, can highlight free speech issues in a manner that leads to transnational dialogue and reconsideration of standards or principles. This, of course, is the theory of the First Amendment – that counter-speech and the clashing of ideas can change minds or at least lead to better understanding.

In any event, we ought not to view the benefits of engagement too narrowly, as if success is achieved only if laws in other nations or international bodies are altered to resemble First Amendment standards. U.S. officials instead ought to take a broader view. They might find that decisions not to punish speakers who denigrate religion, and their refusal to ban racially insensitive speech, will receive a more respectful global reception insofar as these decisions are explained to foreign audiences rather than simply defended on reflexive, exceptionalist grounds. In some quarters, the United States has simply stopped trying to persuade outsiders (and to some extent its own citizens) of the merits of retaining First Amendment standards. Except during times of international crisis, it has become disengaged.

Defending exceptionalism in more universal or cosmopolitan terms will not weaken domestic liberties. Nor will it dilute U.S. power abroad by demonstrating weakness. Rather, it will demonstrate our commitment to the principles we purport to defend in retaining extraordinary speech protections. It may also cause some domestic self-reflection with regard to the costs and benefits of retaining current First Amendment protections.

Cosmopolitan engagement might also lead to some increase in comity by other nations toward U.S. policies and judgments. Indeed, genuine conversation could increase what one scholar refers to as the "overseas trade in American first amendment values."[54] This does not mean that other nations will necessarily adopt American free speech standards. As I explain in Chapter 10, the United States is not in a strong position to export First Amendment standards or doctrines across the globe. However, international courts continue to look to First Amendment doctrines and principles in criminal incitement and other contexts.[55] Further, the United States can export broader values and principles relating to free speech. Toward that end, the United States may improve its credibility in the world community as a defender of free speech by showing due regard for the opinions and laws of the international community.

Finally, we ought not to view the benefits of engagement as directed solely to the world community. Engagement with the transnational can actually *increase* some domestic free speech protections. For example, U.S. participation in the Helsinki Accords, which among other things addressed cross-border movement and information flow, was a precipitating factor behind congressional liberalization of U.S. laws that limited such activities. Further, as mentioned earlier, some European protections relating to governmental transparency and access to information are more robust than those provided in the United States. It is possible that engagement with the transnational, including a more informed comparison between U.S. and other nations' models, could produce more robust expressive rights under U.S. laws.

Most of the benefits I have mentioned must be couched in tentative terms because the United States has not pursued an official policy of cosmopolitan engagement. These benefits ought to be weighed against the minimal costs of the sort of engagement I am proposing. Cosmopolitan engagement would not eliminate or make deep inroads into First Amendment exclusivity. Nor would it pose any general threat to First Amendment exceptionalism, although it would require that the United States explain its standards in more global or cosmopolitan terms.

Adjudication and Interpretation

International treaties and diplomacy are not the only possible entry points for transnational constitutional standards. Through engagement with other transnational legal processes and sources, U.S. courts could also play a role in this process. Thus, courts might interpret the First

Amendment to adopt an international baseline for expressive rights or, in less direct and formal ways, they could interpret domestic rights in such a manner that they more closely resemble the substance of transnational liberties.

On a few occasions, American courts, including the U.S. Supreme Court, have taken transnational legal sources and concerns into account when adjudicating domestic speech rights. What these decisions show is that it is sometimes appropriate, perhaps necessary, to take international law into account in adjudicating certain domestic speech claims. For example, in *Boos v. Barry*, the Supreme Court invalidated a law limiting protests within a certain distance of foreign embassies in Washington, D.C. on the ground that it was not narrowly tailored to address the government's safety concerns.[56] However, the Court suggested that compliance with international laws relating to protection of embassy properties might be recognized as a compelling interest supporting the protest restrictions. As the Court put it, somewhat ambiguously, "the dictates of international law [might] require that First Amendment analysis be adjusted to accommodate the interests of foreign officials."[57]

Professor Spiro cites *Boos* as an example of judicial *subordination* of domestic First Amendment standards.[58] According to Spiro, whenever a domestic court adjusts the First Amendment analysis to accommodate foreign concerns, the United States is thereby "ceding rights autonomy" to international law – in *Boos*, the Vienna Convention on Diplomatic Relations.[59] However, *Boos* did not signal any broad subordination of the First Amendment's Free Speech Clause to an international baseline or standard. The Vienna Convention merely requires signatory nations, including the United States, to take all appropriate steps to protect foreign embassy property and personnel. In *Boos*, the Court actually declined to hold that the interest advanced under international law was compelling. Moreover, the Court strongly suggested that foreign officials are granted no greater protection from offensive expression than are American citizens.[60] The Court's recognition that international law protects the dignity of embassy properties and personnel does not suggest, much less hold, that First Amendment libel, incitement, and other speech doctrines are to be subordinated to international standards. Rather, the Court was merely showing due respect for basic principles of international law and comity.

Although Spiro overstates the case against judicial consideration of transnational sources in *Boos*, transnational sources certainly can adversely affect domestic free speech rights. In *Holder v. Humanitarian Law Project*, which I have discussed in previous chapters, the Supreme Court relied heavily on foreign affairs concerns in upholding federal laws prohibiting the provision of material support to foreign terrorist organizations.[61] Specifically, the Court was concerned that allowing U.S. citizens to provide any type of support to foreign terrorist organizations, including through peaceful forms of expression, would undermine international efforts to combat terrorism and might cause U.S. allies abroad to "react sharply."[62] Thus, unlike *Boos*, *Humanitarian Law Project* arguably does subordinate domestic free speech rights to international concerns.

Here, again, we must be careful not to provoke unwarranted fear of transnational engagement. First Amendment adjudication is highly contextual. Where relevant, U.S. courts certainly ought to consider the interests of foreign embassies, officials, and governments. This is one aspect of cosmopolitan judicial engagement. Thus, in *Boos*, the Court appropriately considered U.S. international obligations when defining the government's interests in the protest restrictions. The United States would expect the same consideration in any case affecting its own embassies abroad.

Moreover, as I explained, my criticism of *Humanitarian Law Project* is not that it considered transnational relations and concerns at all, but rather that the Court treated potential foreign "offense" to peaceful and lawful domestic speech as a compelling reason to limit cross-border conversation and commingling. If U.S. courts are going to engage in a cosmopolitan analysis of domestic speech laws, they ought to consider the transborder costs of enforcement – including the adverse effects on cross-border information flow and association. The Supreme Court failed to do this in *Humanitarian Law Project*, and thereby missed an important opportunity to support transborder speech and association rights.

As *Boos* and *Humanitarian Law Project* show, cosmopolitan adjudication sometimes requires engagement with transnational legal sources and concerns. This sort of engagement is distinct from judicial citation and explicit reliance on transnational law. The Supreme Court and lower U.S. courts have not engaged in this particular form of engagement in First Amendment cases. In the limited circumstances in which the Supreme Court has explicitly referred to foreign precedents and practices in constitutional decisions, it has done so partly because the history and tradition regarding the relevant constitutional norm was uncertain. This was true, for example, with regard to imposition of the death penalty for the mentally retarded and punishment for private consensual sexual activities.[63]

Fundamental free speech doctrines are far more settled and entrenched. With regard to free speech and other First Amendment standards, the United States views itself exclusively as an exporter. As the controversy over enforcement of foreign libel judgments shows, U.S. officials are not about to jettison *New York Times Co. v. Sullivan* in favor of a transnational libel standard.[64] Nor, despite some persistent complaints about its supposedly overprotective nature, is the standard for unlawful incitement adopted in *Brandenburg v. Ohio* likely to be overturned in favor of some less protective transnational approach.[65] In general, wholesale changes in terms of protected categories of speech content seem unlikely to occur.

This does not mean that transnational processes and judicial engagement are irrelevant, or beside the point. In terms of engagement, U.S. jurists can learn something valuable from transnational interactions, sources, and models. As Vicki Jackson has observed, "understanding how roughly comparable bodies have interpreted roughly similar constitutional provisions can help illuminate constitutional commitments to shared constitutional values, like the idea of limited government or of freedom of speech."[66]

Justice Stephen Breyer made a similar point in a conversation with Justice Antonin Scalia regarding the relevance of foreign constitutional interpretation in U.S. adjudication. He said: "If, for example, a foreign court, in a particular decision, had shown that a particular interpretation of similar language in a similar document had had an adverse effect on free expression, to read that decision might help me to apply the American Constitution."[67] The sentiment behind this kind of engagement is neither new nor novel. As Judge Cardozo once wrote, "We are not so provincial as to say that every solution of a problem is wrong because we deal with it otherwise at home."[68]

That said, in many cases, cosmopolitan engagement will likely confirm the conclusion that current First Amendment free speech standards ought to be retained. However, in the spirit of the First Amendment, it is certainly worth asking how other models and experiments have fared.

For example, American libel law is deeply rooted in our own unique historical experiences relating to seditious libel and criticism of public officials. Still, the approach taken by the Supreme Court is not without critics, both domestic and foreign. Accounting, insofar as possible, for cultural and other differences, what does experience abroad suggest with regard to the possible effect of changing the American approach? Further, as Justice Breyer's comment suggests, in some contexts it is possible that judges who have studied transnational approaches will draw on this information in answering new questions. For example, how have foreign courts addressed freedom of the press in the digital era? How have they interpreted privacy and intellectual property rights in online forums? What do other nations' experiences with protection for confidential information tell us about our own standards?

Or, perhaps, as a result of transnational engagement, judges will question some of the basic suppositions behind certain free speech doctrines. For example, although he does not cite transnational sources, Justice Alito's dissent in *Snyder v. Phelps*, which overturned a civil verdict imposing tort liability for a public protest directed at a military funeral, might have been written by a European judge.[69] Justice Alito emphasized the "brutalization" of the fallen soldier's family and the lack of respect the protesters showed for the serenity and dignity of the funeral ceremony.[70] Although he might blanch at the comparison, Justice Alito's dissent argued for a dignity-based approach that is far more consistent with European speech laws and precedents than with First Amendment doctrine. Is it possible that Justice Alito's participation in judicial conferences with European judges indirectly, or even subconsciously, affected his views? Would this be entirely unwelcome, assuming it was the case? After all, judges are influenced by many sources. If the transnational perspective gives American judges some pause in extending a contested principle or edifies them with regard to a common free speech problem, on what basis would this be illegitimate?

Like other officials, American judges may benefit from viewing First Amendment principles and commitments through a transnational lens. Engagement with the transnational offers a distinct vantage point from which to study common concerns and subjects, such as hate speech regulation, privacy, and libel. This may inform, sharpen, and even improve domestic speech doctrines and principles. Jeremy Waldron, who has examined hate speech regulations from a comparative perspective, recently observed:

> The point is not to condemn or reinterpret the U.S. constitutional provisions, but to consider whether American free-speech jurisprudence has really come to terms with the best that can be said for hate speech regulations. Often, in the American debate, the philosophical arguments about hate speech are knee-jerk, impulsive, and thoughtless.[71]

In sum, judicial engagement with the transnational may produce some of the same benefits discussed earlier in the context of treaty negotiations. Judicial decisions provide forums for cosmopolitan conversation regarding problems that are common to members of the community of nations. Better-reasoned explanations for exceptional American free speech protections would contribute to an important international dialogue concerning the costs and benefits of freedom of speech. Again, there are U.S. credibility concerns. First Amendment free speech principles support the search for truth, which often requires comparative assessments. Provincial and reflexive refusals to engage transnational approaches to free speech and other expressive concerns are fundamentally inconsistent with these fundamental principles.

Cosmopolitan Choice of Law and Foreign Judgment Recognition

In some contexts, officials actually have no choice but to engage with transnational legal sources. This occurs, for example, when digital speech originating in one nation crosses international borders, or when plaintiffs seek recognition and enforcement of foreign libel and other judgments in American courts.

As I noted earlier, American courts and legislatures have adopted a provincial approach under which foreign speech laws and judgments generally cannot be enforced in the United States. An alternative approach based on principles of engagement would require application of choice of law and judgment recognition principles in these contexts. This creates some limited opportunities for recognition and enforcement of foreign speech and other laws in the United States. Again, however, this form of engagement would not result in broad displacement of domestic laws or standards.

As I have emphasized throughout the book, it is critically important to preserve the free speech rights of U.S. citizens who communicate across and beyond international borders. Thus, I have argued that the First Amendment ought to be interpreted to protect speech and associational activities that cross international borders. I have argued that citizens' speech and other First Amendment liberties ought to be considered portable – that is, they ought to apply extraterritorially.

At the same time, however, when U.S. citizens visit abroad, their speech and other activities are subject to regulation under the libel, hate speech, and other laws in force in host nations. As Google and several other American businesses have learned, the First Amendment is not a shield against application of Chinese, Italian, or other laws in countries where American companies do business. Multinational corporations, in particular those in the business of distributing information, must comply with multiple national laws relating to free speech. Cross-cutting jurisdiction is an increasingly important part of the twenty-first century free speech landscape.

One question that has arisen in the digital era is what to do when multiple sovereigns have legal jurisdiction over communication. In other words, which nation's law applies to digital speech? This issue spawned a debate between what David Post refers to as "exceptionalists" and "un-exceptionalists."[72] As Post explains, exceptionalists claim that the Internet has fundamentally altered traditional territorial governance. They assert that a speaker who uses the Internet ought not to be subject to the obscenity, libel, hate speech, and other laws in force across the globe.[73] What is needed, according to exceptionalists, is a uniform, globally applicable expressive standard: "Global law for a global Internet."[74]

Un-exceptionalists, by contrast, assert that the Internet has not fundamentally altered traditional models of territorial governance and sovereignty. They maintain that, when speech crosses territorial borders and produces extraterritorial effects, any affected sovereign can potentially assert jurisdiction over the speaker based on those effects.

For the reasons discussed earlier, global convergence with regard to free speech standards is not likely to occur. There is no global law of free speech on our horizon. Although the burdens imposed on Internet speakers and distributors by multijurisdictional standards are high, there is too much variation among speech laws to expect global convergence. Moreover, as I noted earlier, there is no governance structure for enforcing universal standards. As un-exceptionalists point out, in the absence of global standards, nations have a strong interest in enforcing their own laws against speech that enters their territory. If we are unlikely to have a global or universal standard, then we must develop a framework for resolving conflicts of laws issues relating to free speech. This situation calls for an approach to transnational conflicts that takes the interests of multiple nations into account.

Paul Schiff Berman has articulated such an approach to transnational choice of law questions.[75] Berman's approach, which is explicitly based on cosmopolitan principles, is consistent with the type of engagement I am proposing.

Berman's choice of law approach "starts from the premise that community affiliations are always plural and can be detached from mere spatial location."[76] It acknowledges the primacy of local affiliations but, at the same time, recognizes that community affiliations extend across territorial borders. Like transnational engagement, Berman's cosmopolitan approach to multi-jurisdictional conflicts rejects the principles of universalism and convergence.[77] Rather, Berman expressly encourages courts that are faced with transnational choice of law questions to view themselves "as international and transnational actors who are engaging in an international dialogue about legal norms."[78]

Specifically, cosmopolitan choice of law urges courts to look to a variety of transnational legal sources, including domestic constitutional norms, international treaties and agreements, the community affiliations of the parties, and traditional conflicts principles.[79] As Berman explains, "rather than 'localize' a transaction in territorial space, cosmopolitanism would engage in an a priori debate about community affiliation, definition, and effects in order to determine whether a given community may appropriately (or legitimately) apply its norms to a dispute."[80] A cosmopolitan choice of law regime focuses less on territorial connections and territorial sovereignty, and more on "the extent to which the various parties might be deemed to have affiliations with the possible communities seeking to impose their norms."[81]

As Berman notes, this approach to choice of law requires "a nuanced inquiry concerning whether the affiliations of the parties render the original court judgment legitimate."[82] In cases brought in the United States, for example, the local policies of the forum, including the interest in retaining First Amendment standards, are plainly relevant and indeed substantial. However, according to Berman, these interests must be weighed against "the overall systemic interest in creating an interlocking system of international adjudication."[83] As he states, under a cosmopolitan approach, "courts cannot effectively further state interests by parochially making sure that the law applied to any given multistate case will always benefit its own citizens."[84]

Berman's approach represents a departure from traditional choice of law approaches to transnational conflicts, which are based primarily on territoriality and thus define state interests narrowly. It is "ultimately moored to an expanded conception of how governments must operate in an interconnected world."[85] As Berman argues, this cosmopolitan approach "is better suited to a world of interconnection, interrelationship, and multiple community affiliations."[86] It views choice of law questions as part of a cosmopolitan conversation among national courts and legislatures regarding community affiliation and transnational norms.

According to Berman, the cosmopolitan approach to transnational choice of law also extends to recognition of foreign judgments. We can get a sense of the manner in which cosmopolitan principles would resolve choice of law and judgment recognition issues in free speech contexts by examining U.S. recognition of foreign libel judgments and enforcement of foreign hate speech laws.

As discussed earlier, enforcement of foreign libel judgments sets up a conflict between the *New York Times Co. v. Sullivan*[87] standard applicable in the United States and the less protective libel laws of the United

Kingdom and other foreign nations.[88] Ultimately, American courts
and legislatures barred recognition of these judgments. Courts generally rejected the foreign libel judgments on public policy grounds.[89]
Congress and state legislatures reportedly acted out of concerns that
foreign plaintiffs were attempting to silence U.S. authors and to preserve free speech exclusivity and exceptionalism.

The SPEECH Act is an anomaly. In fact, the U.S. treatment of
foreign libel and other speech judgments is itself exceptional. Foreign
judgments are routinely enforced in the United States – even where the
original claim could not have been maintained, whether as a matter of
law or public policy, within the United States.[90] Moreover, under traditional conflicts principles, courts typically at least *consider* the forum's
nexus to the dispute.[91] Indeed, in libel cases, the place of publication
and the victim's domicile are both principal considerations.[92] In contrast, the American approach to foreign libel judgments bars enforcement even when the U.S. has a minimal territorial or other nexus to
the dispute and the foreign nation has a substantial nexus or at least an
interest worthy of some consideration.[93]

As some constitutional scholars have observed, the American
approach to enforcement of foreign libel judgments effectively means
that *New York Times v. Sullivan* is applicable across the globe. For example, Mark Rosen has argued that "[c]ategorically refusing to enforce
such Un-American Judgments is tantamount to imposing U.S. constitutional norms on foreign countries."[94]

Professor Rosen and other scholars argue that this categorical
approach is not compelled by the First Amendment – specifically, they
assert that U.S. courts would not be violating the First Amendment by
enforcing judgments that are based on speech standards that are less
protective than *Sullivan*'s.[95] Although the state action doctrine is notoriously complex and confused, scholars and some courts have persuasively demonstrated that mere enforcement of a foreign judgment does
not itself constitute state action for First Amendment purposes. As one
court addressing the state action argument observed, "*Recognizing and
enforcing* a foreign-country money judgment is distinct from *rendering*
that judgment in the first instance."[96] Thus, courts ought not generally
to refuse recognition and enforcement of foreign judgments on state
action grounds.[97]

Nor ought courts to generally refuse recognition and enforcement of a foreign judgment that does not comport specifically with First Amendment standards on public policy grounds. Rather, under a cosmopolitanism choice of law approach to foreign libel judgments, courts would engage in a conflicts analysis to determine whether the First Amendment rule ought to limit or bar recognition and enforcement of any foreign judgment. Berman's approach "asks judges to consider the independent value of enforcing a foreign judgment, even when that judgment is contrary to local policy choices."[98] As Berman notes, the question in judgment recognition contexts is not whether the forum could have issued the judgment in the first instance, but rather whether it is appropriate under the circumstances to grant international comity to the foreign judgment.[99]

Thus, rather than simply assuming U.S. law applies, domestic courts ought to consider such things as the community affiliations of the parties, their relationship to the forum, and the values of transnational reciprocity and interstate harmony. Further, they ought to base recognition and enforcement decisions on the conflicts values that would be served by enforcement, the balance between those values and the domestic speech norm, and the communal affiliations of the parties. Under this approach, when the United States has a minimal interest or connection to the libel or other claim at issue, enforcement of the foreign judgment might be warranted. Conversely, where the foreign forum has only a minimal connection to the dispute, a U.S. court could validly refuse to enforce the foreign judgment.

Enforcement of foreign libel and other judgments under this approach would not broadly eliminate the exceptional protection for political speech granted to domestic speakers in the United States. Nor would it generally undermine the cosmopolitan protection granted to citizens' cross-border and extraterritorial expression. Rather, in specific cases where the United States has only a minimal interest in the speech conflict and the benefits of comity are significant, judgment recognition would acknowledge the pluralistic nature of community affiliations and recognize the plural national interests in the global, interconnected legal system. In place of a categorical rule, courts would "take seriously the conflicts values that would be effectuated by enforcing the foreign judgment, weigh the importance of such values against the relative importance of the local public policy or constitutional norm, and then consider the degree to which the parties have affiliated themselves with the forum."[100]

This approach can also inform resolution of digital and other speech conflicts. As I mentioned earlier, in the *Yahoo!* case, a French court ordered an American company to remove Nazi paraphernalia from its U.S. servers so that consumers in France would not be able to purchase them in violation of French hate speech laws. Yahoo! argued that the French assertion of jurisdiction, and the attempt to enforce the French judgment in a U.S. court, violated the First Amendment. A federal district court judge held that enforcement of the French judgment would indeed violate Yahoo!'s First Amendment rights, by restricting lawful speech based on its content within U.S. borders.[101] The district court did not perform a choice of law analysis, but merely assumed that the First Amendment applied to Yahoo!'s communications.

As Berman notes, *Yahoo!* is a difficult conflicts case.[102] The company had significant contacts and affiliations in France.[103] However, Yahoo! is an American company, and thus presumptively entitled to First Amendment protection when it engages in expressive activity. Still, Berman tentatively concludes that the company's substantial affiliations with France ought to have rendered the French court's judgment enforceable in the United States.[104] As he notes, this does not mean that every Web publisher in the United States who distributes information in France would be subject to French jurisdiction and to enforcement of French judgments in the United States. Indeed, in many cases, the websites' "utter lack of community affiliation with France" would likely result in the foreign judgment not being considered enforceable in the United States.[105] However, where these affiliations do exist, and where cosmopolitan principles support recognition and enforcement of the foreign court's judgment, a U.S. court ought to oblige – notwithstanding that the First Amendment would protect the speech if distributed solely within the United States.

Again, this form of transnational engagement does not pose a general threat to the First Amendment. It does not undermine any deeply held free speech commitment. Rather, it requires that in the case of conflicting laws and foreign judgments, the United States must respect the interests other nations have in enforcing their own speech laws. As Berman observes, "in an era when ideas of bounded nation-state communities operating within fixed territorial borders are under challenge," parochial conceptions of legal jurisdiction and categorical bans on judgment enforcement are out of place.[106]

Of course, there may be foreign speech judgments that, owing to their content, cannot be enforced in the United States. My analysis assumes that the nations in question generally agree on basic liberal free speech values and principles, but disagree regarding how those principles ought to be enforced or competing interests balanced. Judgments imported from autocratic nations may well be unenforceable in the United States on various grounds, including that the domestic costs of enforcement are simply too great relative to the international or cosmopolitan benefits that comity might produce.[107] As Mark Rosen has argued, where enforcement might significantly endanger American norms or create the impression that domestic courts are broadly endorsing norms or standards inconsistent with core First Amendment free speech, press, or other rights, then enforcement may properly be denied.[108]

Judicial cosmopolitanism is one possible answer to the dilemma of transnational speech conflicts. Mark Rosen has argued that despite the recent American experience with state laws and the federal SPEECH Act, political actors are generally better suited to resolve such conflicts.[109] He has proposed that approaches to transnational judgment recognition be resolved by international agreement, specifically through development by the Hague Conference or in a series of bilateral or multilateral agreements. This approach would also entail cosmopolitan exchange and negotiation by all affected nations, rather than unilateral denial of recognition for what Rosen calls "Un-American Judgments." As Rosen acknowledges, it would be quite difficult to achieve anything approaching international consensus regarding foreign judgment recognition. Nevertheless, this is an alternative worth pursuing. Whether cosmopolitan engagement occurs in judicial or political forums, it would mark a significant improvement over the current provincial U.S. approach to foreign speech and other judgments.

TRANSNATIONAL ENGAGEMENT AND RELIGION

Cosmopolitan engagement with transnational sources relating to religious liberties presents complexities similar to those associated with transnational speech laws and judgments. As I discussed in Chapter 1, the United States has a unique perspective on church–state relations. Its basic views on religious neutrality differ from those of many democratic and other nations around the world. Nevertheless, cosmopolitan engagement with religious sources and religious pluralism can be undertaken without undermining core domestic rights or values. Like the Free Speech Clause and the Free Press Clause, the First Amendment's religion clauses are not in any danger of being displaced by the sort of transnational engagement I have in mind. Thus, international treaties will not act as import channels for foreign standards regarding free exercise or religious practices. Nor will the U.S. church–state model be fundamentally altered as result of transnational engagement.

I begin this section with a positive example of the sort of engagement I am proposing. I then argue against the sort of resistance I believe some portion of the American populace has recently embraced, particularly in the aftermath of the September 11, 2001 terrorist attacks. Finally, I discuss enforcement of foreign judgments that implicate religious liberties.

Transnational Religious Pluralism

The positive example dates, oddly enough, from the Cold War period. In 1952, the U.S. Supreme Court decided *Kedroff v. St. Nicholas Cathedral*.[110] A dispute had arisen over the right to use St. Nicholas Russian Orthodox Cathedral in New York City. An American group claimed that the appointment of the archbishop in New York by the Patriarch of Moscow was void because the Patriarch was under the direct control of the Soviet government. New York's legislature and courts had relied on and sustained this claim. The Supreme Court overruled them, holding that the Free Exercise Clause required that New York uphold the Patriarch's appointment. The Court concluded that deference was owed to the decisions of an international hierarchical church, and that New York's officials erred in interpreting their law of trusts to prohibit granting control of the property to a foreign church that was controlled by a foreign government.

Kedroff is a significant decision regarding free exercise protection regarding internal matters of church governance. But it also has a significant and less-discussed transnational aspect. The Court held that, under the First Amendment's Free Exercise Clause, New York's officials had to respect the decision of a foreign government that dominated both the church and its appointees. As one scholar characterized the decision, it "seems to mean that the free exercise clause entitles donors in the United States to spend their money to support a religion, one of whose characteristics is that it permits a foreign government to perform a function in regard to religion that no American government is allowed to perform[.]"[111]

In this respect, *Kedroff* bears some resemblance to a precedent recognizing a foreign libel judgment or a trademark judgment obtained under foreign intellectual property laws. It is in some ways the mirror image of *Lamont v. Postmaster General* which, as I discussed in Chapter 4, held that foreign political propaganda could not be prevented from entering the U.S. postal stream, even though the foreign nation from which it originated would not allow similar protection for distribution of American materials.[112]

Kedroff interpreted the Free Exercise Clause to require recognition and respect for decisions emanating from a foreign nation that rejects the American view regarding separation of church and state. This form of engagement with the transnational did not threaten to upset or undermine domestic principles with regard to separation of church and state. Indeed, viewed from the perspective of religious neutrality and free exercise, the decision could not have come out any other way. New York's trust laws could not be used to discriminate against the appointee on the ground that the religious beliefs of his church were disfavored. Neither, said the Court, could it reject the church's decision on the ground that it was aligned with or dominated by the state. Ultimately, the decision not only protects the ability of a foreign government to control trust property located in the United States, but it also protects the rights of U.S. citizens to associate with foreign religious organizations of their choosing.

Kedroff is a positive example of transnational engagement. As a negative illustration, I would point to the resistance that has recently developed in the United States with respect to Shari'a law. As discussed earlier, many states have enacted or considered bans on *any* reference to or enforcement of foreign or international law. Some have expressly included reference to or enforcement of Shari'a law within these transnational prohibitions.

State bans on any reference to transnational legal sources are plainly overbroad. If enforced, those bans would effectively preclude courts from enforcing foreign judgments or referring to international law in a variety of civil cases. They are contrary to longstanding principles of international comity and choice of law.

In an interconnected legal system in which citizens from different nations enter into bargains and other transactions, flat bans on engagement with transnational legal sources are untenable and unwise. They convey a generalized disrespect for international and foreign legal systems. Banning all reference to or engagement with the transnational demonstrates an unwillingness to respect and recognize foreign laws, international laws, and bargains entered into between citizens of different nations. In a globalized world, states that adopt this parochial posture may incur significant economic, social, and political costs.

With regard specifically to Shari'a bans, the First Amendment itself forbids the singling out of particular faiths for burdensome and discriminatory treatment. We need only refer and recommit to this principle to reject such laws. The Free Exercise Clause proscribes official discrimination against religion – whether against specific religions or religion in general. Further, the Establishment Clause broadly prohibits governmental establishment of, or specific preferences for, religion or specific religious faiths. If state courts enforce more mainstream religious laws in the context of civil divorce and arbitration, they cannot generally be barred from doing so with respect to Islam or other faiths. Similarly, if state legislatures are going to fund education generally, they cannot deny funding only to those schools that teach Islam.[113]

Some degree of cosmopolitan engagement is thus baked into the religion clause doctrines, in the sense that the First Amendment bars official discrimination against foreign religions and religious tenets. Moreover, discrimination against foreign faiths is inconsistent with America's own cosmopolitan history. Generations of aliens have come to the United States seeking refuge from precisely this sort of discriminatory treatment at the hands of foreign governments.

Recognition and Enforcement of Foreign Judgments

While Shari'a bans plainly offend the First Amendment's religion clauses, more specific forms of transnational engagement with religious laws raise sharper and more difficult questions. Specifically, to what extent can or should U.S. courts recognize and enforce foreign judgments that may violate First Amendment religious liberty standards or norms?

U.S. courts have only begun to struggle with this transnational concern. As discussed earlier, cosmopolitan engagement rejects any blanket ban on consideration and enforcement of judgments and decrees, merely because they are motivated by or premised on foreign laws. This is as true with regard to foreign judgments based on religion as it is with regard to foreign judgments based on speech laws or doctrines that differ from those applicable within the United States.

As in the speech context, state action principles should not generally be relied upon as a ground for U.S. courts to refuse enforcement of foreign judgments affecting religious liberties.[114] Further, as a general matter, Berman's cosmopolitan conflicts principles are transferable to the religion context. Thus, a court faced with the question whether to enforce a foreign judgment entered against a church operating in Japan but incorporated under the laws of the United States, where the judgment is based solely on activities that occurred abroad, should ordinarily recognize and enforce the foreign judgment even if it could not have been entered against the church by a U.S. court in the first instance.[115] The controversy is similar to the *Yahoo!* case, which I discussed earlier in the free speech context.

Foreign courts and officials are not bound by U.S. constitutional limitations. Where the United States has no stake in the action other than to see its laws applied to a controversy that occurred and was adjudicated in Japan, principles of international comity and judgment recognition ought to lead to recognition and enforcement of the foreign judgment. In this and other contexts, public policy objections ought to be read as narrowly as possible. That does not mean that a foreign judgment might not so offend core religious liberty freedoms as to be deemed unenforceable in the United States. However, the mere fact that the foreign judgment does not comport with First Amendment standards or specific doctrines applicable in the United States ought not to bar recognition and enforcement. Note that there is no inconsistency here, in terms of arguing for an expansive First Amendment extraterritorial domain. The defendants are operating on foreign soil and are thus subject to foreign laws and judicial processes and no U.S. official is restricting citizens' rights; thus, the First Amendment does not act as a constitutional constraint.

Some of the most contentious and controversial cases involving importation of foreign judgments have focused on Shari'a laws. The objection, as noted earlier, is that Shari'a is a form of foreign law that is based on principles rejected by domestic religious communities. Of course, nearly all religious faiths now practicing in the United States have transnational roots. Roman Canon law, Jewish Halaka law, and even the Ten Commandments can all be characterized as "foreign" legal sources. Yet judgments that are based on these religious laws are frequently enforced in U.S. courts. So long as courts are not required to interpret the tenets of religious doctrines or beliefs to give effect to the contract or judgment – an analysis that would implicate and perhaps violate the Establishment Clause – the mere fact that the instrument is based on foreign religious principles is not itself a ground for refusing judicial enforcement.[116]

The foregoing conclusion holds even if the terms of the agreement would offend principles or norms of equality that are commonly accepted in the United States. As Eugene Volokh has noted, there is a difference between interpreting religious doctrine and "applying a contract or will according to its secularly ascertainable terms, which is permissible even if the motivation behind the contracting parties' or testator's decisions were religious or sexist."[117] In other words, the fact that state law would not generally apply or impose the same sexist provisions is not a ground for denying enforcement to a foreign contract or agreement that is based on Islamic or other religious tenets. Domestic courts cannot simply refuse to enforce all contracts that are based on Islamic law on the ground that the laws are inherently discriminatory. This approach would violate the Free Exercise Clause by discriminating against parties based on religious cultures or practices.

To be sure, enforcement of some Islamic decrees will intersect with important constitutional and public policy concerns, most notably equal protection guarantees that prohibit gender discrimination. Suppose, for example, that a husband and wife obtain a divorce under Pakistani law. Further assume that, under Pakistani law, women are accorded no marital property rights. Can a U.S. court refuse to recognize the divorce on equal protection and public policy grounds? There are two basic approaches in this situation. One approach is for domestic courts to deny enforcement to any contract that is based on foreign law that fails to grant the same rights to parties that are generally available under U.S. constitutional law. This is essentially the SPEECH Act's approach to foreign libel judgments, and the general provincial American approach. The other approach is to apply choice of law principles, as suggested earlier in the free speech context.[118]

As in the speech context, it may be that under a cosmopolitan choice of law analysis, which again ought to take foreign (forum) interests as well as state public policy concerns into account, the foreign judgment will be enforceable in domestic courts. Or, it may be the case that under cosmopolitan choice of law principles, the foreign interests are outweighed by public policy concerns, and the judgment thus ought not to be enforced. This might be the case, for example, where certain Islamic divorce practices are concerned. Thus, for example, American courts have refused to enforce *talaq* divorces, which are effected by husbands without cause, judicial process, or even the wife's consent.[119] These divorces are sometimes performed opportunistically, by husbands seeking to circumvent American divorce laws.

The choice of law approach requires that an American judge engage the transnational, rather than simply and categorically refuse to enforce the foreign judgments because they might not have been validly entered by a U.S. court in the first instance. Of course, even limited engagement requires that American judges understand foreign laws and non-Christian religious principles. Nathan Oman has written of the difficulties American courts face when interpreting foreign contracts that are based on religious laws and principles. Writing specifically about Muslim *mahr* contracts, under which a husband agrees to pay a sum of money to his wife, Professor Oman notes that courts must first attempt to interpret the contract terms and then must decide whether to enforce them. As he observes, "both inquiries require that courts make sense of contracts embedded in a legal and cultural context that most American judges find foreign and bewildering."[120] While he acknowledges the difficulties courts face in interpreting *mahr* and other Islamic contracts, Professor Oman contends that the argument for blanket refusal to enforce these contracts based primarily on equality concerns proceeds at "too high a level of legal abstraction."[121] He argues that courts can use contract doctrine to resolve marital property issues raised by *mahr* contracts.

Like Professor Oman, I do not argue that domestic courts are required to or ought to displace domestic law in favor of foreign or Islamic religious laws. Cosmopolitan engagement does not press this far. It requires, as exhibited in Professor Oman's work on religious contracts, a sensitivity and understanding of the foreign context in which Islamic principles are applied. This kind of engagement with the transnational requires a delicate balance in the religion context, owing in particular to the requirement that domestic courts apply neutral principles when adjudicating religious contracts and property disputes. Moreover, as Oman notes, "the dominant paradigms for thinking about the relationship between law and religion in American jurisprudence are drawn from the Christian tradition."[122] As Muslims bring their claims to American courts, judges will naturally struggle to frame and adjudicate them. However, in an interconnected world where religious principles migrate among national legal systems, some form of engagement is unavoidable.

Many Americans see Islam as foreign, and thus as inherently threatening. Along with local movements against the building of mosques and public funding of Islamic schools, Shari'a bans are manifestations of public fear, anxiety, and xenophobia in the face of difference. One of the primary purposes of cosmopolitan engagement is to learn from foreign sources, practices, and cultures.[123] Indeed, engagement with the transnational is perhaps most needed where religious creeds or ideologies are deemed foreign, and thus more difficult to understand. As in other transnational contexts, engagement can help to break down differences and facilitate an understanding of diverse beliefs. As one scholar, addressing the First Amendment's religion clauses, justified this orientation:

When we see ourselves as one society among many, some very different from our own, and ponder the perspective of the Constitution on this confrontation and interaction, we can deepen our insight into the philosophy that underlies the Constitution. Perhaps this philosophy endorses neither heavy-handed cultural imperialism nor complete cultural relativism, but while insisting on certain fundamentals, also gives recognition to the many paths by which humanity makes its way.[124]

10   EXPORTING THE FIRST AMENDMENT

As I have made clear throughout the book, the orientation or perspective I am advancing is not intended to render the First Amendment universally applicable to all the peoples and nations of the world. Rather, it is cosmopolitan primarily in the sense that it protects United States citizens and others subject to American laws in cross-border and beyond-border contexts and also serves as a useful guide for U.S. officials and others who participate in international exchanges within the broader community of nations.

The First Amendment is cosmopolitan in another important respect. As the discussion in Chapter 9 showed, in an interconnected world, the First Amendment shares global space with an array of diverse liberty models. If we think of these constitutional models as competing in global marketplaces, it is clear that the First Amendment's exceptional doctrines and standards have now been soundly rejected by the community of nations. The United States has generally not been successful in terms of exporting the First Amendment in the formal or legal sense, even to western democracies with which it shares much in common. Although they have rejected many of the First Amendment's doctrines and standards, many nations have embraced its general norms, principles, and ideals. Indeed, the American First Amendment has had a profound and lasting effect on expressive and religious liberties throughout the world.[1] It is part of the reason why there is such considerable normative overlap among the constitutions of liberal democracies including with respect to recognition of expressive and religious freedoms.

The question I want to address in this final chapter is how, going forward, the United States ought to approach the exportation of free speech, press, and religious liberty standards, norms, and principles. Which mechanisms are most likely to be successful in terms of advancing freedoms of speech and religion in parts of the world where they have not yet been adopted? What general perspective or attitude ought the United States to adopt as it seeks to export freedom of speech and other liberty principles to non-liberal democracies and other nations? What kind and degree of extraterritorial influence can we expect the First Amendment to have in the twenty-first century?

Throughout American history, the United States has adopted the perspective that First Amendment-like rights and values would benefit all citizens in the world community. This sentiment has long been reflected in U.S. foreign policy. Prior to U.S. participation in World War II, President Roosevelt articulated four freedoms he said were necessary for global peace: freedom of worship, freedom from want, freedom from fear, and freedom of the press. He emphasized that global peace and stability depended on the recognition and enjoyment of fundamental expressive and religious liberties.[2] This commitment to liberty did not prevent the United States from establishing an Office of War Information, which was charged with disseminating propaganda overseas. Nor did it prevent the creation of an Office of Censorship that chilled speech within the United States, or the enactment of numerous laws criminalizing domestic criticism of government and restricting cross-border movement and information flow. U.S. domestic laws and policies have not always measured up to the nation's public commitment to global expressive and religious freedoms.

A genuine commitment to exporting First Amendment principles and values must be supported by a strong commitment to respecting those things at home. This claim links the issues addressed in Parts II and III of the book. As Rodney Smolla argued in his important work, *Free Speech in an Open Society*:

> Americans are challenged to ask themselves to what extent, if at all, we should expect or require other nations to adopt our peculiar notions of free speech, and to what extent, if at all, we should at least make our own conduct consistent, so that our behavior toward speech in our foreign relations is equivalent to our behavior toward the speech of our own citizens.[3]

This chapter examines the mechanics and normative aspects of First Amendment exportation. I begin with a description of the means or mechanisms by which First Amendment standards and norms might be exported abroad. Freedoms of speech, press, and religion are global concerns. The United States should continue to adopt and support policies that facilitate the enjoyment of universal expressive and religious human rights.

Both of the competing perspectives discussed in the book, provincialism and cosmopolitanism, share a commitment to First Amendment exportation. However, these perspectives differ rather sharply as to posture, means, and results. Provincialism's approach to exportation is grounded in deep-seated nationalistic pride concerning First Amendment exceptionalism. Thus, it supports protectionist policies regarding foreign laws and judgments, free trade policies that export American cultural goods without regard to their effect on foreign cultures, and unilateral action to enforce human rights regarding expressive and religious liberties.

I will advance a more cosmopolitan perspective with regard to exporting the First Amendment. My approach acknowledges exceptionalism, but rejects protectionism and anything that might resemble rights imperialism. It focuses on empowering individuals through access to information technologies; balances support for cross-border and global information flow with respect for local institutions and cultures; supports a global free press; and relies on a combination of multilateral and unilateral mechanisms to export norms and practices relating to expressive and religious liberty.

EXPORT MECHANISMS

When I refer to *exporting* the First Amendment, I am referring to both specific constitutional standards and more general norms or principles. The United States has at times sought to directly export First Amendment standards and doctrines. It has also adopted certain policies that could indirectly extend First Amendment standards beyond its shores. The United States has also sought, through various mechanisms, to export general norms, principles, and practices that are the product of its own experience with expressive and religious liberties. The principal First Amendment export mechanisms are described briefly in the sections that follow. This description is followed by discussion of a strategy for First Amendment exportation in the twenty-first century.

Treaties and Transnational Processes

As part of a broad foreign policy agenda, the United States has long advocated exportation of First Amendment standards and doctrines. Indeed, at one point, American officials were somewhat confident that the First Amendment would serve as a constitutional model for the rest of the world. After World War II, in the wake of wartime triumph, American officials and press members boldly asserted that the American model was the best hope for global peace. At the United Nations, press associations and American officials, led by Zechariah Chafee, engaged in what Margaret Blanchard has referred to as a "crusade" to enshrine First Amendment press and other standards in international law.[4]

As Blanchard and others have concluded, this crusade was ultimately unsuccessful. Press members were initially dismayed that the American delegation did not forcefully advocate a freedom of expression clause in the United Nations charter. However, President Truman did not want to "cram anything down the throat of an independent nation that will interfere with the peace settlement."[5]

American press professionals argued for the removal of all obstacles to the flow of information and robust protections for freedom of the press. However, Russian and some European delegations were concerned as well with press responsibilities and press abuses. Smaller nations also feared U.S. dominance of international news agencies, and the effects of the American definition of free press on their own domestic papers and other media. There were also complications back in the United States. As Blanchard observed in her detailed account, the free press "crusade" died in part owing to domestic pressures on the American press arising from the postwar Red Scare.[6]

The press crusade and resulting conflict among delegations ultimately produced Article 19 of the Universal Declaration of Human Rights (1948), which states: "Everyone has a right to freedom of thought, conscience and religion; this right includes freedom to hold opinions without interference and to seek, receive and impart information and ideas through any media and regardless of frontiers."[7] However, these broad protections were expressly limited by Article 29, which provides that "[e]veryone has duties to the community in which alone the free and full development of his personality is possible."[8] Thus, the liberty model under international law was, and remains, one that limits expressive and religious liberties in the interest of peace, order, and other communal values.

Despite winning approval of general expressive and religious rights in the U.N. Declaration, the American First Amendment model was not ultimately adopted. One of the principal lessons Blanchard extracted from the postwar press–government crusade on behalf of the First Amendment was that "freedom of the press was culturally based and that no nation could impose its press system on another nation, just as no nation could impose its system of religion or government on another nation."[9]

Although the United States was not successful in its efforts to enshrine First Amendment standards as international law after World War II, its participation influenced the transborder flow and transplant of constitutional norms regarding freedom of speech, press, and religion.[10] The crusade set the world on a path toward recognizing expressive and religious liberties as international human rights. Later, the United States would play a leading role in drafting and negotiating other international instruments, such as the 1975 Helsinki Final Act, under which Communist states were to undertake efforts to respect human rights including expressive and religious liberties.[11] As a result of these agreements, a number of U.S. and international restrictions on cross-border movement and information flow were repealed.

Treaty-making is merely one of many transnational processes by which First Amendment exportation can occur. Other mechanisms provide important alternative channels for expanding the First Amendment's geographic influence. For example, judicial processes are important in this respect. Some foreign courts have found aspects of the First Amendment model persuasive, and many have at least considered First Amendment precedents when interpreting their own liberty guarantees.[12] This engagement with the First Amendment has led to a modest degree of exportation, as foreign courts have adopted or relied on First Amendment precedents, methods, or doctrines in interpreting their own nations' liberty guarantees.[13]

Although some foreign courts will look to American free speech and other precedents for guidance, they generally will adjust these standards to specific national laws and circumstances.[14] As I suggested in the previous chapter, foreign courts' incentives to engage in even this sort of limited borrowing may be declining. First Amendment standards are becoming more exceptional outliers in the world community. Moreover, U.S. courts have steadfastly refused to engage with transnational legal sources in First Amendment cases. In the absence of any meaningful dialogue with the United States Supreme Court on these issues, high courts in other nations may decide not to consider the Court's decisions or to import First Amendment precedents and approaches. Thus, insofar as the Supreme Court wishes to influence the interpretation of transnational law, engagement with foreign sources is a desirable and perhaps even necessary posture.[15]

Since World War II, as the rest of the world has moved steadily in a different direction in terms of interpreting expressive and religious liberties, the American posture has become increasingly defensive rather than offensive. In treaty negotiations and other transnational processes, U.S. officials have focused primarily on preserving and protecting exceptional First Amendment standards from perceived foreign encroachments. Thus, the United States has refused to participate in international and multilateral agreements that diverge from First Amendment standards, or has entered such agreements provisionally with reservations, declarations, and understandings regarding domestic expressive and religious liberties.

Despite this defensive posture, the campaign to export First Amendment standards has not ended. For example, in an effort to combat the practice of "libel tourism" the United States has both enacted domestic legislation and pressed Great Britain to amend its libel rules to conform more closely to First Amendment standards. Further, the United States continues to advocate for a First Amendment model in treaty negotiations and many diplomatic contexts. However, in the postwar period, the U.S. campaign has been far less formal and comprehensive than the 1950s government–press crusade at the United Nations.

International Statecraft and Foreign Relations

Since the 1950s, U.S. export efforts have focused more on broad principles, norms, and practices than transplantation of specific First Amendment standards or doctrines through treaties or other formal instruments. As aspects of international statecraft and foreign relations, the United States has adopted an agenda for exporting broad principles of democratic liberty, which has included freedoms of speech, press, and religion.

This extensive campaign has relied on a variety of mechanisms. For example, the United States funds numerous programs and initiatives that disseminate information about freedom of speech, press, and religion across the world. It funds educational programs in foreign countries. These programs emphasize the political and cultural benefits of self-government, the free flow of information, and freedom of belief to audiences across the world. U.S. funding supports the Voice of America, Radio Free Europe, Al Hurra, and other global media outlets. Through these media, the United States disseminates information regarding expressive and religious freedoms to millions of citizens in both democratic and autocratic nations.

Through these foreign affairs policies and initiatives, the United States exports ideas and principles associated with the First Amendment. For example, Radio Free Europe's official mission is to "promote democratic values and institutions by disseminating factual information and ideas." It is charged with providing "objective news analysis, and discussion of domestic and regional issues crucial to democratic and free-market transformations," supporting "civil societies by projecting democratic values," combating "ethnic and religious intolerance and promot[ing] mutual understanding among peoples," and providing "a model for local media."[16] Similarly, Al Hurra is intended to operate as a model for freedom of the press in a number of Arab-speaking nations.

Recently, support for Internet access and other digital liberties has become a focus of American foreign policy. American officials have embraced the Internet as a distinct mechanism for exporting freedoms of speech and press across the globe. For the first time in U.S. diplomatic history, Secretary of State Hillary Clinton announced that

Internet freedom is an official plank of American foreign policy. As part of what Secretary Clinton called "Twenty-First Century Statecraft," an initiative she discussed in visits to many foreign countries, the United States has pledged support for Internet freedom and digital free speech and press. Some of the projects funded by the State Department thus far have included the construction and operation of independent cell-phone and wireless networks within foreign countries.

Statecraft and foreign relations initiatives such as these do not export formal First Amendment standards or doctrines. Rather, they focus on exporting norms and principles derived from American experience with First Amendment freedoms. The United States exports First Amendment practices and principles by educating citizens around the world, setting examples for local media, and facilitating global access to the Internet.

International Trade Policies

The United States has also sought to facilitate the export of free speech and press principles through its trade policies. Again, what the United States is exporting in this context is not formal rules but rather practices and norms that are related to or derived from the First Amendment

For example, the United States exports a substantial amount of cultural and media products to foreign nations. These commodities are economically important to their producers and, of course, to the American economy. However, they also embody principles of free access to information and media diversity.

As discussed later, proponents of free trade rules with regard to media products stress both economic and democracy-facilitating jus-tifications for open markets and free trade. Opponents question both the economic and democratic justifications of free trade with regard to media and cultural products. Some worry, in particular, about the magnitude and effect of outside influences on local (foreign) cultural and democratic institutions including the press. [17]

Other free trade policies are more directly related to facilitating global freedoms. In conjunction with the State Department Internet initiative described above, the United States has taken steps to liberal-ize export restrictions affecting trade to repressive regimes like Iran,

Cuba, and Sudan. Some U.S. companies have been granted licenses to provide Internet services and software to citizens in these and other countries. These technologies can be used to thwart efforts by repressive governments to censor communications and restrict press freedoms. As the Arab Spring and other democracy movements around the world have demonstrated, by allowing export of these services and technologies the United States can assist oppressed aliens who seek information located outside their countries and who wish to communicate with audiences located beyond their borders.

Like transnational processes and foreign relations, free trade can open global channels of information. It can facilitate the spread of democratic norms and practices, including free speech and press.

Human Rights Monitoring

In an effort to enforce free speech, religion, and other rights across the globe, the United States also monitors the human rights practices of other nations. For instance, the United States frequently condemns Chinese efforts to censor the Internet. In some cases, the United States imposes unilateral monetary and other sanctions against nations that it determines have violated fundamental expressive and religious freedoms.

The United States does not formally insist that foreign nations comply with First Amendment standards in order to be deemed compliant. Rather, when assessing human rights records in foreign nations, U.S. officials generally purport to be applying and enforcing international human rights standards. For instance, President Obama signed the Daniel Pearl Freedom of the Press Act, which requires the U.S. State Department to expand its scrutiny of media restrictions and intimidation as part of its annual review of human rights. Among other things, under the Act, the State Department is required to determine whether foreign governments participate in or condone violations of international press freedoms.

Similarly, in an effort to ensure that religious liberties are protected across the world, the United States has enacted laws and policies under which it monitors other nations to ensure that they do not violate international human rights relating to religious freedoms. The International Religious Freedom Act of 1998 (IRFA) requires such monitoring by

American officials and authorizes a menu of actions and sanctions from which the president may choose in order to admonish or punish foreign nations that persecute religious groups or otherwise violate their citizens' religious liberties.

Of course, in the eyes of many nations, U.S. global rights policing is inappropriate and illegitimate. Among other things, foreign nations claim that the United States applies its own constitutional standards to their behavior, imposes sanctions inconsistently, and refuses itself to be bound by international human rights treaties.[18] From the U.S. perspective, however, the impetus for these oversight and sanctions mechanisms arises from a deep-seated American belief that First Amendment–like freedoms provide the best hope for world peace and democracy.[19]

Extraterritorial Application of the First Amendment

The United States can also export First Amendment standards and norms by determining that its own citizens are entitled to, or bound by, these limits while they are abroad. There are different mechanisms by which this might occur.

I argued in Chapters 6 and 7 that First Amendment expressive and religious liberty protections ought to follow the U.S. flag or, more precisely, its government. This does not excuse American citizens from compliance with foreign speech and other laws. However, when it respects and enforces those rights abroad, the United States exports First Amendment limits to some degree. In doing so, it both respects the rights of citizens (and, in some limited circumstances, aliens) and signals to the rest of the world community that it is committed to respecting speech and religious liberties without regard to frontiers.

The United States could also expand the First Amendment's extraterritorial domain through legislative enactments extending free speech and other standards to American businesses operating abroad. For example, the Global Online Freedom Act of 2007 (GOFA)[20] was proposed in response to news reports that certain American businesses were assisting China and other repressive regimes in their efforts to censor citizens' access to the Internet and invade their privacy.[21] Had it become law, GOFA would have provided for imposition of civil and criminal penalties against U.S. companies that worked in "Internet-restricting countries" if they engaged in content filtering, censoring, or data storage activities on behalf of such nations. GOFA also provided for a private right of action in U.S. federal court for any person whose identifying information had been disclosed to an official in an Internet-restricting country. GOFA purported to enforce the universal rights to freedom of speech and freedom of the press referred to in Article 19 of the UDHR.[22] However, like IRFA and other human rights enforcement measures, U.S. determinations of free speech and other rights violations might have been influenced by First Amendment standards and norms.[23]

Similarly, although it has not done so, the United States could provide for the extraterritorial application of U.S. copyright and trademark laws. In essence, this would export the balance struck in the United States regarding rights to intellectual property and freedom of speech to foreign speakers.[24] U.S. laws that regulate online intellectual property rights could have a similar effect.

For example, as discussed in Chapter 4, had they been enacted, recent congressional proposals targeting foreign online piracy might have had a significant impact on certain foreign information distributors. Extraditing foreign content providers for the purpose of criminal prosecution under U.S. copyright laws is another means of extending the reach of the free speech balance under American intellectual property laws.

Expansion of extraterritorial domain can result in a degree of exportation of First Amendment standards and norms. By enforcing First Amendment limits abroad and expanding the reach of certain U.S. laws, the United States can extend both the geographic reach and the global influence of the First Amendment. It can also signal to the community of nations its commitment to global protection for freedom of speech and other rights.

Defensive Measures and Extraterritorial Effects

Finally, certain domestic laws and policies could indirectly result in the exportation and application of First Amendment standards abroad. In particular, efforts by the United States to preserve First Amendment exceptionalism at home could produce this extraterritorial effect.

As discussed in Chapter 9, the United States has generally refused to recognize foreign speech judgments and laws that do not satisfy the First Amendment's substantive standards. This defensive or protectionist posture may lead to the exportation of First Amendment standards. As some scholars have argued, a blanket refusal by the United States to recognize any foreign speech laws or judgments will effectively result in the extraterritorial application of First Amendment standards.[25]

Thus, to return to an example from the previous chapter, a French court issued an injunction against an American company that was distributing Nazi paraphernalia in France, an act that violates French hate speech laws.[26] The company insisted that enforcement of the judgment in a U.S. court would violate the First Amendment. However, there are two sides to the recognition coin. As Paul Berman has observed, "If France is *not* able to block the access of French citizens to proscribed material, then the United States will effectively be imposing First Amendment norms on the entire world."[27]

PROTECTING GLOBAL EXPRESSIVE AND RELIGIOUS FREEDOMS

The world has changed drastically since the unsuccessful 1950s press–government crusade at the United Nations. The United States has become more of an outlier in terms of substantive expressive and, to a lesser extent, religious liberties. It cannot impose its standards on the world community. However, some U.S. policies may still have an export effect.

As Vicki Jackson has observed, "The degree of normative overlap between the U.S. Constitution and those of many other liberal democracies is considerable."[28] The most significant challenges regarding exportation in the twenty-first century will center not on liberal democracies, but rather on repressive and authoritarian regimes where expressive and religious liberties are frequently restricted or denied altogether. The United States needs to think systematically about this challenge, and in particular about how to best cooperate with nations that share its commitment to *global* expressive and religious freedoms.

General Orientation

Americans view the First Amendment's exceptional expressive and religious liberties with justifiable pride. The urge to share the First Amendment's model, which Americans generally consider a signature accomplishment, with the rest of the world is strong. However, as the U.N. crusade demonstrated more than half a century ago, sharp differences exist among the world's liberty models. Notwithstanding this fact, First Amendment exceptionalism continues to produce strong undercurrents of protectionism, nationalism, and unilateralism.

Americans are not generally accustomed to thinking about First Amendment freedoms in global terms. For a number of reasons, U.S. courts and officials have been reluctant to adopt expansive interpretations of the First Amendment's geographic domain. This is true even with respect to citizens, who have been granted only weak forms of cross-border and beyond-border First Amendment protections. Indeed, as discussed in Chapter 6, according to some courts, First Amendment rights can be waived when citizens publish or disseminate information in foreign speech marketplaces. This suggests that expressive and religious liberty protections are not fully enforceable by citizens when they are beyond U.S. borders.

On the other hand, however, some U.S. policies suggest just the opposite – that is, that First Amendment standards ought to be universally applicable. With regard to recognition of foreign libel judgments, protectionist U.S. policies may result in the exportation of First Amendment standards to foreign countries. The primary reason given by courts and legislators for this approach is that enforcement of foreign speech laws within the United States would violate the First Amendment. As I have argued, this approach disregards the interests of foreign sovereigns in interpreting and enforcing their own laws.

In essence, although the United States generally talks a good game in terms of the universality of expressive and religious liberties and the need for global protection, its own orientation has not been entirely consistent. Perhaps the most consistent aspect of its policy approach has been its territorial and nationalistic orientation. In important respects, First Amendment rights continue to be viewed as domestic rights that have little or no connection to audiences or events beyond U.S. borders.

This provincial attitude extends to the foreign policy realm. There, the U.S. approach has generally been to condemn human rights violations as foreign problems that can best be solved by U.S. monitoring, criticism, and sanctions. As Louis Henkin has observed, U.S. foreign policy has consistently viewed international human rights as being for "export only."[29] Americans are, by now, rather accustomed to judging other nations' liberty protections and human rights records. In some cases, this judgment is rendered despite the fact that the United States has refused to be bound by the instrument that it alleges some other nation has violated.

For some time, U.S. officials and diplomats have acted with a nationalist and unilateral orientation. Backed by the strong tailwinds created by U.S. economic and military supremacy, the United States has asserted the supremacy of the First Amendment model. It has insisted on free trade policies, including with respect to cultural and media exports. Whenever the First Amendment model has been questioned in international forums and processes, the United States has simply withdrawn support or reflexively conditioned its participation in human rights instruments on substantial reservations, declarations, and understandings.

As I have noted, this approach has produced some significant benefits. Over time, it has led to the global spread of important First Amendment norms and principles. But this approach is not well suited to twenty-first century realities. By this point, the list of circumstances is well known. It includes globalization; the decreasing salience of territorial sovereignty; the digitization of expression and global information exchange; and the rise of internationalism. In these circumstances, an orientation that focuses on shared normative commitments to expressive and religious liberties will be better suited to exporting First Amendment norms, principles, and practices than is the traditional provincial approach. The most effective export mechanisms will be international law, international dialogue, and perhaps most importantly, facilitation of global information flow and freedom of the press.

In some sense, Part II was an extended argument for a more global orientation regarding expressive and religious liberties. The United

States cannot herald international human rights abroad while failing to recognize fully its own citizens' expressive and religious liberties regardless of location. Nor can it do so without acknowledging its obligation to respect the First Amendment rights of aliens abroad – at least when it exercises custody and control over them, and insists on obedience to U.S. laws. Recognizing that First Amendment limits apply without regard to borders is an important step in globalizing our orientation regarding expressive and religious freedoms. Similarly, rejection of libel protectionism and similar policies would acknowledge the need to account for transnational law and legal pluralism when considering global expressive and religious freedoms. In this and other contexts, the United States has been dogged by charges of unilateralism, protectionism, and even forms of rights imperialism.[30]

Although it is both normatively and symbolically important for the United States to respect First Amendment limitations abroad, the central focus ought to be on the normative convergence throughout the world community regarding commitments to expressive and religious freedoms. This is to be distinguished from convergence regarding constitutional standards, which is far less likely to occur.[31] As a general matter, global diversity with regard to liberty models does not "negate the possibility of a meaningful international discourse regarding the existence and scope of universal human rights."[32] This discourse can lead to agreement on broad principles relating to expressive and religious freedom.

As Ronald Krotoszynski noted in his comparative study of free speech models, "The ideology of free speech seems to have serious transnational salience."[33] In particular, primarily as a result of American influence First Amendment marketplace and self-government principles have now been widely adopted across the world. As Krotoszynski has observed with regard to expressive rights, "It seems entirely fitting that the free speech project itself should serve as an object of national – and international – debate. A commitment to free speech without a commitment to discourse and debate on the substance of the right would be more than a little bit ironic."[34]

This same commitment to discourse could also facilitate transnational adoption of religious freedoms as well. As Article 19 of the UDHR and other international legal instruments show, ideologies of free conscience and belief also have broad transnational salience and support. There is evidence that, in many parts of the world, nations are starting to converge on a sort of transnational baseline for church-state relations that, in some ways, resembles U.S. separation of church and state principles.[35] Again, the point is not to seek or encourage constitutional convergence in terms of particular First Amendment doctrines or standards. Owing to the diversity of governance systems and constitutional regimes across the world, any actual convergence would be only partly attributable to intentional efforts to export norms relating to religious freedom. However, these efforts could result in general forms of global norm convergence that favor First Amendment–like principles and practices.

Finally, as a matter of general orientation, the United States ought not to view censorship, religious persecution, and other human rights wrongs as *foreign* problems subject to (unilateral) *domestic* solutions. Instead, it ought to view these violations as global problems that may require regional, multilateral, and international solutions. American moral condemnation, unilateral sanctions, and other policies are important and indeed may even sometimes be necessary. However, they are not likely to be sufficient to achieve meaningful protection for global expressive and religious freedoms.

In sum, what the United States ought to be striving for is not exportation of a First Amendment model as such, but rather expansion of broader principles of free speech, press, and religion that have historically been associated with that model. In this regard, Americans can lead by example; but they will not generally be able to convince other nations to adopt or impose specific First Amendment standards. This will not please the ardent nationalist who, despite its exceptional character, views the First Amendment model as the very embodiment of human rights. Nor will it please those who desire international or universal convergence with regard to constitutional standards. However, in a world that is characterized by constitutional and legal pluralism, these aspirations are increasingly dated and unrealistic.

Global Free Speech and Information Flow

Perhaps the primary consideration that ought to drive U.S. policy with regard to exportation of First Amendment norms, policies, and practices is the global free flow of information. As Assistant Secretary of State Adolf A. Berle observed during the United Nations press crusade of the 1950s, "With freedom of information there is always a possibility of understanding between peoples. Without it the way is always open to build up misunderstandings, suspicion, fear, and finally, hatred."[36] Although modern information technologies facilitate transborder communication on an unprecedented scale, governmental censorship still poses a serious and continuing threat to global free speech and information flow.

There are a variety of opportunities, some traditional and others newly presented, to pursue an exportation agenda in this area. As Part II of the book showed, one general way to facilitate global information flow is to liberalize or domesticate cross-border restrictions. As discussed later, exportation of certain cultural and media products may raise special considerations in terms of their effects on foreign cultures and institutions. So might certain forms of government speech, including propaganda, and some harmful forms of expression. However, in general, freedom of information without regard to borders will be critical in terms of connecting the peoples of the world and encouraging global dialogue regarding free speech and other human rights.

Global information flow is also critical to the export of democratic norms, including freedom of speech and religion. As Jack Balkin has observed, the Internet and other technologies facilitate international cooperation and the spread of democratic culture.[37] Thus, communications and technology policies will create some of the principal twentieth-century mechanisms for exporting First Amendment norms. As Balkin has argued, in the future, Internet and intellectual property laws will substantially determine the ease and robustness of global information flow. Regulators must adopt and adjust policies such that cross-border information flow and collaboration are maximized. This means ensuring, to the fullest extent possible, that the Internet's architecture and governance models remain open and flexible and that intellectual property laws encourage information-sharing across international borders.

In addressing global information flow, government officials ought to consult and collaborate with technology industry leaders and freedom of information activists who have been working on their own policies and standards regarding Internet access and other issues. American officials will need also to work with multinational corporations that provide Internet access and other technology services abroad. Government officials must understand that these companies operate within diverse regimes and liberty models, some of which have repressive speech laws and weak privacy protections. Punishing American corporate participation in Internet censorship abroad, as bills like GOFA have proposed, could drive American companies from some foreign markets and thereby eliminate any influence they might have over Internet policies and norms in repressive regimes.[38] As Google has demonstrated in its relations with China, American companies can effectively advocate for Internet freedom abroad. But to do so, they must be able to work and compete beyond U.S. borders.

As the United States has already recognized, perhaps the most effective means of exporting First Amendment norms and practices is to provide people across the world with the tools necessary for thwarting repression and participating in global conversations. The United States has lifted trade restrictions on certain communications technologies and anti-censorship products. As noted earlier, this has become one of the central aspects of the State Department's "Twenty-First Century Statecraft" initiative.

Congress has also considered measures that provide support for the development of software and technologies that prevent Internet jamming and other forms of censorship.[39] Of course, if these methods are to be effective, the United States must ensure that American companies are not simultaneously supplying both anti-jamming and censorship technologies. Access to communications technologies will enable foreign citizens to communicate not just among themselves, but also to an interested global audience. Through a robust trade in communications technology, the United States can export First Amendment self-governance, marketplace, dissent, and transparency norms that are critical to the development of democratic culture in foreign nations.

In its efforts to export free speech norms and practices through free trade, the United States must respect international law and the sovereignty of foreign nations.[40] It ought to keep in mind that the object is to provide the citizens of repressive regimes with the means to defend themselves against censorious policies, not to circumvent the laws of a foreign sovereign, dictate political outcomes, or insist on a First Amendment model with regard to freedom of information. In the case of authoritarian regimes, supporting basic free speech rights in the form of access to technology will generally be warranted.

However, in some cases, fine distinctions may need to be drawn. Thus, it may not be clear what a majority of a foreign nation's citizens want. Moreover, the distinction between facilitating domestic speech rights, and imposing American will through technological intervention, may not be clear. As it develops policies and initiatives regarding circumvention technologies, the United States must carefully consider the scope and consequences of its intervention in the internal processes of foreign nations.[41]

Similarly, although free international trade can facilitate the spread of First Amendment norms and practices, the United States must be careful in implementing its trade policies not to inflict damage on foreign cultures and institutions, including domestic media. C. Edwin Baker has argued that this is a particular concern with regard to American exports of cultural and media products, which could displace or marginalize domestic content and institutions.[42] Baker did not argue against robust free trade in media products. As he observed, such exports "can introduce new and potentially transformative values, perspectives, and cultural resources that can be particularly important for individuals or groups that are oppressed or marginalized by the dominant local culture."[43]

However, as Baker observed, we ought not to simply assume that free trade in this particular area is an unmitigated good in terms of exporting First Amendment–like norms and principles. Baker raised serious objections to the economic and democratic defenses of American free trade policy with regard to media products. The details of his claims are beyond the scope of the present discussion. Summarizing his analysis of trade in media-related products, Baker stated:

> In sum, a country's own domestic media products potentially better provide (or provide in ways not duplicated by imports) domestic content that people need for a democratic political process to function well and, more generally, for their cultural discourses of identity, meaning, and value. In this regard, domestic media can

have tremendous positive externalities not supplied by the imports that threaten to replace them.[44]

Baker also questioned whether free trade in media products is a necessary condition for the creation of a "global public sphere" that supports the spread of democracy or democratic culture.[45] Indeed, he claimed that a pure free trade regime "can seriously undermine the struggle to create less distorted, more robust public spheres;" it could "enable foreign commercialized media to overwhelm domestic non-commercialized media" and "make subsidization much more expensive if it is allowed at all."[46] Adopting what he called a "dialogic" rather than an "artifact" conception of culture, Baker argued that it may be necessary for foreign governments to adopt measures to prevent importation of American and other nations' media products from suppressing local democratic processes, discourses, and identities. As he observed, "In other words, global democracy requires national capacity to restrain and supplement free trade precisely in the ways called for here – interventions designed to assure vigorous domestic media serving national, cultural, and political discourse functions."[47]

Of course, trade protectionism directly inhibits global information flow. According to Baker, protectionist measures ought to be subject to review under international human rights laws governing the free flow of information rather than free trade standards and processes.[48] This result, he noted, "parallels the American use of the First Amendment to forbid objectionable restrictions on communications while allowing governmental structural regulation of the communications industries."[49] Although Baker made his proposal in the late twentieth century, before the rise of the Internet, the blending of First Amendment and international human rights principles provides a possible blueprint for a twenty-first century orientation regarding the export of some uniquely American cultural and media products.

The United States might begin to think in terms of a similar balance with regard to its foreign propaganda policies and practices. Government speech creates additional avenues for exportation of First Amendment principles through various forms of education and the dissemination of information. However, foreign propaganda may also pose serious threats to local democratic institutions. In general, the

United States ought to continue to pursue the dissemination of information regarding democratic speech and press norms throughout the
world. These efforts contribute significantly to cosmopolitan conversations regarding freedom of speech, press, and religion. However, the
United States must take care that its propaganda activities do not stifle
or displace local media, or stunt their growth in ways that produce
long-term damage. This would offend both First Amendment values
and international human rights principles relating to freedom of the
press, self-determination, and self-governance.

In developing an approach to exportation of First Amendment
principles and norms in the twenty-first century, the United States
ought to be guided by two general principles. First, American officials ought to view censorship and information suppression as global
human rights concerns. In addition to traditional means of diplomatic
persuasion, the United States ought to use more tangible measures
involving trade and technology in order to encourage the spread of
democratic culture. Second, in seeking to export First Amendment
norms and principles beyond its shores, the United States must be
careful to temper its interventions in a manner that is respectful of
local institutions and cultures. Foreign democratic processes may differ significantly from the American model. This perspective ought to
inform, and in some cases could limit, resort to technological, propaganda, and some trade interventions.

A Twenty-First Century Global Free Press

If information is going to flow freely across borders, global press freedoms will have to be fully recognized, supported, and enforced. Lee
Bollinger has provided a cosmopolitan vision, as well as a prescriptive
blueprint, for a twenty-first century free press. Bollinger focuses in
particular on the American free press model, and the lessons this experience provides for establishing a more globally oriented and operative
free press – although not one formally governed by First Amendment
press standards. His work provides important suggestions for how the
United States can effectively export free press norms and practices to
other nations.

Bollinger and I disagree regarding certain particulars. For example,
he supports U.S. efforts to prohibit U.S. courts from enforcing foreign

libel judgments. Bollinger posits that courts should "give less weight to the traditional principle of comity in enforcing libel judgments and refuse enforcement in cases where a similar case in the United States would result in protection for speech under the First Amendment."[50] As I have argued, among other things, libel protectionism fails to acknowledge the pluralistic nature of the world's free speech and free press models. It is thus inconsistent with participation in a global society. Bollinger also suggests that international free trade principles ought to be used to promote the global free press agenda. As I discussed earlier, however, international trade in media-related products may raise special concerns. Although the free flow of information across borders is critically important, the United States must be careful not to insist on free trade to the detriment of foreign press and other media institutions. Despite these differences, I find much to agree with in Bollinger's analysis and want here to summarize some of its major points.

Bollinger's first recommendation relates to orientation or perspective. He argues, in essence, that the United States ought to adopt a more cosmopolitan perspective with regard to freedom of the press. Bollinger writes:

> No longer can we divide the world into what happens with press freedom in our own country and then view what happens in the rest of the world as 'human rights.' Now we are all – local press everywhere and new global media – part of a world community looking for understanding about how each part relates to the global whole and about what the global whole itself should be. All of the press is 'our' press, because what we need to know will come from these sources. And we need to ensure that the U.S. press is out there in the world reporting on what is important – to the broader world as well as, of course, to Americans. All of this stems from our own self-interest and needs as part of a world community.[51]

Bollinger argues that the "projection outward of the principle of freedom of the press onto the world stage should become a primary goal as we build the rudiments of a global society."[52] He offers several concrete recommendations for exporting the principle of a global free press. These recommendations relate to possible actions by U.S. courts, legislators, and regulatory officials.

Bollinger envisions a distinct and primary role for the U.S. Supreme Court. He urges the Supreme Court to apply the First Amendment concept of the public forum on a global scale and to "try to do for this new forum what [*New York Times v.*] *Sullivan* did to facilitate the shift to a national forum in the United States."[53] Although he acknowledges the limits of the Court's power in terms of addressing global press censorship, Bollinger claims that it can play a central role in terms of changing the nature and terms of debate. In order to do this, "the Court must appreciate the power of the example that the First Amendment sets for the world."[54]

Bollinger emphasizes what he calls the "gravitational pull of American law," a force that, as I have argued, is somewhat limited by America's own provincial approach to free speech – in particular, its refusal to engage with the transnational.[55] More generally, he argues, the Court "must speak more directly to the broader world" and must "actively and deliberately try to influence the rest of the world to embrace what we have come to believe is vital to good society."[56]

Bollinger concedes that the rest of the world is not going to adopt a Madisonian free speech and free press model. Accordingly, he urges the Court to "rethink how it articulates the basic rationales for its choices under the First Amendment."[57] It can do this, Bollinger argues, by emphasizing broader principles concerning openness and its effect on authoritarian governments and by drawing explicitly on language and concepts in international covenants and laws.[58] Bollinger urges the Court to "create a narrative of a global public forum with a widely accepted standard of press freedom."[59] Finally, he urges the Court to recognize a press right to gather information and to apply that right in an international or global context. Bollinger claims that this would provide a "powerful example to the world" of the U.S. commitment to global information flow.[60]

Bollinger also proposes some prescriptive measures for American legislators and regulators. As he observes, in part owing to the rise of digital media, the institutional press is experiencing dire financial circumstances. For this and other reasons, Bollinger argues, "we must develop a better system of public funding of the press."[61] He advocates maintenance of a strong U.S. global press corps capable of disseminating information about the world to American and foreign audiences.

In terms of global press concerns, Bollinger is highly critical of Voice of America, Al Hurra, and other U.S.-funded media, which

Bollinger describes as "either a pale version of what America stands for or completely inconsistent with America's fundamental values."[62] Instead, Bollinger argues, "[i]t would be an enormous improvement in the overall goal of projecting American values around the world to have a vital and responsible press embodied, for example, in the programming of NPR and made available to the world in many languages."[63]

In terms of developing mechanisms for protecting a global free press, Bollinger argues in favor of greater reliance on international human rights law. He argues that the United States ought to ratify the American Convention on Human Rights and submit to the jurisdiction of the Inter-American Court of Human Rights.[64] This participation, he argues, will enable the United States to encourage other nations to conform to human rights standards and judgments without being charged with inconsistency or hypocrisy. Bollinger argues that "the United States must recommit itself to the expansion of the international principle of freedom of expression that it helped to establish more than sixty years ago."[65] As he notes, "the norms at the core of international human rights law are largely consistent with the traditional conception of the First Amendment" and "could help to provide the base for legal protection of freedom of the press in the twenty-first century."[66]

Finally, Bollinger offers a few additional ideas that relate to exportation of free press norms. He urges not only the Supreme Court, but other public officials, including the president, to speak more frequently and forcefully about global press freedom. As Bollinger states, "We need fewer of the traditional perorations on human rights and more hard-headed analyses of the critical role of meaningful flows of information in an increasingly integrated and pluralistic globe."[67] He also argues in favor of broader access for foreign journalists through liberalization of visa and accreditation policies, which Bollinger says "can have a very significant impact on the development of a free press both in the United States and around the world."[68] Through participation in transnational processes such as press exchange, constitutional norms may cross international borders.

Bollinger has offered an attractive blueprint for thinking globally about and exporting First Amendment freedom of press and freedom of speech norms. As he notes, a significant amount of international consensus already exists with regard to the core principles and functions of a free and independent press.[69] As Bollinger emphasizes, developing a global free press does not entail "imposing an American view of rights on others solely for their sake but rather trying to secure what we believe that the United States, as well as the world, needs to live successfully with globalization."[70]

Trade, Transnationalism, and Religious Liberties

Thus far, I have considered economic and human rights mechanisms as distinct and separate means of export. Further, the discussion has assumed that the United States acts unilaterally when pursuing export goals. However, trade and transnationalism mechanisms are sometimes used in combination. Further, the United States ought to use both unilateral and multilateral approaches to exporting First Amendment norms and principles.

A potential example of this hybrid approach is the International Religious Freedom Act of 1998 (IRFA). Although it has long been proud of its tradition of protecting religious liberties and religious pluralism, it has been only in the past couple of decades that the United States has focused, as a distinct aspect of its foreign policy, on exporting religious liberty principles.[71] IRFA, which first came to life when activists pushed for protection against persecution of Christians abroad, relies on a system of U.S. monitoring for violation of international human rights relating to religious freedom. Violations may be answered by a range of presidential actions, from various diplomatic measures to economic sanctions.

Scholars have raised two primary objections to this approach, one grounded in concerns relating to ends and the other focusing on the means of enforcement. The first objection is that American policy seeks to export First Amendment free exercise and anti-establishment standards to other nations. Some scholars have expressed concern that IRFA might be used as a vehicle for coercing other nations into adopting First Amendment religious liberty standards.

Thus, David Smolin has noted the special difficulties involved in American assessment, pursuant to IRFA, of foreign nations' treatment of proselytizing and evangelism.[72] In the United States, these activities are clearly protected by First Amendment freedom of speech and free exercise guarantees. This is not true in many other nations, some of which criminalize efforts to evangelize adherents of different faiths as well as blasphemous speech.[73] Nations differ markedly in terms of their protection for religious minorities, the connection between church and state, and the extent to which laws may take account of religious status or identity.

As Smolin argues, "If we wish to export certain core values, such as religious liberty, we need to define them in such a way that they can fit more comfortably within a variety of cultures."[74] He claims that the United States ought to "target the most egregious violations of the core principle of religious liberty, and must seek to export a form of religious liberty that can be culturally adaptable."[75] At the same time, Smolin argues, "It would belittle religion and our religious heritage to maintain that religious liberty demands a right to proactively demean or desecrate the religion of others or to maintain that all such societies must attach as little public significance as we do to religious affiliation."[76] Smolin's point is similar to the one I made earlier with regard to expressive rights, namely, that the United States must be careful to insist on application of international law and human rights standards rather than its own unique model of religious liberty.

The second objection is that the United States has adopted a unilateral, punitive approach rather than more legitimate and effective multilateral and diplomatic mechanisms. Thus, critics claim, the problem with IRFA lies not in its ends, but rather its means. Peter Danchin insists that the "rationale of the Act is to use U.S. economic and political power to punish those states that engage in egregious violations of the rights of minority religious groups of special concern to U.S. interests."[77] He offers four primary objections or criticisms of IRFA and similar domestic legislation.

First, Danchin argues, IRFA "creates an irrational hierarchy of human rights in U.S. foreign policy that makes the act vulnerable to politicization and abuse of the human rights agenda."[78] Second, he claims that IRFA "demonstrates a failure of international participation and cooperation."[79] Specifically, he claims that, by relying upon domestic or "exceptional" sanctions, the United States is undermining and weakening "not only the legitimacy and progressive development of existing multilateral and regional human rights regimes, but also the universality that lies at the heart of the human rights idea itself."[80] Third, Danchin argues that IRFA's core rationale is based upon a misunderstanding of human rights enforcement. He claims that, in an era of declining statist conceptions of sovereignty and penetration of international legal process, individuals should rely more on multilateral human rights regimes to counter religious persecution and other human rights violations.[81] Finally, Danchin criticizes IRFA on the ground that it divides regimes along liberal and illiberal axes in a manner that "will ultimately prove to be destructive of the universal values ... that the United States seeks to promote and protect abroad."[82]

These criticisms raise issues regarding enforcement of international human rights that are beyond the scope of my discussion. With regard to IRFA, however, other commentators have taken sharp issue with Danchin's description and, in particular, his criticism of American unilateralism. Jeremy Gunn, who has worked in the State Department on IRFA matters, argues that Danchin mischaracterizes the law and its intent.[83] He insists that IRFA is not a unilateral and punitive measure, but one that specifically contemplates multilateral cooperation on religious freedom issues and relies on a range of mostly diplomatic mechanisms. In any event, Gunn points out that while the European Court of Human Rights has addressed religious human rights effectively in some cases, other multilateral institutions such as the U.N. Human Rights Commission have done little to address such concerns.

The exchange between Danchin and Gunn demonstrates that there are reasonable differences of opinion regarding the best way to ensure respect for global religious freedoms. The case against unilateral economic sanctions should not be overstated. As Sarah Cleveland has argued, unilateral sanctions such as those contemplated in extreme cases under IRFA are consistent with international law and "are an important weapon in transnational efforts to promote respect for fundamental rights and can have substantial behavior-modifying potential."[84] Cleveland situates economic sanctions within the larger context of transnational processes and argues that they "assist[] in the international definition, promulgation, recognition, and domestic internalization of human rights norms."[85] They create "a forum for various domestic and foreign governmental agencies and nongovernmental entities to conduct an ongoing dialogue with foreign states regarding international human rights compliance."[86]

At the same time, the case for multilateralism should also not be oversold. Multilateral institutions operate in the face of political and other complexities and, as Gunn notes, have a rather uneven record in terms of enforcing international human rights laws.

Experience with IRFA supports adoption of a hybrid U.S. export approach that relies upon a combination of unilateral sanctions, multilateral collaboration, and participation in transnational processes. To the extent possible, the United States ought to embrace core human rights principles and conventions. It ought to participate in the ongoing dialogue Cleveland mentions, with regard to expressive and religious freedoms as well as other human rights. As Smolin observes, this process will not only assist foreign nations and their citizens in realizing the benefits of religious and other freedoms, but may also encourage U.S. officials and American citizens to "learn to look more critically at ourselves, and become willing to question some of our easy assumptions and overconfidence about the state of liberty and religion in contemporary America."[87]

The First Amendment in the Twenty-First Century

The American First Amendment remains a beacon of freedom around the world. As President Franklin Roosevelt, participants in the U.S. press-government crusade, and countless others since have argued, its principles offer the best hope for world peace and the spread of democracy. However, the First Amendment's substantive standards and doctrines are increasingly out of step with the liberty models adopted across the community of nations. This poses a rather serious question regarding the extent to which the First Amendment can continue to support and influence the causes of global expressive and religious freedom in the twenty-first century and beyond.

To a large degree, the answer depends on the actions of American officials and the American people. Will we be able to defend First Amendment exceptionalism to foreign audiences who are increasingly skeptical of its benefits? Will we refuse to engage with transnational approaches, even if only to confirm our commitment to First

Amendment standards and doctrines? Will we exhibit a commitment to those standards and doctrines with respect to Americans and aliens who engage in cross-border and beyond-border conversations and collaborations? Will Americans insist that executive surveillance programs that sweep in masses of data relating to transnational conversations be limited or discontinued? These questions will have significant bearing on the relevance and influence of the First Amendment in the world community.

For a mature, but still evolving, First Amendment, these are critical questions. But we ought not to focus too narrowly on preservation of First Amendment liberties in their most formal sense. The First Amendment is not going to be repealed. Nor is it likely to be interpreted by courts and elected officials as coextensive with international human rights laws or transnational instruments. Rather, the real battle in the twenty-first century will be between democratic regimes, in which there is now broad convergence on principles such as access to information, freedom of press, and freedom of belief, and authoritarian regimes in which these principles are rejected and violated.

What the people of the world will need – indeed, what they have always needed – in order to prevail in that battle is a repository of wisdom and experience that demonstrates these things: Why freedom must prevail over repression; why access to information is a universal good; why respect for expressive and religious pluralism is critical to global peace; and why self-governance and self-determination are the destiny of all mankind. These are the familiar lessons of the First Amendment. We ought to continue to share them with the world community – not in the hope that they will adopt American standards, but to the end that they might be inspired by the First Amendment's exceptional principles.

NOTES

Introduction

1 There have been a few notable exceptions. With regard to speech, see, e.g., Burt Neuborne and Steven R. Shapiro, "The Nylon Curtain: America's National Border and the Free Flow of Ideas," 26 *Wm. & Mary L. Rev.* 719, 728–33 (1985). With regard to religious liberties, see J. Bruce Nichols, *The Uneasy Alliance: Religion, Refugee Work, and U.S. Foreign Policy* (New York: Oxford University Press, 1988); John H. Mansfield, "The Religion Clauses of the First Amendment and Foreign Relations," 36 *DePaul L. Rev.* 1 (1986).

2 Examples of this work include Lee C. Bollinger, *Uninhibited, Robust, and Wide-Open; A Free Press for a New Century* (New York: Oxford University Press 2010); Jack Goldsmith and Tim Wu, *Who Controls the Internet?: Illusions of a Borderless World* (New York: Oxford University Press, 2006); Harold Hongju Koh, "On American Exceptionalism," 55 *Stan. L. Rev.* 1479 (2003); Alexander Tsesis, *Destructive Messages: How Hate Speech Paves the Way for Harmful Social Movements* (New York: NYU Press, 2002); David A. Richards, *Free Speech and the Politics of Identity* (New York: Oxford University Press, 2000); and Jeremy Harris Lipschultz, *Free Expression in the Age of the Internet: Social and Legal Boundaries* (Boulder, Colo.: Westview Press, 2000).

3 See, e.g., Jeremy Waldron, *The Harm in Hate Speech* (Cambridge, Ma.: Harvard University Press, 2012); Alan Brownstein and Leslie Gielow Jacobs (eds.), *Global Issues in Freedom of Speech and Religion* (Eagan, Minn.: West, 2009); Ronald J. Krotoszynski, *The First Amendment in Cross-Cultural Perspective: A Comparative Legal Analysis of the Freedom of Speech* (New York: NYU Press, 2006).

4 See, e.g., David G. Post, *In Search of Jefferson's Moose: Notes on the State of Cyberspace* (New York: Oxford University Press, 2009); Jack M. Balkin, "Digital Speech and Democratic Culture: A Theory of Freedom of Expression for the Information Society," 79 *N.Y.U. L. Rev.* 1 (2004).

5 For an early and comprehensive treatment of the system of free expression in the United States, see Thomas I. Emerson, *The System of Freedom of Expression* (New York: Random House [Vintage Books], 1971).

6 381 U.S. 301 (1965). *Lamont* was the first decision by the Supreme Court to invalidate a federal law on First Amendment grounds.

7 Jan Aart Scholte, *Globalization: A Critical Introduction* (Palgrave, 2000), 49.

8 As will become clear, unless otherwise indicated, references to First Amendment "expressive" liberties include freedom of speech, press, assembly, petition, and association, while references to "religious" liberties or freedoms refer collectively to the First Amendment's free exercise and anti-establishment guarantees.

9 See Yochai Benkler, "A Free Irresponsible Press: Wikileaks and the Battle over the Soul of the Networked Fourth Estate," 46 *Harv. Civ. Rts.-Civ. Liberties L. Rev.* 311 (2011).

10 See generally Deibert, Palfrey, Rohozinski & Zittrain, *Access Controlled* (Cambridge, MA.: MIT Press, 2010).

11 This is not to say the intersection has been entirely ignored. During the Cold War, for example, scholars challenged restrictions on immigration, cross-border communications, and other transborder activities. But only recently, roughly coinciding with the advent and widespread use of digital communication technologies, has significant attention turned outward. This change in communicative habits does not necessarily portend a corresponding shift in attitudes or arguments regarding the First Amendment's scope or application. From a provincial perspective, the fact that communications can traverse international borders does not necessarily mean that those communications are or ought to be regarded as within the First Amendment's protective domain.

12 As I explain in Chapter 2, the term "cosmopolitan" is not intended to track or adopt particular philosophic treatments of cosmopolitanism. Rather, the term is used primarily in its more basic definitional senses. However, as I suggest, philosophical and other treatments of cosmopolitanism provide a useful conceptual framework for thinking about the First Amendment's transborder dimension. Thus, I do not shy entirely away from certain aspects of philosophical cosmopolitanism. See, e.g., Kwame Anthony Appiah, *Cosmopolitanism: Ethics in a World of Strangers* (New York: W. W. Norton, 2006); Martha C. Nussbaum, "Patriotism and Cosmopolitanism," in Joshua Cohen (ed.), *For Love of Country?* (Boston, Ma.: Beacon Press, 2002), 3.

13 Appiah, supra note 12, at xiii.

14 Id.

15 Id. at 72. See also Sheldon Bernard Lyke, "Brown Abroad: An Empirical Analysis of Foreign Judicial Citation and the Metaphor of Cosmopolitan Conversation," 45 *Vand. J. Int'l L.* 83, 128 (2012).

16 See generally Cass R. Sunstein, *Democracy and the Problem of Free Speech* (New York: The Free Press, 1995).

17 Vicki C. Jackson, *Constitutional Engagement in a Transnational Era* (New York: Oxford University Press, 2010).

The First Amendment's Transborder Dimension

1 Although I have changed the terminology somewhat, the basic concept is set forth in Timothy Zick, "Territoriality and the First Amendment: Free Speech at – and Beyond – Our Borders," 85 *Notre Dame L. Rev.* 1543 (2010).

2 United States territories are, in many important respects, governed by federal laws and constitutional provisions. Accordingly, I include them within the First Amendment's intraterritorial domain and do not discuss them at length in the book. Insofar as they are relevant to matters of constitutional scope or domain, U.S. territories are discussed in Chapters 6 and 7.

3 See Peter J. Spiro, *Beyond Citizenship: American Identity after Globalization* (New York: Oxford University Press, 2008), 60.

4 Indeed, one scholar has argued that the act of leaving the country is *itself* a form of expressive conduct that is protected by the Free Speech Clause. See Jeanne M. Woods, "Travel That Talks: Toward First Amendment Protection for Freedom of Movement," 65 *Geo. Wash. L. Rev.* 106, 110 (1996).

5 Zechariah Chafee, *Three Human Rights in the Constitution of 1787* (Lawrence: University of Kansas Press, 1956).

6 See generally Marketa Trimble, "The Future of Cybertravel: Legal Implications of the Evasion of Geolocation," 22 *Fordham Intell. Prop. Media & Ent. L.J.* 567 (2012).

7 See Saskia Sassen, *Territory, Authority, Rights: From Medieval to Global Assemblages* (Princeton, NJ: Princeton University Press, 2006).

8 See, e.g., Jeffrey Kahn, "International Travel and the Constitution," 56 *UCLA L. Rev.* 271 (2008); Thomas E. Laursen, "Constitutional Protection of Foreign Travel," 81 *Colum. L. Rev.* 902 (1981).

9 Kleindienst v. Mandel, 408 U.S. 753, 769 (1972).

10 See Gerald L. Neuman, *Strangers to the Constitution: Immigrants, Borders, and Fundamental Law* (Princeton, NJ: Princeton University Press, 1996), 151

11 18 U.S.C. § 953 (2006).

12 See Foreign Agents Registration Act of 1938, 22 U.S.C. §§ 611–621 (2006) (restricting distribution of foreign political propaganda in the United States); Cass R. Sunstein, "Government Control of Information," 74 *Calif. L. Rev.* 889, 905–12 (1986) (discussing the "deemed export" rule, which limits the sharing of scientific and technical information with aliens in the United States).

13 Allen W. Palmer & Edward L. Carter, "The Smith-Mundt Act's Ban on Domestic Propaganda: An Analysis of the Cold War Statute Limiting Access to Public Diplomacy," 11 *Commun. Law & Policy* 1, 29–30 (Winter 2006). The Smith-Mundt Act's ban on domestic receipt and dissemination of foreign propaganda has been partially repealed, as to certain State Department materials and broadcasts by foreign stations controlled by the Broadcast Board of Governors. Smith-Mundt Modernization Act of 2012, H.R. 5736, 112th Cong., 2d Sess.

14 See Clapper v. Amnesty International USA, 132 S. Ct. 2341 (2012); ACLU v. NSA, 493 F.3d 644 (6th Cir. 2007).

15 Rasha Alzahabi, "Should You Leave Your Laptop at Home When Traveling Abroad?: The Fourth Amendment and Border Searches of Laptop Computers," 41 *Ind. L. Rev.* 161 (2008).

16 Lamont v. Postmaster General, 381 U.S. 301 (1965).

17 Delbert, Palfrey, Rohozinski, & Zittrain, *Access Controlled* xvi (Cambridge, MA: MIT Press, 2010).

18 See Jack Goldsmith & Tim Wu, *Who Controls the Internet?: Illusions of a Borderless World* (New York: Oxford University Press, 2006).

19 See Citizens United v. Federal Election Comm'n, 558 U.S. 310, 362 (2010).

20 American Civil Liberties Union, *Blocking Faith, Freezing Charity: Chilling Muslim Charitable Giving in the "War on Terrorism" Financing* 16 (June 2009).

21 See Holder v. Humanitarian Law Project, 130 S. Ct. 534 (2010) (holding that a federal prohibition on the provision of material support to foreign terrorist organizations does not violate First Amendment expressive or associative rights).

22 With regard to freedom of speech, see, e.g., Frederick Schauer, "The Exceptional First Amendment," in *American Exceptionalism and Human Rights* (Michael Ignatieff, ed., 2005); Ronald Krotoszynski, Jr., *The First Amendment in Cross-Cultural Perspective* (2006); Kent Greenawalt, "Free Speech in the United States and Canada," 55 *Law & Contemp. Probs.* 5 (1992). With regard to freedom of speech and religion, see generally Alan E. Brownstein and Leslie Jacobs, *Global Issues in Freedom of Speech and Religion: Cases and Materials* (Thomson Reuters 2009), on which some of the following discussion regarding comparative constitutional principles is based.

23 G.A. Res. 217 A (III), U.N. Doc. A/810 (Dec. 12, 1948).

24 ICCPR, at. 18, 6 I.L.M. 368, 999 U.N.T.S. 171 (Dec. 16, 1966).

25 Gerald L. Neuman, "Human Rights and Constitutional Rights: Harmony and Dissonance," 55 *Stan. L. Rev.* 1863, 1890 (2003).

26 Id.

27 ECHR, art. 10.

28 Id.

29 U.S. Const., art. VI; art. I, § 8, cl. 18.

30 For an explanation of the sometimes elusive distinction between self-executing and non-self-executing treaties, see, e.g., Carlos Manuel Vazquez, "The Four Doctrines of Self-Executing Treaties," 89 *Am. J. Int'l L.* 695 (1995).

31 Reid v. Covert, 354 U.S. 1 (1957).

32 These include The Framework Convention for Tobacco Control; The Council of Europe Convention on Cybercrime; The Optional Protocol to the Convention on the Rights of the Child on the Sale of Children, Child Prostitution and Child Pornography; the International Covenant on Civil and Political Rights; and the International Convention on the Elimination of all Forms of Racial Discrimination.

33 See William A. Schabas, "Invalid Reservations to the International Covenant on Civil and Political Rights: Is the United States Still a Party?," 21 *Brook J. Int'l L.* 277, 280 (1995) (discussing the reservations made by the United States in negotiating the terms of the ICCPR); Kristina Ash, "U.S. Reservations to the International Covenant on Civil and Political Rights: Credibility Maximization and Global Influence," 3 *Nw. U.J. Int'l Hum. Rts.* 7 (2005) (examining ICCPR reservations and questioning their legitimacy).

34 See, e.g., "The Relevance of Foreign Legal Materials in U.S. Constitutional Cases: A Conversation Between Justice Antonin Scalia and Justice Stephen Breyer, 3 *Int'l J. Const. L.* 519, 525–29 (2005); Lawrence v. Texas, 539 U.S. 558, 598 (2003) (Scalia, J., dissenting) (arguing that "this Court should not impose foreign moods, fads, or fashions on Americans").

35 With regard to First Amendment exceptionalism, see Schauer, supra note 22.

36 This discussion thus tracks the U.S. focus on categorical distinctions with regard to speech content. However, most nations do not approach the interpretation of free speech protections in this manner.

37 Brandenburg v. Ohio, 395 U.S. 444 (1969).

38 See Terrorism Act, 2006, c. 11 (U.K.).

39 Council of Europe, Convention on the Prevention of Terrorism, opened for signature May 16, 2005, C.E.T.S. 196, art. 5.

40 376 U.S. 254 (1964).

41 See Hustler Magazine v. Falwell, 485 U.S. 46 (1988) (applying the "actual malice" standard to parody of public figure).

42 Schauer, supra note 22, at 40.

43 Id. at 41.

44 See Krotoszynski, supra note 22, at 102–03 (discussing rejection of Sullivan by the German Federal Constitutional Court).

45 See, e.g., James Q. Whitman, "The Two Western Cultures of Privacy: Dignity Versus Liberty," 113 *Yale L.J.* 1151 (2004).

46 R.A.V. v. City of St. Paul, 505 U.S. 377 (1992); Virginia v. Black, 538 U.S. 343 (2003).

47 See, e.g., Jeremy Waldron, *The Harm in Hate Speech* (Cambridge, MA: Harvard University Press 2012); Richard Delgado & Jean Stefancic, *Must We Defend Nazis? Hate Speech, Pornography, and the New First Amendment* (1997); Richard Delgado, "Words That Wound: A Tort Action for Racial Insults, Epithets, and Name-Calling," 17 *Harv. C.R.-C.L. L. Rev.* 133 (1982).

48 Waldron, supra note 47, at 14. *See also* id. at 8 (describing European hate speech laws).

49 See, e.g., Isabelle Rorive, "Strategies to Tackle Racism and Xenophobia on the Internet – Where Are We in Europe?," 7 *Int'l J. Comm. L. & Pol'y* 1–9 (2002/2003).

50 Rodney A. Smolla, *Free Speech in an Open Society* (New York: Alfread A. Knopf, Inc., 1992), 352.

51   Carolyn Evans and Christopher A. Thomas, "Church-State Relations in the European Court of Human Rights," 2006 *B.Y.U. L. Rev.* 699, 700.

52   Employment Div. v. Smith, 494 U.S. 872 (1990). See also Church of the Lukumi Babalu Aye v. City of Hialeah, 508 U.S. 520 (1993); Hosanna-Tabor Evangelical Lutheran Church v. EEOC, 132 S.Ct. 694 (2012).

53   Larson v. Valente, 456 U.S. 228 (1982); Lynch v. Donnelly, 465 U.S. 668 (1984). For a discussion of the original understanding of the Establishment Clause, see Michael W. McConnell, "Establishment and Disestablishment at the Founding, Part I: Establishment of Religion," 44 *Wm. & Mary L. Rev.* 2105 (2003).

54   Leszek Lech Garlicki, "Perspectives on Freedom of Conscience and Religion in the Jurisprudence of Constitutional Courts," 2001 *B.Y.U. L. Rev.* 467, 489–93.

55   Id.

56   See Evans and Thomas, supra note 51.

57   Garlicki, supra note 54, at 498.

58   Id. at 501–6. See also Hasan and Eylim Zengin v. Turkey, 46 E.C.H.R. 44 (2008) (noting that 43 Council of Europe member States provide religious education classes in state schools and that in 25 of the member States, religious education is a compulsory subject).

59   Garlicki, supra note 54, at 507–8.

60   See Mark L. Movsesian, "Crosses and Culture: State-Sponsored Religious Displays in the U.S. and Europe," 1(2) *Ox. J. Law and Religion* 338–62 (2012).

61   See, e.g., Multani v. Commission Scolaire Marguerite-Bourgeoys, 1 S.C.R. 256 (Can. 2006) (applying a "proportionality" test to free exercise claim).

62   See Daniel O. Conkle, "Congressional Alternatives in the Wake of *City of Boerne v. Flores*: The (Limited) Role of Congress in Protecting Religious Freedom from State and Local Infringement," 20 *U. Ark. Little Rock L.J.* 633, 661 (1998) ("Article 18 thus appears to demand more protection of religious freedom than is required by the Supreme Court's decisions in Smith and Boerne."); Gerald L. Neuman, "The Global Dimension of RFRA," 14 *Const. Commentary* 33, 43 (1997) (stating that Article 18 expresses a broader conception of religious liberty than the *Smith* interpretation of free exercise).

63   Peter G. Danchin and Lisa Forman, "The Evolving Jurisprudence of the European Court of Human Rights and the Protection of Religious Minorities," in *Protecting the Human Rights of Religious Minorities in Eastern Europe* (Peter G. Danchin & Elizabeth A. Cole eds., Columbia University Press, 2002), 192, 198–99.

64   See Leyla Sahin v. Turkey, App. No. 44774/98 Eur. Ct. H. R. (2005) (upholding Turkish prohibition on wearing of Islamic headscarf at a university).

65   Ruti Teitel, "Militating Constitutional Democracy: Comparative Perspectives," in Andras Sajo ed., *Issues in Constitutional Law 4. Censorial*

Sensitivities: Free Speech and Religion in a Fundamentalist World (The Hague: Eleven Publishing, 2007), 71, 75–76.

66 Peter G. Danchin, "Of Prophets and Proselytes: Freedom of Religion and the Conflict of Rights in International Law," 49 *Harv. Int'l L. J.* 249 (2008).

67 See, e.g., Lee v. Weisman, 505 U.S. 577 (1992) (holding that offering prayer at public high school graduation ceremony was unconstitutionally coercive).

68 See Ohno v. Yasuma, – – F.3d – –, 2013 WL 3306351 (9th Cir. 2013) (rejecting Free Exercise Clause and public policy arguments against recognition of citizen's money judgment against a church located in Japan).

69 Yahoo! Inc. v. La Ligue Contre le Racisme et l'Antisemitisme, 433 F.3d 1199 (9th Cir. 2006).

70 See Adam Shinar and Anna Su, "Religious Law as Foreign Law," 11(1) *Int'l J. Const'l. Law* 74–100 (2012).

71 Vicki C. Jackson, *Constitutional Engagement in a Transnational Era* (New York : Oxford University Press, 2010).

72 Id. at 69.

73 See SPEECH Act, P.L. No. 111–223. SPEECH stands for "Securing the Protection of our Enduring and Established Heritage."

74 See Awad v. Ziriax, 670 F.3d 1111 (10th Cir. 2012) (invalidating Oklahoma's 'Save Our State" Amendment).

75 See Louis Henkin, *The Age of Rights* (New York: Columbia University Press, 1990), 74.

76 *The Declaration of Independence* para. 1 (U.S. 1776).

77 See John H. Mansfield, "The Religion Clauses of the First Amendment and Foreign Relations," 36 *DePaul L. Rev.* 1 (1986).

78 J. Bruce Nichols, *The Uneasy Alliance: Religion, Refugee Work, and U.S. Foreign Policy* (New York: Oxford University Press, 1988).

79 Jessica Powley Hayden, "Mullahs on a Bus: The Establishment Clause and U.S. Foreign Aid," 95 *Geo. L. J.* 171 (2006).

80 See generally Kal Raustiala, *Does the Constitution Follow the Flag? The Evolution of Territoriality in American Law* (New York: Oxford University Press 2009).

81 Haig v. Agee, 453 U.S. 280, 308 (1981).

82 See David A. Anderson, "Freedom of the Press in Wartime," 77 *U. Colo. L. Rev.* 49, 66 (2006) ("So far as existing case law is concerned, there appears to be nothing to prevent the Pentagon from eliminating on-scene coverage of military operations, detention facilities, military hospitals, and other auxiliaries of war.").

83 Only one federal appeals court has addressed the question of the Establishment Clause's extraterritorial application on the merits. See Lamont v. Woods, 948 F.2d 825, 843 (2d Cir. 1991) (holding that Establishment Clause applies to overseas projects funded by United States). See also Ohno v. Yasuma, – – F.3d – –, 2013 WL 3306351 *12 (9th Cir. 2013) (in case of first impression,

declining to decide whether the Free Exercise Clause applies beyond U.S. borders)

84 Peter G. Danchin, "U.S. Unilateralism and the Protection of Religious Freedom: The Multinational Alternative," 41 *Colum. J. Transnat'l L.* 33, 35–36 (2002–3).

85 Margaret A. Blanchard, *Exporting the First Amendment: The Press-Government Crusade of 1945–1952* (New York: Longman, 1986); Mary Ann Glendon, *A World Made New: Eleanor Roosevelt and the Universal Declaration of Human Rights* (New York: Random House, 2001).

86 See Ian Loveland (ed.), *Importing the First Amendment: Freedom of Speech and Expression in Britain, Europe and the USA* (Oxford: Hart Publishing, 1998); Anthony Lester, "The Overseas Trade in the American Bill of Rights," 88 *Colum. L. Rev.* 537 (1988). But see C. Edwin Baker, *Media, Markets, and Democracy* (Cambridge: Cambridge University Press, 2002), chapter 11 (questioning whether free trade in media-related products actually leads to greater free speech and information flow in foreign markets).

87 See Krotoszynski, supra note 22; David M. Smolin, "Exporting the First Amendment?: Evangelism, Proselytism, and the International Religious Freedom Act," 31 *Cumb. L. Rev.* 685 (2000–2001).

88 David Law & Mila Versteeg, "The Declining Influence of the U.S. Constitution," 87 *N.Y.U.L. Rev.* 762 (2012).

89 See id. See also Mark Tushnet, "The Inevitable Globalization of Constitutional Law," 49 *Va. J. Int'l L.* 985, 987 (2009) (observing that "globalization does not entail uniformity").

90 U.S. Const., art. II, § 1, cl. 5; art. I, § 9, cl. 8.

91 See Geoffrey R. Stone, *Perilous Times: Free Speech in Wartime* (New York: W. W. Norton, 2004).

92 Act of July 14, 1798, ch. 74, 1 Stat. 596; Act of July 6, 1798, ch. 66, 1 Stat. 577; Act of June 25, 1798, ch. 58, 1 Stat. 570; Act of June 18, 1798, ch. 54, 1 Stat. 566.

93 Anthony Lewis, *Freedom for the Thought That We Hate: A Biography of the First Amendment* (New York: Basic Books, 2006), 22.

94 Schenck v. United States, 249 U.S. 47 (1919).

95 See generally Zick, supra note 1.

96 See Jan Aart Scholte, *Globalization: A Critical Introduction* 49 (2000) (describing deterritorialization as consisting of "*trans*-border exchanges *without distance*").

97 See David G. Post, *In Search of Jefferson's Moose: Notes on the State of Cyberspace* (New York: Oxford University Press, 2009) 166–69; Goldsmith and Wu, supra note 18.

98 Smolla, supra note 50, at 361–67.

99 For general treatments of globalization, see Miles Kahler and David A. Lake, "Globalization and Governance," in *Governance in a Global Economy: Political*

Authority in Transition (Princeton, NJ: Princeton University Press, 2003), 10–14; Boaventura de Sousa Santos, *Toward a New Legal Common Sense: Law, Globalization, and Emancipation* (Chicago: Northwestern University Press, 2d ed. 2002), 178.

100 With regard to new challenges to freedom of the press, see Lee C. Bollinger, *Uninhibited, Robust, and Wide-Open: A Free Press for a New Century* (New York: Oxford University Press, 2010).

101 See Jack M. Balkin, "Digital Speech and Democratic Culture: A Theory of Freedom of Expression for the Information Society," 79 *N.Y.U. L. Rev.* 1 (2004).

102 See Anthony Giddens, *Runaway World: How Globalization Is Reshaping Our Lives* (New York: Routledge, 2000), 24–37

103 See Goldsmith and Wu, supra note 18.

104 Harold Hongju Koh, "How Is International Human Rights Law Enforced?", 74 *Ind. L. J.* 1397, 1399–1408 (1999); Harold Hongju Koh, "On American Exceptionalism," 55 *Stan. L. Rev.* 1479, 1501–3 (2003).

Transborder Perspectives: Provincialism and Cosmopolitanism

1 In a previous book, I emphasized the importance of domestic expressive liberties. See generally Timothy Zick, *Speech Out of Doors: Preserving First Amendment Liberties in Public Places* (New York: Cambridge University Press, 2008).

2 See Kwame Anthony Appiah, *Cosmopolitanism: Ethics in a World of Strangers* (New York: W. W. Norton, 2006), xvii ("The position worth defending might be called ... a partial cosmopolitanism.").

3 David M. Golove and Daniel J. Hulsebosch, "A Civilized Nation: The Early American Constitution, the Law of Nations, and the Pursuit of International Recognition," 85 *N.Y.U. L. Rev.* 932, 934 (2010).

4 See, e.g., Michael Walzer, *Spheres of Justice: A Defense of Pluralism and Equality* (New York: Basic Books, 1983), Chapter 2.

5 See Anarchist Act of 1918, chapter 186, 40 Stat. 1012 (authorizing the removal of alien anarchists); Harisiades v. Shaughnessy, 342 U.S. 580, 592 (1952) (rejecting a First Amendment challenge to a law providing for the deportation of communists); United States *ex rel.* Turner v. Williams, 194 U.S. 279, 290–91 (1904) (upholding the removal of an alien anarchist).

6 See Harisiades, 342 U.S. at 591–92 (First Amendment does not protect aliens from deportation on grounds of membership in the Communist Party).

7 See 2 U.S.C. § 441e(a) (banning political contributions by foreign nationals). Aliens are subject to other restrictions that would violate the First Amendment as applied to citizens. See W. Scott Hastings, Note, "Foreign Ownership of Broadcasting: The Telecommunications Act of 1996 and Beyond," 29 *Vand. J. Transnat'l L.* 817, 821 (1996) (discussing limits on foreign ownership of

telecommunications interests); Cass R. Sunstein, "Government Control of Information," 74 *Calif. L. Rev.* 889, 905–12 (1986) (defending export controls relating to aliens' receipt of information on ground that they do not affect domestic political debate).

8   See Andrew Kent, "A Textual and Historical Case against a Global Constitution," 95 *Geo. L. J.* 463 (2007) (arguing against extraterritorial application of the Bill of Rights); United States v. Verdugo-Urquidez, 494 U.S. 259, 265–66 (1990) (plurality opinion) (rejecting Fourth Amendment claim of foreign national, in part on ground that he was not among "the people" protected by the warrant requirement). See also Gerald L. Neuman, *Strangers to the Constitution: Immigrants, Borders, and Fundamental Law* (Princeton, NJ: Princeton University Press, 1996), 109 ("citizens are always subject to the nation's law, and so always protected by constitutional rights").

9   *The Federalist* No. 41 (James Madison) (internal quotation marks omitted).

10 See U.S. Const., art. I, § 9, cl. 8 (forbidding grants of titles of nobility from kings, princes, and foreign states); id. (prohibiting those holding an office of "profit or trust" from accepting any gift, office or title from "any King, Prince, or foreign state" without the consent of Congress); art. I, § 2, cl. 2 (seven-year citizenship requirement for House members). See also Peter Margulies, "Advising Terrorism: Material Support, Safe Harbors, and Freedom of Speech," 63 *Hastings L. J.* 455, 471–74 (2012) (discussing framers' concerns regarding foreign influence).

11 See generally Dennis v. United States, 341 U.S. 494 (1951); Whitney v. California, 274 U.S. 357 (1927); Gitlow v. New York, 268 U.S. 652 (1925); Abrams v. United States, 250 U.S. 616 (1919); Debs v. United States, 249 U.S. 211 (1919).

12 Anthony Lewis, *Freedom for the Thought That We Hate: A Biography of the First Amendment* (New York: Basic Books, 2007), 12.

13 U.S. Const., art. VI, cl. 3.

14 U.S. Const., art. I, § 8, cl. 3, 4, 10.

15 Id., art. I, § 8, cl. 11–15.

16 See id., art. II, §§ 2, 3 (entry of treaties, appointment of ambassadors, receipt of foreign ambassadors).

17 See, e.g., Hiroshi Motomura, "Immigration Law after a Century of Plenary Power: Phantom Constitutional Norms and Statutory Interpretation," 100 *Yale L. J.* 545 (1990).

18 U.S. Const., art. III, § 2.

19 Id., art. I, § 10.

20 Stephen D. Krasner, *Sovereignty: Organized Hypocrisy* (Princeton, NJ: Princeton University Press, 1999), 12; United States v. Ramsey, 431 U.S. 606, 619 (1977).

21 United States v. Flores-Montano, 541 U.S. 149, 153 (2004).

22 See United States v. Ramsey, 431 U.S. 606 (1977) (upholding suspicion less border search).

23 See John A. Scanlan, "Aliens in the Marketplace of Ideas: The Government, the Academy, and the McCarran-Walter Act," 66 *Tex. L. Rev.* 1481, 1496–97 (1988); Steven R. Shapiro, "Ideological Exclusions: Closing the Border to Political Dissidents," 100 *Harv. L. Rev.* 930, 935, 940–41 (1987); Murray L. Schwartz & James C. N. Paul, "Foreign Communist Propaganda in the Mails: A Report on Some Problems of Federal Censorship," 107 *U. Pa. L. Rev.* 621, 633–49 (1959); Louis L. Jaffe, "The Right to Travel: The Passport Problem," 35 *Foreign Aff.* 1, 17–28 (1956); Eugene Gressman, "The Undue Process of Passports," 127 *New Republic* 13, 14 (Sept. 8, 1952).

24 Timothy Zick, "The First Amendment and Territoriality: Free Speech at – and Beyond – Our Borders," 85 *Notre Dame L. Rev.* 1543 (2010).

25 For a summary of basic free speech theories, see Ronald J. Krotoszynski, Jr., *The First Amendment in Cross-Cultural Perspective: A Comparative Legal Analysis of the Freedom of Speech* (New York: N.Y.U. Press, 2006), 13–21.

26 Alexander Meiklejohn, *Free Speech and Its Relation to Self-Government* (New York: Harper Brothers, 1948), 22–25.

27 See, e.g., Cass R. Sunstein, "Government Control of Information," 74 *Calif. L. Rev.* 889, 905–12 (1986) (defending export controls on the ground that they do not affect domestic political debates); William W. Van Alstyne, "The First Amendment and the Suppression of Warmongering Propaganda in the United States," 31 *Law & Contemp. Probs.* 530, 540–41 (1966) (arguing that speech addressed to foreign audiences is beyond the First Amendment's domain because "such speech is not addressed to our public forum, to sear *our* consciences").

28 Robert D. Kamenshine, "Embargoes on Exports of Ideas and Information: First Amendment Issues," 26 *Wm. & Mary L. Rev.* 863, 866 (1985). See also Sharon E. Foster, "Does the First Amendment Restrict Recognition and Enforcement of Foreign Copyright Judgments and Arbitration Awards?," 10 *Pace Int'l L. Rev.* 361, 390 (1998) ("[F]ree speech in the United States … should be the focus of the Court's concern."); Jeremy Maltby, "Juggling Comity and Self-Government: The Enforcement of Foreign Libel Judgments in U.S. Courts," 94 *Colum. L. Rev.* 1978, 2007 n.160 (1994) (suggesting that First Amendment concerns are limited to the domestic sphere); Joel R. Reidenberg, "Yahoo and Democracy on the Internet," 42 *Jurimetrics J.* 261, 267 (2002) (arguing that Yahoo's right to disseminate reprehensible ideas "is a national right and does not extend extra-territorially beyond the U.S. border").

29 Kamenshine, supra note 28, at 869.

30 See Kermit Roosevelt III, "Guantanamo and the Conflict of Laws: *Rasul* and Beyond," 153 *U. Pa. L. Rev.* 2017, 2066 (2005) (arguing that "it is hard to see why the Constitution would be concerned with the self-actualization

of aliens abroad"). See also Gerald L. Neuman, *Extraterritorial Rights and Constitutional Methodology After* Rasul v. Bush, 153 *U. Pa. L. Rev.* 2073, 2082 (2005) (agreeing with Roosevelt that self-government principles are of limited relevance with respect to alien-to-alien communications, and that the First Amendment does not obligate the United States to facilitate aliens' self-actualization abroad).

31   See Lee Bollinger, *Uninhibited, Robust, and Wide-Open: A Free Press for a New Century* (New York: Oxford University Press, 2010), 116–17 (urging the Supreme Court to shift the "constitutional paradigm" from a national to a global forum with regard to press freedoms).

32   For an interesting anthology on press freedoms, see Garrett Epps, ed., *The First Amendment Freedom of the Press* (Amherst, NY: Prometheus Books, 2008).

33   See John H. Mansfield, "The Religion Clauses of the First Amendment and Foreign Relations," 36 *DePaul L. Rev.* 1, 19 (1986).

34   County of Allegheny v. American Civil Liberties Union, Greater Pittsburgh Chapter, 492 U.S. 573, 627 (1989) (opinion of O'Connor, J.).

35   See Ira C. Lupu & Robert W. Tuttle, "The Faith-Based Initiative and the Constitution," 55 *DePaul L. Rev.* 1, 115–16 (2005).

36   See Lamont v. Postmaster General, 381 U.S. 301, 305–06 (1965) (invalidating postal prior restraint on receipt of foreign propaganda); Haig v. Agee, 453 U.S. 280, 308 (1981) (assuming citizen enjoys freedom of speech abroad); Nation Magazine v. U.S. Dep't of Def., 762 F. Supp. 1558, 1571–74 (S.D.N.Y. 1991) (stating that, in the context of gathering news, abroad "it is arguable that generally there is at least some minimal constitutional right to access"); Lamont v. Woods, 948 F.2d 825, 838 (2d Cir. 1991) (holding that Establishment Clause applies to foreign projects funded with U.S. dollars).

37   See, e.g., Flynt v. Rumsfeld, 180 F. Supp. 2d 174, 175–76 (D.D.C. 2002) (declining to decide whether the American press had certain access rights abroad).

38   See, e.g., Briggs & Stratton Corp. v. Baldridge, 728 F.2d 915, 917 (7th Cir. 1984) (assuming that application of export controls to an American company's desire to respond to a questionnaire from an Arab trade group regarding its business dealings with Israel raised a justiciable First Amendment question); United States v. Edler Indus., 579 F.2d 516, 519–20 (9th Cir. 1978) (applying the First Amendment to regulations that prohibited communication of technical data by a U.S. company to a French company).

39   See, e.g., Carlson v. Schlesinger, 511 F.2d 1327, 1331–33 (D.C. Cir. 1975) (applying First Amendment speech protection to pamphleteering on a military base in Vietnam); Nation Magazine v. U.S. Dep't of Def., 762 F. Supp. 1558, 1571 (S.D.N.Y. 1991) (concluding it was "arguable" that First Amendment press protections applied abroad). Compare Lamont v. Woods, 948 F.2d 825 (2d Cir. 1991) (explaining why Establishment Clause restrictions apply to projects funded by United States abroad).

40   Haig v. Agee, 453 U.S. 280, 308 (1981).

41 See *Yahoo!*, 433 F.3d at 1217 (noting that the extent to which the First Amendment's Free Speech Clause protects cross-border communications remains an open question).

42 Desai v. Hersh, 719 F.Supp. 670, 680 (N.D. Ill. 1989).

43 DKT Mem. Fund Ltd. v. Agency for Int'l Dev., 887 F.2d 275, 290, 292 (D.C. Cir. 1989).

44 Zemel v. Rusk, 381 U.S. 1, 16–17 (1965).

45 *Agee*, 453 U.S. at 309.

46 Palestine Info. Office v. Shultz, 853 F.2d 932, 939–40 (D.C. Cir. 1988).

47 Clancy v. Office of Foreign Assets Control, 559 F.3d 595, 604–05 (7th Cir. 2009).

48 One notable, recent exception is *Holder v. Humanitarian Law Project*, in which the Supreme Court rejected the government's argument that the act of speaking to members of a foreign terrorist organization amounted to unprotected conduct. 130 S. Ct. 2705, 2724 (2010). The fact that the government led with this argument itself says something about the quasi-recognition of transborder liberties.

49 Aptheker v. Sec'y of State, 378 U.S. 500, 505 (1964) (invalidating a statute that made it unlawful for a Communist Party member to apply for a passport); Kent v. Dulles, 357 U.S. 116, 130 (1958) (holding that the secretary of state could not deny passports to those wishing to travel abroad to further Communist ideals).

50 See *Agee*, 453 U.S. at 306–7.

51 See Jeffrey Kahn, "International Travel and the Constitution," 56 *UCLA L. Rev.* 271 (2008).

52 See *DKT*, 887 F.2d at 295; *Palestine Info. Office*, 853 F.2d at 940.

53 See *Clancy*, 559 F.2d at 604 (noting that travel restrictions need only be based on a "rational foreign policy consideration").

54 Compare this approach to the statement of Justice Holmes in Abrams v. United States, 250 U.S. 616, 628 (1919) (Holmes, J., dissenting) ("[A]s against dangers peculiar to war, as against others, the principle of the right to free speech is always the same.").

55 Mark D. Rosen, "Exporting the Constitution," 53 *Emory L.J.* 171, 172 (2004) ("Categorically refusing to enforce such Un-American Judgments is tantamount to imposing U.S. constitutional norms on foreign countries.").

56 For philosophical treatments of cosmopolitanism, see Appiah, supra note 2; Martha C. Nussbaum, "Patriotism and Cosmopolitanism," in *For Love of Country?* (Boston, MA: Beacon Press, 2002).

57 In particular, see Appiah, supra note 2.

58 Kwame Anthony Appiah, "Cosmopolitan Patriots," in Nussbaum, supra note 56, at 22.

59 David A. Strauss, *The Living Constitution* 55 (New York: Oxford University Press, 2010). One could make a similar claim regarding the First Amendment's religion clauses, whose history, despite significant effort, has not been

completely recovered. However, in both contexts history remains relevant to the provincialism/cosmopolitanism debate. Insofar as each approach is based in part on historical accounts and suppositions, it is appropriate to consult historical materials and engage in historical arguments.

60 Daniel Farber, "Constitutional Cadenzas," 56 *Drake L. Rev.* 833 (2008).

61 See Gordon S. Wood, *The Radicalism of the American Revolution* (New York: Vintage Books, 1991), 222 ("The revolutionary generation was the most cosmopolitan of any in American history.").

62 Gordon S. Wood, *Revolutionary Characters: What Made the Founders Different* (New York: Penguin Press, 2006), 15.

63 Golove and Hulsebosch, supra note 3 at 974. See Anthony Grafton, "A Sketch Map of a Lost Continent: The Republic of Letters," in *World Made by Words: Scholarship and Community in the Modern West* (Cambridge, MA: Harvard University Press, 2009), 9–34.

64 *The Declaration of Independence* para. 1 (U.S. 1776). See David Armitage, *The Declaration of Independence: A Global History* (Cambridge, MA: Harvard University Press, 2007).

65 See generally Zecharia Chafee, *Three Human Rights in the Constitution of 1787* (Lawrence, KS: University of Kansas Press, 1956).

66 *The Federalist No. 63*, at 422 (James Madison) (Jacob E. Cooke ed., 1961).

67 See Golove and Hulsebosch, supra note 3; Thomas Bender, *A Nation Among Nations: America's Place in World History* (New York: Farrar Straus, 2006).

68 Golove and Hulsebosch, supra note 3 at 935.

69 Id. at 932. See David J. Hancock, *Citizens of the World*: London Merchants and the Integration of the British Atlantic Community, 1735–1785 (New York: Cambridge University Press, 1995).

70 This connection has existed throughout American history. See, e.g., Mary L. Dudziak, *Cold War Civil Rights: Race and the Image of American Democracy* (Princeton, NJ: Princeton University Press, 2000) (noting the connection between Cold War diplomacy and the constitutional conception of equality).

71 Golove and Hulsebosch, supra note 3 at 945.

72 See Jack M. Balkin, *Living Originalism* (Cambridge, MA: Harvard University Press, 2011), 155 (discussing the eighteenth century conception of "commerce," which included a broad range of interactions and affairs with foreign nations).

73 See, e.g., Sarah H. Cleveland, "Powers Inherent in Sovereignty: Indians, Aliens, Territories, and the Nineteenth Century Origins of Plenary Power over Foreign Affairs," 81 *Tex. L. Rev.* 1, 19 (2002) (observing that "most of the Constitution's provisions are not textually restricted by either the population or the geographic area to which they apply").

74 I discuss the First Amendment's geographic domain in Chapters 6 and 7.

75 See N.Y. Times Co. v. United States, 403 U.S. 713, 717 (1971) (praising the publication of the Pentagon Papers by the press as "precisely that which the Founders hoped and trusted they would do").

76 See Jack N. Rakove, *Original Meanings: Politics and Ideas in the Making of the Constitution* (New York: Alfred A. Knopf, Inc., 1996), 18–22 (discussing influence of international thinkers and practices on the formation of the Constitution).

77 See Joseph Story, Commentaries on the Constitution of the United States § 1879 (1833) (defining liberty of press as "the right to publish without any previous restraint or license").

78 See Reynolds v. United States, 98 U.S. 145, 162 (1878) ("Congress cannot pass a law for the government of the Territories which shall prohibit the free exercise of religion").

79 See N.Y. Times Co. v. Sullivan, 376 U.S. 254, 270 (1964) (observing that Americans share a "profound national commitment to the principle that debate on public issues should be uninhibited, robust, and wide open, and that [speech] may well include vehement, caustic, and sometimes unpleasantly sharp attacks on government and public officials"); Leonard W. Levy, *Legacy of Suppression: Freedom of Speech and Press in Early American History* (Cambridge, MA: Harvard University Press, 1960), 258 (noting that controversy regarding the Sedition Act helped focus national attention on the central meaning of freedom of speech).

80 See Bollinger, supra note 31, at 5 (noting that globalization is "tightening connections among open markets and systems of communication and helping us to perceive issues and problems as transcending national borders").

81 See Appiah, supra note 2, at xx (discussing the concept of the "rooted" cosmopolitan).

82 See, e.g., Nussbaum, supra note 56; Bollinger, supra note 31.

83 Golove and Hulsebosch, supra note 3 at 974; see also Grafton, supra note 63.

84 See Steven Kull and I. M. Destler, *Misreading the Public: The Myth of a New Isolationism* (Washington, D.C.: Brookings Press, 1999), 122–24.

85 See Peter J. Spiro, *Beyond Citizenship: American Identity after Globalization* (New York: Oxford University Press, 2008), 60 (describing plural citizenship as "a sort of international version of the First Amendment protection for free association").

86 See Sabrina Tavernise and Robert Gebeloff, "Immigrants Make Paths to Suburbia, Not Cities," *New York Times*, December 15, 2010, at A15 (noting that census data showed immigrants "fanned out across the United States in the last decade, settling in greater numbers in small towns and suburbs").

87 Nussbaum, supra note 56, at 9.

88 Appiah, supra note 2, at xx.

89 Rodney A. Smolla, *Free Speech in an Open Society* (New York: Alfred A. Knopf, Inc. 1992), 367.

90 See *Bollinger*, supra note 31, at 131 (arguing that, with respect to a free press, "[w]hat is fundamentally needed is a change in our orientation, characterized by the task of opening up the world to a press that is independent and free").

91 There are of course many more theories or justifications. See gener-
    ally Frederick Schauer, *Free Speech: A Philosophical Enquiry* (New York:
    Cambridge University Press, 1982).

92 Alexander Meiklejohn, *Free Speech and Its Relation to Self-Government* (New
    York: Harper Brothers, 1948).

93 See id. at 22–25.

94 See Vincent Blasi, "The Checking Value in First Amendment Theory," 1977
    Am. B. Found. Res. J. 521, 529–44.

95 The marketplace idea or metaphor is generally thought to have originated
    in the work of John Stuart Mill. See *John Stuart Mill, On Liberty* (Elizabeth
    Rapaport ed., 1978) (1859), 16. For elaborations of the metaphor, see
    Abrams v. United States, 250 U.S. 616, 630 (1919) (Holmes, J., dissenting)
    ("[T]he best test of truth is the power of the thought to get itself accepted in
    the competition of the market.") and *Zechariah Chafee, Jr., Free Speech in the
    United States* (The Lawbook Exchange, Ltd., 1969), 559–66.

96 Smolla, supra note 89, at 367.

97 See C. Edwin Baker, *Human Liberty and Freedom of Speech* (New York:
    Oxford University Press, 1989).

98 Akhil Reed Amar, "The Bill of Rights as a Constitution," 100 *Yale L. J.* 1131,
    1196 (1991).

99 See Jack M. Balkin, "The Future of Free Expression in a Digital Age," 36
    Pepp. L. Rev. 427, 438 (2009).

100 Id.

101 Id. at 438–39.

102 Jack M. Balkin, "Digital Speech and Democratic Culture: A Theory of Freedom
    of Expression for the Information Society," 79 *N.Y.U. L. Rev.* 1 (2004).

103 Id. at 4.

104 Smolla, supra note 89, at 367.

105 See Universal Declaration of Human Rights, G.A. Res. 217A, U.N. GAOR,
    3d Sess., 1st plen. Mtg., U.N. Doc. A/810 (Dec. 10, 1948), art. 19 [herein-
    after UDHR] ("Everyone has the right to freedom of opinion and expres-
    sion; this right includes freedom to hold opinions without interference
    and to seek, receive and impart information and ideas through any media
    regardless of frontiers") (emphasis added); International Covenant on Civil
    and Political Rights, G.A. Res. 2200A (XXI), U.N. GAOR, 21st Sess.,
    Supp. No. 16, U.N. Doc. A/6316, art. 19, ¶¶ 1–2 (Dec. 16, 1966) (stating
    that every person has the right to hold opinions "without interference"
    and that freedom of expression includes the "freedom to seek, receive and
    impart information of all kinds, *regardless of frontiers*, either orally, in writing
    or in print, in the form of art, or through any other media of his choice")
    (emphasis added); UDHR, art. 18 (providing that "[e]veryone has the
    right to freedom of thought, conscience, and religion," including the right

to teach, practice and observe religion or belief in public or private contexts); International Religious Freedom Act (IRFA) of 1998 § 401, Pub. L. No. 105–292, 112 Stat. 2787 (codified as amended in scattered sections of 8 and 22 U.S.C.); 22 U.S.C. § 6441(a) (i)–(ii) (2006) (obligating Congress and the President to "oppose violations of religious freedom that are or have been engaged in or tolerated by the governments of foreign countries" and "to promote the right to freedom of religion in those countries").

106 See also Mary Ann Glendon, *A World Made New: Eleanor Roosevelt and the Universal Declaration of Human Rights* (New York: Random House, 2001); Louis Henkin, "Rights: American and Human," 79 *Colum. L. Rev.* 405, 415 (1979).

107 See Appiah, supra note 2, at 30 (discussing the benefits of shared values and common language of values).

108 Id. at xxi.

109 Appiah, supra note 2, at 72.

110 Kal Raustiala, *Does the Constitution Follow the Flag?* The Evolution of Territoriality in American Law (New York: Oxford University Press, 2009), v.

111 Krasner, supra note 20.

112 See Lawrence Lessig, *Code and Other Laws of Cyberspace: Version 2.0* (New York: Basic Books, 2006); Jack Goldsmith and Tim Wu, *Who Controls the Internet? Illusions of a Borderless World* (New York: Oxford University Press 2006).

113 See Goldsmith and Wu, supra note 112, at 247; Saskia Sassen, *Territory, Authority, Rights: From Medieval to Global Assemblages* (Princeton, NJ: Princeton University Press, 2006); T. Alexander Aleinikoff, *Semblances of Sovereignty: The Constitution, the State, and American Citizenship* (Cambridge, MA: Harvard University Press, 2002).

114 Raustiala, supra note 110, at 247.

115 See id.

116 See Akhil Reed Amar, "The Bill of Rights as a Constitution," 100 *Yale L. J.* 1131, 1196 (1991).

117 See generally Jules Lobel, "The Constitution Abroad," 83 *Am. J. Int'l L.* 871, 879 (1989).

118 Louis Henkin, "The Constitution as Compact and as Conscience: Individual Rights Abroad and at Our Gates," 27 *Wm. & Mary L. Rev.* 18, 32 (1985).

119 United States v. Verdugo-Urquidez, 494 U.S. 259, 277 (1990) (Kennedy, J., concurring).

120 Boumediene v. Bush, 553 U.S. 723 (2008).

121 Raustiala, supra note 110, at 247. See id. at 107–17 (discussing assertion of extraterritorial jurisdiction through use of the "effects" standard).

122 See Nina J. Crimm, "The Global Gag Rule: Undermining National Interests by Doing unto Foreign Women and NGOs What Cannot Be Done at Home," 40 *Cornell Int'l L.J.* 587, 592–608 (2007) (explaining that the "global gag rule" prevents foreign nongovernmental organizations from using U.S.

government funds to provide abortion counseling to women, to lobby for or against legalized abortions, and to facilitate or offer abortions to women).

123 See United States v. Curtiss-Wright Export Corporation, 299 U.S. 304, 315–18 (1936).

124 For criticisms of federal plenary authority over immigration, see Gerald L. Neuman, *Strangers to the Constitution: Immigrants, Borders, and Fundamental Law* (Princeton, NJ: Princeton University Press. 1996), 119–25; 134–38; Louis Henkin, "The Constitution and United States Sovereignty: A Century of Chinese Exclusion and Its Progeny," 100 *Harv. L. Rev.* 853 (1987).

125 See Crosby v. National Foreign Trade Council, 530 U.S. 363 (2000); Sarah H. Cleveland, "Crosby and the 'One-Voice' Myth in U.S. Foreign Relations," 46 *Vill L. Rev.* 975 (2001).

126 See Paul Schiff Berman, "Towards a Cosmopolitan Vision of Conflicts of Laws: Redefining Governmental Interests in a Global Era," 153 *U. Pa. L. Rev.* 1819 (2005).

127 See generally Vicki C. Jackson, *Constitutional Engagement in a Transnational Era* (New York: Oxford University Press, 2010).

128 See, e.g., Jeremy Waldron, *The Harm in Hate Speech* (Cambridge, MA: Harvard University Press, 2012); Martha C. Nussbaum, *The New Religious Intolerance: Overcoming the Politics of Fear in an Anxious Age* (Cambridge, MA: Harvard University Press, 2012).

129 Appiah, supra note 2, at 97.

130 See Steven R. Swanson, "Forcing Facebook on Foreign Dictators: A Violation of International Law?," 79 *Tenn. L. Rev.* 851 (2012).

131 Appiah, supra note 56, at 29.

Mobility and Expressive Liberties

1 Zemel v. Rusk, 381 U.S. 1, 3, 4, 16 (1965).

2 Id. at 16.

3 Id.

4 Id.

5 Id. at 17.

6 Id.

7 See John Schwartz, "U.S. Is Urged to Lift Antiterror Ban on Foreign Scholars," *New York Times*, March 18, 2009, at A19; Brief for Defendants Appellees, Am. Acad. of Religion v. Napolitano, 573 F.3d 115 (2d Cir. 2009) (No. 08–0826-CV) at 52–59.

8 The relationship between religious liberty and cross-border movement is discussed in Chapter 7, which examines religious freedoms in transborder perspective.

9 Stephen D. Krasner, *Sovereignty: Organized Hypocrisy* (Princeton, NJ: Princeton University Press, 1999), 12.

10 Peter Adey, *Mobility* (New York: Routledge, 2009).
11 Burt Neuborne and Steven R. Shapiro, "The Nylon Curtain: America's National Border and the Free Flow of Ideas," 26 *Wm. & Mary L. Rev.* 719, 734–35 (1985).
12 Act of May 22, 1918, ch. 81, §§ 1–2, 40 Stat. 559, 559.
13 Neuborne and Shapiro, supra note 11, at 734.
14 Jeffrey Kahn, *Mrs. Shipley's Ghost: The Right to Travel and Terrorist Watchlists* (University of Michigan Press, forthcoming).
15 Louis L. Jaffe, "The Right to Travel: The Passport Problem," 35 *Foreign Aff.* 1, 17–28 (1956).
16 Aptheker v. Sec'y of State, 378 U.S. 500, 501–02 (1964); Kent v. Dulles, 357 U.S. 116, 117–20 (1958).
17 See, e.g., 31 C.F.R. § 515.560 (2009) (listing restricted activities and expenses relating to travel to Cuba).
18 78 Pub. L. No. 95–426, 92 Stat. 963 (codified as amended at 22 U.S.C. § 211a). See id. § 124, 92 Stat. at 971. Today, area restrictions may only be imposed with the acquiescence of Congress pursuant to the International Emergency Economic Powers Act, 50 U.S.C. §§ 1701–1706 (2006).
19 See Jeffrey Kahn, "International Travel and the Constitution," 56 *UCLA L. Rev.* 271, 321–22 (2008) (describing the compilation and use of the No Fly List).
20 357 U.S. 116, 130 (1958).
21 Id. at 125–30.
22 Id. at 125.
23 378 U.S. 500, 505 (1964).
24 Id. at 505–08. See also id. at 517 (noting the connection between the First Amendment and international travel). Although the Court has never specifically addressed the issue, the same due process protections would presumably apply to compelled renunciation of one's religious beliefs or associations.
25 381 U.S. 1 (1965).
26 Id. at 16.
27 Id.
28 Id. at 17.
29 391 U.S. 367, 376 (1968).
30 453 U.S. 280, 310 (1981).
31 The extraterritorial First Amendment rights of citizens and aliens are discussed in Chapters 6 and 7.
32 *Agee*, 453 U.S. at 309.
33 Id.
34 Id. at 306.
35 Id. at 307.
36 See Regan v. Wald, 468 U.S. 222, 242–43 (1984) (holding that Cuba travel restrictions do not violate the freedom to travel abroad). See also Clancy v. Office of Foreign Assets Control, 559 F.3d 595, 605 (7th Cir. 2009) (rejecting

a First Amendment challenge to the imposition of sanctions on a person who traveled to Iraq to act as a "human shield" on the ground that sanctions applied to conduct rather than speech); Emergency Coal. to Defend Educ. Travel v. U.S. Dep't of the Treasury, 545 F.3d 4, 13–14 (D.C. Cir. 2008) (holding that regulations restricting educational programs offered in Cuba by U.S. academic institutions did not violate the First Amendment); Karpova v. Snow, 402 F. Supp. 2d 459, 473–74 (S.D.N.Y. 2005) (holding that enforcement of regulations restricting travel to Iraq did not give rise to any First Amendment claim and that, insofar as traveler's actions as a human shield were expressive conduct, the travel regulations satisfied First Amendment standards); Freedom to Travel Campaign v. Newcomb, 82 F.3d 1431, 1441 (9th Cir. 1996) (holding that Cuba travel restrictions did not implicate the First Amendment); Walsh v. Brady, 927 F.2d 1229, 1231–34 (D.C. Cir. 1991) (deferring to agency's interpretation that denial of license to travel to Cuba for purposes of negotiating purchase of political posters did not violate federal law).

37 Zechariah Chafee, *Three Human Rights in the Constitution of 1787* (Lawrence, KS: University of Kansas Press, 1956).

38 Id. at 187–204.

39 Id. at 195.

40 Id.

41 Id. See Roberts v. U.S. Jaycees, 468 U.S. 609, 617–18 (1984) (recognizing that the First Amendment protects both "intimate" associations, such as families, and "expressive" associations).

42 Chafee, supra note 37, at 197.

43 Id. at 195–96.

44 Id. at 196.

45 Id.

46 *Kent*, 357 U.S. at 126–27 (praising Chafee for showing "how deeply engrained in our history this freedom of movement is").

47 *Zemel*, 381 U.S. at 24 (Douglas, J., dissenting).

48 *Aptheker*, 378 U.S. at 519–20 (Douglas, J., concurring) (emphasis added).

49 Id. at 520.

50 *Zemel*, 381 U.S. at 24 (Douglas, J., dissenting).

51 Id.

52 *Aptheker*, 378 U.S. at 520.

53 See also Rodney A. Smolla, *Free Speech in an Open Society* (New York: Alfred A. Knopf, Inc., 1992), 361–67.

54 *Aptheker*, 378 U.S. at 519–20 (Douglas, J., concurring).

55 See Saskia Sassen, *Territory, Authority, Rights: From Medieval to Global Assemblages* (Princeton, NJ: Princeton University Press, 2006), 379 ("Digital domains cannot (at least for now) fully encompass the lived experience of users or the domain of institutional orders and cultural formations.").

56 Jeanne M. Woods, "Travel That Talks: Toward First Amendment Protection for Freedom of Movement," 65 *Geo. Wash. L. Rev.* 106, 110 (1996).

57 See Jeffrey Kahn, "International Travel and the Constitution," 56 *UCLA L. Rev.* 271 (2008) (arguing that international travel is protected by the Citizenship Clause of the Fourteenth Amendment).

58 See Barry P. McDonald, "The First Amendment and the Free Flow of Information: Towards a Realistic Right to Gather Information in the Information Age," 65 *Ohio St. L.J.* 249, 340–55 (2004). Cf. also Lee C. Bollinger, *Uninhibited, Robust, and Wide-Open; A Free Press for a New Century* (Oxford University Press, 2010), 120–21 (arguing that the Court should recognize a broad international newsgathering right under the First Amendment).

59 McDonald, supra note 58, at 345, 348, 350.

60 United States v. O'Brien, 391 U.S. 367 (1968).

61 22 U.S.C. § 2721 (2006). Not all expressive grounds have been eliminated. For example, an alien who is an officer, official, representative, or *spokesman* of the Palestine Liberation Organization is deemed excludable on the ground of participation in terrorist activity. 8 U.S.C. § 1182(a)(3)(B)(i) (2006).

62 31 C.F.R. §§ 515.560(a)(1)–(12) (2009).

63 See id. §§ 515.561, 515.566, 515.575, 515.567.

64 See, e.g., Brad R. Roth, "The First Amendment in the Foreign Affairs Realm: 'Domesticating' the Restrictions on Citizen Participation," 2 *Temp. Pol. & Civ. Rts. L. Rev.* 255, 276 (1993).

65 22 C.F.R. § 51.60(c)(4) (2011).

66 See Freedom to Travel to Cuba Act, H.R. 874, 111th Cong. § 2 (2009).

67 Office of Foreign Assets Control, Dep't of the Treasury, Guidance on Implementation of Cuba Travel and Trade-Related Provisions Act, at 1 (2009). See Omnibus Appropriations Act, 2009, Pub. L. No. 111–8, § 621, 123 Stat. 524, 678 (directing the Treasury Department to defund certain travel restrictions); William E. Gibson, "More Cuba Trips Expected," *L.A. Times*, March 15, 2009, at A20 (suggesting that the Obama administration may lift the Cuba travel embargo).

68 John F. Burns, "Britain Identifies 16 People Barred from Entering the Country in the Past 6 Months," *New York Times*, May 6, 2009, at A6.

69 See, e.g., Alien Immigration Act, ch. 1012, § 2, 32 Stat. 1213, 1214 (1903).

70 See Gerald Neuman, *Strangers to the Constitution: Immigrants, Borders, and Fundamental Law* (Princeton, NJ: Princeton University Press, 1996), 149–50.

71 Act of July 14, 1798, ch. 74, 1 Stat. 596 (expired 1801); Act of July 6, 1798, ch. 66, 1 Stat. 577 (expired 1801); Act of June 25, 1798, ch. 58, 1 Stat. 570 (expired 1800); Act of June 18, 1798, ch. 54, 1 Stat. 566 (repealed 1802).

72 See, e.g., Anarchist Act of 1918, ch. 186, 40 Stat. 1012 (authorizing the removal alien anarchists); Harisiades v. Shaughnessy, 342 U.S. 580, 592 (1952) (rejecting aFirst Amendment challenge to a law providing for the deportation of communists);United States *ex rel.* Turner v. Williams, 194 U.S. 279, 290–91 (1904) (upholding the removal of an alien anarchist).

73 Immigration and Nationality Act, ch. 477, 66 Stat. 163 (1952) (codified as amended at 8 U.S.C. §§ 1101–1537 (2006)).

74 Id. at § 212(a)(27), 66 Stat. at 184 (repealed 1990).

75 Id. at § 212(a)(28)(A)–(C), 66 Stat. at 184–85 (current version at 8 U.S.C. § 1182(a)(3)(D)).

76 Neuborne and Shapiro, supra note 11, at 723.

77 See John A. Scanlan, "Aliens in the Marketplace of Ideas: The Government, the Academy, and the McCarran-Walter Act," 66 *Tex. L. Rev.* 1481, 1496–97 (1988) (discussing the effect of ideological deportation and exclusion on the American academy and on academic freedom); Steven R. Shapiro, "Ideological Exclusions: Closing the Border to Political Dissidents," 100 *Harv. L. Rev.* 930, 935, 940–41 (1987) (discussing ideological exclusions).

78 Pub. L. No. 95–105, 91 Stat. 844 (1977) (repealed 1990).

79 Id. at § 112, 91 Stat. at 848.

80 H.R. REP. No. 100–475, at 162–63 (1987) (Conf. Rep.).

81 See Immigration and Nationality Act of 1952, ch. 477, § 212(a)(27), 66 Stat. 163, 184 (repealed 1990); see also Neuborne & Shapiro, supra note 11, at 726–27 (describing exclusions under the Reagan administration).

82 See Neuborne and Shapiro, supra note 11, at 726–27.

83 Immigration Act of 1990, Pub. L. No. 101–649, 104 Stat. 4978.

84 Id. at § 601, 104 Stat. at 5071.

85 For example, immigration laws make a person who has engaged in terrorist activities ineligible for certain visas. 8 U.S.C. § 1182(a)(3)(B)(i)(I) (2006).

86 8 U.S.C. § 1182(a)(3)(C)(i).

87 50 U.S.C. § 21 (2006).

88 See Antiterrorism and Effective Death Penalty Act of 1996, Pub. L. No. 104–132,§ 411, 110 Stat. 1214, 1268–69 (codified as amended at 8 U.S.C. § 1182 (2006)).

89 See, e.g., Uniting and Strengthening America by Providing Appropriate Tools Required to Intercept and Obstruct Terrorism (USA PATRIOT) Act of 2001, Pub. L. No. 107–56, 115 Stat. 272 (codified in scattered sections of 8, 12, 15, 18, 22, 28, 31, 42, 49, and 50 U.S.C.) (imposing more restrictive rules on the immigration of suspected terrorists).

90 Id. at § 411(a)(1)(A), 115 Stat. at 345–46.

91 U.S. Dep't of State, *Foreign Affairs Manual* § 40.32 at n.6.2(3) (2005).

92 Pub. L. No. 109–13, div. B, 119 Stat. 302 (codified as amended in scattered sections of 8 and 49 U.S.C.), § 103(a), 119 Stat. at 306–07.

93 J. David Goodman, "Travelers Say They Were Denied Entry to U.S. for Twitter Jokes," *New York Times*, January 30, 2012.

94 See, e.g., Juan Forero, "U.S. Denies Visa for Colombian Writer," *Wash. Post*, July 10, 2010, at A7 (reporting that prominent Colombian journalist Hollman Morris, who had planned to study at Harvard University, was

ineligible for a U.S. student visa under the "terrorist activities" section of the USA PATRIOT Act).

95 Am. Civil Liberties Union, *The Excluded*, 8 (2007), available at http://www. aclu.org/files/pdfs/safefree/the_Excluded_report.pdf.

96 See Am. Sociological Ass'n v. Chertoff, 588 F. Supp. 2d 166, 172–73 (D. Mass. 2008) (ordering the government to provide some specific basis for exclusion); Am. Acad. of Religion v. Chertoff, No. 06 CV 588(PAC), 2007 WL 4527504, at *15–16 (S.D.N.Y. Dec. 20, 2007) (finding that alien was excluded not under PATRIOT Act's "endorse or espouse" provision, but on basis of donations made to organizations supporting known terrorist groups), *vacated sub nom.* Am. Acad. of Religion v. Napolitano, 573 F.3d 115 (2d Cir. 2009).

97 See *Am. Acad. of Religion*, 2007 WL 4527504, at *3–4 (noting that government alleged alien was excluded based on his provision of financial assistance to terrorists).

98 See Brief for Defendants-Appellees at 52–59, Am. Acad. of Religion v. Napolitano, 573 F.3d 115 (2d Cir. 2009) (No. 08–0826-CV).

99 United States *ex rel.* Knauff v. Shaughnessy, 338 U.S. 537, 542 (1950). See Zadvydas v. Davis, 533 U.S. 678, 693 (2001) (discussing relationship between political membership and territorial borders); Krasner, supra note 9, at 12 (describing the ability to control admission as "interdependence sovereignty").

100 See United States *ex rel.* Turner v. Williams, 194 U.S. 279, 290–91 (1904) (upholding the removal of an alien anarchist); Harisiades v. Shaughnessy, 342 U.S. 580, 592 (1952) (rejecting a First Amendment challenge to a law providing for the deportation of communists).

101 408 U.S. 753 (1972).

102 Id. at 767–78.

103 Id. at 769; see also Lamont v. Postmaster Gen., 381 U.S. 301, 307 (1965) (recognizing a right to receive communist political propaganda through the mail).

104 *Mandel*, 408 U.S. at 764–65 (quoting Mandel v. Mitchell, 325 F. Supp. 620, 631 (E.D.N.Y. 1971)).

105 See id. at 765 (emphasizing the "particular qualities inherent in sustained, face-to-face debate, discussion and questioning").

106 Id. at 770.

107 Id. at 762; see United States *ex rel.* Turner v. Williams, 194 U.S. 279, 279 (1904) (upholding ideological exclusion of alien).

108 Id. at 768–69; *see* Harisiades v. Shaughnessy, 342 U.S. 580, 585–92 (1952) (upholding the Alien Registration Act of 1940, which barred the entry of aliens who advocated for the violent overthrow of the U.S. government or associated with others who did so, against a First Amendment challenge).

109 Shapiro, supra note 77, at 936.

110 Compare El-Werfalli v. Smith, 547 F. Supp. 152, 153–54 (S.D.N.Y. 1982) (concluding that *Mandel* does not permit courts to probe the wisdom or basis of proffered reasons for exclusion), *with* Allende v. Shultz, 605 F. Supp. 1220, 1225 (D. Mass. 1985) (holding that mere membership in an organization alleged to be a communist-front association was not a sufficient statutory basis for denial under the McCarran–Walter Act) *and* Abourezk v. Reagan, 592 F. Supp. 880, 887 (D.D.C. 1984) (holding that the government lacks authority to exclude an alien under section 212(a)(27) of the McCarran-Walter Act based solely on a proposed message), *vacated,* 785 F.2d 1043 (D.C. Cir. 1986).

111 See *Mandel,* 408 U.S. at 770 ("What First Amendment or other grounds may be available for attacking exercise of discretion for which no justification whatsoever is advanced is a question we neither address nor decide in this case.").

112 David Cole, "Are Foreign Nationals Entitled to the Same Constitutional Rights as Citizens?," 25 *T. Jefferson L. Rev.* 367 (2003).

113 Bridges v. Wixon, 326 U.S. 135, 148 (1945).

114 Harisiades v. Shaughnessy, 342 U.S. 580 (1952).

115 See, e.g., Scales v. United States, 367 U.S. 203 (1961) (holding that Congress cannot criminalize mere membership in the Communist Party).

116 *Compare* American-Arab Anti-Discrim. Comm. v. Reno, 70 F.3d 1045 (9th Cir. 1995), *rev'd on other grounds,* 525 U.S. 471 (1999) *and* Parcham v. INS, 769 F.2d 1001 (4th Cir. 1985) (removal of aliens cannot be based solely on protected speech) *with* Price v. INS, 941 F.2d 878 (9th Cir. 1991) (government has nearly unlimited powers to deny naturalization and remove aliens).

117 See Reno v. American-Arab Anti-Discrim. Comm., 525 U.S. 471, 488–91 (1999).

118 Cole, supra note 112, at 368.

119 Chafee, supra note 37, at 198.

120 Id. at 199–200.

121 Id. at 200.

122 Id. at 149–61 (addressing, and finding wanting, possible governmental justifications for ideological exclusions).

123 Id. at 201.

124 Neuman, supra note 70, at 134–38.

125 Id. at 138. Thus far, we have assumed that the First Amendment rights at issue are those belonging to citizens – specifically, their rights to receive and participate in exchanges with aliens who wish to travel to the United States. In *Mandel,* the Supreme Court concluded that aliens do not possess enforceable First Amendment rights. However, some scholars have suggested that aliens subject to ideological exclusions possess First Amendment rights. See Neuman, supra note 70, at 127 (arguing that under a "mutuality of legal

obligation" approach, aliens subjected to exclusion orders can assert their own First Amendment claims). I address the extent to which the First Amendment extends to aliens located beyond U.S. borders in Chapters 6 and 7.

126 See John T. Inazu, *Liberty's Refuge: The Forgotten Freedom of Assembly* (New Haven, CT: Yale University Press, 2012).

127 U.S. Dep't of State, *Foreign Affairs Manual* § 40.32 at n.6.2(3) (2005).

128 See Kwong Hai Chew v. Colding, 344 U.S. 590, 598 n.5 (1953).

129 Cole, supra note 112, at 377.

130 I am drawing here on Kant's conception of hospitality. See Immanuel Kant, *Toward Perpetual Peace and Other Writings on Politics, Peace, and History* (1795; trans. D. Clocasure) (New Haven, CT: Yale University Press, 2006).

131 Id. at 82.

132 Cole, supra note 112, at 372.

Cross-Border Communication and Association

1 See Murray L. Schwartz and James C. N. Paul, "Foreign Communist Propaganda in the Mails: A Report on Some Problems of Federal Censorship," 107 *Pa. L. Rev.* 621, 633–49 (1959) (reporting that foreign materials deemed to be communist propaganda were frequently seized or subject to federal licensure).

2 381 U.S. 301 (1965).

3 Holder v. Humanitarian Law Project, 130 S. Ct. 2705 (2010).

4 Lawrence Lessig, *Code: And Other Laws of Cyberspace* (New York: Basic Books, 2000); Lawrence Lessig, *Code: And Other Laws of Cyberspace, Version 2.0* (New York: Basic Books, 2006).

5 United States v. 12 200-Ft. Reels of Super 8MM. Film, 413 U.S. 123, 125 (1973). See also United States v. Ickes, 393 F.3d 501 (4th Cir. 2005) (refusing to recognize any First Amendment exception to broad customs authority in the context of searches of laptops and other computing devices); United States v. Arnold, 533 F.3d 1003 (9th Cir. 2008) (same); United States v. Seljan, 547 F.3d 993, 1011–12 (9th Cir. 2008) (Callahan, J., concurring) (same).

6 See Jack Goldsmith and Tim Wu, *Who Controls the Internet?* Illusions of a Borderless World (New York; Oxford University Press, 2006), 49–65; see also Jack L. Goldsmith, "Against Cyberanarchy," 65 *U. Chi. L. Rev.* 1199, 1212–50 (1998).

7 With respect to commercial information, the Supreme Court first held that this form of expression was entitled to First Amendment protection in the 1970s. Virginia State Bd. of Pharmacy v. Virginia Citizens Consumer Council, 425 U.S. 748 (1976).

8 50 U.S.C. §§ 1–44 (2006). See Burt Neuborne and Steven R. Shapiro, "The Nylon Curtain: America's National Border and the Free Flow of Ideas," 26 *Wm. & Mary L. Rev.* 719, 728–33 (1985).

9   Id. at 730.

10 Id.

11 19 U.S.C. § 1202–1681b (2006).

12 Neuborne and Shapiro, supra note 8, at 733. In 1973, the Supreme Court held that the Tariff Act was unconstitutional as applied to the importation of obscene materials for private use. United States v. 12 200-Ft. Reels of Super 8MM Film, 413 U.S. 123, 139 (1973).

13 19 U.S.C. §1305(a).

14 Id.

15 19 C.F.R. § 12.40(g) (2009).

16 Agreement for Facilitating the International Circulation of Visual and Auditory Materials of an Educational, Scientific and Cultural Character, opened for signature July 15, 1949, 17 U.S.T. 1578, 197 U.N.T.S. 3. Congress passed an implementing statute in 1966, and formal operations under the agreement began in 1967. See Joint Resolution of Oct. 8, 1966, Pub. L. No. 89–634, 80 Stat. 879 (formal ratification).

17 22 C.F.R. § 502.6(b)(3)-(5) (repealed).

18 Bullfrog Films, Inc. v. Wick, 847 F.2d 502, 512 (9th Cir. 1988). After successor regulations were also challenged as restrictions on expression, Congress enacted a law prohibiting federal regulators from denying customs exemptions to materials on the ground that they advocate a particular position or viewpoint, might lend themselves to misinterpretation, or are in the opinion of the agency propaganda. Foreign Relations Authorization Act, 19 U.S.C. § 2051(1)-(5).

19 Omnibus Trade and Competitiveness Act of 1988, Pub. L. No. 100–418, § 2502, 102 Stat. 1107, 1371 (codified at 50 U.S.C. app. § 5 (2006)).

20 31 C.F.R. § 500.332 (2009).

21 A federal district court rejected this interpretation. Cernuda v. Heavy, 720 F. Supp. 1544, 1546 (S.D. Fla. 1989).

22 A federal district court found this interpretation to be reasonable. Capital Cities/ABC, Inc. v. Brady, 740 F. Supp. 1007, 1014–15 (S.D.N.Y. 1990).

23 Pub. L. No. 103–236, § 525, 108 Stat. 382, 474 (codified as amended at 12 U.S.C. § 95a(4) (2006), 50 U.S.C. § 1702 (2006)).

24 See Tracy J. Chin, "An Unfree Trade in Ideas: How OFAC's Regulations Restrain First Amendment Rights," 83 N.Y.U. L. Rev. 1883, 1890 (2008).

25 The EAA expired in 1989, and was thereafter periodically reauthorized for short periods. Currently, the export licensing system created by the EAA is continued under the International Emergency Economic Powers Act, 50 U.S.C. §§ 1701–1707 (2006). The cross-border exchange of materials and information with military applications is regulated under another federal law. See International Security Assistance and Arms Export Control Act of 1976, 22 U.S.C. §§ 2751–2799aa-2 (2006).

26 15 C.F.R. §§ 730.1–774.1 (2009).

27 50 U.S.C. app. § 2415.

28 See Ian Ferguson, Cong. Research Serv., *The Export Administration Act* (2009), 10, 18.

29 See Junger v. Daley, 209 F.3d 481, 485 (6th Cir. 2000) (holding that source code is expressive and remanding for consideration in light of EAR source code amendments); Bernstein v. Dep't of Justice, 176 F.3d 1132, 1147 (9th Cir. 1999) (holding that source code is expressive and that the EAR constitute an invalid prior restraint), *reh'g granted, opinion withdrawn by* 192 F.3d 1308 (9th Cir. 1999).

30 See generally E. John Park, "Protecting the Core Values of the First Amendment in an Age of New Technologies: Scientific Expression vs. National Security," 2 *Va. J.L. & Tech.* 3 (1997).

31 15 C.F.R. § 734.2.

32 18 U.S.C. § 953 (2006). The ban applies regardless of the citizen's location. I discuss the Logan Act further in Chapter 8.

33 Prosecutions under the Logan Act have been threatened, but rarely commenced. See Detlev F. Vagts, "The Logan Act: Paper Tiger or Sleeping Giant?," 60 *Am. J. Int'l L.* 268 (1966). As scholars and some courts have observed, the Act may be vulnerable to vagueness or other constitutional objections. See Waldron v. British Petroleum Co., 231 F. Supp. 72, 89 (S.D.N.Y. 1964).

34 See Clapper v. Amnesty International USA, 132 S. Ct. 2341 (2012) (holding that plaintiffs lacked standing to challenge governmental surveillance program on First Amendment and Fourth Amendment grounds); ACLU v. Nat'l Sec. Agency, 493 F.3d 644, 667–73 (6th Cir. 2007) (same).

35 381 U.S. 301 (1965).

36 See Murray L. Schwartz and James C. N. Paul, "Foreign Communist Propaganda in the Mails: A Report on Some Problems of Federal Censorship," 107 *Pa. L. Rev.* 621, 633–49 (1959) (reporting that foreign materials deemed to be communist propaganda were frequently seized or subject to federal licensure).

37 *Lamont*, 381 U.S. at 307.

38 22 U.S.C. §§ 611–621 (2006). "Political propaganda" is defined as material that:

is reasonably adapted … to influence a recipient of any section of the public within the United States with reference to the political or public interests, policies, or relations of a government or a foreign country or a foreign political party or with reference to the foreign policies of the United States or promote in the United States racial, religious, or social dissension.

22 U.S.C. § 611(j).

39 481 U.S. 465, 485 (1987).

40 *Keene*, 481 U.S. at 480.

41 For empirical and other analyses questioning this and certain other claims made by the Court, see Rodney A. Smolla and Stephen A. Smith,

"Propaganda, Xenophobia, and the First Amendment," 68 *Oregon L. Rev.* 253 (1988).

42 Smith-Mundt Act, ch. 36, § 501, 62 Stat. 6, 9 (1948) (codified at 22 U.S.C. § 1461 (2006)).

43 22 U.S.C. § 1461–1a.

44 Gartner v. U.S. Info. Agency, 726 F. Supp. 1183, 1189 (S.D. Iowa 1989). Efforts to force disclosure of U.S. international propaganda materials under the Freedom of Information Act were unsuccessful. Essential Info., Inc. v. U.S. Info. Agency, 134 F.3d 1165, 1169 (D.C. Cir. 1998); Judicial Watch, Inc. v. U.S. Dep't of Commerce, 337 F. Supp. 2d 146, 168 (D.D.C. 2004).

45 *Gartner*, 726 F. Supp. at 1189 (quoting *Zemel*, 381 U.S. at 17).

46 See National Defense Authorization Act for Fiscal Year 2013, P.L. 112–239, Div. A, Title X, Sec. 1078, 22 USC §1461–1a.

47 2 U.S.C. § 441e (2006).

48 Lori F. Damrosch, "Politics across Borders: Nonintervention and Nonforcible Influence over Domestic Affairs," 83 *Am. J. Int'l L.* 1, 21–25 (1989).

49 558 U.S. 310, 362 (2010).

50 Id. at 423 (Stevens, J., dissenting).

51 See John H. Mansfield, "The Religion Clauses of the First Amendment and Foreign Relations," 36 *DePaul L. Rev.* 1, 19 (1986) (observing that "there are no judicial statements about an unlimited governmental power to exclude information that originates outside the country, such as mail or electronic transmissions").

52 *Lamont*, 381 U.S. at 307.

53 Anuj C. Desai, "The Transformation of Statutes into Constitutional Law: How Early Post Office Policy Shaped Modern First Amendment Doctrine," 58 *Hastings L.J.* 671, 724 (2007).

54 See Teague v. Reg'l Comm'r of Customs, 404 F.2d 441, 447 (2d Cir. 1968).

55 Yahoo! Inc. v. La Ligue Contre le Racisme et l'Antisemitisme, 433 F.3d 1199, 1217, 1221 (9th Cir. 2006).

56 See Briggs & Stratton Corp. v. Baldridge, 728 F.2d 915, 917 (7th Cir. 1984) (assuming that application of export controls to an American company's desire to respond to a questionnaire from an Arab trade group regarding its business dealings with Israel implicated First Amendment); United States v. Edler Indus., 579 F.2d 516, 519–20 (9th Cir. 1978) (applying First Amendment to regulations that prohibited communication of technical data by a U.S. company to a French company).

57 As discussed further in Chapter 7, the situation is the same with regard to distinctly religious expression or activities. See Ohno v. Yasuma, – – F.3d – –, 2013 WL 3306351 ★ 12 (9th Cir. 2013) ("Nor has any court yet decided whether the First Amendment's Free Exercise Clause applies to religious expression initiated domestically but directed to a foreign audience.").

58 Bullfrog Films, Inc. v. Wick, 646 F. Supp. 492, 503 (C.D. Cal. 1986), *aff'd* 847 F.2d 502, 512 (9th Cir. 1988).

59 646 F. Supp. at 503.

60 Id. at 503 n. 16.

61 Id. at 502.

62 See id. at 503 n. 16.

63 See, e.g., Rodney A. Smolla, *Free Speech in an Open Society* (New York: Alfred A. Knopf, Inc., 1992), 367 (arguing that all nations "must come to respect the free flow of information across all international borders," and encouraging the United States "to set the example"); Neuborne and Shapiro, supra note 8.

64 Robert D. Kamenshine, "Embargoes on Exports of Ideas and Information: First Amendment Issues," 26 *Wm. & Mary L. Rev.* 863, 867 (1985).

65 Kamenshine did allow that the First Amendment might be implicated where the foreign audience consists of a mixture of aliens and citizens. Id. at 873–75.

66 Id. at 867–68.

67 William W. Van Alstyne, "The First Amendment and the Suppression of Warmongering Propaganda in the United States," 31 *Law & Contemp. Problems* 530, 540–41 (1966).

68 Id. at 541.

69 Cass R. Sunstein, "Government Control of Information," 74 *Calif. L. Rev.* 889, 905–12 (1986).

70 See, e.g., Sharon E. Foster, "Does the First Amendment Restrict Recognition and Enforcement of Foreign Copyright Judgments and Arbitration Awards?," 10 *Pace Int'l. L. Rev.* 361, 390 (1998); Jeremy Maltby, "Juggling Comity and Self-Government: The Enforcement of Foreign Libel Judgments in U.S. Courts," 94 *Colum. L. Rev.* 1978, 2007 n. 160 (1994); Joel R. Reidenberg, "Yahoo and Democracy on the Internet," 42 *Jurimetrics* 261, 267 (2002). But see Molly S. Van Houweling, "Enforcement of Foreign Judgments, the First Amendment, and Internet Speech: Notes for the Next Yahoo v. LICRA," 24 *Mich. J. Int'l L.* 697, 714 (2003) ("The First Amendment should protect speech to foreign audiences even if the amendment is concerned primarily with domestic self-government.").

71 Of course, foreign laws and regulations may prevent a communication from reaching its intended audience. Here I am concerned solely with U.S. restrictions, which implicate the First Amendment.

72 Allen W. Palmer and Edward L. Carter, "The Smith-Mundt Act's Ban on Domestic Propaganda: An Analysis of the Cold War Statute Limiting Access to Public Diplomacy," 11 *Comm. L. & Pol'y* 1, 29–30 (2006).

73 David G. Post, *In Search of Jefferson's Moose*: Notes on the State of Cyberspace 166–69 (New York: Oxford University Press, 2009); David R. Johnson & David Post, "Law and Borders – The Rise of Law in Cyberspace," 48 *Stan. L. Rev.* 1367, 1372 (1996).

74 See Goldsmith and Wu, supra note 6, at 49–65 (2006).

75 Id. at 68–72.

76 Id. at 81.

77 Id.

78 Stephen D. Krasner, *Sovereignty: Organized Hypocrisy* (Princeton, NJ: Princeton University Press, 1999), 12.

79 Palestinian Information Office v. Shultz, 853 F.2d 932, 939–40 (D.C. Cir. 1988).

80 Id. at 941–42.

81 See id. at 935 (noting that the mission closure operated "in that subtle realm in which foreign policy matters brush up against rights of free speech").

82 DKT Memorial Fund, Ltd. v. Agency for Int'l Dev., 887 F.2d 275, 294–95 (D.C. Cir. 1989).

83 See Brown v. Socialist Workers '74 Campaign Comm., 459 U.S. 87, 98 (1982).

84 *DKT*, 887 F.2d at 294.

85 130 S. Ct. 2705 (2010). Chapter 5 contains a fuller analysis and critique of *Humanitarian Law Project*. The discussion in this chapter focuses on the cross-border associational aspects of the case.

86 Id. at 2731.

87 Id. at 2713–14.

88 Id. at 2729–30.

89 Id. at 2717–28, 2728. Under the relevant provisions, it is enough that the speakers provide material support knowing that the recipient is a foreign terrorist organization. The law does not require a specific intent to aid violent or other terrorist causes. Id. at 2717.

90 Id. at 2723.

91 Id. at 2724.

92 Id. at 2730–31.

93 David Cole, "The First Amendment's Borders: The Place of Holder v. Humanitarian Law Project in First Amendment Doctrine," 6 *Harv. L. & Pol'y Rev.* 147, 162–63 (2012).

94 *HLP*, 130 S. Ct. at 2730.

95 See Jack M. Balkin, "The Future of Free Expression in a Digital Age," 36 *Pepp. L. Rev.* 427, 438 (2009). See also Jack M. Balkin, "Digital Speech and Democratic Culture: A Theory of Freedom of Expression for the Information Society," 79 *N.Y.U. L. Rev.* 1 (2004).

96 Lee C. Bollinger, *Uninhibited, Robust, and Wide-Open: A Free Press for a New Century* (New York: Oxford University Press, 2010), 116–17.

97 Id. at 117.

98 *Mandel*, 408 U.S. at 784–85 (Marshall, J., dissenting).

99 Reno v. ACLU, 521 U.S. 844, 850, 868 (1999). Although the Court noted that some of the material to which Congress sought to restrict access originated beyond U.S. borders, it did not decide any specific issue relating to cross-border expression.

100 Saskia Sassen, *Losing Control?: Sovereignty in an Age of Globalization* (New York: Columbia University Press, 1996), 59.

101 See Zephyr Teachout, "Extraterritorial Electioneering and the Globalization of Elections," 27 *Berkeley J. of Int'l L.* 161 (2009).

102 For arguments that the absolute ban is unconstitutional, see Note, "'Foreign' Campaign Contributions and the First Amendment," 110 *Harv. L. Rev.* 1886 (1997); Toni M. Massaro, "Corporate Speech and Electoral Spending: Foreign Nationals, Electoral Spending, and the First Amendment," 34 *Harv. J. L. & Pub. Pol.* 663 (2011).

103 See generally Balkin, "Digital Speech and Democratic Culture," supra note 95.

104 Balkin, "The Future of Free Expression in a Digital Age," supra note 95, at 438.

105 Id.

106 Id. at 440.

107 Id. at 444.

108 I discuss whether aliens ought to have due process and First Amendment rights in Chapters 6 and 7.

109 Derek E. Bambauer, "Orwell's Armchair," 79 *U. Chi. L. Rev.* 863 (2012).

110 See Yochai Benkler, "A Free Irresponsible Press: Wikileaks and the Battle Over the Soul of the Networked Fourth Estate," 46 *Harv. Civ. Rts.-Civ. Lib. L. Rev.* 311, 338–42 (2010) (discussing the extensive denial-of-service campaign against WikiLeaks).

111 See id. at 365 (noting the use of Blacklisting during the McCarthy era).

112 Id. at 367–69.

113 Id. at 370.

114 See Cole, supra note 93.

115 Id. at 172.

116 Id. at 172–73.

117 Id. at 172.

118 See Nat'l Council of Resistance of Iran v. Dep't of State, 251 F.3d 192 (D.C. Cir. 2001) ("the Secretary has deemed the Council to be nothing but a foreign terrorist organization, and it is as such that the Secretary must litigate against that entity").

119 Cole, supra note 93, at 173.

120 Id.

121 Id. at 173–74.

122 Principled or not, some lower courts have relied upon this distinction. See, e.g., Al- Haramain Islamic Foundation, Inc. v. U.S. Dept of the Treasury, 660 F.3d 1019 (9th Cir. 2011).

Falsely Shouting Fire in a Global Theater

1 Schenck v. United States, 249 U.S. 47, 52 (1919).

2 Reno v. ACLU, 521 U.S. 844, 850, 868 (1999) (describing the Internet as "a unique and wholly new medium of worldwide human communication," and

a "new marketplace of ideas" containing "vast democratic forums," from which "any person with a phone line can become a town crier with a voice that resonates farther than it could from any soapbox").

3 See Timothy Zick, "Falsely Shouting Fire in a Global Theater: Emerging Complexities of Transborder Expression," 65 *Vand. L. Rev.* 112 (2012).

4 Charlie Savage, "U.S. Weighs Prosecution of WikiLeaks Founder, but Legal Scholars Warn of Steep Hurdles," *New York Times*, December 2, 2010, A13.

5 To be clear, I am not claiming that a global marketplace of ideas presently exists. Repressive regimes and other limitations obviously prevent such a marketplace from fully forming and functioning. See Jack Goldsmith and Tim Wu, *Who Controls the Internet?: Illusions of a Borderless World* (New York: Oxford University Press, 2006), 92–95 (discussing Chinese Internet filtering technologies). Rather, my claim is that transborder information flow is creating a global marketplace in which more and more of the world's population may participate. See Rodney A. Smolla, *Free Speech in an Open Society* (New York: Alfred A. Knopf, Inc., 1992), 352 (suggesting that "the new technologies that increasingly knit the globe into one giant electronic village will tend to create an international marketplace for free speech").

6 See, e.g., David G. Post, *In Search of Jefferson's Moose: Notes on the State of Cyberspace* (New York: Oxford University Press, 2009), 90–99 (discussing Internet and network connectivity).

7 See generally Jack M. Balkin, "The Future of Free Expression in a Digital Age," 36 *Pepperdine L. Rev.* 427 (2009).

8 Jack M. Balkin, "Digital Speech and Democratic Culture: A Theory of Freedom of Expression for the Information Society," 79 *N.Y.U. L. Rev.* 1 (2004).

9 See, e.g., Alexander Tsesis, "Hate in Cyberspace: Regulating Hate Speech on the Internet," 38 *San Diego L. Rev.* 817 (2001).

10 Id. at 858–63 (discussing approaches to Internet hate speech in various Western democracies).

11 See id. at 858 (noting, in particular, that U.S. protection of hateful expression complicates other nations' efforts to regulate it).

12 See Yahoo! Inc. v. La Ligue Contre Le Racisme et L'Antisemitisme, 433 F.3d 1199, 1217 (9th Cir. 2006) (addressing enforceability of French judgment ordering U.S. website to prevent display of Nazi memorabilia for sale in France).

13 These concerns are discussed in Chapter 9.

14 See Anthony Grafton, "A Sketch Map of a Lost Continent: The Republic of Letters," in *World Made by Words: Scholarship and Community in the Modern West* (Cambridge, MA: Harvard University Press, 2009), 9–34.

15 Damien Cave and Anne Barnard, "Minister Wavers on Plans to Burn Koran," *New York Times*, September 9, 2010, A3.

16 See Holder v. Humanitarian Law Project, 130 S. Ct. 2705, 2726 (2010) (upholding "material support" laws as applied to transborder collaboration, based in part on national security and foreign affairs concerns).

17 Sheryl Gay Stolberg, "Obama Strongly Backs Islam Center Near 9/11 Site," *New York Times*, August 14, 2010, A1.

18 See Lillian BeVier, "The First Amendment and Political Speech: An Inquiry into the Substance and Limits of Principle," 30 *Stan. L. Rev.* 299, 331–42 (1978) (discussing evolution of incitement standard).

19 Brandenburg v. Ohio, 395 U.S. 444, 447 (1969).

20 Dennis v. United States, 341 U.S. 494, 509 (1951).

21 *Schenck*, 249 U.S. at 52.

22 See, e.g., Debs v. United States, 249 U.S. 211 (1919) (giving a public speech with intent to obstruct the military draft); *Schenck*, 249 U.S. at 49–51 (distributing pamphlets with intent to interfere with military recruitment and enlistment); Gitlow v. New York, 268 U.S. 652 (1925) (advocating socialist uprising and overthrow of domestic government); Whitney v. California, 274 U.S. 357 (1927) (associating with others to teach and advocate violent overthrow of government).

23 *Cf.* Timothy Zick, "Clouds, Cameras, and Computers: The First Amendment and Networked Public Places," 59 *Fla. L. Rev.* 1, 34–36 (2007) (discussing the effects that technologies, in particular computer networks, may have on definition and regulation of incitement).

24 The fact that U.S. assets or interests potentially imperiled by domestic expression are located abroad ought not to make any difference. The United States can seek to protect its foreign military and other interests from domestic interferences, whether these take the form of tangible aid to enemies, unlawful possession of state secrets, or incitements to unlawful action or violence. If the United States can prosecute foreign speakers based upon the negative effects of their speech inside its territorial borders, surely it may prosecute a domestic speaker who threatens imminent harm to its extraterritorial assets and interests. For discussions of extraterritorial application of U.S. laws, particularly on the basis of domestic effects, see Jeffrey A. Meyer, "Dual Illegality and Geoambiguous Law: A New Rule for Extraterritorial Application of U.S. Law," 95 *Minn. L. Rev.* 110, 125–30 (2010); Austen Parrish, "The Effects Test: Extraterritoriality's Fifth Business," 61 *Vand. L. Rev.* 1455, 1478–82 (2008); Kal Raustiala, "The Geography of Justice," 73 *Fordham L. Rev.* 2501, 2525 (2005).

25 Compare the Ninth Circuit's decision in Planned Parenthood v. American Coalition of Life Activists, 290 F.3d 1058 (9th Cir. 2002) (en banc) (concluding that anti-abortion activists had not incited violence by placing "Wanted" posters identifying physicians who perform abortions and certain identifying information on the Internet, but that materials constituted an unprotected true threat).

26 See, e.g., Gerald Gunther, "Learned Hand and the Origins of Modern First Amendment Doctrine: Some Fragments of History," 27 *Stan. L. Rev.* 719, 755 (1975) (calling the *Brandenburg* formulation "the most speech-protective standard yet evolved by the Supreme Court").

27   See Richard A. Posner, *Not a Suicide Pact:The Constitution in a Time of National Emergency* (New York: Oxford University Press, 2006), 120–25 (suggesting that imminence and other requirements under *Brandenburg* may lack the necessary flexibility to address the threat of extremist expression in the digital era); Robert S. Tanenbaum, Comment, "Preaching Terror: Free Speech or Wartime Incitement?," 55 *Am. U. L. Rev.* 785, 790 (2006) (arguing that the incitement standard "should be recast in the context of the War on Terror"); Laura K. Donohue, "Terrorist Speech and the Future of Free Expression," 27 *Cardozo L. Rev.* 233 (2005) (questioning whether the *Brandenburg* test will ultimately survive new threats to security); Tiffany Kamasara, "Planting the Seeds of Hatred: Why Imminence Should No Longer Be Required to Impose Liability on Internet Communications," 29 *Capital University L. Rev.* 835, 837 (2002).

28   Alexander Tsesis, "Prohibiting Incitement on the Internet," 7 *Va. J.L. & Tech.* 5 (2002).

29   Id.

30   Steven G. Gey, "The Brandenburg Paradigm and Other First Amendments," 12 *U. Pa. J. Const. L.* 971 (2010).

31   Abrams v. United States, 250 U.S. 616, 630 (1919) (Holmes, J., dissenting).

32   Texas v. Johnson, 491 U.S. 397 (1989) (flag burning); United States v. O'Brien, 391 U.S. 367 (1968) (burning of draft card); R.A.V. v. City of St. Paul, 505 U.S. 377 (1992) (cross burning); Virginia v. Black, 538 U.S. 343 (2003) (cross burning).

33   See Cohen v. California, 403 U.S. 15, 26 (1971) (invalidating breach of peace conviction based on wearing of offensive jacket in courthouse corridor). See also Edwards v. South Carolina, 372 U.S. 229 (1963); Cox v. Louisiana, 379 U.S. 536 (1965); Brown v. Louisiana, 383 U.S. 131 (1966); Gregory v. City of Chicago, 394 U.S. 111 (1969); Bachellar v. Maryland, 397 U.S. 564 (1970).

34   See Boos v. Barry, 485 U.S. 312, 316 (1988) (invalidating D.C. ordinance limiting assemblies and protests near foreign embassies).

35   Arch Puddington, "Freedom of Expression after the Cartoon Wars," in Karin Dutsch Karlekar (ed.), *Freedom of the Press 2006: A Global Survey of Media Independence* (Lanham, Md.: Rowman & Littlefield, 2006), 19–29.

36   Steven J. Heyman, *Free Speech and Human Dignity* (New Haven, CT: Yale University Press, 2008).

37   See Lyrissa Barnett Lidsky, "Incendiary Speech and Social Media," 44 *Tex. Tech. L. Rev.* 147 (2012).

38   Helene Cooper, "Obama Tells U.N. New Democracies Need Free Speech," *New York Times*, September 25, 2012, A1.

39   Id. at A8.

40   See Feiner v. New York, 340 U.S. 315, 321 (1951) (upholding official interference with public speech on grounds of hostile audience reaction to speaker). See id. at 326 (Holmes, J., dissenting) (rejecting "the implication of

the Court's opinion that the police had no obligation to protect petitioner's constitutional right to talk").

41 "Enemies of the state" would include persons formally designated as enemy combatants and persons or groups designated as terrorist threats by United States officials, as well as persons or groups not formally aligned with designated enemies who are nevertheless committed to taking or encouraging hostile action against the United States. Aiding the enemy is a specific charge in the military justice system. My discussion focuses primarily on civilian contexts.

42 U.S. Const., art. III, § 3.

43 See Eugene Volokh, "Speech as Conduct: Generally Applicable Laws, Illegal Courses of Conduct, 'Situation-Altering Utterances,' and the Uncharted Zones," 90 *Cornell L. Rev.* 1277, 1342 (2005) (arguing that domestic antiwar speech should "probably" be protected because it may "contribute valuable arguments to an important public debate").

44 See id. (noting the dangers of reliance on an intent standard in this and other contexts).

45 Id. at 1341.

46 *Humanitarian Law Project*, 130 S. Ct. at 2731.

47 Id. at 2713–14.

48 Id. at 2729–30.

49 See David Cole, "The First Amendment's Borders: The Place of Holder v. Humanitarian Law Project in First Amendment Doctrine," 6 *Harv. L. & Pol'y Rev.* 147, 158–60 (2012).

50 See, e.g., Citizens United v. Federal Election Comm'n, 558 U.S. 310, 350 (2010); New York Times Co. v. Sullivan, 376 U.S. 254, 269 (1964); Whitney v. California, 274 U.S. 357, 375 (1927) (Brandeis, J., concurring); NAACP v. Claiborne Hardware Co., 458 U.S. 886, 908 (1982); Scales v. United States, 367 U.S. 203, 229 (1961); De Jonge v. Oregon, 299 U.S. 353, 365 (1937).

51 *Humanitarian Law Project*, 130 S. Ct. at 2732–34 (Breyer, J., dissenting). See also Cole, supra note 49, at 155.

52 See Cole, supra note 49, at 156–58.

53 DeJonge v. Oregon, 299 U.S. 353 (1937).

54 *Humanitarian Law Project*, 130 S. Ct. at 2725.

55 Id.

56 Id.

57 Id.

58 Id. at 2729.

59 There is some irony in this, as the Court specifically rejected the government's argument that the material support provisions regulated only conduct and not speech. Id. at 2724.

60 United States v. O'Brien, 391 U.S. 367, 377 (1968).

61 See, e.g., Linmark Assocs., Inc. v. Twp. of Willingboro, 431 U.S. 85, 97 (1977) (invalidating municipal ban on posting of "for sale" or "sold" signs on homeowners' properties, put in place to prevent so-called "white flight").

62 *Humanitarian Law Project*, 130 S. Ct. at 2725.

63 Cole, supra note 49, at 160–62.

64 Id. at 161.

65 Id. at 154–61.

66 *Humanitarian Law Project*, 130 S. Ct. at 2726.

67 Id.

68 But see Boos v. Barry, 485 U.S. 312, 316 (1988) (refusing to defer to Congress in determining whether restriction on protests near foreign embassies violated free speech and assembly rights).

69 *Humanitarian Law Project*, 130 S. Ct. at 2729.

70 Id. at 2731.

71 For a contrary view, arguing that *Humanitarian Law Project* preserves a number of safe havens for protected speech, see Peter Marguiles, "Advising Terrorism: Hybrid Scrutiny, Safe Harbors, and Freedom of Speech," 63 *Hastings L. J.* 455 (2011). Marguiles argues that the Court's decision has been subject to unwarranted criticism and that the decision and statutory scheme preserve substantial opportunities for lawful and peaceful forms of communication and association.

72 See generally Timothy Zick, "The First Amendment in Trans-Border Perspective: Toward a More Cosmopolitan Orientation," 52 *B.C. L. Rev.* 941 (2011).

73 *Humanitarian Law Project*, 130 S. Ct. at 2740 (Breyer, J., dissenting).

74 U.S. Const. art. III, § 3, cl. 1. The federal crime of treason is codified at 18 U.S.C. § 2381.

75 See generally Tom W. Bell, "Treason, Technology, and Freedom of Expression," 37 *Ariz. St. L. J.* 999, 1005–06 (2005).

76 See United States v. Aguilar, 515 U.S. 593, 606 (1995) (upholding criminal punishment for publishing confidential information in violation of governmental restrictions).

77 See Bell, supra note 75, at 1004 (citing as a possible example Jane Fonda's activities in Vietnam).

78 See Gabriel H. Teninbaum, "American Volunteer Human Shields in Iraq: Free Speech or Treason?," 28 *Suffolk Transnat'l L. Rev.* 139, 158 (2004) (arguing that "human shields" may have acted treasonously, but that for several reasons prosecution was not likely).

79 See Bell, supra note 75, at 1006–09 (positing a hypothetical "Al Qaeda Al," who posts messages to his own blog that could benefit global terrorist networks).

80 See id. at 1010–26 (discussing elements of treason law, as interpreted and applied by courts).

81 See D'Aquino v. United States, 192 F.2d 338 (9th Cir. 1951); Burgman v. United States, 188 F.2d 637 (D.C. Cir. 1951); Gillars v. United States, 182 F.2d 962 (D.C. Cir. 1950); Best v. United States, 184 F.2d 131 (1st Cir. 1950); Chandler v. United States 171 F.2d 921 (1st Cir. 1949).

82 See Bell, supra note 75, at 1012–1026 (addressing application of treas[on] requirements to instances of pure speech); Volokh, supra note 43, at 1341–42 (discussing whether a speaker could be punished for treason merely for making antiwar statements).

83 See Bell, supra note 75, at 1027–28 (arguing that prosecution of pure speech subverts the original meaning of the Treason Clause); David P. Currie, *The Constitution in the Supreme Court: The Second Century, 1888–1986* (Chicago: University of Chicago Press, 1990), 298–99 ("[S]trong arguments have been made that the Framers did mean to forbid punishment of mere 'treasonable' words under any label; otherwise their central goal of eliminating punishment for acts earlier viewed as 'constructive' treason would not have been achieved."); James Willard Hurst, *The Law of Treason in the United States* (Westport, Conn.: Greenwood, 1971), 143 (1945) (discussing framers' views that Treason Clause would prevent "the suppression of political opposition or the legitimate expression of views on the conduct of public policy").

84 Brandenburg v. Ohio, 395 U.S. 444, 447 (1969).

85 Id.

86 See, e.g., Citizens United v. Federal Election Comm'n, 558 U.S. 310, 350 (2010); New York Times Co. v. Sullivan, 376 U.S. 254, 269 (1964); NAACP v. Claiborne Hardware Co., 458 U.S. 886, 908 (1982).

87 See Bell, supra note 75, at 1032–34 (discussing overbreadth problems under current treason law).

88 Geoffrey R. Stone, *Perilous Times: Free Speech in Wartime* (New York: W. W. Norton, 2004).

89 See Bell, supra note 75, at 1040–41 (suggesting an employment standard be used to demonstrate "adherence" to the enemy); Volokh, supra note 43, at 1342 (suggesting that proper test might be whether speaker was being paid by the enemy or otherwise coordinated his activities with the enemy).

90 See Matthew Lippman, "The New Terrorism and International Law," 10 *Tulsa J. Comp. & Int'l L.* 297, 302–03 (2003) (describing the functional structure of contemporary terrorist organizations).

91 See Best, 184 F.2d at 135 (describing defendant's preparation of propaganda broadcast to the U.S. via shortwave radio); Gillars, 182 F.2d at 966 (noting that defendant helped in preparation of German propaganda broadcast to the U.S.); United States v. Burgman, 87 F. Supp. 568, 569 (D.D.C. 1949) (observing that defendant was employed by the German government to prepare propaganda broadcast to the U.S.), aff'd, 188 F.2d 637 (D.C. Cir. 1951).

92 I focus here on citizens. As I discuss in Chapter 6, in narrow circumstances, aliens abroad may also be entitled to some free speech protections.

93 See Haig v. Agee, 453 U.S. 280, 308–09 (1981) (upholding, against First Amendment challenge, revocation of U.S. passport where citizen traveled

411

aged in various efforts to expose Central Intelligence Agency
ations to foreign audiences).

"A Free Irresponsible Press: Wikileaks and the Battle Over
Networked Fourth Estate," 46 *Harv. Civ. Rts.-Civ. Lib. L. Rev.*

es Co. v. Rhinehart, 467 U.S. 20 (1984); Robert C. Post,
"The Management of Speech: Discretion and Rights," 1984 *Sup. Ct. Rev.*
169. See also Snepp v. United States, 444 U.S. 507, 511 (1980); *Haig v. Agee*,
453 U.S. 280 (1981).

97 Benkler, supra note 94, at 371–85. See Lee Bollinger, *Uninhibited, Robust,
and Wide-Open: A Free Press for a New Century* (New York: Oxford University
Press, 2010), 116–17 (urging a shift in the "constitutional paradigm" from a
national to a global forum with regard to press freedoms).

98 See U.S. v. Zehe, 601 F.Supp. 196 (D. Mass. 1985) (Espionage Act applies
to acts of foreign nationals abroad); United States v. Helmich, 521 F.
Supp. 1246, 1252 (M.D. Fla. 1981) ("[I]t is clear that the legislative intent
behind the repeal of section 791 was to extend application of the Espionage
Act to cover acts committed anywhere in the world.").

99 See Gerald L. Neuman, *Strangers to the Constitution*: Immigrants, Borders,
and Fundamental Law (Princeton, NJ: Princeton University Press, 1996),
199 (noting that under a "mutuality of obligation" approach to constitutional
domain, aliens "are within the sphere either when they are within the nation's
territory or on specific occasions when the nation attempts to extract obedience to its laws"); Benkler, supra note 94, at 360 (concluding that Wikileaks
is entitled to the protections afforded to other press entities). I discuss the
extraterritorial domain of free speech protections in Chapter 6.

100 403 U.S. 713 (1971).

101 Id. at 730 (Stewart, J., concurring); id. at 736–40 (White, J., concurring); id.
at 745 (Marshall, J., concurring).

102 Bartnicki v. Vopper, 532 U.S. 514, 528 (2001). The government might
argue that, as a matter of statutory interpretation, the Espionage Act makes
knowing dissemination of confidential materials a criminal offense and that
Assange's sharing of information with the press was thus a criminal offense.
See United States v. Morrison, 604 F. Supp. 655, 660 (D. Md. 1985) (holding that 18 U.S.C. §§ 793(d) and (e) apply to individuals who leak classified material to the press, because the recipients are "not entitled to receive
[the classified material]"). See also Posner, supra note 27, at 108–09 ("[S]
ince the Espionage Act does punish the *communication* of material relating
to the national defense … that could be used to injure the nation, … publication of such material … would seem … to violate the act."). As noted
below, however, that theory would seem to apply with equal measure to outlets like *The New York Times*. The government might also argue that Assange
entered a conspiracy with the person who stole the government information

by providing him with certain forms of assistance in disseminating the files. Prosecution for this sort of criminal conduct would presumably not raise serious First Amendment questions.

103 *Bartnicki*, 532 U.S. at 530. See also New York Times, 403 U.S. at 729–30 (Stewart, J., concurring) (arguing that the responsibility for ensuring confidentiality rests with the executive).

104 Some harmful or deadly disclosures can be restrained in advance of publication or subject to punishment. See Near. v. Minnesota, 283 U.S. 697, 716 (1931) ("No one would question but that a government might prevent actual obstruction to its recruiting service or the publication of the sailing dates of transports or the number and location of troops."). However, the disclosed wartime logs and diplomatic cables do not constitute the sort of "crime-facilitating" speech that lies outside the First Amendment's domain. See Eugene Volokh, "Crime-Facilitating Speech," 57 *Stan. L. Rev.* 1095 (2005). See also Geoffrey R. Stone, "Government Secrecy v. Freedom of the Press," 1 *Harv. L. & Pol'y Rev.* 185, 203–04 (2007) (arguing that to justify punishing the press for publishing confidential information, government must prove the publisher knew the information was confidential, that publication would result in imminent and serious harm, and publication would not meaningfully contribute to public debate).

Expressive Liberties Beyond U.S. Borders

1 See generally Kal Raustiala, *Does the Constitution Follow the Flag? The Evolution of Territoriality in American Law* (New York: Oxford University Press, 2009).

2 Boumediene v. Bush, 553 U.S. 723 (2008) (habeas corpus); In re Iraq and Afghanistan Detainees Litigation, 479 F. Supp. 2d 85 (D.D.C. 2007) (Eighth Amendment's Cruel and Unusual Punishments Clause); Harbury v. Deutch, 233 F.3d 596, 602–04 (D.C. Cir. 2000), *rev'd on other grounds sub nom.* Christopher v. Harbury, 536 U.S. 403 (2002) (Fifth Amendment Due Process Clause).

3 140 U.S. 453, 464 (1891).

4 See Downes v. Bidwell, 182 U.S. 244 (1901); Hawaii v. Mankichi, 190 U.S. 197 (1903); Dorr v. United States, 195 U.S. 138 (1904); Balzac v. Porto Rico, 258 U.S. 298 (1922). For an illuminating discussion of these cases, see Sarah H. Cleveland, "Powers Inherent in Sovereignty: Indians, Aliens, Territories, and the Nineteenth Century Origins of Plenary Power over Foreign Affairs," 81 *Tex. L. Rev.* 1 (2002).

5 *Downes*, 182 U.S. at 277.

6 Louis Henkin, "The Constitution as Compact and as Conscience: Individual Rights Abroad and at Our Gates," 27 *Wm. & Mary L. Rev.* 11, 21 (1985); Kal Raustiala, "The Geography of Justice," 73 *Fordham L. Rev.* 2501, 2516–17 (2005); Raustiala, *Does the Constitution Follow the Flag?*, supra note 1.

7   Raustiala, "The Geography of Justice," supra note 6, at 2504.

8   354 U.S. 1 (1957).

9   Id. at 18–19.

10 Id. at 5–6 (plurality opinion).

11 Id. at 6.

12 Id. at 12.

13 See id. at 53 (Frankfurter, J., concurring); id. at 75–76 (Harlan, J., concurring).

14 See id. at 75 (Harlan, J., concurring).

15 494 U.S. 259, 274–75 (1990).

16 Id. at 270.

17 Id. at 265–66. See also Johnson v. Eisentrager, 339 U.S. 763, 769–72 (1950) (suggesting that enemy aliens held abroad were not entitled to writ of habeas corpus in part owing to the fact that the U.S. government had no obligation to protect the rights of those who had no duty of loyalty to the United States).

18 *Verdugo-Urquidez*, 494 U.S. at 276 (Kennedy, J., concurring).

19 Id. at 278.

20 Id. at 284 (Brennan, J., dissenting).

21 Id.

22 553 U.S. 723, 765 (2008).

23 Id. at 765 (quoting Murphy v. Ramsey, 114 U.S. 15, 44 (1885)).

24 Id. at 760.

25 Id.

26 Id. at 766.

27 A sampling of this literature includes Sarah H. Cleveland, "Embedded International Law and the Constitution Abroad," 110 *Colum. L. Rev.* 225 (2010); Eric A. Posner, "Boumediene and the Uncertain March of Judicial Cosmopolitanism," 2008 *Cato Sup. Ct. Rev.* 23, 43–46; J. Andrew Kent, "A Textual and Historical Case Against a Global Constitution," 95 Geo. L. J. 463 (2007); Raustiala, "The Geography of Justice," supra note 6; and Jules Lobel, "The Constitution Abroad," 83 *Am. J. Int'l. L.* 871 (1989).

28 See, e.g., Posner, supra note 27, at 43–46.

29 Gerald L. Neuman, "The Extraterritorial Constitution after Boumediene v. Bush," 82 *S. Cal. L. Rev.* 259, 282 (2009).

30 See Reid v. Covert, 354 U.S. 1, 6 (1957). See also Henkin, supra note 6.

31 This has, however, been the position of the American Law Institute since 1987. See Restatement (Third) of Foreign Relations Law of the United States § 721 (1987) ("The provisions of the United States Constitution safeguarding individual rights ... generally limit governmental authority whether it is exercised in the United States or abroad").

32 Gerald L. Neuman, *Strangers to the Constitution*: Immigrants, Borders, and Fundamental Law (Princeton, NJ: Princeton University Press, 1996), 7–8.

33 *But* see Lobel, supra note 27, at 315.

34 Gerald L. Neuman, "Extraterritorial Rights and Constitutional Methodology After Rasul v. Bush," 153 *U. Pa. L. Rev.* 2073, 2077 (2005); *Verdugo-Urquidez*, 494 U.S. at 284 (Brennan, J., dissenting).

35 See Laker Airways Ltd. v. Pan Am. World Airways, Inc., 604 F. Supp. 280, 287 (D.D.C. 1984) (noting that it is not clear "whether even American citizens are protected specifically by the First Amendment with respect to their activities abroad").

36 See Haig v. Agee, 453 U.S. 280, 308 (1981) (upholding revocation of citizen's passport based in part on the nature of his overseas expression).

37 Id. at 308.

38 Id. at 309.

39 See Carlson v. Schlesinger, 511 F.2d 1327, 1331–33 (D.C. Cir. 1975) (applying First Amendment time, place, and manner standards to restrictions on soldiers' pamphleteering on military bases in Vietnam).

40 United States v. Aguilar, 883 F.2d 662 (9th Cir. 1989), *cert. denied*, 498 U.S. 1046 (1991), *abrogated on other grounds by* Pub. L. 99–603, Title I, Part B, § 112 (1986).

41 See Clancy v. Office of Foreign Assets Control, 559 F.3d 595, 605 (7th Cir. 2009); Karpova v. Snow, 402 F. Supp. 2d 459, 473–74 (S.D.N.Y. 2005).

42 Bullfrog Films, Inc. v. Wick, 646 F. Supp. 492 (C.D. Cal. 1986), *aff'd* 847 F.2d 502, 512 (9th Cir. 1988).

43 646 F. Supp. at 503.

44 Id. at 503 n. 16.

45 Id.

46 See, e.g., *Laker Airways Ltd.*, 604 F. Supp. at 287.

47 719 F. Supp. 670, 676 (N.D. Ill. 1989).

48 Id. at 672.

49 Id.

50 Id. at 675.

51 Id. at 676.

52 Id.

53 See id. at 678, 680. The court did adopt an elastic conception of the U.S. information market. For example, it treated as within the U.S. speech marketplace a book "being sent to, or brought into, a foreign country by an American diplomat, an American national studying abroad, or even an American doing a little reading on a vacation." Id. at 676.

54 Id. at 676–77.

55 Id. at 677.

56 Id. at 680–81.

57 381 U.S. 301, 305 (1965).

58 433 F.3d 1199, 1217 (9th Cir. 2006).

59 Id.

60 Id. at 1217–18.

61 Jeremy W. Peters, "News Media Seek Loosening of the Pentagon's Rules at Guantanamo," *New York Times*, July 21, 2010, at A15.

62 See Leo Shane III, "Army Used Profiles to Reject Reports," *Stars & Stripes* (Mideast ed.), August 29, 2009, at 1, 2 (reporting that the Pentagon used secret profiles of journalists' work to influence coverage of the war in Afghanistan).

63 See, e.g., Citizens United v. FEC, 558 U.S. 310, 350–51 (2010) (rejecting the proposition that the institutional press has any constitutional privilege beyond that of other speakers).

64 See Nation Magazine v. U.S. Dep't of Def., 762 F. Supp. 1558, 1572 (S.D.N.Y. 1991) (acknowledging the press's "affirmative right to gather news, ideas and information" in Iraq).

65 See Flynt v. Rumsfeld, 180 F. Supp. 2d 174, 175–76 (D.D.C. 2002), aff'd, 355 F.3d 697 (D.C. Cir. 2004) (declining publisher's request to enjoin the secretary of defense from interfering with a plan to have correspondents accompany American troops during combat in Afghanistan); Nation Magazine v. U.S. Dep't of Def., 762 F. Supp. 1558, 1572 (S.D.N.Y. 1991) (acknowledging that the "affirmative right to gather news, ideas and information" was implicated by Defense Department restrictions on coverage of Operation Desert Storm, but refusing to grant the journalists' requested injunctive relief).

66 David A. Anderson, "Freedom of the Press in Wartime," 77 *Colo. L. Rev.* 49, 66 (2006).

67 See David Cole, "Are Foreign Nationals Entitled to the Same Constitutional Rights as Citizens?," 23 *T. Jefferson L. Rev.* 367 (2003) ("The difficulty of the question is reflected in the deeply ambivalent approach of the Supreme Court, an ambivalence matched only by the alternately xenophobic and xenophilic attitude of the American public toward immigrants."). See also Galvan v. Press, 347 U.S. 522 (1954) (allowing deportation of foreign nationals based on political associations).

68 Kleindienst v. Mandel, 408 U.S. 753, 762 (1972). Nor, it has held, do they have any First Amendment right to remain in the country if they arrived illegally and are deemed excludable. See United States *ex rel.* Turner v. Williams, 194 U.S. 279, 292 (1904) (holding that an excludable alien is not entitled to First Amendment rights because he "does not become one of the people to whom these things are secured by our Constitution").

69 339 U.S. 763, 784 (1950).

70 See, e.g., DKT Mem'l Fund Ltd. v. Agency for Int'l Dev., 887 F.2d 275, 283–85 (D.C. Cir. 1989).

71 See Nina J. Crimm, "The Global Gag Rule: Undermining National Interests by Doing unto Foreign Women and NGOs What Cannot Be Done at Home," 40 *Cornell Int'l L. J.* 587 (2007).

72 Laker Airways Ltd., 604 F. Supp. at 287, 290.

73 Kermit Roosevelt III, "Guantanamo and the Conflict of Laws: *Rasul* and Beyond," 153 *U. Pa. L. Rev.* 2017, 2066 (2005).

74 See, e.g., Michael J. Lebowitz, "'Terrorist Speech': Detained Propagandists and the Issue of Extraterritorial Application of the First Amendment," 9 *First Am. L. Rev.* 573, 589 (2010–11) ("it seems quite likely that overseas alien propagandists cannot hang their hats on First Amendment protections").

75 Neuman, "Extraterritorial Rights," supra note 34, at 2082.

76 Id.

77 Id.

78 See Neuman, "The Extraterritorial Constitution," supra note 29, at 287 (observing that the extent of First Amendment protection abroad may depend on such factors as "where the speech originated, where its intended audience was, and the location of detention and trial").

79 Neuman, "Extraterritorial Rights," supra note 34, at 2082.

80 See William Magnuson, "The Responsibility to Protect and the Decline of Sovereignty: Free Speech Protection Under International Law," 43 *Vand. J. Transnat'l L.* 255, 290–91 (2010) (proposing an international duty to intervene on behalf of free speech rights in repressive regimes).

81 See generally Raustiala, *Does the Constitution Follow the Flag?*, supra note 1; Cleveland, "Embedded International Law," supra note 27.

82 Lee C. Bollinger, *Uninhibited, Robust, and Wide-Open: A Free Press for a New Century* (New York: Oxford University Press, 2010), 5.

83 See generally Jack Goldsmith & Tim Wu, *Who Controls the Internet?: Illusions of a Borderless World* (New York: Oxford University Press, 2006) (arguing that the Internet has not eradicated territorial control of national governments).

84 Jack M. Balkin, "The Future of Free Expression in a Digital Age," 36 *Pepp. L. Rev.* 427, 438 (2009).

85 Chimiene I. Keitner, "Rights Beyond Borders," 36 *Yale J. Int'l L.* 55, 71–81 (2011).

86 See Peter Spiro, *Beyond Citizenship: American Identity after Globalization* (New York: Oxford University Press, 2008), 60 (describing plural citizenship as "a sort of international version of the First Amendment protection for free association").

87 See, e.g., N.Y. Times Co. v. United States, 403 U.S. 713, 717 (1971) (praising the publication of the Pentagon Papers by the press as "precisely that which the Founders hoped and trusted they would do").

88 See Bollinger, supra note 82, at 5 (noting that large number of American press report on global events from foreign locations).

89 See Barry P. McDonald, "The First Amendment and the Free Flow of Information: Towards a Realistic Right to Gather Information in the Information Age," 65 *Ohio St. L. J.* 249, 345–50 (2004) (arguing in favor of a limited right to gather information abroad). As I argued in Chapter 4, McDonald's conception of the right to gather information abroad is too narrow. Among other things, it is limited to the institutional press and requires

that the rights-holder intend to communicate with American audiences on matters of public concern to those audiences. In Chapter 4, I explained why these limitations unduly narrow the transborder right to seek, gather, and distribute information.

90 But see Afroyim v. Rusk, 387 U.S. 292 (1967) (holding that the U.S. government could not revoke citizenship on the ground that a citizen had voted in a foreign election, even though such voting may embarrass the United States in its foreign relations).

91 Jack M. Balkin, "Digital Speech and Democratic Culture: A Theory of Freedom of Expression for the Information Society," 79 *N.Y.U. L. Rev.* 1 (2004).

92 See Bollinger, supra note 82, at 121.

93 Universal Declaration of Human Rights, G.A. Res. 217A, U.N. GAOR, 3d Sess., 1st plen. Mtg., U.N. Doc. A/810 (December 10, 1948), art. 19 [hereinafter UDHR]; International Covenant on Civil and Political Rights, G.A. Res. 2200A (XXI), U.N. GAOR, 21st Sess., Supp. No. 16, U.N. Doc. A/6316, art. 19, ¶¶ 1–2 (December 16, 1966).

94 See Cole, supra note 67.

95 Neuman, *Strangers to the Constitution*, supra note 32, at 110–11.

96 See Neuman, "The Extraterritorial Constitution," supra note 29, at 287.

97 Neuman, *Strangers to the Constitution*, supra note 32, at 111.

98 Id.

99 Id. at 109.

100 Id.

101 Balkin, "Digital Speech and Democratic Culture," supra note 91, at 1.

102 See Cleveland, "Embedded International Law," supra note 27. See also Lobel, supra note 27 (arguing that constitutional domain ought to be determined by reference to *jus cogens*, or customary international law principles).

103 See Neuman, "The Extraterritorial Constitution," supra note 29, at 287.

104 See Neuman, "Extraterritorial Rights," supra note 34, at 2082.

105 Bollinger, supra note 82, at 75–76.

106 See *Laker Airways Ltd.*, 604 F. Supp. at 287.

107 Kleindienst v. Mandel, 408 U.S. 753, 762 (1972).

108 See DKT Mem'l Fund Ltd. v. Agency for Int'l Dev., 887 F.2d 275, 283–85 (D.C. Cir. 1989); see id. at 308 (Ginsburg, J., concurring in part and dissenting in part) (suggesting that alien grant recipients ought to be permitted to raise First Amendment claims).

109 See Crimm, supra note 71, at 592–608 (explaining that the "global gag rule" prevents foreign NGOs from using U.S. government funds to provide abortion counseling to women, to lobby for or against legalized abortions, and to facilitate or offer abortions to women).

110 See Garcetti v. Ceballos, 547 U.S. 410 (2006) (rejecting First Amendment free speech claim of government employee who was acting pursuant to his employment duties when statements were made).

111 See Rosenberger v. Rector and Visitors of University of Va., 515 U.S. 819, 833 (1995) ("[W]hen the government appropriates public funds to promote a particular policy of its own it is entitled to say what it wishes").

112 *Eisentrager,* 339 U.S. at 784.

113 See Holder v. Humanitarian Law Project, 130 S. Ct. 2705, 2726 (2010) (upholding material support provisions under strict scrutiny standard).

114 See Bollinger, supra note 82, at 139–41.

115 See Magnuson, supra note 80.

Transborder Religious Liberties

1 See, e.g., William W. Van Alstyne, "What Is 'An Establishment of Religion'?", 65 *N.C. L. Rev.* 909 (1987); Thomas v. Review Bd. 450 U.S. 707, 722 (Rehnquist, J., dissenting) (noting that "we simply do not know how [the framers] would view the scope of the two [religion] Clauses").

2 The establishment prohibition was extended to the states in 1947. See Everson v. Board of Educ., 330 U.S. 1, 15–16 (1947).

3 See Reynolds v. United States, 98 U.S. 145, 162 (1878) ("Congress cannot pass a law for the government of the Territories which shall prohibit the free exercise of religion").

4 See Bruce Nichols, *The Uneasy Alliance: Religion, Refugee Work, and U.S. Foreign Policy* (New York: Oxford University Press, 1988).

5 Universal Declaration of Human Rights (UDHR), art. 18.

6 Articles 18 and 27 of the International Covenant on Civil and Political Rights, adopted in 1966 and entered into force in 1976, expand on the rights identified in article 18 of the UDHR.

7 International Religious Freedom Act of 1988 § 401, Pub. L. No. 105–292, 112 Stat. 2787 (codified as amended in scattered portions of 8 and 22 U.S.C.).

8 Employment Div. v. Smith, 494 U.S. 872, 879–80 (1990).

9 Church of Lukumi Babalu Aye, Inc. v. City of Hialeah, 508 U.S. 520, 534 (1993).

10 Pub. L. No. 103–141, 107 Stat. 1488 (November 16, 1993), codified at 42 U.S.C. §2000bb through 42 U.S. C. §2000bb-4.

11 City of Boerne v. Flores, 521 U.S. 507 (1997).

12 See John H. Mansfield, "The Religion Clauses of the First Amendment and Foreign Relations," 36 *DePaul L. Rev.* 1, 18 (1986).

13 Church of the Holy Trinity v. United States, 143 U.S. 457, 464–72 (1892).

14 Harisiades v. Shaughnessy, 342 U.S. 580, 597 (1952) (Frankfurter, J., concurring).

15 Kleindienst v. Mandel, 408 U.S. 753, 772 (Douglas, J., dissenting).

16 Lamont v. Postmaster General, 381 U.S. 301 (1965).

17 See Ohno v. Yasuma, – – F.3d – -, 2013 WL 3306351 *12 (9th Cir. 2013) ("Nor has any court yet decided whether the First Amendment's Free

Exercise Clause applies to religious expression initiated domestically but directed to a foreign audience.").

18 See Mansfield, supra note 12, at 19 (noting the lack of precedent regarding the "unlimited governmental power to exclude information that originates outside the country, such as mail or electronic transmissions, including information important to religion").

19 319 F. Supp. 945, 946 (D.D.C. 1970).

20 Id.

21 Id. at 947–48.

22 It is possible that cross-border free exercise activities could constitute a "hybrid" speech-free exercise claim subject to heightened scrutiny under *Smith*. See *Smith*, 494 U.S. at 881. However, given the analysis in other cross-border communication cases, it is perhaps more likely that a court would find that the restriction affected conduct rather than pure speech and was thus not entitled to hybrid claim review.

23 130 S. Ct. 2705 (2010).

24 18 U.S.C. § 2339 (B)(j).

25 See American Civil Liberties Union, "Blocking Faith, Freezing Charity: Chilling Muslim Charitable Giving in the 'War on Terrorism Financing'" (published June, 2009).

26 Id. at 15.

27 See Nat'l Council of Resistance of Iran v. Dep't of State, 251 F. 3d 192 (D.C. Cir. 2001).

28 See Zemel v. Rusk, 381 U.S. 1, 16–17 (1965) (upholding the secretary of state's decision to refuse to issue passports for travel to Cuba in part on the ground that travel to Cuba was action not speech); Haig v. Agee, 453 U.S. 280, 310 (1981) (sustaining the secretary of state's revocation of citizen's passport in part on the ground that he was engaged in action rather than speech).

29 For criticisms of *Smith*, see, e.g., Michael W. McConnell, "Free Exercise Revisionism and the *Smith* Decision," 57 *U. Chi. L. Rev.* 1109 (1990); Douglas Laycock, "The Remnants of Free Exercise," 1990 *Sup. Ct. Rev.* 1. Although it has many detractors, *Smith* does have some supporters in the academy. See, e.g., Marci A. Hamilton, *God vs. The Gavel: Religion and the Rule of Law* (New York: Cambridge University Press, 2005).

30 Mansfield, supra note 12, at 29–33.

31 Id. at 29.

32 Id.

33 Id. at 39, 31.

34 In some parts of the world, attempts at religious conversion remain illegal. See, e.g., Stanislaus v. State of Madhya Pradesh, 1977 A.I.R. (S.C.) 908 (India). However, international or supranational laws may negate or call some of these laws into question.

35 Mansfield, supra note 12, at 31.

36 Id. at 32.

37 Id.

38 See Michael G. Freedman, "Prosecuting Terrorism: The Material Support Statute and Muslim Charities," 38 *Hastings Const. L. Q.* 1113 (2011); Kathryn A. Ruff, "Scared to Donate: An Examination of the Effects of Designating Muslim Charities as Terrorist Organizations on the First Amendment Rights of Donors," 9 *N.Y.U. J. Leg. & Pub. Pol'y* 447 (2005).

39 Holy Land Found. for Relief & Dev. v. Ashcroft, 333 F.3d 156, 167 (D.C. Cir. 2003).

40 President Barack Obama, "The President's Speech in Cairo: A New Beginning" (June 4, 2009).

41 Id.

42 See Ruff, supra note 38, at 495–502 (offering regulatory and policy suggestions for clarifying terrorism financing laws).

43 Mansfield, supra note 12, at 32.

44 Id. at 35–37.

45 But see Rasul v. Myers, 512 F.3d 644, 668–69 (D.C. Cir. 2008) (declining to decide whether the federal Religious Freedom Restoration Act applies extraterritorially to aliens held at Guantanamo Bay, Cuba).

46 98 U.S. 145, 168 (1878).

47 Reid v. Covert, 354 U.S. 1, 74–75 (1957) (Harlan, J., concurring).

48 See Boumediene v. Bush, 128 S.Ct. 2229, 2259 (2008).

49 Chimene I. Keitner, "Rights Beyond Borders," 36 *Yale J. Intl. L.* 55, 66 (2011).

50 Mansfield, supra note 12, at 35.

51 Id. at 36.

52 Id.

53 Id.

54 Kern v. Dynalectron, 577 F. Supp. 1196 (N.D. Tex. 1983), *aff'd* 746 F.2d 810 (5th Cir. 1984).

55 Id. at 1200. See 42 U.S.C. § 2000e-(2)(e).

56 See Mansfield, supra note 12, at 37–38 (suggesting that the same restriction applied to a pilgrimage route in Oregon might be invalid).

57 As one scholar has noted, religious missionaries and others who are dependent on federal logistical and other support overseas are not likely to assert free exercise claims in many cases. See Nichols, supra note 4, at 8 (noting that domestic and international law may be of limited value in terms of enforcing religious liberties in foreign contexts).

58 Boumediene, 533 U.S. at 765 (quoting Murphy v. Ramsey, 114 U.S. 15, 44 (1885)).

59 See Boumediene, 553 U.S. at 766.

60 See Rasul v. Myers, 512 F.3d 644, 668–69 (D.C. Cir. 2008) (declining to decide whether the Religious Freedom Restoration Act applies to aliens held at Guantanamo Bay).

61 See Gerald L. Neuman, *Strangers to the Constitution: Immigrants, Borders, and Fundamental Law* (Princeton, NJ: Princeton University Press, 1996), 109 (expressing concern that expansion of First Amendment rights to aliens abroad will dilute core rights at home).

62 See id. at 109.

63 See id. at 134–38 (discussing judicial review of alien exclusions).

64 For practical and constitutional reasons, free exercise limits would not apply on the battlefield and perhaps in other military contexts.

65 Title VII of the Civil Rights Act exempts aliens employed by the government outside the limits of the United States. 42 U.S.C. § 2000e-16.

66 See Office of Inspector Gen., No. 9–000–09–009-P, "Audit of USAID's Faith-Based and Community Initiatives, Audit Report" 5–7 (2009).

67 Restatement (Third) of Foreign Relations Law of the United States § 721 & cmts. a, b & d (1987 & Supp. 2008).

68 For example, in the case of employer-sponsored religious displays or official prayers, U.S. government employees stationed abroad would be entitled to assert Establishment Clause claims.

69 521 F.2d 234, 235 (5th Cir. 1975) (per curiam).

70 948 F.2d 825, 843 (2d Cir. 1991).

71 Compare Flast v. Cohen, 392 U.S. 83, 102 (1968) (allowing taxpayers to challenge congressional appropriations under Establishment Clause) with Hein v. Freedom from Religion Foundation, Inc., 551 U.S. 587 (2007) (denying taxpayer standing to challenge faith-based executive expenditures made from general congressional appropriations).

72 The schools were located in the Philippines, Egypt, Jamaica, Micronesia, and South Korea. *Woods*, 948 F.2d at 828. The ASHA program authorizes the president to furnish assistance to schools located outside the United States or sponsored by U.S. citizens and serving as study and demonstration centers for ideas and practices of the United States. 22 U.S.C. § 2174(a) (2006). The foreign affiliates are required to operate as "centers for American educational ideas and practices, with programs of study that reflect favorably on and increase understanding of the United States." Final Program Criteria for Screening of Applications for Grants Made by American Schools and Hospitals Abroad (ASHA) Program, 44 Fed. Reg. 67,543, 67,544 (Nov. 26, 1979).

73 *Woods*, 948 F.2d at 828.

74 Final Program Criteria for Screening of Applications for Grants Made by American Schools and Hospitals Abroad (ASHA) Program, 44 Fed. Reg. at 67,544.

75 *Woods*, 948 F.2d at 834.

76 494 U.S. 259 (1990).

77 *Woods*, 948 F.2d at 834–41.

78 Id. at 835.

79 Id. at 835–39. The Court did acknowledge that, in some post-ratification contexts, Congress had directly supported religion in the Northwest Territories and had given funds to the Kaskaskia Indians for religious purposes. Id. at 838. But it observed that these grants were discontinued. It ultimately dismissed this limited post-ratification history as unreliable and, in any event, insufficient to demonstrate that the Establishment Clause did not apply beyond U.S. territories.

80 Id.

81 Id. at 834.

82 Id. at 840.

83 For example, the court treated certain U.S. territories, including the Philippines, as if they were located abroad rather than within U.S. territorial limits. Id. at 828. It also failed to clarify whether the situs of the funding was a crucial aspect of its decision – in other words, whether the same rationale would apply where funds are given directly to foreign recipients rather than U.S. sponsors. See id. at 834.

84 See Ira C. Lupu & Robert W. Tuttle, "The Faith-Based Initiative and the Constitution," 55 *DePaul L. Rev.* 1, 116–17 (2005).

85 For example, what, if any, role would concerns regarding psychological coercion play in school contexts abroad? Is the "reasonable observer," which we may assume to be a U.S. citizen or permanent resident alien, deemed to have knowledge of the foreign religious culture? Do foreign policy considerations that are related to working with religious leaders and communities constitute a secular purpose?

86 See Mansfield, supra note 12, at 25–26 (ultimately rejecting this proposal).

87 Id. at 34.

88 See Lemon v. Kurtzman, 403 U.S. 602 (1971); Committee for Pub. Educ. v. Nyquist, 413 U.S. 756 (1973); Lynch v. Donnelly, 465 U.S. 668 (1984); Bowen v. Kendrick, 487 U.S. 589 (1988).

89 Mansfield, supra note 12, at 34.

90 Woods, 948 F.2d at 842.

91 Id.

92 Id.

93 Mansfield, supra note 12, at 34.

94 Id.

95 Neuman, supra note 61, at 110–11.

96 Mansfield, supra note 12, at 3.

97 Id. at 40.

The First Amendment in International Forums

1   See U.S. Const., art. I, §8, cl. 1 (Spending Clause), cl. 11 (power to declare war), cl. 14 (power to make rules for government and regulation of land and

naval forces), cl. 18 (Necessary and Proper Clause); art. II, § 1 (Executive Vesting Clause); § 2, cl. 2 (Treaty Clause); § 3 (executive power to receive ambassadors and other public ministers). See also United States v. Curtiss-Wright Co., 299 U.S. 304, 318 (1936) (discussing the express and implied powers of "external sovereignty").

2 Curtiss-Wright, 299 U.S. at 319.

3 Louis Henkin, *Foreign Affairs and the Constitution* (New York: Oxford University Press, 1996), 41.

4 Id.

5 Id.

6 Id. See U.S. Const., art. II.

7 Henkin, supra note 3, at 41–42.

8 Id. at 42.

9 Id. at 43.

10 U.S. Const., art. I, § 8.

11 Henkin, supra note 3, at 63–64.

12 See Agency for Int'l Development v. Alliance for Open Society Int'l, Inc., 133 S. Ct 2321 (2013) (invalidating federal funding condition that required recipients to adopt and espouse an anti-prostitution message).

13 Rust v. Sullivan, 500 U.S. 173 (1991).

14 B. S. Murty, *The International Law of Propaganda: The Ideological Instrument and World Public Order* lxvii (New Haven, Conn.: Yale University Press, 1989).

15 U.S. Const., art. III, § 2, cl. 1.

16 U.S. Const., art. I, § 9.

17 Earl Fry, *The Expanding Role of State and Local Governments in U.S. Foreign Affairs* (Council on Foreign Relations Press, 1998); John Kincaid, "Constituent Diplomacy in Federal Politics and the Nation-State: Conflict and Co-operation," in H.J. Michelmann and P. Soldatos (eds.), *Federalism and International Relations: The Role of Subnational Units* (New York: Oxford University Press, 1990); Richard Bilder, "The Role of States and Cities in Foreign Relations," 83 *Am. J. Int'l L.* 821 (1989).

18 Sarah H. Cleveland, "Crosby and the 'One-Voice' Myth in U.S. Foreign Relations," 46 *Vill L. Rev.* 975 (2001).

19 Matthew C. Porterfield, "State and Local Foreign Policy Initiatives and Free Speech: The First Amendment as an Instrument of Federalism," 35 *Stan. J. Int'l. L.* 1 (1999).

20 See Robert A. Schapiro, "Foreword: In The Twilight of the Nation-State: Subnational Constitutions in the New World Order," 39 *Rutgers L. Rev.* 801, 802 (2008) ("Foreign policymaking is no longer the exclusive preserve of the federal government.").

21 See Boos v. Barry, 485 U.S. 312 (1988).

22 Holder v. Humanitarian Law Project, 130 S. Ct. 2705, 2725 (2010) (expressing concern that foreign allies might "react sharply" if the United States did not prevent citizens from assisting foreign terrorist organizations).

23 For discussions of the government speech principle, see generally Randall P. Bezanson and William G. Buss, "The Many Faces of Government Speech," 86 *Iowa L. Rev.* 1377 (2001); Mark G. Yudof, *When Government Speaks: Politics, Law, and Government Expression in America* (Berkeley: University of Cal. Press, 1983).

24 Cleveland, supra note 18.

25 U.S. Const., art. VI.

26 Zschernig v. Miller, 389 U.S. 429 (1968).

27 Id. at 435.

28 The United States did not claim that the state judges' speech would actually disrupt foreign relations; nor was there any record evidence of diplomatic protests or other foreign relations repercussions.

29 Crosby v. National Foreign Trade Council, 530 U.S. 363 (2000).

30 American Insurance Ass'n v. Garamendi, 539 U.S. 396 (2003).

31 Id. at 420 n. 11.

32 Holder v. Humanitarian Law Project, 130 S. Ct. 2705 (2010).

33 See DKT Memorial Fund, Ltd. v. Agency for International Development, 887 F.2d 275, 295 (D.C. Cir. 1989) (deferring to Congress's foreign policy concerns regarding limitations on use of federal funds by foreign organizations that provide abortion counseling abroad); Palestine Information Office v. Shultz, 853 F.2d 932, 935 (D.C. Cir. 1988) (noting that the State Department's decision to close a foreign mission "operates in that subtle realm in which foreign policy matters brush up against rights of free speech and free expression").

34 Meese v. Keene, 481 U.S. 465, 485 (1987).

35 See Gartner v. U.S. Info. Agency, 726 F. Supp. 1183, 1189 (S.D. Iowa 1989) (rejecting Free Speech Clause challenge); Essential Info., Inc. v. U.S. Info. Agency, 134 F.3d 1165, 1169 (D.C. Cir. 1998) (holding that propaganda materials are exempt from disclosure); Judicial Watch, Inc. v. U.S. Dept. of Commerce, 337 F. Supp 2d 146, 168 (D.D.C. 2004) (same) As discussed in Chapter 4, the Smith-Mundt Act's ban on distribution of U.S. foreign propaganda was partially repealed by the Smith-Mundt Modernization Act of 2012. See H.R. 5736, 112th Cong., 2d sess.

36 8 U.S.C. § 1182.

37 See, e.g., Bd. of Trustees of Employees' Ret. Sys. v. Mayor of Baltimore City, 562 A.2d 720, 726 (Md. 1989) (rejecting constitutional and statutory preemption challenges to Baltimore's South Africa divestment ordinances).

38 Cleveland, supra note 18.

39 What we might think of as *horizontal* speech conflicts between presidential administrations and congressional committees are not uncommon. These conflicts have been resolved in the political realm, rather than through litigation in federal courts.

40 Schapiro, supra note 20, at 810–13.

41 The example is drawn from Porterfield, supra note 19, at 38.

42 See, e.g., Pleasant Grove City, Utah v. Summum, 555 U.S. 460 (2009).

43 See Porterfield, supra note 19, at 35–38. See also David Fagundes, "State Actors as First Amendment Speakers," 100 *Nw. U. L. Rev.* 1637 (2006) (arguing for protection in limited circumstances).

44 Andrea L. McArdle, "In Defense of State and Local Government Anti-Apartheid Measures: Infusing Democratic Values into Foreign Policymaking," 62 *Temple L. Rev.* 813 (1989); Perry S. Bechky, "Darfur, Divestment, and Dialogue," 30 *U. Pa. J. Int'l L.* 823 (2009).

45 See Student Gov't Ass'n v. Board of Trustees, 868 F.2d 473, 481 (1st Cir. 1989) ("a state entity … has no First Amendment rights"); Muir v. Alabama Educ. Television Comm'n, 688 F.2d 1033, 1038 (5th Cir. 1982); Estiverne v. Louisiana State Bar Ass'n, 863 F.2d 371, 379 (5th Cir. 1989); Warner Cable Communications Sys., Inc. v. City of Niceville, 911 F.2d 634, 638 (11th Cir. 1990); NAACP v. Hunt, 891 F.2d 1555, 1565 (11th Cir. 1990); *but* see Creek v. Village of Westhaven, 80 F.3d 186, 193 (7th Cir. 1996) (suggesting that curtailment of municipality's speech may raise First Amendment concerns).

46 See Ernest A. Young, "Welcome to the Dark Side," 69 *Brook. L. Rev.* 1277, 1295–1301 (2004); Fagundes, supra note 43.

47 Akhil Reed Amar, "Some New World Lessons for the Old World," 58 *U. Chi. L. Rev.* 483, 504 (1991).

48 558 U.S. 50 (2010).

49 Pleasant Grove City, Utah v. Summum, 555 U.S. 460 (2009).

50 See Creek v. Village of Westhaven, 80 F.3d 186, 192 (7th Cir. 1996) (suggesting that municipalities have First Amendment free speech rights).

51 Jessica Bulman-Pozer and Heather K. Gerken, "Uncooperative Federalism," 118 *Yale L. J.* 1256 (2009).

52 Many of these complications are discussed in Young, supra note 46.

53 See id.

54 Meir Dan-Cohen, "Freedom of Collective Speech: A Theory of Protected Communications by Organizations, Communities, and the State," 79 *Calif. L. Rev.* 1229, 1258–66 (1991).

55 See Pleasant Grove City, Utah v. Summum, 555 U.S. 460 (2009).

56 There are a number of reasons why the government speech doctrine may not be applicable. In the government speech context, a substantial part of the rationale for allowing government speakers to silence others relates to preservation of public resources under the management and control of the government speaker. Thus, when the government funds speech, or employs individuals who speak on its behalf, or regulates speech on public properties which it manages, it is permitted to restrict the use of public resources even where its own message may not be patently clear. No such resource allocation issues arise with respect to state and local enactments that communicate foreign affairs positions. One might argue that subnational

measures that impose divestiture requirements tread on international commerce and thus affect a "federal" resource. However, these measures principally regulate local business practices; their expressive components have only an attenuated connection to federal resources. In sum, the resource rationale for applying the single voice principle is much weaker in vertical speech conflicts than in other conflicts between private and governmental speakers. Moreover, in many government speech contexts the forum remains open to some speech even though the government is itself present as a speaker. By contrast, the single voice principle purports to monopolize and distort an entire forum owing to the fact that the subnational speech may conflict to some degree with foreign affairs policymaking. The First Amendment's democratic principles are arguably less offended when the government acts as a participant in the forum rather than as a monopolist.

57 But see Stephen Gey, "Why Should the First Amendment Protect Government Speech When the Government Has Nothing to Say?," 95 *Iowa L. Rev.* 1259 (2010) (arguing that the Court has accepted government speech arguments without requiring that the governmental entity express any message).

58 See id. Other expressive issues would also arise. For example, the Supreme Court has never addressed in detail whose voice "counts" in the foreign affairs context. Can high-level diplomats express a binding and preemptive position on behalf of the national government? Which diplomatic instruments should courts look to in divining the national message?

59 Catherine Powell, "Dialogic Federalism: Constitutional Possibilities for Incorporation of Human Rights Law in the United States," 150 *U. Pa. L. Rev.* 245 (2001).

60 Perry S. Bechky, "The Politics of Divestment," in Tomer Broude, et al., (eds.), *The Politics of International Economic Law* (New York: Cambridge University Press, 2010).

61 Pub. L. No. 110–174, § 3(b) (2007).

62 See Jo Becker and Ron Nixon, "U.S. Enriches Companies Defying Its Policy on Iran," *New York Times*, March 7, 2010, A8 (reporting that nineteen states have enacted state pension divestment measures, and that the federal government was considering similar legislation with respect to federal contracts).

63 See Bechky, supra notes 49, 60.

64 Mark Landler, "Google Searches for a Foreign Policy," *New York Times*, March 28, 2010, at WK 4.

65 Brad R. Roth, "The First Amendment in the Foreign Affairs Realm: 'Domesticating' the Restrictions on Citizen Participation," 2 *Temp. Pol. & Civ. Rts. L. Rev.* 255, 266 (1993).

66 William W. Van Alstyne, "The First Amendment and the Suppression of Warmongering Propaganda in the United States: Comments and Footnotes," 31 *Law & Cont. Probs.* 530 (1966).

67 See generally Murty, supra note 14. With respect to the specific problem of war propaganda, see Michael G. Kearney, *The Prohibition of Propaganda for War in International Law* (New York: Oxford University Press, 2008).

68 Van Alstyne, supra note 66, at 549.

69 Even if the term "propaganda" could be defined with the requisite specificity, for the reasons discussed in Part II, I do not think such limits would be consistent with the First Amendment. But see id., at 540 (arguing that the U.S. could prohibit private propaganda that conflicts with its own foreign policy).

70 See id. at 531–33 (discussing free speech problems associated with domestic propaganda).

71 Lee C. Bollinger, *Uninhibited, Robust, and Wide-Open: A Free Press for a New Century* (New York: Oxford University Press, 2010), 75.

72 Id. at 137.

73 Id.

74 The Smith-Mundt Act's decades-long ban on distribution of U.S. foreign propaganda on American soil was partially repealed, as to certain State Department materials and foreign broadcasts under the control of the Broadcast Board of Governors, in 2012. See National Defense Authorization Act for Fiscal Year 2013, P.L. 112–239, Div. A, Title X, Sec. 1078, 22 USC §1461–1a.

75 See Mark Yudof, *When Government Speaks: Politics, Law, and Government Expression in America* (Berkeley: University of California Press, 1983), Ch. 14.

76 See, e.g., Murty, supra note 14, at 142.

77 In general, owing to justiciability doctrines, courts are not the most likely source of guidance in this area. See, e.g., Baker v. Carr, 369 U.S. 186 (1962) (discussion the political question doctrine); Hein v. Freedom From Religion Found., 551 U.S. 587 (2007) (limiting standing to challenge government funding for religious projects).

78 See "Engaging Religious Communities Abroad: A New Imperative for U.S. Foreign Policy," in R. Scott Appleby, Richard Cizik, & Thomas Wright (eds.), *Report of the Task Force on Religion and the Making of U.S. Foreign Policy* (The Chicago Council on Global Affairs, 2010).

79 Lemon v. Kurtzman, 403 U.S. 602, 612–13 (1971); Agostini v. Felton, 521 U.S. 203, 223–33 (1997).

80 See, e.g., Allegheny County v. ACLU, 492 U.S. 573, 593 (1989).

81 See McCreary County v. ACLU, 545 U.S. 844, 861 (2005); Santa Fe Indep. Sch. Dist. v. Doe, 530 U.S. 290, 308 (2000).

Cosmopolitan Engagement

1 Yahoo! Inc. v. La Ligue Contre Le Racisme et l'Antisemitisme, 169 F. Supp.2d 1181 (N.D.Cal. 2001) (refusal to recognize a foreign injunction against the posting on the Internet of Nazi-related materials), *rev'd on other grounds*, 433 F.3d 1199 (9th Cir. 2006).

2 With regard to America's exceptional protection for freedom of speech in particular, see Frederick Schauer, "The Exceptional First Amendment," in Michael Ignatieff ed., *American Exceptionalism and Human Rights* (Princeton, N.J.: Princeton University Press, 2005), 29.

3 Schauer, supra note 2.

4 For a comparative analysis of speech guarantees in several constitutional democracies, see Ronald J. Krotoszynski, Jr., *The First Amendment in Cross-Cultural Perspective: A Comparative Legal Analysis of the Freedom of Speech* (New York: NYU Press, 2006).

5 Reid v. Covert, 354 U.S. 1, 16–17 (1957).

6 For a discussion of transnational processes, see Harold Hongju Koh, "On American Exceptionalism," 55 *Stan. L. Rev.* 1479, 1501–03 (2003); Harold Hongju Koh, "How Is International Human Rights Law Enforced?", 74 *Ind. L. J.* 1397, 1399–1408 (1999).

7 See Harold Hongju Koh, "International Law as Part of Our Law," 98 *Am. J. Int'l L.* 43, 53–54 (2004).

8 Atkins v. Virginia, 536 U.S. 304, 316 n.21 (2002); Lawrence v. Texas, 539 U.S. 558 (2003).

9 Citation of international and foreign authority by U.S. courts has engendered a robust debate among American academics and jurists. See, e.g., Roger P. Alford, "Misusing International Sources to Interpret the Constitution," 98 *Am. J. Int'l L.* 57 (2004); Vicki C. Jackson, "Constitutional Comparisons: Convergence, Resistance, Engagement," 119 *Harv. L. Rev.* 109 (2005); Eugene Kontorovich, "Disrespecting the 'Opinions of Mankind': International Law in Constitutional Interpretation," 8 *Green Bag 2d* 261 (2005); Sanford Levinson, "Looking Abroad when Interpreting the U.S. Constitution: Some Reflections," 39 *Tex. Int'l L. J.* 353 (2004); Mark Tushnet, "When Is Knowing Less Better than Knowing More? Unpacking the Controversy over Supreme Court Reference to Non-U.S. Law," 90 *Minn. L. Rev.* 1275 (2006); Ernest A. Young, "Foreign Law and the Denominator Problem," 119 *Harv. L. Rev.* 148 (2005); John O. McGinnis, "Foreign to Our Constitution," 100 *Nw. U. L. Rev.* 303 (2006).

10 But see Boos v. Barry, 484 U.S. 312, 324 (1988) (suggesting, in a case involving a protest near a foreign embassy, that "the dictates of international law [might] require that First Amendment analysis be adjusted to accommodate the interests of foreign officials").

11 See Sarl Louis Feraud Int'l v. Viewfinder, Inc., 489 F.3d 474, 478–80 (2d Cir. 2007); Telnikoff v. Matusevitch, 702 A.2d 230, 240–51 (Md. 1997); Matusevitch v. Telnikoff, 877 F. Supp. 1, 4–6 (D.D.C. 1995); Bachchan v. India Abroad Publ'ns Inc., 585 N.Y.S. 2d 661, 663–65 (Sup. Ct. 1992).

12 Compare Montré D. Carodine, "Political Judging: When Due Process Goes International," 48 *Wm. & Mary L. Rev.* 1159, 1245 (2007) (arguing that the state action doctrine precludes enforcement of some foreign libel

judgments) *and* Eric P. Enson, "A Roadblock on the Detour Around the First Amendment: Is the Enforcement of English Libel Judgments in the United States Unconstitutional?", 21 *Loy. L.A. Int'l & Comp. L. J.* 159, 160 (same) with Mark D. Rosen, "Exporting the Constitution," 53 *Emory L. J.* 171, 186 (2004) (arguing that enforcement of English libel judgments would not constitute state action) and Molly S. Van Houweling, "Enforcement of Foreign Judgments, the First Amendment, and Internet Speech: Notes for the Next *Yahoo! v. LICRA*," 24 *Mich. J. Int'l L.* 697, 703 (2003) (suggesting that enforcement of foreign judgments might be likened to other generally applicable laws that do not trigger meaningful First Amendment scrutiny).

13 See, e.g., Sharon E. Foster, "Does the First Amendment Restrict Recognition and Enforcement of Foreign Copyright Judgments and Arbitration Awards?", 10 *Pace Int'l. L. Rev.* 361, 390 (1998).

14 See N.Y. C.P.L.R. 302(d), 5304(b)(8) (Consol. 2010); 735 *Ill. Comp. Stat.* 5/12–621(b)(7) (2009).

15 28 U.S.C.A. §§ 4101–4105 (West, 2010).

16 See generally David G. Post, *In Search of Jefferson's Moose*: Notes on the State of Cyberspace (New York: Oxford University Press, 2009).

17 See Rosen, supra note 12. See also Paul Schiff Berman, "Towards a Cosmopolitan Vision of Conflicts of Laws: Redefining Governmental Interests in a Global Era," 153 *U. Pa. L. Rev.* 1819, 1834–39 (2005).

18 Yahoo! Inc. v. La Ligue Contre Le Racisme et l'Antisemitisme, 169 F. Supp. 2d 1181 (N.D.Cal. 2001) (refusal to recognize a French court's injunction barring the posting of Nazi-related materials on the Internet), *rev'd on other grounds*, 433 F.3d 1199 (9th Cir. 2006).

19 The myriad choice of law problems associated with these measures are discussed in John T. Parry, "Oklahoma's Save Our State Amendment and the Conflict of Laws," 64 *Oklahoma L. Rev* . 161 (2012) and Penny M. Venetis, "The Unconstitutionality of Oklahoma's SQ 755 and Other Provisions Like It, Which Bar State Courts from Considering International Law," 59 *Clev. St. L. Rev.* 1 (2011).

20 See Nathan B. Oman, "How to Judge Shari'a Contracts: A Guide to Islamic Marriage Agreements in American Courts," 2011 *Utah L. Rev.* 287.

21 Awad v. Ziriax, 670 F.3d 1111 (10th Cir., 2012).

22 Vicki C. Jackson, *Constitutional Engagement in a Transnational Era* (New York: Oxford University Press, 2010).

23 Id. at 8–9.

24 Roper v. Simmons, 543 U.S. 551, 624 (2005) (Scalia, J., dissenting).

25 See sources cited supra, note 9.

26 For decisions discussing the tension between anti-establishment and equality principles in enforcement of foreign marital judgments, see Soleimani v. Soleimani (Kan. Dist. Ct.., No. 11CV4668, Aug. 28, 2012); Tarikonda v. Pinjari, 2009 WL 930007 (Mich. Ct. App. April 7, 2009).

27 Jackson, supra note 22, at 9.
28 See id. at 66 ("There are relatively few areas of human rights law where a strong transnational consensus has developed; it is clearly lacking in such areas as regulation of religious garb in the public sphere, of abortions, of access to information and many others."). See also Mark Tushnet, "The Inevitable Globalization of Constitutional Law," 49 *Va. J. Int'l L.* 985, 987 (2009) ("globalization does not entail uniformity").
29 See Jackson, supra note 22, at 68 (noting that one of the main obstacles to strong convergence is the lack of a "hierarchically final and authoritative interpreter of international human rights law").
30 For discussion of the benefits of constitutional pluralism and transnational exchange, see Mark D. Rosen, "The SPEECH Act's Unfortunate Parochialism: Of Libel Tourism and Legitimate Pluralism," 53 *Va. J. Int'l L.* 99, 114–17 (2012).
31 Jackson, supra note 22, at 72.
32 Id. at 75.
33 Id. at 71.
34 Id. at 77.
35 Id. at 73.
36 McDonald v. City of Chicago, 130 S. Ct. 3020, 3111 (Stevens, J., dissenting).
37 Jackson, supra note 22, at 118.
38 Id. at 125.
39 Id. at 121.
40 Id. at 85.
41 Id.
42 See Reid v. Covert, 354 U.S. 1, 16–17 (1957) (plurality opinion).
43 Peter J. Spiro, "Treaties, International Law, and Constitutional Rights," 55 *Stan. L. Rev.* 1999, 2001 (2003).
44 Id. at 2017–27.
45 See id. at 2019 (discussing, as an example, the Chemical Weapons Convention and domestic Fourth Amendment adjudication).
46 Spiro, supra note 43, at 2022, 2025.
47 Id. at 2025.
48 Id. at 2018.
49 See Richard B. Lillich, "The Constitution and International Human Rights," 83 *Am. J. Int'l L.* 851, 855 (1989) (discussing U.S. qualification and avoidance of international human rights provisions).
50 See Amy Oberdorfer Nyberg, "Is All Speech Local?: Balancing Conflicting Free Speech Principles on the Internet," 92 *Geo. L. J.* 663, 664 (2004) (discussing U.S. participation in the Council of Europe's Additional Protocol to the Convention on Cybercrime Concerning the Criminalisation of Acts of a Racist and Xenophobic Nature Committed Through Computer Systems).

51 See, e.g., Clive Walker, "Global speech and global terrorism: A tall tale of two cities," 63 *NILQ* 119 (2012).

52 Id. at 132–36.

53 Transcript of Remarks of President Barack Obama, Speech to the United Nations General Assembly (September 25, 2012).

54 See Anthony Lester, "The Overseas Trade in the American Bill of Rights," 88 *Colum. L. Rev.* 537, 552–58 (1988).

55 See Jean-Marie Kamatali, "The U.S. First Amendment Versus Freedom of Expression in Other Liberal Democracies and How Each Influenced the Development of International Law on Hate Speech," 36 *Ohio N.U. L. Rev.* 721 (2010) (concluding that while First Amendment incitement doctrine has been rejected under international human rights law, it has influenced judicial decisions under international criminal law).

56 485 U.S. 312 (1988).

57 *Boos*, 485 U.S. at 324.

58 See Spiro, supra note 43, at 2019–20.

59 Id. at 2020.

60 *Boos*, 485 U.S. at 322.

61 130 S. Ct. 2705 (2010).

62 Id. at 2725.

63 Atkins v. Virginia, 536 U.S. 304, 316 n. 21 (2002); Lawrence v. Texas, 539 U.S. 558 (2003).

64 376 U.S. 254 (1964).

65 395 U.S. 444 (1969).

66 Jackson, supra note 22, at 117.

67 "The Relevance of Foreign Legal Materials in U.S. Constitutional Cases: A Conversation between Justice Antonin Scalia and Justice Stephen Breyer," 3 *Int'l J. Const. L.* 519, 522–37 (2005).

68 Loucks v. Standard Oil Co., 120 N.E. 198, 201 (1918).

69 131 S. Ct. 1207 (2011).

70 Id. at 1229 (Alito, J., dissenting).

71 Jeremy Waldron, *The Harm in Hate Speech* (Cambridge, Ma.: Harvard University Press, 2012), 11.

72 See Post, supra note 16, at 166–67.

73 David G. Post, "Against Cyberanarchy," 17 *Berkeley Tech. L. J.* 1365 (2002).

74 Post, *In Search of Jefferson's Moose*, supra note 16, at 170.

75 See Berman, "Towards a Cosmopolitan Vision," supra note 17. See also Paul Schiff Berman, "The Globalization of Jurisdiction," 151 *U. Pa. L. Rev.* 311 (2002); Paul Schiff Berman, "Global Legal Pluralism," 80 *S. Cal. L. Rev.* 1155 (2007).

76 Berman, "Towards a Cosmopolitan Vision," supra note 17, at 1857.

77 Id. at 1860.

78 Id. at 1865.
79 Id. at 1862.
80 Id. at 1845.
81 Id.
82 Id. at 1868.
83 Id.
84 Id. at 1851.
85 Id. at 1865.
86 Id. at 1862.
87 376 U.S. 254 (1964).
88 U.K. libel law places the burden on the defendant to prove truthfulness, while *Sullivan* requires that the plaintiff in cases involving public officials, public figures, and matters of public concern prove actual malice – that the defendant uttered false statements with knowledge of or reckless disregard as to falsity. *Sullivan*, 376 U.S. at 279–80. See Bachchan, 585 N.Y.S.2d at 663 (describing U.K. libel law).
89 Ehrenfeld v. Mahfouz, 518 F.3d 102, 104 (2d Cir. 2008).
90 See Rosen, supra note 12, at 176–79 (noting that under conflicts-of-law and constitutional principles, U.S. courts almost always enforce foreign judgments).
91 Restatement (Second) of Conflict of Laws §§ 149, 150 (1971).
92 See id.
93 See, e.g., Telnikoff v. Matusevitch, 702 A.2d 230, 232 (Md. 1997) (refusing to enforce U.K. libel judgments where only U.S. connection to the dispute was the fact that the judgment debtor had moved to the United States and had assets there).
94 Rosen, supra note 12, at 172.
95 See sources cited supra note 9.
96 Ohno v. Yasuma, – – F.3d – –, 2013 WL 3306351 * 6 (9th Cir. 2013) (emphasis in original).
97 Of course, in cases involving injunctive decrees, it may be the case that courts are more entangled with carrying out a foreign judgment. The state action analysis could be somewhat different in such circumstances. See id. at *12.
98 Berman, "Toward a Cosmopolitan Vision," supra note 17, at 1822.
99 See id. at 1869 (noting that under cosmopolitan conflicts principles, "we will necessarily reject the idea that, because a judgment could not have been issued by a court in the first instance, that court is simply unable to enforce the judgment").
100 Id. at 1872.
101 Yahoo! Inc. v. La Ligue Contre Le Racisme Et L'Antisemitisme, 169 F. Supp. 2d 1181, 1186 (N.D. Ca. 2001), *rev'd on other grounds*, 379 F.3d 1120 (9th Cir. 2004), *reh'g granted en banc*, 399 F.3d 1010 (9th Cir. 2005). The Ninth Circuit ultimately dismissed Yahoo!'s declaratory judgment action

on ripeness and jurisdictional grounds. Yahoo! Inc. v. La Ligue Contre Le Racisme Et L'Antisemitisme, 433 F.3d 1199, 1201–04 (9th Cir. 2006). Yahoo! eventually removed the contested auction sites from its servers.

102 Berman, "Toward a Cosmopolitan Vision," supra note 17, at 1879.

103 Id. at 1878. See also Joel R. Reidenberg, "Yahoo and Democracy on the Internet," 42 *Jurimetrics* 261, 267 (2002) (discussing Yahoo!'s contacts with France).

104 Berman, "Toward a Cosmopolitan Vision," supra note 17, at 1879.

105 Id.

106 Id. at 1821.

107 See Rosen, supra note 30, at 116 (discussing grounds for non-enforcement of "Un-American Judgments").

108 See id. (discussing limits on enforcement of foreign judgments).

109 Id. at 121–25.

110 344 U.S. 94 (1952). For a fascinating background account of the case, see Richard W. Garnett, "'Things That Are Not Caesar's'": The Story of Kedroff v. St. Nicholas Cathedral," in Richard W. Garnett & Andrew Koppelman, eds., *First Amendment Stories* (New York: Foundation Press, 2012), 171.

111 John H. Mansfield, "The Religion Clauses of the First Amendment and Foreign Relations," 36 *DePaul L. Rev.* 1, 15 (1986).

112 381 U.S. 301 (1965).

113 Larson v. Valente, 456 U.S. 228 (1982); Church of the Lukumi Babalu Aye, Inc. v. City of Hialeah, 508 U.S. 520 (1993).

114 See Ohno v. Yasuma, – – F.3d – –, 2013 WL 3306351 * 6 (9th Cir. 2013) (holding that U.S. district court's recognition and enforcement of a money judgment against a church operating in Japan but incorporated in the United States did not constitute state action).

115 The facts are based on Ohno v. Yasuma, – – F.3d – –, 2013 WL 3306351 (9th Cir. 2013), in which the court recognized and enforced the Japanese judgment based on foreign judgment recognition laws and principles.

116 See Oman, supra note 20, at 324–27 (arguing that domestic courts run afoul of the Establishment Clause when they interpret specific Shari'a doctrines or the revelations of Islam, but not when they consult social facts and the intention of the parties – even when these are based on Islamic law).

117 Eugene Volokh, "Court Refuses to Enforce Islamic Premarital Agreement That Promised Wife $677,000 in the Event of Divorce," *The Volokh Conspiracy,* blog post dated September 10, 2012. Retrieved from http://volokh. com/2012/90/10/court-refuses-to-enforce-islamic-premarital-agreement.

118 See, e.g., Chaudry v. Chaudry, 388 A.2d 1000, 1006 (N.J. Ct. App. 1978) (upholding marital contract derived from Pakistani law on choice of law grounds).

119 See Oman, supra note 20, at 313 n. 180 (citing cases).

120 Id. at 291.

121 Id. at 320.

122 Id. at 334.
123 See Jeff Redding, "What American Legal Theory Might Learn from Islamic Law: Some Lessons About 'The Rule of Law' from 'Shari'a Court' Practice in India," 83 *U. Colo. L. Rev.* 1027 (2012).
124 Mansfield, supra note 111, at 3.

Exporting the First Amendment

1 Vicki C. Jackson, *Constitutional Engagement in a Transnational Era* (New York: Oxford University Press, 2010), 108–10.
2 See Margret A. Blanchard, *Exporting the First Amendment: The Press-Government Crusade of 1945–1952* (New York: Longman, 1986), 17.
3 Rodney Smolla, *Free Speech in an Open Society* (Random House [Vintage Books], 1992), 347.
4 See generally Blanchard, supra note 1.
5 Id. at 57.
6 Id. at 380.
7 Universal Declaration of Human Rights, art. 19, G.A. Res. 217 (III), U.N. Doc A/810 at 71 (1948).
8 Universal Declaration of Human Rights, art. 29(2).
9 Blanchard, supra note 1, at 402.
10 See Saskia Sassen, *Losing Control?*: Sovereignty in an Age of Globalization (New York: Columbia University Press 1996), 17–18 (noting that flow of constitutional norms, including First Amendment norms, has favored U.S. expansionism rather than transnationalism).
11 1975 Final Act of the Conference on Security and Cooperation in Europe, reprinted in 14 I.L.M. 1292 (1975).
12 See Jackson, supra note 1, at 76–77 (discussing examples).
13 See, e.g., Ian Loveland ed., *Importing the First Amendment: Freedom of Speech and Expression in Britain, Europe and the USA* (New York: Oxford University Press, 1998); United Food & Commercial Workers Local 1518 v. Kmart Can. Ltd. [1999] 2 S.C.R 1083, 1118–21 (Can.) (adopting First Amendment distinction between leafleting and picketing).
14 See Anthony Lester, "The Overseas Trade in the American Bill of Rights," 88 *Colum. L. Rev.* 537, 552–58 (1988).
15 Jackson, supra note 1, at 120–21.
16 Radio Free Europe/Radio Liberty, About RFE/RL: Mission Statement. Retrieved July 5, 2013 from http://www.rferl.org/info/about/176.html.
17 See C. Edwin Baker, *Media, Markets, and Democracy* (New York: Cambridge University Press, 2002), 217–21.
18 See Sarah H. Cleveland, "Norm Internalization and U.S. Economic Sanctions," 26 *Yale J. Int'l L.* 1, 69 (2001).
19 See David M. Smolin, "Exporting the First Amendment?: Evangelism, Proselytism, and the International Religious Freedom Act," 31 *Cumb. L. Rev.*

685 (2001); Christy Cutbill McCormick, "Exporting the First Amendment: America's Response to Religious Persecution Abroad," 4 *J. Int'l Legal Stud.* 283 (1998).

20 H.R. 275, 110th Cong. (2007).

21 For an account of the events leading to GOFA's proposal, see William J. Cannici, Jr., "The Global Online Freedom Act: A Critique of Its Objectives, Methods, and Ultimate Effectiveness in Combating American Businesses That Facilitate Internet Censorship in the People's Republic of China," 32 *Seton Hall Legis. J.* 123, 124–25 (2007).

22 H.R. 275, § 2(17).

23 Id. § 105.

24 For an analysis of the tension between intellectual property rights and free-dom of speech, see David L. Lange & H. Jefferson Powell, *No Law: Intellectual Property in the Image of an Absolute First Amendment* (Palo Alto: Stanford University Press, 2009). See also Eldred v. Ashcroft, 537 U.S. 186, 219 (2003) ("Indeed, copyright's purpose is to *promote* the creation and publication of free expression.") (emphasis in original).

25 See Mark D. Rosen, "Exporting the Constitution," 53 *Emory L.J.* 171 (2004); Paul Schiff Berman, "Towards a Cosmopolitan Vision of Conflicts of Laws: Redefining Governmental Interests in a Global Era," 153 *U. Pa. L. Rev.* 1819, 1822 (2005).

26 See Yahoo! Inc. v. La Ligue Contre Le Racisme et l'Antisemitisme, 169 F. Supp.2d 1181 (N.D. Cal. 2001) (refusing to recognize a French court's injunction against the posting of Nazi-related materials on the Internet), *rev'd on other grounds*, 433 F.3d 1199 (9th Cir. 2006).

27 Berman, supra note 25, at 1836.

28 Jackson, supra note 1, at 108.

29 Louis Henkin, *The Age of Rights* (New York: Columbia University Press, 1990), 74.

30 See Rosen, supra note 25, at 172 ("Categorically refusing to enforce such Un-American Judgments is tantamount to imposing U.S. constitutional norms on foreign countries.").

31 See Ronald J. Krotoszynski, Jr., *The First Amendment in Cross-Cultural Perspective: A Comparative Legal Analysis of the Freedom of Speech* (New York: NYU Press, 2006), 214–15 (discussing freedom of speech and glo-bal rights pluralism). See also Mark Tushnet, "The Inevitable Globalization of Constitutional Law," 49 *Va. J. Int'l L.* 985 (2009); David S. Law, "Globalization and the Future of Constitutional Rights," 102 *Nw. U. L. Rev.* 1277 (2008).

32 Krotoszynski, supra note 31, at 221. See Michael J. Perry, *The Idea of Human Rights: Four Inquiries* (New York: Oxford University Press, 1998), 91–92.

33 Krotoszynski, supra note 31, at 215.

34 Id. at 222.

35 See Claudia E. Haupt, "Transnational Nonestablishment", 8 *Geo. Wash. L. Rev.* 991 (2012).

36 Blanchard, supra note 1, at 22.

37 See Jack M. Balkin, "Digital Speech and Democratic Culture: A Theory of Freedom of Expression for the Information Society," 79 *N.Y.U. L. Rev.* 1 (2004).

38 See Cannici, supra note 21; Miriam D. D'Jaen, "Breaching the Great Firewall of China: Congress Overreaches in Attacking Chinese Internet Censorship," 31 *Seattle U. L. Rev.* 327 (2008); Kaydee Smith, "A Global First Amendment," 6 *J. Telecomm. & High Tech. L.* 509 (2008).

39 See, e.g., Global Internet Freedom Act of 2006 (GIFA), H.R. 4741, 109th Cong.

40 See Cleveland, supra note 18, at 48–56 (discussing compliance with sovereignty and customary international law principles in context of unilateral trade sanctions).

41 Steven R. Swanson, "Forcing Facebook on Foreign Dictators: A Violation of International Law?", 79 *Tenn. L. Rev.* 851 (2012).

42 See Baker, supra note 17, at 236–39 (discussing negative and positive externalities of U.S. export of cultural and media products). *But* see Lee C. Bollinger, *Uninhibited, Robust, and Wide-Open: A Free Press For A New Century* (New York: Oxford University Press, 2010), 89 (urging free trade in media and cultural products).

43 Baker, supra note 17, at 237.

44 Id.

45 Id. at 248.

46 Id. at 255.

47 Id. at 266.

48 Id. at 270.

49 Id.

50 Bollinger, supra note 42, at 117.

51 Id. at 6.

52 Id. at 130.

53 Id. at 113.

54 Id. at 117.

55 Id.

56 Id. at 118.

57 Id.

58 Id.

59 Id. at 131.

60 Id. at 125.

61 Id. at 131.

62 Id. at 134–35.

63 Id. at 134.

64 Id. at 143.
65 Id. at 144.
66 Id.
67 Id. at 157.
68 Id.
69 Id. at 163.
70 Id.
71 See Zachary R. Calo, "The Internationalization of Church-State Issues," in Ann W. Duncan and Steven L. Jones (eds.), *Church and State Issues in America Today* (Westport, Conn.: Praeger, 2008).
72 Smolin, supra note 19.
73 See Stephanie Farriorr, "Molding the Matrix: The Historical and Theoretical Foundations of International Law Concerning Hate Speech," 14 *Berkeley J. Int'l Law* 1 (1996).
74 Smolin, supra note 19, at 706.
75 Id.
76 Id. at 707.
77 Peter G. Danchin, "U.S. Unilateralism and the International Protection of Religious Freedom: The Multilateral Alternative," 41 *Colum. J. Transnat'l L.* 33, 38 (2002).
78 Id. at 41.
79 Id.
80 Id.
81 Id.
82 Id. at 42.
83 T. Jeremy Gunn, "American Exceptionalism and Globalist Double Standards: A More Balanced Alternative," 41 *Colum. J. Transnat'l L.* 137 (2002).
84 Cleveland, supra note 18, at 5.
85 Id. at 6.
86 Id. at 87.
87 Danchin, supra note 77, at 42.

INDEX

Afghanistan, 170, 174, 209, 319
Al Hurra, 352, 368
Al Qaeda, 5, 164, 170, 182, 186
al-Awlaki, Anwar, 164, 193, 194
Alien and Sedition Act, 19, 54, 64, 65,
    81, 121
aliens
    campaign contributions of, 10, 35, 56,
        142, 155
    and exclusion based on health, 129
    and exclusion based on religion, 236, 254
    extraterritorial rights of, 10, 18, 200,
        210–12, 220–25, 233, 254
    First Amendment rights of, 9, 94,
        126, 220
    and funding conditions, 224
    ideological exclusion of, 9, 17, 30–31,
        120–25, 126–29, 224, 273, 280
    removal of, 105
Alito, Samuel (Justice), 329
Amar, Akhil, 87
American Civil Liberties Union, 4, 36
American Convention on Human Rights,
    39, 369
American Insurance Association v. Garamendi,
    278, 279, 287
anarchism, 65
apartheid, 271
Appiah, Kwame, 84, 99
Aptheker v. Secretary of State, 108
Arab, 239, 271, 301, 352
Arab Spring, 354
Arabic, 188
Assange, Julian, 6, 7, 165, 196
assembly, freedom of, 40, 50, 60, 78, 111,
    157, 211, 212, 215, 305

in foreign locations, 209
and portability, 215
association, freedom of, 184, 199
    and aliens, 17
    and aliens abroad, 9
    and cross-border relationships, 14, 26,
        35–36, 72, 133, 147–50, 160–63, 209
    and domestic relationships, 148
    and extraterritorial rights, 50
    and foreign missions, 148
    and funding conditions, 148
    and religious charities, 239
    and self-government, 162
Austria, 46

Baker, C. Edwin, 364, 365
Balkin, Jack, 87, 156, 157, 167, 215, 362
    and democratic culture theory, 88, 157,
        167, 217, 362
Beirut Agreement, 136, 144
Belgium, 46
Benghazi, 5, 322
Benkler, Yochai, 159, 195
Berle, Adolf A., 362
Berman Amendment, 137, 142
Berman, Paul Schiff, 332, 336, 357
    and cosmopolitan choice of law, 332,
        333, 335
Bill of Rights, 65, 80, 82, 201, 204, 206,
    210, 231, 275, 307
    as structural safeguard, 87
    and territoriality, 87
Black, Hugo (Justice), 201
Blackstone's Commentaries, 311
Blanchard, Margaret, 349, 350
blasphemy, 315, 322, 324

Bollinger, Lee, 153, 214, 219, 297, 298, 366, 367, 368, 369
  and global press concerns, 366–70
Bono, 273
Boos v. Barry, 326, 327
Boumediene v. Bush, 203, 204, 205, 210, 211, 212, 223
Brandenburg v. Ohio, 176, 189, 328
Brennan, William (Justice), 202
Breyer, Stephen (Justice), 328, 329
Broadcast Board of Governors, 270
Bullfrog Films, Inc. v. Wick, 144
Burma, 278
Bush, George H.W. (President), 50, 107, 123, 209, 273, 299

Cairo, 247
California, 114, 278, 279
Canada, 43, 120
Canon law, 342
Cardozo, Benjamin, 328
Carmichael, Stokely, 273, 281
Carter, James (President), 273
Catholic, 236
Catholic Church, 258
CD-ROM, 32, 137
censorship
  hard forms of, 159
  soft forms of, 158, 159
Chafee, Zechariah, 110, 111, 112, 113, 126, 127, 349
China, 135, 274, 294, 363
choice of law, 331, 332, 343
  cosmopolitan version, 332, 333, 335, 343
Christian, 236, 322, 343, 344, 370
Church of England, 230
Citizens United v. FEC, 142, 287
Cleveland, Sarah, 284, 372, 373
Clinton, Hillary, 4, 104, 160, 352
Clinton, William J. (President), 75, 234, 273, 299
Cold War, 30, 32, 55, 64, 105, 106, 121, 128, 135, 137, 151, 338
Cole, David, 126, 130, 150, 161, 162
Commerce Control List, 138
communism, 19, 55, 65, 111, 126, 261, 271
Communist Party, 108, 125, 161
community of nations, 11, 12, 13, 15, 19, 21, 36, 43, 45, 53, 56, 59, 63, 66, 82, 96, 97, 112, 127, 150, 231, 244, 259, 265, 293, 316, 330, 346, 356

and comity, 36, 304, 324
and framers of the U.S. Constitution, 79, 81, 231
and pluralism, 304
and recognition of expressive and religious liberties, 87
and religious freedom, 250
and transnational legal sources, 315
and treaty negotiations, 320
U.S. membership in, 98
and U.S. rights exceptionalism, 11, 76, 304, 305, 306, 317
conflict of laws, 49, 98, 332
copyright, 308, 356
cosmopolitan engagement, 337
  and religious decrees, 341, 344
cosmopolitan First Amendment
  basic principles of, 2–3, 16–17, 77
  and community of nations, 95–100
  constitutional origins and orientation, 77–82
  and constitutional text, 80
  and cosmopolitan justifications for rights, 87
  and cross-border information flow, 150–56
  and cross-border religious liberties, 240–47
  and democratic culture theory, 88
  and export of U.S. standards or norms, 17, 98, 348
  and extraterritorial domain, 16, 92
  and extraterritorial rights, 212–27
  and First Amendment justifications, 85–90
  and global information policy, 160
  and global standards, 15, 19
  and government facilitation, 16
  and governmental power in transborder dimension, 95
  and interconnectivity, 167
  and international diplomacy, 321–25
  and pluralism, 17, 77, 304
  and press rights, 86
  and protection of transborder liberties, 82–85
  and religious freedom, 89
  and republic of letters, 78, 83
  and rights of aliens, 92, 127–28, 130–31
  and rights portability, 16, 92, 199, 215–20, 250
  and structural theory of rights, 87

and territorial sovereignty, 77, 90–93
and territoriality, 93–94
and transborder borrowing, 81
and transborder commingling, 83
and transborder conversation, 83
and U.S. exceptionalism, 77, 324
cosmopolitanism
    definition of, 15
    and commingling, 16
    and conversation, 16
    rooted form of, 15, 77
Council of Europe, 41
Crosby v. National Foreign Trade Council,
    278, 279
cross-border communication
    and digitization, 147
    U.S. regulation of, 134–42
cross-territorial First Amendment, 25,
    28, 35
Cuba, 30, 103, 106, 108, 118, 119, 135,
    137, 203, 209, 271, 354
customary international law, 268

Danchin, Peter, 371, 372
Daniel Pearl Freedom of the Press Act, 354
Darfur, 266, 271
death penalty, 271
Declaration of Independence, 49, 79
deemed export rule, 10, 155
Denmark, 41
Der Spiegel, 6
Desai v. Hersh, 207, 208
Dickson v. Ford, 256
digitization
    and cross-border communication, 310
    and cross-border religious activities, 246
    and effect on audiences, 146
    and effect on expression, 8, 58, 147
    and harmful speech, 167
    and incitement, 173
    and interconnectivity, 30–31
    and sovereignty, 147, 331
    and speech conflicts, 305, 331
    and spread of democratic culture, 88
Douglas, William O. (Justice), 107, 111,
    112, 113, 236
drone strikes
    and due process, 193
    free speech implications of, 194
Due Process Clause (Fifth Amendment),
    73, 107, 108, 109, 193, 240

Egypt, 247, 319
Employment Division v. Smith, 235, 237,
    240, 243, 245
enemy combatant, 183, 199, 222, 224, 233
enemy-aiding expression. (*see* global
    theater)
    defined, 182
England, 201
Equal Protection Clause, 288, 289
Espionage Act of 1917, 6, 7, 165, 196
Establishment Clause, 45, 50, 51, 68, 70,
    97, 228, 229, 231, 232, 251, 255, 256,
    257, 258, 259, 260, 261, 266, 275,
    300, 301, 302, 340, 342
    and endorsement test, 301
    extraterritorial application of, 255–62
    and foreign aid, 233
    and wall of separation, 45
European Convention on Human Rights
    and freedom of expression, 38
    and religious freedom, 44
European Convention on the Prevention of
    Terrorism, 41
European Court of Human Rights,
    38, 372
    and free exercise of religion, 47
Export Administration Act, 137
Export Administration Regulations, 138
extraterritorial First Amendment , 26,
    49, 199
extraterritoriality
    and Establishment Clause, 255–62
    and export of First Amendment
        standards, 53
    and expressive rights of U.S. citizens,
        205–10
    and First Amendment rights, 10,
        26, 49–50
    and free exercise rights of aliens, 253,
        254, 255
    and free exercise rights of U.S. citizens,
        248, 249, 250, 251, 253
    general approaches, 203–05
    and influence of First Amendment, 347
    limits of, 225–27
    as mechanism of export of First
        Amendment norms and practices,
        355–56
    and mutuality of legal obligation, 200,
        204, 221, 222, 223, 224, 225, 226, 249,
        253, 254

extraterritoriality (*cont.*)
  and pragmatic approach, 204
  and expressive rights of aliens,
    202–03
  and social compact approach, 204,
    216, 249
  and universalist approach, 204

Facebook, 116, 179
faith-based initiative, 50
Farrakhan, Louis, 273
federalism, 114, 287, 288, 291, 292,
  293
Fifth Amendment, 201, 202, 216, 240
First Amendment
  and community of nations, 12–13, 25,
    29, 61, 265, 303, 346, 373
  cosmopolitan approach to, 3, 15–18,
    76–100, 348
  and cross-border association, 35–36,
    133, 147–50, 160, 161, 162,
    163, 238
  and cross-border communication, 3,
    31–35, 67, 133, 138, 139, 141, 142–47,
    151, 153, 154, 156
  and defamation, 41, (*see also* speech,
    freedom of)
  and digitization, 59, 167, 310
  and domestic rights, 3, 20, 44, 49, 61,
    183, 308
  and enemy-aiding speech, 183
  and exceptionalism, 3, 12, 40, 41, 43, 49,
    56, 60, 61, 74–75, 168, 174, 177, 303,
    304, 305, 306, 309, 312, 313, 314, 317,
    321, 322, 323, 346, 348, 351, 357, 358,
    373, 374
  exclusivity in domestic sphere, 305, 306,
    309, 312, 325, 336
  and export of standards and norms, 3,
    12, 44, 52–53, 56, 62, 244, 325,
    346, 347, 348–57, 358, 359, 360,
    361, 370
  and extraterritorial domain, 2, 3, 8, 10,
    20, 44, 49–52, 68, 199, 200, 205–27,
    233, 247–62, 300, 331, 355, 356, 358,
    360, (*see also* extraterritoriality)
  and foreign affairs, 10
  and foreign judgments, 10, 303, 308,
    336, 357
  and foreign relations, 275, 276, 284, 288,
    295, 299, 349, 350, 351, 352

  and foreign travel, 2, 29–30, 73, 103,
    104, 105–20, 244
  and free flow of information, 361–66
  and global free press, 366–70
  in the global theater, 165, 179
  and globalization, 58
  and government propaganda, 282, 296,
    297, 298
  and government speech, 287, 289
  and hate speech, 42, 43, 176,
    (*see also* speech, freedom of)
  and human rights, 354, 355, 361, 374
  and immigration, 2, 30–31, 105, 125,
    126–29
  and incitement, 40, 41, 172, 175, 185,
    194, (*see also* speech, freedom of)
  and international borders, 1, 2, 12,
    134, 235
  in international forums, 12, 265, 266,
    267, 280, 282, 283, 286, 287, 289, 290,
    291, 293, 295, 299, 300, 301, 302, 359
  and judicial quasi-recognition of
    transborder liberties, 70–74
  and justifications for protection, 68–70,
    152, 241, 324
  and offensive speech, 177
  origins of, 54, 64, 65, 78, 81, 82,
    230, 232
  and prosecution of press, 196
  provincial approach to, 14–15,
    62–76, 348
  and religion clauses, 45,
    (*see also* Establishment Clause, Free
    Exercise Clause, religion, freedom of)
  and religious neutrality, 340
  and religious pluralism, 48
  and removal of aliens, 105, 126, 130–31
  and state action, 334
  territorial dimensions of, 25–28
  and territoriality, 67, 80, 187
  and transborder communication, 2
  transborder dimension of, 4, 7–9, 25, 47,
    53–60, 233, 235, 244
  and transborder religious liberties, 228,
    229, 243
  and transnational engagement, 304, 312,
    313, 315, 316, 317, 318, 324, 326, 327,
    328, 329, 330, 336, 350, 351, 374
  and global incitement, 171
  and treaties, 39, 48, 154, 318, 319, 320,
    321, 351, (*see also* treaties)

Florida, 201
Flynt, Larry, 4
Fonda, Jane, 281
foreign affairs
  and congressional powers, 268
  and cosmopolitan principles, 283
  and establishment of religion, 10
  and free speech federalism, 282, 284,
    290–93
  and freedom of speech, 274–99
  and implied preemption of states,
    277, 284
  and international travel, 30
  and judicial deference, 73, 280
  judicial participation in, 270
  and marketplace of ideas concept, 281,
    282, 294
  and private speakers, 272–74
  and quasi-recognition of transborder
    liberties, 71
  and religious neutrality, 299–302
  and single voice principle, 10, 267, 274,
    276, 277, 278, 281, 283, 284
  and speech in international forums,
    17, 51
  and speech rights of states, 51
  state and local participation in, 270–72
  and sub-national speech rights, 290
  and U.S. propaganda, 296–99
  and U.S. spending, 269
Foreign Agent Registration Act, 140,
  141, 154
Foreign Assistance Act, 257
foreign judgments
  and SPEECH Act, 308
  and religious laws, 10
  recognition of by U.S. courts, 10, 18,
    28, 47, 304, 308, 310, 331, 334, 341,
    343, 357
foreign libel judgments, 308, 311, 333, 334,
  335, 343, 358
Fourth Amendment, 202, 257, 258
framers (of the U.S. Constitution), 63
  and cosmopolitanism, 78, 79, 81, 82,
    139, 231
  and dealings with foreign powers, 66
  and extraterritorial rights, 87, 257
  and foreign influence, 54, 65, 80, 187
  and provincialism, 64, 77, 80, 230
  and religious freedom, 64, 80, 230, 231
  and text of First Amendment, 80

and Treason Clause, 190
France, 34, 41, 65, 114, 167, 309, 310,
  336, 357
Frankfurter, Felix (Justice), 201, 202, 203,
  225, 236
Free Exercise Clause, 45, 47, 50, 228, 229,
  232, 233, 235, 237, 238, 240, 245, 246,
  248, 249, 250, 251, 252, 253, 254, 259,
  338, 339, 340, 342
  and cross-border activities, 240–47
  and rights of aliens located abroad,
    253–55
  and rights of citizens located abroad,
    248–53
  transborder dimension of, 235–40
free exercise of religion
  and comparative perspective, 46
  and extraterritorial rights, 10
  and proselytizing, 47
  and religious garb in schools, 47
  and veiling, 47
Free Trade in Ideas Act, 142
French Revolution, 65
Fulbright, J. William (Senator), 142

gag rule, 211
Germany, 46, 167, 205, 309
Ginsburg, Ruth B. (Justice), 279
Global Network Initiative, 158
Global Online Freedom Act, 355,
  356, 363
global theater, 7, 21, 34, 59, 85, 152, 164,
  165, 166, 167, 168, 169, 170, 172, 173,
  174, 175, 176, 178, 179, 180, 181, 182,
  183, 187, 188, 189, 190, 191, 193, 195,
  197, 228, 233
  defined, 165
  and challenges to government authority,
    169–71
  characteristics of, 166–71
  and compression of space and time, 168–69
  and domestic dissent, 183
  and enemy-aiding expression, 182–95
  and foreign hecklers, 181
  and free speech pluralism, 179
  and incitement, 171–76
  and offensive speech, 176–82
globalization
  and effect on expression, 8, 58
  and information flow, 91
  and speech conflicts, 305

Goldsmith, Jack, 146
Golove, David, 79
Google, 266, 274, 294, 331, 363
government speech, 286, 296, 362, 365,
    (*see also* speech, freedom of)
    and foreign affairs, 289
Great Britain, 351
Ground Zero (Manhattan), 168
Guantanamo Bay, 203, 209, 210, 254,
    255
Gunn, Jeremy, 372

habeas corpus, 203
Haig v. Agee, 108, 115, 205, 206
Halaka, 342
Harlan, John (Justice), 202, 203,
    225, 249
hate speech, 315, 319, 320, 323, 324,
    330, 331 (*see also* speech, freedom of)
Hawaii, 201
Helsinki Accords, 113, 325
Helsinki Final Act, 350
Henkin, Louis, 92, 268, 359
Hersh, Seymour, 207
Hinduism, 242
Hofstadter, Richard, 56
Holder v. Humanitarian Law Project, 6, 36,
    133, 134, 143, 149, 150, 152, 160, 161,
    163, 185, 186, 187, 190, 238, 239, 240,
    243, 294, 296, 327
Holmes, Oliver Wendell Jr. (Justice),
    164, 172
Holocaust, 278
Hulsebosch, Daniel, 79
human rights, 1, 15, 37, 44, 46, 52, 60, 62,
    75, 79, 80, 85, 87, 89, 91, 100, 113,
    127, 130, 131, 132, 154, 194, 212,
    219, 229, 234, 242, 243, 266, 268,
    271, 272, 274, 278, 292, 307, 314,
    320, 323, 348, 350, 354, 355, 356,
    359, 360, 361, 362, 365, 366, 367,
    369, 370, 371, 372, 373
human shield, 189, 206, 225
Humanitarian Law Project, 132, 133
Hustler Magazine, 4

In re Ross, 200, 201
incitement. (*see also* speech, freedom of)
    and development of unitary
        standard, 174
    and distant effects, 173

in the global theater, 172, 173,
    174, 175
and laws of other nations, 174
Indonesia, 242, 243
Innocence of Muslims (video), 5, 8, 12, 164,
    168, 176, 179, 180, 322, 324
Insular Cases, 201
intellectual property, 60, 214, 362
    and global information flow, 362
    and global piracy, 59
Inter-American Commission on Human
    Rights, 39
Inter-American Court of Human Rights,
    39, 369
International Convention on the
    Elimination of All Forms of Racial
    Discrimination, 242
International Covenant on Civil and
    Political Rights, 131, 219, 242
    and free exercise of religion, 46
    and freedom of expression, 37
    and hate speech, 42
    and religious freedom, 44
International Religious Freedom Act, 75,
    234, 242, 299, 354, 356, 370, 371,
    372, 373
Internet, 1, 5, 6, 7, 10, 11, 32, 34, 86, 87,
    88, 91, 94, 99, 113, 145, 146, 147, 154,
    156, 157, 158, 160, 164, 169, 170, 173,
    174, 175, 176, 181, 188, 191, 192, 193,
    194, 195, 214, 215, 246, 274, 298, 309,
    323, 331, 332, 352, 353, 354, 355, 362,
    363, 378, 385, 391, 417
    and censorship, 11, 34, 159, 180
    and cross-border information flow, 34
    and exceptionalists, 146, 331
    and global information flow, 362
    and global theater, 59
    and hate speech, 43, 60
    as marketplace of ideas, 154
    and repressive governments, 363
    as republic of letters, 151
    and service providers, 34, 146, 157
    and spread of democratic culture, 362
    and territorial borders, 58, 84, 146
    and un-exceptionalists, 331, 332
    and universal speech standards, 315, 332
    U.S. facilitation of access to, 352, 354
intraterritorial First Amendment, 25, 31
Iran, 261, 271, 281, 292
Iraq, 209

Iraq War, 223
Islam, 46, 50, 66, 182, 239, 242, 251, 260,
    261, 304, 310, 311, 340, 344
Israel, 271

Jackson, Jesse, 273
Jackson, Vicki, 312, 314, 316, 317, 318,
    328, 357
Jacobinism, 65
Jefferson, Thomas, 54, 230
Jehovah's Witnesses, 4
Johnson v. Eisentrager, 211
Jones, Terry, 5, 7, 35, 164, 168, 170, 176, 182
Jong-un, Kim, 33

Kamenshine, Robert, 69, 144, 151
Kedroff v. St. Nicholas Cathedral, 338, 339
Keene, Barry, 140
Kennedy, Anthony (Justice), 93, 202,
    203
Kent v. Dulles, 107
Kleindienst v. Mandel, 124, 125, 127, 128,
    142, 147, 148, 152, 154, 236, 237
Koran, 5, 35, 42, 164, 168, 170, 176, 178,
    182, 186, 233, 310
Kremlin, 139, 266
Krotoszynski, Ronald, 360
Ku Klux Klan, 4
Kurdistan Workers' Party, 132, 149, 184

Lamont, Corliss, 132, 256
Lamont v. Postmaster General, 1, 33, 132,
    133, 134, 140, 141, 142, 143, 148, 152,
    153, 154, 208, 339
Lamont v. Woods, 256, 257, 258, 259,
    260, 261
Le Monde, 6
Lewis, Anthony, 54, 65
libel tourism, 308, 324, 351
Libya, 319, 322
Logan Act, 32, 139, 154, 281, 294,
    295, 297

Madison, James, 54, 65, 230, 257, 368
mahr, 343, 344
Malaysia, 260
Manhattan, 171
Mansfield, John, 242, 243, 244, 245, 246,
    250, 251, 252, 259, 260, 261
margin of appreciation, 46
Marshall, Thurgood (Justice), 154

Massachusetts, 278
McCarran-Walter Act, 121
McCarthy Era, 106
McDonald, Barry, 115, 116, 117
McGovern Amendment, 121
Mecca, 252
Meese v. Keene, 140
Mehanna, Tarek, 5, 7, 164, 187, 188
Meiklejohn, Alexander, 69, 85
Mexico, 202, 206, 257
Middle East, 46, 164, 255, 256
Miller, Arthur, 106
Mohammed, 164, 181, 310, 322
Monroe, Marilyn, 123
Moynihan-Frank Amendment, 122, 128
Muslim, 5, 36, 103, 231, 239, 244, 246,
    247, 250, 251, 252, 299, 322, 343, 344
Myanmar, 271, 292

National Public Radio, 369
national security, 6, 7, 8, 13, 18, 19, 30, 34,
    38, 57, 59, 68, 71, 73, 95, 108, 119,
    120, 122, 127, 134, 137, 138, 144, 147,
    153, 160, 169, 170, 172, 184, 187, 191,
    193, 194, 195, 196, 197, 218, 225, 226,
    237, 241, 246, 247, 251, 252, 258,
    261, 267, 269, 270, 274, 276, 280,
    297, 300
Nazi, 140, 180, 309, 336, 357
networked fourth estate, 195
Neuman, Gerald, 37, 128, 212, 220,
    221, 223
New York, 114
New York City, 168, 338
New York Times, 6
New York Times Co. v. Sullivan, 41, 153, 328,
    333, 334, 368
New York Times v. United States, 196
Nixon, Richard (President), 207
no-fly lists, 30
non-governmental organizations, 68, 267,
    272, 293
North Korea, 33
Northern Ireland, 271
Norway, 42
Notre Dame University, 103
Nussbaum, Martha, 83

Obama, Barack H. (President), 5, 8, 11, 50,
    164, 170, 171, 179, 182, 209, 247, 299,
    322, 323

Oklahoma, 310, 311, 313
Oman, Nathan, 343, 344
Organization for Economic Co-operation and Development, 158
Organization of American States, 39
Orthodox Church (Russia), 46

pacifism, 55
Paine, Thomas, 230
Pakistan, 218, 343
Patriarch of Moscow, 338
PATRIOT Act, 4, 55, 104, 122
Pauling, Linus, 106
Pentagon, 209
petition, right to, 3, 50, 78, 157, 199, 205, 211, 212, 247, 305
  and extraterritorial rights, 50
  in foreign locations, 209
  and portability, 215
Philippines, 201
Poland, 46
Post, David, 331
press, freedom of, 3, 40, 157, 199, 211, 212, 217, 247, 305, 374
  and cross-border information flow, 153
  and espionage prosecutions, 196
  and extraterritorial activities, 84
  and extraterritorial rights, 50, 210, 218
  and foreign affairs, 272
  and foreign reporting, 274
  as global concern, 195, 366–70
  and globalization, 20
  and networked activity, 195
  and portability, 215
  and right to foreign travel, 117
  and U.S. human rights monitoring, 354
  and United Nations crusade, 349, 362
privacy, 308
propaganda, 8, 9, 10, 13, 27, 33, 51, 52, 68, 94, 97, 132, 134, 140, 141, 145, 146, 154, 170, 172, 183, 190, 191, 192, 194, 226, 256, 265, 267, 269, 270, 280, 282, 283, 296, 297, 299, 339, 347, 362, 365, 366, 377, 400, 425
proselytizing, 241
Protect IP Act, 158
Protestantism, 242
provincial
  definition of, 62
provincial First Amendment
  basic principles of, 14–15, 63

on constitutional origins and orientation, 63–66
and export of U.S. standards or norms, 348
and extraterritorial rights, 213
and free speech justifications, 68–70
and nationality, 64
and press rights, 69
and quasi-recognition of transborder liberties, 70–74
and recognition of foreign judgments, 331
and religious freedom, 70
and territorial sovereignty, 66–68
and transnational engagement, 305
and U.S. exceptionalism, 74–76
public forum, 215
Puerto Rico, 201

radicalism, 65
Radio Free Europe, 352
Ramadan, Tariq, 4, 7, 8, 103, 123
Raustiala, Kal, 90, 91, 93, 201
REAL ID Act, 122
Red Scare, 349
Reid v. Covert, 201, 202, 203, 206, 213, 216, 225, 249, 307
religion clauses. (*see also* Free Exercise Clause, Establishment Clause)
  and extraterritorial rights, 232
  origins of, 231, 232
  and transborder activities, 232–34
  in transborder perspective, 229–32
religion, freedom of
  and comparative perspective, 43–47
  and U.S. origins, 81
Religious Freedom Restoration Act, 235, 236, 237, 240, 246
Reno v. ACLU, 154
Restatement (Third) of Foreign Relations, 256, 258, 259, 261
Revolutionary Era, 78, 82
Reynolds v. United States, 248
Robeson, Paul, 106
Rodman, Dennis, 33
Roman Catholic, 257
Roosevelt, Franklin D. (President), 89, 347
Roosevelt, Kermit, 211
Rosen, Mark, 334
Russia, 46

Sassen, Saskia, 154
Saudi Arabia, 223, 250, 252
Save Our State Amendment (Oklahoma),
    310, 311, 313
Scalia, Antonin (Justice), 279, 313, 328
Schauer, Frederick, 41
Securing the Protection of Our Enduring
    and Established Constitutional
    Heritage Act. (see foreign libel
    judgments, SPEECH Act)
Shari'a, 9, 48, 56, 251, 303, 310, 311, 312,
    340, 341, 344
Shipley, Ruth, 106
Sixth Amendment, 201, 202, 216
Smith-Mundt Act, 154, 280, 298
Smolin, David, 370, 371, 373
Smolla, Rodney, 43, 48, 84, 86, 88, 347
Snyder v. Phelps, 329
social media, 179
socialism, 55, 65
South Africa, 120, 271
Southeast Asia, 260
sovereignty
    defined, 90
    and cross-border movement, 91
    and exclusive legal control, 90
    and extraterritoriality, 90
Soviet Union, 271
Spain, 41, 46
SPEECH Act, 343
speech, freedom of
    and clear and present danger
        standard, 191
    and comparative perspective,
        37–43
    and counter-speech, 324
    and cross-border communication,
        32–35, 238
    and cross-border information flow, 8,
        142–45
    and defamation, 40, 41
    and domestic dissent, 182, 183
    and export of U.S. standards or
        norms, 347
    and extraterritorial rights of U.S.
        citizens, (see also extraterritoriality),
        50, 358
    and foreign affairs exception,
        187, 280
    and foreign audiences, 9
    and foreign hecklers, 177

    and funding conditions, 10, 51, 73, 214
    and global information flow, 362
    and government speech, 51, 226
    and hate speech, 40, 42, 43
    and incitement, 40, 172, 175, 185, 305,
        323, 328
    in international forums, 279–81
    and marketplace of ideas concept, 8, 69,
        86, 214, 363
    and material support for terrorism,
        184–89
    and offensive speech, 177
    and private censorship, 180
    and right to receive information, 33, 133,
        208, 209, 237, 298
    and self-actualization, 69, 87
    and self-government, 69, 86, 111, 112,
        116, 151, 184, 215, 363
    and sub-national speech rights, 286–90
    and symbolic conduct, 72
    and time, place, manner regulations, 225
    and transnational engagement, 312
    and treason, 189–92
    and truth-seeking, 69
    and U.S. exceptionalism, 14, 40, 56, 179,
        304, 305, 322
Spiro, Peter, 83, 318, 319, 326, 327
St. Nicholas Russian Orthodox
    Cathedral, 338
Stevens, John P. (Justice), 142, 279, 317
Stop Online Piracy Act, 158
Strasbourg, 38
Strauss, David, 78
Sudan, 354
Sunstein, Cass, 145
Supremacy Clause, 276, 289
Supreme Court of the U.S.
    and admission to U.S., 123
    and approach to territoriality, 94
    and border searches, 67
    and citation of foreign authority, 39,
        328, 351
    and cross-border association, 149, 160
    and defamation, 41
    and extraterritorial application of the
        U.S. Constitution, 253
    and extraterritorial First Amendment
        rights, 71
    and ideological exclusion of
        aliens, 127
    and press rights, 210

Supreme Court of the U.S. (*cont.*)
  and right to foreign travel, 103, 107, 109
surveillance, 2, 11, 33, 55, 139, 147,
    153, 174
Switzerland, 46, 271
Syria, 266

talaq, 343
Tamil Tigers, 149, 184
targeted killing (*see also* drone strikes)
  free speech implications of, 10
Tariff Act, 135, 136
Ten Commandments, 342
territoriality
  and rights, 59, 306
  and sovereignty, 15, 59, 112, 214, 306
terrorism
  and foreign terrorist organizations, 35,
    36, 184, 186, 237, 269
  and incitement, 174
  and Islam, 311
  and material support for religious
    organizations, 238
  and religious freedom, 228
  and U.S. material support law, 5, 6, 35,
    133, 149, 184, 238
The New York Times, 6, 197
The Washington Post, 197
Thomas, Clarence (Justice), 279
Tibet, 120
trade
  as First Amendment export mechanism,
    353, 364, 365, 370
trademark, 356
Trading With the Enemy Act, 135, 137
transborder dimension
  description of, 27–28
  factors influencing, 53–60
transnational judicial discourse, 317
transnational legal processes, 48, 60, 74, 96,
    99, 303, 306, 307, 310, 324, 325, 328,
    348, 351, 354, 369, 372, 373
  and effect on First Amendment rights,
    307, 308
  and export of First Amendment
    standards, 350
transnational legal sources, 312
  convergence with, 314, 315
  engagement with, 312, 314, 315–18
  and religion, 337–45
  resistance to, 313, 315

  in U.S. courts, 326–30
travel, foreign
  and commingling, 111
  constitutional right to, 17, 30,
    109–18, 243
  and embargoes, 106, 117
  as expressive act, 114
  First Amendment aspects of, 29–30, 72,
    110–12
  as human right, 79
  limits on, 9, 11, 30, 72, 105–07
  and no fly lists, 107
  quasi-recognition of right to, 107–09
  and religious free exercise, 236, 241
  and terrorist watchlists, 109, 115
treason, 169
  defined, 189
  and agency relationships, 191, 192
  and online expression, 190, 191
Treason Clause, 190, 191
treaties
  and cross-border information
    flow, 154
  and derogation of First Amendment
    rights, 10, 97, 307, 318–21, 338
  and export of First Amendment
    standards, 349
  and expressive liberties, 312
  and importation of foreign laws, 48
  and protection of transborder rights, 16
  and religious freedom, 43
  self-executing, 39
  status under U.S. law, 38
  and U.S. exceptionalism, 60
  and U.S. reservations, 39, 48, 74, 313,
    320, 351
Treaty of Tripoli, 231
Trotskyism, 55
Truman, Harry S. (President), 121,
    349
Turkey, 132
Twitter, 123, 179

U.N. Human Rights Commission, 372
U.S. Attorney General, 121, 140
U.S. Bureau of Educational and Cultural
    Affairs, 57
U.S. Bureau of Industry and Security, 57
U.S. Central Intelligence Agency, 108
U.S. Customs and Border Protection
    Agency, 57

U.S. Department of Homeland Security, 57, 122
U.S. Department of State, *4*, 57, 103, 104, 105, 121, 122, 129, 133, 149, 261, 269, 270, 281, 353, 354, 363, 372
U.S. Department of Treasury, 106
U.S. Office of Censorship, 347
U.S. Office of Foreign Asset Control, 135, 137
U.S. Office of War Information, 347
U.S. Postal Service, 140
United Arab Emirates, 217, 218
United Kingdom, 41, 308, 334
United Nations, 6, 8, 52, 110, 133, 149, 179, 184, 185, 187, 322, 324, 349, 351, 357, 358, 362
United States Agency for International Development, 57
United States v. O'Brien, 108
United States v. Verdugo-Urquidez, 202, 210, 257, 258
Universal Declaration of Human Rights, 131, 219, 234, 349, 356, 360
  and freedom of expression, 37
  and religious freedom, 44

Van Alstyne, William, 145, 151, 296, 297
Vienna, 34
Vienna Convention on Diplomatic Relations, 326
Vietnam, 135, 237, 273

Vietnam War, 135
Voice of America, 267, 352, 368
Volokh, Eugene, 183, 342

Waldron, Jeremy, 42, 330
Washington, D.C., 326
Washington, George (President), 64
watchlists, 30
Web, 336
Welch v. Kennedy, 237
Westboro Baptist Church, 4
WikiLeaks, 6, 7, 8, 35, 165, 195, 196, 197
Wood, Gordon, 78
World War I, 106, 270
World War II, 33, 56, 89, 190, 191, 192, 347, 349, 350, 351
Wu, Tim, 146

Yahoo!, 274, 309, 310, 336
Yahoo! Inc. v. La Ligue Contre le Racisme et l'Antisemitisme, 208, 336
Yemen, 6, 164, 174, 193, 223
YouTube, 7, 179, 180

zakat, 36, 239, 246, 247
Zemel v. Rusk, 104, 108, 115, 118, 141
Zemel, Louis, 103
Zschernig v. Miller, 278, 279, 284, 285, 291, 293

Made in the USA
Middletown, DE
26 January 2021